THE GREAT EXHIBITION OF 1851

The Great Exhibition of 1851

A NATION ON DISPLAY

JEFFREY A. AUERBACH

YALE UNIVERSITY PRESS
NEW HAVEN AND LONDON

For Nancy

Copyright © 1999 by Yale University

Designed by Adam Freudenheim

Set in Garamond by Best-set Typesetter Ltd., Hong Kong
Printed in Hong Kong through World Print Ltd.

Library of Congress Cataloging-in-Publication Data
Auerbach, Jeffrey A., 1965–
    The Great Exhibition of 1851: a nation on display/Jeffrey A. Auerbach.
    Includes bibliographical references and index.
    ISBN 0–300–08007–7 (hbk.: alk. paper)
    1. Great Exhibition (1851: London, England)   I. Title.
 T690.B1A94   1999
 907.4′421—dc21   99–32177
                                                                      CIP

A catalogue record for this book is available from the British Library.

10 9 8 7 6 5 4 3 2 1

CONTENTS

ACKNOWLEDGMENTS

WRITING THIS BOOK has involved more people, and taken me to more places, than I ever imagined it would, and to all of them I am grateful. Yale University was the birthplace of this project, and I am indebted to those who guided me while I was there. As a graduate student I benefitted enormously from the advice and insights of several outstanding scholars. Peter Gay and Linda Colley supervised this book in its formative stages, and stand as role models for thorough research, careful analysis, and elegant writing. Paul Kennedy, Frank Turner, Frans Coetzee, and Mark Micale provided me with opportunities to try out some of my ideas and approaches. Jennifer Hall-Witt and Cyrus Vakil speedily read chapters at critical times, and offered perceptive and valuable suggestions, as did David Cannadine, who was simultaneously witty, critical, supportive. I owe David a special debt of thanks for his careful reading of the entire manuscript in its later stages.

Financial assistance came most generously from the United States government in the form of a Jacob Javits Fellowship. I also received fellowships from the Macarthur Foundation and the Andrew W. Mellon Foundation, and grants from the John F. Enders fund at Yale University, St Mary's College of Maryland, and Stanford University.

I appreciate having had the opportunity to try out some of the ideas expressed here at the 1992 Northeast Victorian Studies Association Annual Meeting, the 1993 North American Conference on British Studies, and, at the invitation of Fred Leventhal, the 1994 Annual Meeting of the American Historical Association. My thanks to those in the audience, several of whom offered useful and provocative comments.

The directors and staffs at a number of libraries and archives went out of their way to be helpful, foremost among them being Valerie Phillips, Archivist for the Royal Commission for the Exhibition of 1851 at Imperial College of Science, Technology & Medicine, who brought me volume after volume of letters and patiently assisted me while I learned to read nineteenth-century handwriting. At the Yale Center for British Art, Duncan Robinson, Patrick McCaughey, and Elisabeth Fairman all took an interest in my work. My thanks go also to staff at Yale University's Sterling Memorial Library, the British Library, the National Art Library at the Victoria and Albert Museum, the India Office Library, Manchester Central Library, Guildhall Library, the Royal Society for the Arts, Chatsworth, the Bodleian Library, the National Library of Scotland, the Public Record Office, the University of St Andrews Library, the Hartley Library at the University of Southampton, the University College London Library, and the West Sussex Record Office.

Because my research took me away from home for long periods of time, I found myself relying on the generosity of others, not just for food and lodging, but for the less material comforts of home. Special thanks go to Gerry Segal, Edwina Moreton, and Rachel Segal, my surrogate family in London, as well as to two other London friends, Mark Foley and Maya Weil. And, of course, to Chrissie Robertson, who was a formative presence in my life even before I knew how to write, and who took me on a wonderful tour of Scotland so that I could stop at archives in Edinburgh and St Andrews along the way. Other friends who contributed in less tangible but no less important ways include Phil Deloria, Emily Greenwald, David Herrmann, Fred Logevall, Paul Miller, and, more recently, Eric Haskell, Dion Scott-Kakures, Hao and Rachel Huang, and David Andrews. Keith Langston, especially, helped sustain me throughout the project with his friendship, and graciously helped proofread the final version.

In its later stages, this book benefitted greatly from the assistance of Elisheva Urbas, who provided invaluable stylistic suggestions, tempered always by a caustic sense of humor. I also owe a special debt of gratitude to my editors, John Nicoll, who has nurtured this project for several years, and to Candida Brazil, as well as to Adam Freudenheim for his work on the layout and design.

I could not have written this book without the support, encouragement, and assistance of my family. My father read an entire draft and helped me negotiate the dilemmas of multiple meanings even as he refused to solve them for me. My mother drew on her years of editorial experience to help me clarify and prune my prose. Susan, Shira, Rebecca, Pammy, Bart, Cole, Jonah, and, especially, my newborn daughter Dalia, continually remind me that this book is only one part of my life. And finally, above all, Nancy has read every word in this book (most of them more than once), talked me through every major argument and conceptual issue, rescued me from my work at critical moments, and supported me unfailingly in this endeavor. This has truly been a collaborative project in all but name.

Introduction

O N MAY DAY 1851, Queen Victoria opened the Great Exhibition of the Works of Industry of All Nations, at the newly constructed Crystal Palace in Hyde Park, London. *The Times* described the opening as 'the first morning since the creation of the world that all peoples have assembled from all parts of the world and done a common act'.[1] Over 25,000 people mobbed the exhibition building on the first day alone, with thousands more lining the streets to catch a glimpse of the Queen. Inside, visitors found works of art and industry from around the world, from blast furnaces to silk tapestries, from lumps of coal to the first facsimile machine. By the time the exhibition closed in October, there had been more than six million paid entrances to the Crystal Palace, which, allowing for foreign and repeat visits, represented almost one-fifth of the population of Britain.

There has been a whiggish inevitability to most historical accounts of the origins and creation of the exhibition.[2] According to one historian, Prince Albert's announcement of the exhibition at the Society of Arts in 1849 'rang like a trumpet blast through the land;' 'great' was 'the energy and enthusiasm of all concerned;' Joseph Paxton, the architect of the Crystal Palace, was the archetypal self-made man 'born of poor parents;' 'the exhibits were beyond calculation;' the weather for the opening was 'perfect;' and 'It was a triumph for England.'[3] In point of fact, none of these statements was true. Albert was reluctant to become involved in the planning process, and his announcement was not only tentative, but fell, if not on deaf ears, at least on only a few. Many Britons responded with apathy if not outright opposition, even after the exhibition opened. Paxton was not born of poor parents, nor was he without patronage and connections. The exhibits were a hodgepodge at best and severely criticized in many quarters. The morning of the opening was cloudy and raining, although the sun did appear just before the opening ceremony began. Finally, while Britain performed well at the exhibition, premonitions of its decline appeared almost as often as proclamations of victory.

Not only have narratives of the exhibition been teleological; they have also portrayed the exhibition as a monumental and monolithic event with a set of self-evident meanings.[4] Historians have made the Great Exhibition the pre-eminent symbol of the Victorian age. According to traditional accounts, it symbolized 'peace, progress, and prosperity,'[5] and boldly asserted Britain's position not only as the first industrialized nation and as the 'workshop of the world,' but also as the most powerful and advanced state, a paragon of liberalism.[6] It was also, for many historians, the high point of what has been called the 'age of equipoise,' a period of domestic accord, when British society was in balance.[7] G. M. Young proclaimed it a 'pageant of domestic peace.'[8] The Crystal Palace itself has been variously described as the first embodiment of a commodity culture and the first modern building, marking the origin of industrial design and even 'the advent of modernity.'[9]

Scholars have also almost uniformly characterized the exhibition as the product of middle-class cultural ascendancy in mid-Victorian Britain. It 'advanced a particularly middle-class vision' of society, at a time when 'Middle-class ideals set the standard for the nation.'[10] One historian interpreted its motto – 'The workers, of all types, stand forth as the really great men' – as 'not the slogan of "two nations," but of a single nation sharing a single ethos and exulting in the monumental product of that ethos.'[11] There is much evidence for this view, and, on a superficial level, the exhibition can be seen as a testament to the middle class. They had substantial input in the preparations, they attended in large numbers, and they were the target of much of the organizers' promotional efforts. More broadly, the organizers raised funds for the exhibition using public meetings and voluntary societies, both particularly middle-class forms of expression, and the exhibition itself presented and represented a vision of Britain and British society that was appealing to the middle classes.

But there are several problems in asserting that the Great Exhibition was the cultural product of the Victorian middle class. The first is a methodological one, that there is no consensus among historians about who should be considered middle class, and whether class is a useful category of analysis in the first place.[12] Second, it will be argued here that the exhibition was an event that cut across traditional class boundaries and distinctions, both in its formulation and in its popularity. Third, and most importantly, this portrayal of the exhibition as a middle-class event promulgating a middle-class vision of society reduces the many and varied meanings of the exhibition to a single, unequivocal truth.

What is so remarkable about the Great Exhibition is that it included something for almost everyone. In this regard the exhibition was a protean event with numerous possible meanings. This book investigates these meanings by re-inserting the exhibition into the historical context from which it emerged in order to explore the many people and processes that led to its creation. It not only analyzes those who supported and promoted the event, but gives credence to those who opposed it, thus providing a broader and more informed reading of its meanings. Drawing on the unpublished minutes and correspondence of the organizers, along with published accounts, newspapers and periodicals, memoirs, visual material including engravings, and the exhibits themselves, this book investigates the contemporary views of and subsequent meanings ascribed to the Great Exhibition. In three parts, covering eight chapters in total, it considers the making of the event, the meanings encoded within it, and people's memories of it.

The first part tells in narrative form the story of the creation and organization of the exhibition. Chapter 1 discusses the historical context out of which the exhibition emerged, including the inadequate system of industrial education in Britain during the first half of the nineteenth century. It traces the early, unsuccessful attempts to produce a national industrial exhibition, and it examines the organizers of the exhibition, their backgrounds, and their motives. The second chapter turns to some of the difficulties the organizers experienced in planning the exhibition, such as funding and providing an exhibition building. Both of these issues forced the organizers to decide what they meant by a 'national' and 'public' exhibition. Only after the organizers had resolved these issues were they able to turn to the vital task of promoting the exhibition, the subject of Chapter 3.

Contrary to what most historians have suggested, British men and women did not immediately embrace the exhibition. For months subscriptions and exhibits trickled in because Britons simply did not know what to make of it, or did not like what they heard. The organizers had to define for the public, and negotiate with the public, the meaning of the exhibition. They did so by presenting it in multiple and changing forms, as they shifted the focus of their appeal to fit their audience. In other words, giving meaning to the exhibition was less a statement of fact than a process. The exhibition was an idea that had to be sold to the public by means of a sophisticated publicity campaign that involved the careful cultivation of the press, the distribution of pamphlets, posters, and circulars, and the organization of 300 local committees that sponsored large meetings with speeches and resolutions. In the process of promoting the exhibition, not only did the organizers continually redefine it to fit their audience; the exhibition itself was redefined by the public in a symbiotic relationship. Consequently, the story of the exhibition must be told in relation as much to the provincial towns as to London, because towns responded in very different ways that reflected local social, political, and economic issues.

Part II turns from the event's narrative creation to its thematic meanings. The Great Exhibition was a battleground in which different groups within Victorian society fought to present their vision of what sort of nation Britain should be. Chapter 4 analyzes the exhibits on display at the exhibition in order to argue that there were many at the time who did not view commerce and culture as inherently antithetical, and that industrialization in Britain did not have to take the form it did, but could have followed an altogether different path. It also suggests that the Great Exhibition was designed less to celebrate Britain's economic successes than to locate and remedy its deficiencies. In Chapter 5 the focus shifts from the economic system to the social structure. Whereas the organizers and many observers portrayed the exhibition as a tribute to social order and class integration, a careful analysis of attendance patterns discloses deep, underlying divisions. Moreover, the Crystal Palace segregated Victorian society not just along class lines, but on regional, occupational, and gender bases as well.

The final thematic chapter explores the dichotomy between the language used by the organizers and by many commentators which characterized the exhibition as a festival of peace and an opportunity to foster international harmony and trade, and the stridently nationalistic, jingoistic, and xenophobic cartoons and publications that turned the exhibition into a competition not only about products, but about values. As such, the Great Exhibition became a forum for discussions of British national identity in the broadest sense. If the earlier chapters explore the divisions within British society, this chapter elucidates those ties that largely bound it together. Whatever doubts British men and women may have had about the composition of their own society and culture, they had few such doubts about what differentiated them not only from their closest neighbors, but from the exotic, foreign 'other.'

Part III looks at the Great Exhibition as an aspect of both memory and popular culture, a national icon embedded with meanings, some of which date more from 1951, the date of the Festival of Britain that celebrated the centennial of the exhibition, than from 1851. It analyzes the rebuilt version of the Crystal Palace, which stood in the London suburb of Sydenham from 1854 until it burned down in 1936, and discusses what was done with the proceeds from the exhibition. Ultimately, what emerged out of the Great Exhibition was the educational and museum complex in South Kensington that includes the Victoria and Albert Museum, the Science Museum, the Natural History Museum, Imperial College of Science and Technology, and the Royal Albert Hall, all of which were built on land purchased with the profits from the exhibition. Even as these have provided a lasting, tangible memorial to the Great Exhibition, it has been the hill in Sydenham, where the ruins of the Crystal Palace are being turned into a hotel and leisure center, that has become the locus for continuing reinterpretations of the meaning of the exhibition.

There are, then, two stories to tell about the exhibition. One is the 'official' or 'received' version, based largely on the *Reports* of the commissioners, the *Official Descriptive and Illustrated Catalogue* of the exhibition, guidebooks, celebratory poems, the mainstream press such as *The Times* and the *Illustrated London News*, and highbrow periodicals such as *Blackwood's*, the *Edinburgh Review*, and the *Westminster Review*. The narrative that emerges from these sources and from the historians who have employed them treats the exhibition as an inevitable event, sprung from the mind of Prince Albert, embraced by the broadest spectrum of the British public, and symbolic of the middle-class ideals of peace, progress, and prosperity. The other story, less publicized, focuses on what occurred beneath the official veneer. This story is based on the less accessible and unpublished records of the 1851 commission, the exhibits themselves, the more peripheral but not necessarily less important newspapers such as *John Bull*, the *Britannia*, and the *Mechanics' Magazine*, the provincial press, and popular penny publications. This is the story of reluctant manufacturers, nationalistic and jingoistic rivalries, petty political disputes, and, in many areas of Britain, outright antipathy toward the exhibition. The Great Exhibition was not an immediately popular or successful event. Both its popularity and its success were carefully crafted and created by a small group of men over a considerable period of time.

Since 1983, Benedict Anderson's idea of the nation as 'an imagined political community' has become something of a cliché, but there have been few studies that explore the social, political, and cultural process by which a people come to imagine themselves as a distinct nation.[13] Anderson's much cited definition also begs at least two important questions, both of which this book seeks to address. By whom is the political community imagined? And of what does this imagined community consist? Both questions complicate the notion of British national identity, and are reminders of how widely contested and differently conceived the British polity was during the mid-century years. From this perspective, the nation is less a given to be pursued or rejected than it is a site of contention, a source of conflict and debate. Moreover, whatever method is used to address the formation of national identity must also rectify what one scholar has identified as 'the artificial dichotomy between nationalism from above and from below, by exploring nationhood as a process by which people from all walks of life redefine concepts of space, time, and kin.'[14] The Great Exhibition provides just such an opportunity, for it can tell us how British men and women devised 'a common denominator between their intimate, immediate, and real local place and the distinct and abstract national world.'[15]

The Great Exhibition was arguably the greatest defining occasion for nineteenth-century Britons between the Battle of Waterloo in 1815 and Queen Victoria's Diamond Jubilee in 1897, containing not one but many different narratives. As such, it reveals much about the ordering and disordering of Victorian society, which was undergoing profound social, economic, political, and cultural changes during the mid-nineteenth century. Walking through the nave of the building, the axial line of power, and then veering off into the side courts and galleries, men and women from all classes and regions learned much about themselves, their country, and their place in the world.

The analysis put forward here suggests that Victorians used the exhibition to define themselves as a nation. They were able to do so because the organizers of the exhibition constructed it as a protean event with numerous possible meanings, even as they used it to disseminate liberal ideas about society, the economy, and Britain's relationship with the rest of the world. From the outset, different individuals and groups were able to interpret the meaning of the exhibition in localized, individualized ways. The Great Exhibition was, in essence, a cultural battlefield, in which proponents of different and at times competing visions of Britain fought for ascendancy in a struggle to define Britain's past, present, and future. The analysis that follows considers the Great Exhibition as evidence of the cultural ties that bound Britons together, as well as those that were contested and potentially divisive. By marshaling a variety of sources, and by employing an interdisciplinary approach, it seeks to contribute to our understanding of British national identity in the nineteenth century, as well as of how national identity is formed more generally.

PART I   MAKING

CHAPTER 1

Origins: Conceiving the Exhibition

O N 6 DECEMBER 1844, the Society for the Encouragement of Arts, Manufactures, and Commerce held a small exhibition of paintings and 'useful inventions' in the Society's rooms at Adelphi. It was organized by the secretary, Francis Whishaw, who offered £300 in prize money out of his own pocket. In all likelihood Whishaw drew his inspiration either from the local exhibitions that had been held with some regularity at mechanics' institutes in the North and Midlands since the late 1830s, or from two continental exhibitions that had occurred earlier in the year: one in Berlin, for the Zollverein, the German Customs Union; the other in Paris, the most recent in a series of quincennial French national exhibitions that had begun during the Napoleonic Wars as 'economic weapons in the fight against England' and which turned out to be so beneficial to French industry that they were continued long after the wars ended. The success of these expositions led many other European countries to experiment with the idea between 1815 and 1830. Most were directed toward, and even catered to, foreigners. Organizers had their eyes on foreign investors and consumers, and intended their exhibitions to showcase national identities. But none of these exhibitions risked opening their doors to foreign exhibitors, largely out of fear of economic competition, especially from the British, who were rightly perceived to be capable of flooding almost any market with inexpensive, mass-produced goods.[1] The evening at the Society of Arts, however, attracted only 150 people, and Whishaw considered it a failure. He had experienced great difficulty in persuading manufacturers to exhibit their products, and must have been disappointed by the paltry attendance.[2]

Just over six years later, on 1 May 1851, Queen Victoria opened the Great Exhibition of the Works of Industry of All Nations in Hyde Park. Housed in the newly built Crystal Palace, the Great Exhibition displayed 100,000 exhibits from around the world. More than 20,000 people attended that first day alone, and during the next five months men, women, and children from all classes, regions, and religions flocked to London to see what many considered to be the eighth wonder of the world. It was the most popular event of its age, and became the first in a long line of international exhibitions and world fairs. What in 1844 was for the few became by 1851 for the nation. Whishaw's failure had become a national and international success.

The very idea of the exhibition, and the fact that it took place, not to mention its stunning success, merits explanation, because there was nothing inevitable about it. The process of organizing the Great Exhibition was as much a matter of overcoming a succession of unforeseen setbacks as it was executing a carefully articulated plan of action, and there were many points at which the entire enterprise could have fallen apart. It is possible to explain the exhibition only with reference to the men who organized it, most of whom were members of the Society of Arts, which was desperately in need of funds, but had an enduring interest in improving British arts, manufacturing, and commerce; and to several economic trends that served as the backdrop for the endeavor and the motivating forces behind it. These include the state of the British economy, which was by no means uniformly or consistently robust during the 1840s, and the system of industrial education in Britain, which was embryonic and widely perceived as inadequate. There was, in short, nothing grandiose about the origins of the exhibition. It was years in the making; Prince Albert's involvement was restrained and even reluctant; and it was organized less to demonstrate Britain's industrial successes than to identify and rectify Britain's manufacturing deficiencies.

INDUSTRIAL EDUCATION

From its position as 'the first industrial nation,' Britain had by the mid-nineteenth century become the world's leading industrialized power.[3] But the foundations of that strength were not uniformly strong, and the 'Hungry Forties' were difficult years economically. There were severe trade dislocations following the repeal of the Corn Laws in 1846 that reflected widespread disjunctures within the British economic system. The Commercial Crisis of 1847 was brought about by problems of industrial production and the relaxation of certain trade restrictions, and was exacerbated by the Whig budgets as well as the discount policy of the Bank of England.[4] An exhibition of works of industry certainly offered an opportunity to bring together men of industry, banking, and commerce in the hopes of improving a sputtering economy.

One of the most important issues facing Britain as a nation throughout the 1840s was its system of workers' education, and, by extension, the production of goods both for domestic use and for export. The Great Exhibition occurred at a time when there was a resurgence of interest in technical education as an element of national industrial performance, and it cannot be understood outside the context of industrial education and production in Britain.[5] In the mid-1840s, technical education in Britain was minimal. This was true not only in the absolute sense, but also relatively, in comparison with other nations. According to Henry Brougham, who in 1824 wrote an influential article in the *Edinburgh Review* on scientific education, British artisans were the least trained, and middle-class manufacturers the worst educated, in Europe. Most skilled occupations up to the late eighteenth century were handicrafts passed down from generation to generation. In an economic system based on cottage industries and craft apprenticeships there had been little need for formal teaching. But the Industrial Revolution and the attendant growth of the factory system made the old system of apprenticeship obsolete, and called for a new educational process that increasingly emphasized science and technology.[6]

There were two principal attempts to improve workers' skills and education levels in Britain during the first half of the nineteenth century – mechanics' institutes and schools of design – neither of which proved very successful. The mechanics' institutes, which dated from the turn of the century, provided lectures, classes, and books for workers and artisans who wished to learn the scientific principles underlying their trades. They taught the practical application of science to art.[7] Initially support came from the radical wing of the Whig party: James Mill, David Ricardo, William Cobbett, Francis Place, and Jeremy Bentham, as well as from Henry Brougham, who in addition to his widely read *Edinburgh Review* article also authored *Practical Observa-tions upon the Education of the People, addressed to the Working Classes, and their Employers* (1825). But the early success of the movement also attracted some support from Tories, including Robert Peel, William Gladstone, and Walter Scott. It was, then, primarily men of property and status who were concerned for the future of British industry who supplied the impetus behind the movement.[8] There was a fairly wide-spread and bipartisan perception that Britain needed to educate its workers because its industry was falling behind that of other nations, especially France. There may also have been an element of indoctrination involved, a belief that educating workers would foster stronger social ties and keep them out of Chartist mischief. Already by the 1820s, when trade conditions began to improve following a period of post-war economic malaise, there were institutes in Glasgow, London, and Sheffield, and by 1850 there were more than 600 mechanics' institutes in England, Scotland, and Wales, with more than half a million members.[9]

But the inadequacy of primary education in Britain was an insurmountable barrier to the success of these institutes.[10] By the mid-1840s the mechanics' institutes had almost universally ceased to be regarded as a medium for the instruction of the masses. Rather than drawing from the poorer working and artisan classes, they served the lower-middle and respectable working classes (clerks and shop assistants earning 20s–30s per week in wages, or less than £75 per annum).[11] While they drew many people, and increased literacy, the mechanics' institutes failed to fulfill their intended function. Many of them, however, held periodic small-scale exhibitions, and in this regard they were quite successful, especially in their publicity and fund-raising. In Leeds, for example, an exhibition of 'arts and manufactures' in 1839 attracted almost 200,000 people and enabled the institute there to purchase a larger building.[12] Although the mechanics' institutes did not substantially improve scientific education or British design, they did suggest that industrial exhibitions could be popular and financially renumerative.

The second means of educating workers and improving the quality of industrial design in the early nineteenth century were the schools of design. By the second quarter of the century, growth rates for major industries were no longer increasing as quickly as they had twenty or thirty years earlier.[13] Many manufacturers of pottery, textiles, furniture, and other ornamented goods were of the opinion that British con-sumers did not want British products, and in order to rectify this situation manu-facturers began to spend large sums on foreign designers. In 1835 the House of Commons, through the Select Committee on Arts and Manufactures, began to take an interest in these trends, inquiring 'into the best means of extending a knowledge of the arts and of the principles of design among the people (especially the manufac-turing population) of the country.' The committee's report, which received consid-erable public attention, concluded that, whereas at one time British workmanship and products had been of a very high quality and had dominated foreign markets, the Napoleonic Wars had slowed the export of British goods, and, overseas, consumers had learned to do without. In Britain, producers had devoted their competitive and inventive energies to issues of quantity and economy, rather than the aesthetics of design. The result was that by the third decade of the nineteenth century the British were producing goods that were inexpensive but sometimes unattractive. More importantly, the committee pointed out that continental European governments were devoting a great deal of time and money to the education of their artists and artisans, in stark contrast to the British government, which was doing very little. It therefore recommended setting up a school of design, for which the government provided £15,000, which opened at Somerset House in 1837 under the aegis of the Board of Trade. Within the decade there were approximately twenty local and provincial schools of design, in addition to the government school in London.[14]

The schools of design, however, were not uniformly successful, and the nature and worth of the education they provided remained under question through the 1840s. The principal dispute was over what they should teach, and whether the purpose of the schools was to produce artists as well as to supply industry. In September 1846 the painter and designer Richard Redgrave sent a letter to Lord John Russell, drawing attention 'to the failure of the schools of design to attain the objects for which they were founded,' namely 'the improvement of art in manufactures.'[15] Neither the mechanics' institutes nor the schools of design had made a significant impact. The next option was to expand on the mini-exhibitions that the Society of Arts was arranging, and create a national exhibition of works of industry that would provide a spur to the nation.

There was, however, another side to the whole issue of industrial education, and that concerned the consumer. According to a number of British manufacturers, one of the greatest hindrances facing them in their quest for profits was that their products were not reaching consumers, and consumers did not seem to want the products to which they had access. The introduction to the catalogue for the 1847 exhibition at the Society of Arts described the problem faced by manufacturers in detail:

> It is a universal complaint among manufacturers that the taste for good art does not exist in sufficient extent to reward them for the cost of producing superior works; that the public prefers the vulgar, the gaudy, the ugly even, to the beautiful and perfect.
>
> We are persuaded that, if artistic manufactures are not appreciated, it is because they are not widely enough known. We believe that when works of high merit, of British origin, are brought forward they will be thoroughly appreciated and thoroughly enjoyed. We believe that this exhibition, when thrown open gratuitously to all, will tend to improve the public taste.[16]

One functional solution to this problem was the exhibition, the modern form of the trade fairs and regional markets that had been popular since the late Middle Ages in places such as Bury St Edmunds, Northampton, Westminster, and Boston. These fairs were extraordinary gatherings, mobilizing the inhabitants and economies of entire regions. There was entertainment in the form of plays, jugglers, and fortune-tellers; there were processions and displays of power and authority; and, of course, there were economic exchanges, settling of accounts, and displays of new products (fig. 1).[17] As would be the case at the Great Exhibition, they combined business and pleasure. Certainly in their eighteenth-century form, exhibitions and trade fairs provided manufactures with a forum in which they could display their wares, and they provided consumers with an opportunity to examine and compare a diversity of products.

In Britain, there had also been industrial exhibitions of a sort by the mid-eighteenth century, though these had not been of a national character. One of the primary objectives of the Society of Arts in its early years was to stimulate the invention of mechanical devices by offering prizes and awards for different categories of

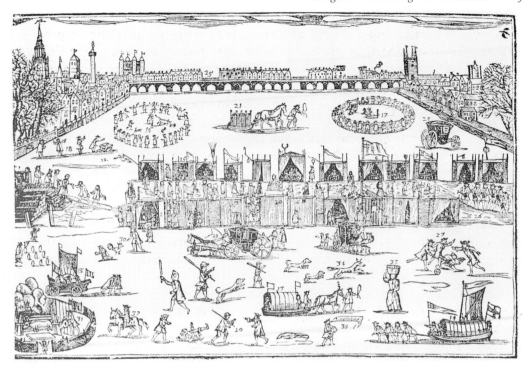

1. *Fair on the Thames, 1683.*

new industrial products, which were then displayed in small exhibitions. The Society, however, experienced financial difficulties during the second quarter of the nineteenth century, as advances in industry made obsolete the idea of encouraging industrial progress through the award of prizes. The system of prizes and exhibitions had at one time been of significant value in stimulating inventors, but as industry itself became increasingly capable of rewarding its inventors, the distribution of prizes by the Society became less important and had less of an impact.[18] The locus then shifted to the northern manufacturing towns, where there were a number of regional and provincial trade fairs beginning in the late 1830s, some of them drawing in excess of 100,000 people.[19] There was a brief movement to establish industrial exhibitions on a national basis, but this had petered out by the early 1830s.[20] There was in Britain a long-standing reluctance to involve the state in individual affairs, and, despite increasing evidence to the contrary, many manufacturers thought their products too good to need such a thing.

In addition to these, by the early nineteenth century there existed what have been called the 'shows of London', combinations of fair, theatre, art, and scientific collection. Shows such as the Leicester Square Panorama and the Diorama were 'the scene of the perennial conflict between the claims of amusement and those of earnest instruction,' a clash that would continue in the Crystal Palace. These shows were all privately owned, advertised in widely circulating weeklies such as the *Athenaeum* and the *Illustrated London News*, and at various points drew large crowds, usually from the middle and upper classes who were eager to escape the streets of London for an evening to explore a fantasy world of exotic foreign nations. The shows appealed to the curious, the patriotic, and those desiring edification.[21]

When the idea of a national industrial exhibition arose in Britain, therefore, it brought together many threads: the national industrial expositions in France, the displays at mechanics' institutes, the commercial shows of London, the perceived need to improve the education and training of workers, and, perhaps most importantly, the need manufacturers had to display and promote their products. But despite the many small-scale exhibitions that had been held by the Society of Arts and in the northern manufacturing towns over the previous fifty years, and the obvious need to improve certain areas of the economy and the manufacturing process, there was still nothing inevitable about the Great Exhibition. Its organization was a long-drawn-out process that took place slowly over a period of about five years. It is worthwhile, therefore, tracing in some detail how it came about that Whishaw's 1844 failure should have become, seven years later, such a success.

THE SOCIETY OF ARTS

The Royal Society of Arts, as it would be called after 1847, was established in 1753 for the encouragement of the arts, manufactures, and commerce. It accomplished this aim by bestowing prizes for inventions or improvements that increased trade or the employment of the poor.[22] Tangible results from the more than £16,000 in prizes paid out by the Society during its first twenty-two years included the introduction of several new crops in Britain and the invention of new agricultural implements and mechanical devices. The Society also sponsored papers and discussions on topics as diverse as trade with the Baltics, drill ploughs, and sheep rot. Initially a collection of 'noblemen, clergy, gentlemen and merchants,' as the first minute book described them, membership expanded rapidly, reaching 2,500 within a few years of its founding.[23] The success of the Society, however, did not extend into the nineteenth century, and by the early 1840s it was in severe debt. When the Society reinstated its prize competitions and exhibitions in the mid-1840s under the guidance of Francis Whishaw, it did so not so much to encourage industry – although the desire to do so was certainly present – as to raise money.[24]

Although Whishaw considered the 1844 exhibition a failure, the officers of the Society encouraged him to hold a second one in January 1845. It drew 800 people, and achieved at least one of Whishaw's objectives, which was to set people talking about an annual exhibition on a grand scale.[25] The result was that at the Society's annual meeting in May 1845 the council resolved to begin 'immediate preparation' for a periodic exhibition of works of industry, noting in its discussion the benefits foreign countries had derived from exhibitions, that they had stimulated industrial growth through competition, and that Britain too could reap these benefits.[26] Again, it is important to emphasize here that the impetus for the exhibition grew out of perceived economic weaknesses, rather than a desire to celebrate economic supremacy. Two weeks later, on 1 June 1845, Prince Albert made his annual visit to present the prizes as President of the Society of Arts, at which time Whishaw reported both publicly to the Society and privately to Albert on the proceedings of the previous fortnight.

In Albert, Whishaw had a sympathetic audience. The subject of design as applied to manufactured goods – or arts manufactures – was one in which the Prince Consort had shown personal interest. He had accepted the presidency of the Society of Arts in 1844, and had served as chairman of the Royal Commission appointed to decide how the rebuilding of the House of Commons might be utilized to promote the fine arts in Britain. At the time he had expressed his hope that developing a taste for art would elevate the character and habits of British men and women and provide greater incentive for British manufacturers to produce high-quality, aesthetically pleasing work.[27] In Francis Xavier Winterhalter's portrait (fig. 2) one can see books and drawings to Albert's left that testify to his interest in the arts. Since his arrival from Germany, he had perceived that the taste of the British public in the arts was underdeveloped, and believed this to be an area where his interests and the needs of the country coincided. In a constitutional framework which provided no place for a Queen's husband, Albert's involvement in issues of manufacturing and design enabled him to augment the role of the Crown in the elevation of the moral, cultural, and economic well-being of the country, as well as to boost his own importance. So when Whishaw presented him with a plan for an annual exhibition of well-designed products, the Prince expressed interest. He directed that he should be further informed if and when the plan reached the stage at which it appeared plausible, a response that constituted both a challenge and a caution.[28] He was clearly concerned not to become too closely associated with a plan that so far had failed to demonstrate much popularity or drawing power among the public.

Whishaw, however, took Albert's response as an indication of royal encouragement, and lost no time in getting his project under way. He convened a committee to implement the plan for a national exhibition, which included John Scott Russell, Francis Fuller, Charles Wentworth Dilke, and Robert Stephenson: In short, it comprised the nucleus of the committee (with the prominent exception at this stage of Henry Cole) that would, four years hence, begin formally planning the Great Exhibition. Their idea was that competitions would provide material for small annual exhibitions, which would in turn prepare the way for the proposed national exhibition. The committee realized, given the relatively paltry attendance and reluctance on the part of manufacturers to exhibit at the exhibitions in December 1844 and January 1845, that public opinion and the support of manufacturers was essential to the success of the project. Accordingly, some on the committee began to canvass towns to gauge – and perhaps encourage – support for their venture. But as Scott Russell put it: 'This attempt failed. The public was indifferent. Manufacturers lukewarm – some of the most eminent even hostile to the proposition. The Committee neither met with sufficient promise of support or money, sufficient public sympathy, nor sufficient cooperation among manufacturers, to see their way to success. The attempt was abandoned.'[29] This raises a very important question: Why were manufacturers so reluctant to support the idea of an exhibition of works of industry?

There are several possible explanations. Even though manufacturers had had some exposure to exhibitions or trade fairs, they may not have believed that exhibitions could produce commercial gains by bringing together producers, products, and consumers; in fact, it seems manufacturers believed that they would be hurt commercially by exhibitions, because their goods would be exposed to competitors who might steal their ideas.[30] The nascent system of communication between British cities and towns, and the primitive rail network that was only beginning to draw together the British nation geographically (map 1), may have made the idea seem impractical.

2. Francis Xavier Winterhalter, *Prince Albert of Saxe-Coburg-Gotha* (1867; original 1859). National Portrait Gallery, London.

Map 1. The railway network in 1840.

Even as late as 1851, rail lines had to be built and special excursion fares offered to enable much of the nation to reach London. Five years earlier, with 50 per cent fewer miles of railway tracks, the task would have been that much more difficult.[31] Finally, of course, manufacturers might have failed to support the idea of an exhibition simply because they believed they were sufficiently successful without its stimulus.

It was John Scott Russell who kept alive Whishaw's idea of a national industrial exhibition after the disappointment of 1845.[32] His explanation of the failure of 1845 was that the British were unaware of the value of exhibitions on 'the character as well as the commerce of the Nation.' He realized that what was needed was education, and it was this tack that the Society pursued. On 6 December 1845, Scott Russell offered £50 in 'prizes for a series of models and designs of useful objects calculated to improve general taste.' That is, the first step would be simply to encourage the production of new manufactures, in effect a return to the eighteenth-century origins of the Society. The Society also decided to collect and exhibit models of works of art for the improvement of the taste of metal workers and manufacturers, for which it offered £100. Progress, however, was slow, and as of 1846 there were still hardly any competitors, and it was only with difficulty that the judges could find objects to honor with prizes. The entries were inadequate for even a small exhibition.[33]

The brightest light in the 1846 annual exhibition was a plain and simple white tea service designed by Henry Cole under the pseudonym 'Felix Summerly.' Cole had learned of the upcoming 1846 exhibition around the time Scott Russell announced the special prizes, and had convinced Herbert Minton, the china manufacturer, to submit a design for beer mugs; Cole himself worked on the tea service. At Minton's factory in Stoke-upon-Trent, Cole personally supervised the modeling and production of the tea service he had designed, guided by a few basic principles: simplicity, cheapness, elegance, and harmony (fig. 3). Both the beer mugs and the tea service won prizes at the 1846 show. While 'Summerly's tea service' is today far from striking, at the time, after years of ornate decoration in all classes of industrial wares, especially the lower-priced ones, it represented a return to aesthetic simplicity. It also caught the attention of Prince Albert, who purchased the earthenware tea set for Buckingham Palace, and invited Cole and the other prize winners to meet with him. Albert commented on Cole's success at having united quality, elegance, and price in

3. Felix Summerly's Tea Service, designed by Henry Cole and manufactured by Minton & Co., bone china, 1846. Victoria and Albert Museum, London.

his tea service. Cole had successfully wed high art and mechanical skill, and, buoyed by his success, he joined the Society of Arts.[34]

Henry Cole was a remarkably versatile and industrious man who without question lived up to the motto from Ecclesiastes that he chose for his memoirs: 'Whatsoever thy hand findeth to do, do it with all thy might.' He began his career as a civil servant at the Record Commission, where he designed a cataloguing system for the Public Record Office. While he held this job he also studied art and exhibited sketches at the Royal Academy; he helped the novelist Thomas Love Peacock write musical reviews; he became editor of the *Historical Register*, the *Journal of Design*, and the *Railway Chronicle*, and was a contributor to the *Westminster Review*, the *British and Foreign Review*, and the *Athenaeum*. Beginning in 1838, he worked with Rowland Hill on the introduction of the penny postage. In the 1840s he agitated for a single railway gauge and for patent-law reform. He also published the first Christmas card and wrote children's books on the side, along with popular guidebooks to the National Gallery, Westminster Abbey, and Hampton Court. In his work at the Public Record Office and with Rowland Hill, he learned, among other things, how to influence public opinion by means of pamphlets, articles, and letters in newspapers and was so successful in this respect that Richard Cobden offered to make him secretary of the Anti-Corn Law League. Cole reluctantly declined this offer, probably to avoid being linked to any one partisan group, perhaps to keep future political opportunities open. He was, above all, practical.[35]

Several themes guided Cole's work. He sought to make basic services such as postage and rail travel available to the masses. He believed in progress, freedom of thought, commerce, and free trade. And like Prince Albert, whom he first met in 1842 in connection with his work at the Public Record Office, he believed in the importance of applying science and art to industrial manufactures.[36] He possessed a dominating personality, and was, for the most part, an astute administrator. Cobden wrote to his friend, the publisher John Cassell, about him: 'He is a clever agitator, and a public spirited fellow.'[37] Cole's talents and connections were well known to the members of the Society of Arts, and soon after joining he was promoted to the council, which was arranging for a new and enlarged series of prizes and making preparations for a more extensive competition and exhibition in 1847.[38]

This 1847 exhibition, which took place in March at the Society, was the first national exhibition of any magnitude in Britain. Its objective, unabashedly educational and forward-looking, was to correct some of the problems that the organizers had found in the previous exhibitions, and in fact throughout Britain: that the public was not well educated in matters of taste, which meant, in its most blunt form, that certain segments tended to prefer foreign and especially French products to those made in Britain.[39] Putting the exhibition together, however, was not easy. Cole and Russell had spent days trying to persuade manufacturers to lend articles for exhibit, but they managed to secure only a few hundred, although some came from famous manufacturers such as Wedgwood. The result, however, was 'triumphant' in Scott Russell's opinion, particularly given expectations. Some 20,000 people attended the exhibition, and as Scott Russell perceived it, 'The lesson was given. The manufactuers found that 20,000 customers had seen their wares, and had learned to select good from bad.'[40] The results of this success were readily apparent the following year, in 1848, when, instead of the Society having to scrounge for exhibits, they had to limit them. Upwards of 70,000 people filled their rooms.

Scott Russell's pithy remark about the significance of the 1847 exhibition – that manufacturers discovered consumers, and that consumers learned to discriminate between products – charts a fundamental change in the British economic system. Despite the rapid commercialization and increased consumption of goods that occurred during the second half of the eighteenth century, until roughly the 1840s, manufacturers were unable to reach consumers in truly large numbers. A survey of consumer behavior and material culture in the late seventeenth or eighteenth century has found no evidence that there was a 'mass market' for various consumer goods or even a 'humble consumer society.' And, while one historian has claimed that 'between about 1650 and 1750, tobacco, sugar products and caffeine drinks became items of mass consumption,' the definition of 'mass' employed was that 25 percent of the adult population used them regularly.[41] Only with the growth in the number of newspapers, the attendant proliferation of advertisements, and the increase in railway track mileage, not to mention improvements in the technology of production (such as the sewing machine, which was first exhibited in 1851), in the second quarter of the nineteenth century at the earliest, could manufacturers deliver large quantities of goods quickly to a diversity of markets.[42] Insofar as there had been any growth in the market for consumer goods in the late eighteenth century it had been enjoyed largely by the upper classes; to a great extent businessmen, shopkeepers, and the middle classes only benefitted a generation or two later, in the 1830s, and it was not until the second half of the *nineteenth* century that middle-class homes would take on the cluttered appearance now so commonly associated with the Victorians.[43]

Russell's analysis of the reasons underlying the success of 1847 also speaks to a shorter-term change in the economy. The mid-1840s, the 'Hungry Forties', were economically disastrous years for many in Britain and Ireland. It is not surprising that in the midst of recession manufacturers would be wary of investing money in new products and paying the cost of sending those products to London to an exhibition at the Society of Arts. Nor is it surprising that consumers would fail to evince much enthusiasm for such an exhibition, given the poor state of the economy. But by 1847 the situation was looking marginally better: the controversy over the Corn Laws was abating, Russell's Whig government was continuing the gradual move towards free trade, and the standard of living was improving for the poorer segments of society, partly because of cheaper bread prices, which meant more money for other things.[44] The exhibition of 1847 represented the first fruits of some of these changes.

Building on its success, Henry Cole prepared and sent to Prince Albert in January 1848 a prospectus outlining the Society's plans for a national exhibition, in what was obviously an attempt to push Albert to renew the interest he had expressed a few years earlier.[45] The response from Colonel Phipps, Albert's personal secretary, was not encouraging. Albert had considered the plan and conferred with 'several members of the Cabinet,' but Phipps was sorry to report that 'opinion does not appear to be favourable to any such plans, nor do I think that any reasonable hope could be entertained of any co-operation or assistance at any rate at present, from the government.' Lord John Russell's Whig government, in which laissez-faire doctrines of self-help with a minimum of government intervention prevailed, was unlikely to provide any official sanction for a private proposal that would involve a grant of public money. Phipps added, 'Under these circumstances I conclude that you will agree that it would not be advisable at this time to press the proposal.'[46] In other words, Albert was not going to stand behind the idea, at least for the time being, and it would not be politically astute to push him to do so.

Cole was undaunted. Though the Cabinet had not supported his plan, there were still other governmental organizations that he could approach, especially if he minimized the financial aspects of government involvement. In early 1848, therefore, at Cole's suggestion, a delegation from the Society of Arts met in turn with the President of the Board of Trade, Henry Labouchere, and the Commissioner of Woods and Forests, Charles Wood, and secured their cooperation, and by extension that of the government.[47] Although commentators would later laud the exhibition as a symbol of the benefits of laissez-faire government, and as a testament to what could be accomplished through voluntarism and public subscription, at this early stage the members of the Society of Arts who were planning the exhibition had no doubt but that the government should be involved. The idea of the exhibition came from the private sector, but its success depended on cooperation between both private and public sectors. In part this reflected the poor fiscal standing of the Society of Arts at this time. It was indicative as well of the scale of the planned exhibition that it was conceived to be so grandiose that it was only proper to include the government. It is also likely that the Society of Arts' predeliction for official involvement derived from the government's previous participation in industrial arts education.

It was propitious that during the summer and fall of 1848 the government began to worry once again about the ailing schools of design. In the autumn, Lord Granville, President of the Board of Trade, and two of his assistants, John George Shaw Lefevre and Stafford Northcote, began to look for someone to investigate and reform the schools, which were beset by administrative, financial, and educational problems.

Thus the government's goal of educating artisans in matters of industrial design and the Society of Arts' interest in holding a national exhibition of works of industry coincided. In September 1848, Northcote wrote to Cole asking for suggestions to improve the government school of design. Cole responded that the schools were unworkable in their present form. As with the Record Office, the broad-gauge railways, and the Post Office, Cole had decided that total reform was needed, and that he should be the reformer. This created tension between Northcote and Cole that would continue throughout their mutual association with the exhibition. Meanwhile, however, in his usual manner Cole began to 'create a climate of opinion.' He launched a new periodical, the *Journal of Design*, to challenge the *Art Union Journal*, which was the established magazine in the field of arts manufactures and a supporter of the current administration of the schools of design. Cole used his journal to criticize the council of the London School of Design at Somerset House. By the mid-1840s, he claimed, the school of design had become a school of high art; no one was allowed 'to study for his business.'[48] He, on the other hand, firmly believed that the schools of design should be geared to manufacturers, that they should be practical, and that the tests of their success would be whether the graduates of the schools of design found employment and whether the designs produced by students at the schools of design sold. His journal was aimed directly at manufacturers, and sold well. Almost as soon as it was published, the *Journal of Design* – and Felix Summerly's manufactures – came under vitriolic attack from the *Art Union Journal*, which sought to discredit Cole in the eyes of industrial manufacturers. Cole did not let the attacks go unanswered, and a virtual war was under way.[49]

In need of allies, Cole turned to Parliament, first to Richard Cobden, then to Thomas Milner Gibson, the Liberal MP from Manchester who had been Vice President of the Board of Trade and involved in the agitation for Post Office reform. He was a member of the Society of Arts as well. Milner Gibson agreed to work with Cole, and in March he called for and obtained a select committee to consider the constitution and management of the Schools of Design. The committee, which heard evidence during the same period in which the Society of Arts was preparing for its next national exhibition of arts manufactures, was stacked in Cole's favor. As one historian has written, 'It is clear that the Committee was invented for and by Cole and that its management was in his hands.' Numerous manufactures testified to their dissatisfaction with the system of industrial education and the schools of design.[50]

There were two issues facing the Select Committee of 1849: How to revive or reform the production of arts manufactures in Britain, and what role the state should play in doing so. These were the same two issues that were central to the Society of Arts' preparations for the Great Exhibition, and it was Henry Cole, more than anyone else, who brought the two together. Cole was the central figure throughout the School of Design proceedings, just as he was in the organization of the exhibition before 1850. He was a man with a vision, and was prepared to do whatever was necessary to achieve it. In February 1849 he wrote to Granville:

I believe the time will come when the government and the public will thank me for what I am doing and that it will then be quite consistent that your Lordship should avowedly sanction the object I have in view, which is not merely to obtain a reform of the School of Design – but a recognition and conduct of all the interests of commercial design worthy of their national importance.[51]

What Cole envisioned was an entire restructuring of the system of design and manufacturing in Britain. For him, the exhibition was a means to a broader end. He was sure of the importance of his vision, and convinced that in the long run history would see that he was right.

The publicity generated by the School of Design hearings provided the Society with a boost. The 1849 exhibition was by far the most successful one in Britain to date, in large part because manufacturers were eager to participate.[52] Albert himself offered prizes, and Queen Victoria loaned a gilt centerpiece which the Society took as a royal seal of approval for the exhibition venture.[53] Henry Cole, enterprising as ever, took advantage of the public enthusiasm surrounding the exhibition and invited signatures for a Parliamentary petition seeking support for a quincennial national exhibition of works of industry, commencing in 1851. In April 1849 Milner Gibson presented the petition to Parliament, where it was referred to the Select Committee on the Schools of Design, which expressed its support.[54]

Having thus received at least tacit consent from the government, the next step for the Society of Arts in their campaign for an 1851 exhibition was to produce a comprehensive plan. Towards this end, they commissioned Matthew Digby Wyatt, a young architect, to report on the eleventh national exposition being held on the Champs-Elysées in Paris. Wyatt wrote up a detailed report, but it was Cole, who had accompanied him, who returned with a visionary idea.[55] While in Paris, Cole had heard that the French Minister for Agriculture and Commerce had proposed that the exposition be conducted on an international scale. The French Chamber of Commerce, under pressure from protectionist French industrialists, had rejected the idea, but it fired Cole's imagination. For years he had harbored a utopian vision of free trade ushering in an era of international peace and prosperity, as industrial competition replaced military aggression. Cole shared his ideas with Wyatt, and collected as many opinions as he could on the question of whether the still hypothetical exhibition of 1851 should be national or international. Herbert Minton, among others, encouraged Cole to pursue the internationalist approach.[56]

In June 1849, Scott Russell again suggested to Albert, and then stated publicly at the annual distribution of prizes at the Society of Arts, that the time had arrived for the Society to contemplate carrying out the idea of a national exhibition.[57] Soon thereafter Albert asked Scott Russell to Buckingham Palace to present his reasons for believing an exhibition would be successful. Scott Russell said that the public was no longer apathetic, that better information on the nature and effects of such exhibitions had been communicated to manufacturers, and that the cooperation of the community at large could be expected. He also mentioned to Albert that Cole, Wyatt, and Francis Fuller had all recently made trips to the Paris exposition and that each had reported back favorably.

Albert finally took matters into his own hands. The government had given its approval; Fuller had outlined a financial plan; it was time to move, even more so because on 1 August Albert and Victoria were scheduled to leave for Ireland, and from there travel first to Balmoral, their Scottish holiday home, and then to Osborne, their newly-built stuccoed Italianate villa on the Isle of Wight, for the remainder of the summer. Albert called Cole to Buckingham Palace on 29 June. The discussion centered on possible locations for the exhibition, until Cole broke in to inquire about the 'character' of the exhibition – whether it should be national or international. The

Prince deliberated for a moment, and then declared: 'It must embrace foreign productions . . . international, certainly.'[58] After years of laying the groundwork, the time had finally come to turn the vision into a plan of action.

PLANS AND PREPARATIONS

On 30 June 1849, the very next day, Albert met with Cole, Fuller, Scott Russell, and Thomas Cubitt, the London developer and self-taught architect who had built the new Osborne House in 1845–6 and was continuing to make improvements to it. This was the meeting that launched the Great Exhibition of 1851 by establishing a structural framework around which the exhibition could be organized. The original draft of the minutes of this meeting, with corrections made by Albert himself, provides fascinating clues to what was on the minds of those who met that day at Buckingham Palace.[59] It lends further weight to the argument that the exhibition was fundamentally an attempt to improve British design, rather than to celebrate Britain's economic prowess; it reveals the tension that was present throughout the exhibition between nationalism and internationalism; and it suggests that the form and meaning of the exhibition were protean from the beginning.

The meeting began with Albert suggesting three reasons for organizing 'a great collection of works of industry and art in London in 1851:' exhibition, competition, encouragement. He then expressed his belief that such a collection and exhibition should consist of four divisions. What stands out first is that these categories are in a different order from that ultimately adopted. Albert's corrections to the original minutes added numbers, shown below in square brackets, which determined the categorization of exhibits at the exhibition:

[2] Machinery and Mechanical Inventions
[3] Decorative Manufactures
[1] Raw Materials of Manufactures, British Colonial and Foreign
[4] Sculpture connected with Architecture and Plastic Art Generally

It is significant that the first category listed, and probably the first one that came to mind, was 'machinery and mechanical inventions.' The Great Exhibition of 1851, for all it said about the industrial process, and for all it became a trade and consumer fair of finished manufactured goods that could be bought and sold, was at heart an exhibition of 'machinery and mechanical inventions.' It was to be about new ideas, possibilities.

Another significant correction to this list was Albert crossing out the word 'decorative' in 'Decorative Manufactures,' a decision which reveals much about how, upon reflection, he and the others viewed manufactured goods as intrinsically reflecting the quality of their design. After all, the idea of the exhibition emerged in part out of Cole's plans to reform the schools of design, and the vision he and Albert shared of marrying arts and manufactures. In all likelihood, they saw manufactures not exclusively as commercial products, but equally as educational devices, in which decoration was a key component. The primary deficiency of British manufactures, compared especially to the French but also to those in other European nations, was in design and workmanship, and only secondarily in sales. Decoration and ornamentation were critical issues.

Finally, Albert raised the issue of whether the exhibition should be international or whether it 'should be exclusively limited to British industry.' The original draft stated that 'advantages would arise from collecting the scattered productions of all nations and that foreign productions ought not to be excluded. The occasion would be one on which the visits of foreigners to England should be encouraged as extensively as possible.' The corrected version emphasized the advantages that would accrue to *British* industry: 'It was considered that, whilst it appears an error to fix any limitations in the productions of machinery, science and taste which are of no country but belong as a whole to the civilized world, particular advantage to British industry might be derived from placing it in fair competition with that of other nations.' In other words, a competition not just with general benefits for all nations, but with specific benefits for Britain. At the same time, however, the planners deleted a clause stating that the exhibition 'might prove of great service to the city of London, by the concourse of visitors whom it would bring there and to the manufacturing towns of the kingdom to whose productions it would be introduced.' The minutes, therefore, present a picture of the organizers struggling to balance their personally held belief in Benthamite internationalism with their realization that in order to promote the exhibition they would need to present it in more nationalistic and commercially beneficial terms.

Even at this early stage of the exhibition's planning, the organizers were expressing, in their own private deliberations, conflicting goals, opinions, and objectives. The form the exhibition took, and more importantly the meanings being ascribed to it, were already changeable and contested. From the outset there was uncertainty about how nationalist or internationalist the event should be, and about what aspects of British industry the exhibition represented, whether it was to showcase finished decorative products, finished goods regardless of their decorative merits, machinery, or a more general process of production. These were all issues that were present at the creation, and continued to be interpreted, misinterpreted, and refined before, during, and after the Great Exhibition.

Another major issue at the 30 June 1849 meeting was money. Cubitt estimated that they would need £75,000, which included £50,000 for the building, £20,000 for prizes, and £5,000 for preliminary and administrative expenses. Fuller thought that this could be obtained by public donation, provided the exhibition was carried out under the auspices of the Society of Arts, with Albert's name prominently behind the undertaking. The plan was to obtain large credits in advance which would be guaranteed by wealthy individuals. Fuller and the others perhaps rather optimistically considered the Society of Arts to have sufficient powers to collect money and organize subscriptions, in addition to working out the plan. They also greatly overestimated Albert's willingness to throw his name publicly behind the proposal at this early stage. From 30 June until 14 July the question of funds was a source of great anxiety to Cole, Fuller, and Scott Russell. The problem was how to raise funds *before* invoking Albert's name, in case the plan came to naught.

Those present at the meeting also decided to offer 'very large premiums in money' as inducement to manufacturers 'to produce works which, although they might not form a manufacture profitable in the general market, would, by the effort necessary for their accomplishment permanently raise the calibre of production and improve the character of the manufacture itself.' Once again, the focus was on long-term improvements in the manufacturing and production process, rather than a short-term boost to sales. They further proposed to establish a royal commission with Albert as its head in order to raise the plan to 'a sufficiently elevated position in the eyes of the public and to place beyond all possibility any accusation of partiality or undue influence.'

Two weeks later, on 14 July, Cole, Fuller, Scott Russell, Labouchere, and Albert all met at Osborne. The primary purpose of the meeting was to present Cole, Fuller, and Scott Russell to some of the government ministers, including Sir Robert Peel. Peel declared that he approved of the idea of the exhibition, but cautioned that, until a sufficient number of manufacturers were found to be supportive of the scheme, he would strongly advise Albert and the government to have nothing to do with it. Since manufacturers had not yet been consulted, the meeting came to a close. Over lunch, following the meeting, Fuller expressed, for himself and his colleagues, determination to canvass every manufacturer in the country. They drafted a plan, and departed, agreeing to report to Albert at Balmoral in September.[60] Albert, full of enthusiasm for the direction in which the plan was proceeding, wrote to his brother, Duke Ernst of Saxe-Coburg, 'I am working out a plan for a large industrial exhibition in London, for the whole civilized world.'[61]

There was, however, still substantial disagreement about how quickly to proceed. It was mid-July, and the Parliamentary session was about to come to a close; nothing more could be done on that front. The advice of Peel and Labouchere was to use the summer intercession to rouse support for the exhibition among manufacturers, but Cole thought this too slow a route. He was frustrated by the lack of a commission, impatient with the state bureaucracy, and wanted strong, immediate action. He was, as ever, enthusiastic, impetuous, and self-righteous.[62] Once again, however, Albert urged caution. He believed that the government should not commit itself, by means of a commission, 'without mature consideration in the Cabinet,' and that he should be the person, in his position as President of the Society of Arts (and not as Prince Consort) to approach the cabinet ministers. Phipps reiterated to Cole that the Society of Arts 'may very usefully and beneficially exert themselves without any delay, in feeling more extensively the public pulse . . . and in getting more exact data as to the probable amount of the subscriptions to be expected.'[63] Whereas Cole had wanted to publicize the upcoming exhibition by naming a royal commission immediately, and then let the Society of Arts begin raising funds for what would therefore be a guaranteed event, Albert believed that before his name – or that of the government – was invoked, the Society had to make sure that the idea would be supported. Whereas Cole was (perhaps arrogantly) convinced that he was right, and was prepared to lead and bring public opinion along with him, Albert had to be more prudent, and move only after being assured that he would have widespread support.[64] Albert, apparently, wanted to make very sure he was in control of the arrangements, and he was understandably being careful with his name and reputation. It is also possible he was worried about seeming to interfere in politics when constitutionally he had no official role or powers.

The lack of a commission, however, made financial backers difficult to find. At the 14 July meeting Albert, Cole, and the others had decided to enlist the Society of Arts to organize the fund-raising effort, irrespective of what happened in the short term with the royal commission. Accordingly, the council of the Society resolved to find 'capitalists,' or investors, to advance the money. The council turned to private sources of money because it did not have sufficient funds itself, and was unable to persuade the government to advance them.[65] The Society decided that it needed £20,000 to begin work on the exhibition. Needless to say it was not easy finding a person to advance such a large sum of money with so minimal a guarantee. How could the Society convince someone to take the risk without committing the Prince to the proposal? The Society approached half a dozen men, all of whom rejected the offer. Then Fuller wrote to his father-in-law, George Drew, who was the solicitor for a public works contracting firm, Messrs James and George Munday. Fuller revealed to Drew, in confidence, copies of the minutes of the meetings that had been held at Buckingham Palace and Osborne, as proof of Prince Albert's personal interest in the plan. In the absence of any commercial security, this would have to suffice.[66] On 23 August 1849 the Mundays and the Society of Arts reached an agreement which solved the Society's financial problems, and provided the necessary funds to begin working on the exhibition.[67]

It was the Mundays' commitment to advance the prize money that enabled the organization of the exhibition to proceed. Without prizes to offer the Society believed it would be unable to secure public opinion in support of the exhibition; without public support there would be no royal commission; without a royal commission it was unlikely that there would be a national, let alone an international, exhibition. Once the Society could offer prizes, Cole, Fuller, and Scott Russell could travel to the manufacturing districts of the United Kingdom, armed with letters of introduction and with instructions to report back to Albert in September so that he could submit the results of their findings to the government.[68]

During the early fall, the men of the Society of Arts commenced the critical task of seeking popular support for the project. At the 14 July meeting at Osborne both Peel and Labouchere had suggested that before October, when Parliament would be back in session, it would be useful if the Society could collect 'more evidence as to the readiness of the great manufacturing and commercial interests to subscribe to and support the undertaking.'[69] Labouchere's emphasis on the Society contacting 'the great manufacturing and commercial interests' is revealing about who the organizers oriented the Great Exhibition toward, and whose support they thought they required in order to insure its success. When, in a letter to Sir George Grey, the Home Secretary, on 31 July, Albert wrote of 'preparing the public mind,' what he meant was preparing the minds of certain people, particularly manufacturers, industrialists, and men of commerce, who would be needed to provide both subscriptions and exhibits. In early September, Cole, Fuller, and the others presented the lists of support to Albert at Balmoral, and a month later they reported to the Society of Arts on the positive response of both manufacturers and agriculturalists. By the end of November there were 3,000 names on the list of subscribers, 6,000 by the end of January 1850.[70] The organizers' reward for their tour of the manufacturing districts was an overwhelmingly positive article in *The Times*, the first on the subject of the exhibition.[71] Preliminary indications of support also came from France, Germany, America, and the East India Company.[72]

Only after Albert had heard the opinions of manufacturers did he decide it was time to hold a more public meeting, this time in London. And so about thirty members of the Society of Arts were invited to meet with City magnates at the

Mansion House on 17 October 1849. 'The hall was well filled,' reported *The Times*, with three or four hundred merchants and bankers.[73] Cole's performance at the meeting was a *tour de force*. He reported on the proceedings up to that point, drawing on the minutes of the first meeting at Buckingham Palace; he quoted from a number of supporters; and he listed many of the more famous firms that already supported the idea. He painted a picture of a cornucopia of raw materials from around the world, and of an exhibition that would represent the very best that the world could produce. He spoke of the advantages that would accrue to British industry from competition with other nations, and of the direct benefits to London of foreign buyers and tourists flocking to the metropolis. And, on the issue of funding, he suggested that the best course was to leave contributions optional, rather than to raise funds through taxation, claiming that the British differed from their neighbors in that they 'do much better for themselves than any government can do for them,' a line which received loud cheers.[74] It was an inspiring appeal, and Cole had the crowd firmly behind him, the proposal, and his vision of how the plan should be carried out.[75] The following week Phipps called Cole to Buckingham Palace. The Mansion House meeting had eased the constraints of official caution, and on 24 October 1849 Albert finally spoke with Cole about forming a commission.

THE ROYAL COMMISSION

The formation of the commission was a lengthy and delicate task, and Albert and Cole tried out many people and combinations before they settled on a final list. During the month of December there was frantic and almost continuous behind-the-scenes activity, and both Cole and Labouchere ended up having to work on Christmas day.[76] At one point Albert eliminated several names 'on the ground of the list being too aristocratic.'[77] More problematic was the degree to which manufacturers and industrialists would be included, an issue that had less to do with wariness about giving manufacturers too much *de facto* political power than it reflected manufacturers' trade jealousies and concerns that some of their competitors would be unduly advantaged.[78] The designer and manufacturer Herbert Minton's opinion was 'very decidedly . . . that no manufacturer should be upon it [the commission],' and Alderman Neild of Manchester 'laughed at the notion of manufacturers judging on the interests of cotton printing.'[79] When Labouchere, in a draft list to Albert, included a number of manufacturers, Albert responded that 'if manufacturers are to be upon it, it appears to me a very good one,' but that he still had 'strong apprehensions' and Labouchere should 'try to ascertain the feelings of the manufacturers themselves' before launching into it.[80] What eased some of these difficulties was the plan to create local committees, which provided an opportunity for the representation of manufacturers in the planning process, without involving them at the highest levels.[81] But the issue was not easily or quickly resolved. Although few records survive regarding the many discussions that must have taken place, as late as 14 December the problem was still under consideration, with Albert 'doubting the policy [replacing the word 'propriety,' which had been crossed out] of manufacturers being on the commission.'[82]

4. Henry Windham Phillips, *The Royal Commissioners for the Great Exhibition of 1851*. Victoria and Albert Museum, London.

The Royal Commission was announced on 3 January 1850 (fig. 4). It was appointed to inquire into the general conduct of the exhibition, the most suitable site for the exhibition building, the best mode of introducing foreign manufactures into Britain for the exhibition, and the best way of determining the nature of the prizes and their impartial distribution.[83] It included the following:

Prince Albert (President), President, Royal Society for the Arts
Earl Granville (Vice President)
Duke of Buccleuch
Earl of Ellesmere, President, Royal Asiatic Society; Rector, King's College, Aberdeen
Earl of Rosse, President, Royal Society
Lord John Russell, Prime Minister
Lord Stanley (Earl of Derby), Leader of the Opposition
Robert Peel MP
Thomas Baring MP, Chairman, Lloyd's and Baring Brothers
Charles Barry, Architect
Thomas Bazley, Chairman, Manchester Chamber of Commerce
Richard Cobden MP, Leader, Anti-Corn Law League
William Cubitt, President, Institute of Civil Engineers
Charles Lock Eastlake, President, Royal Academy
Archibald Galloway, Chairman, East India Company
Thomas Field Gibson, Spitalfields Silk Merchant

William Gladstone MP
John Gott, Leeds Wool Manufacturer
Henry Labouchere MP, President of the Board of Trade
Samuel Jones Loyd (Baron Overstone), Chairman, Jones, Loyd, and Company
Charles Lyell, President, Geological Society
Philip Pusey MP, Founder, Royal Agricultural Society
William Thompson MP, Alderman, City of London
Richard Westmacott, Sculptor, Marble Arch Reliefs

The Times praised its composition as proof that the government was acting with 'perfect impartiality,' that 'every shade of political opinion in the country, and every great interest in the State,' was represented on the commission, and that 'Protectionism, the Peerage, the commonality, science, art, [and] the East India Company' were all to 'have a voice' in the preparations.[84] But who were these men in reality? What were their backgrounds? What values and priorities did they bring to the commission?

The commissioners ranged in age from Albert and Granville, who were thirty-one and thirty-five respectively, to Cubitt (Thomas Cubitt's younger brother) and Galloway, who were the oldest, at ages sixty-four and seventy. Most were in their fifties, and slightly fewer than half had been born in the nineteenth century. As a group they were wealthy and well educated, one-third having attended one of the elite public schools as well as Oxford or Cambridge. Most had political careers, which meant not only election to Parliament, but also service on various national public interest committees. Loyd, for example, had served on the Commission on Hand Loom Weavers, and Bazley was one of the earliest supporters of the Lancashire Public Schools Association. The vast majority had been supportive of political reform and were committed to free trade. Granville, Gladstone, and Labouchere had all lessened trade restrictions during their tenures at the Board of Trade, and Peel, Cobden, Bazley, and Loyd were leaders in the fight to repeal the Corn Laws. It was difficult to miss the fact that there were only four protectionists on the commission (Stanley, Baring, Thompson, and Pusey); that only two had opposed franchise reform in 1832 (Gladstone and Peel); and that there were more men of finance, industry, and commerce than there were men of the peerage, although these categories were by no means exclusive. As a group, these men believed in 'progress,' and were deeply interested in science and technological innovation. Rosse, for example, had funded at a cost of £20,000 an enormous telescope, the 'Leviathan of Parsonstown,' to probe 'the abyss of the heavenly wilderness' – the Great Nebula in Orion. He joined the commission out of his belief that the exhibition would encourage engineers and scientists to become more practical and to make their work more relevant for industry and manufacturing.[85] Even Pusey, who had strongly supported the Corn Laws, urged agriculturalists to make the best of their position after the restrictions on the import of foreign grains were lifted in 1846, and to adopt scientific improvements in order to enable them to compete with foreign producers. It was he who introduced McCormick's reaper into Britain, on his estates in Berkshire in 1851.[86]

These were also men who had sought to improve the plight of the poor. Bazley was the first large employer to pay weekly wages on Fridays, not Saturdays, and Gladstone, as President of the Board of Trade, had worked diligently to establish the Parliamentary trains, whereby railroad companies were required to run one train with covered carriages each weekday, stopping at every station, at a speed of at least twelve miles per hour, at a rate of not more than one penny per mile, which had the effect of making railway travel affordable to the masses.[87]

The Times was certainly correct in that the commissioners had been chosen to represent certain sectors of society. These included the aristocracy, the political establishment, science, industry, the arts, commerce and finance, agriculture, and the empire. Scotland was also represented, in Buccleuch (by virtue of his estates) and Ellesmere (as Rector of King's College, Aberdeen). That only about one-quarter of the commissioners were active participants in the organization of the exhibition suggests that what many of them symbolized – the arts (Barry, Eastlake, and Westmacott), the political establishment (Russell and Stanley) – was more important that what they actually contributed. But the commission was in no way representative of Great Britain. Wales and Ireland were both without representation, as were the working classes, because anyone who could claim to speak for them (such as John Bright) would probably have been seen as too radical, democratic, and threatening. And, while Gladstone and Peel were devout churchmen, there was no one on the commission representing the religious community, either Church of England or Dissenting.

Despite their various similarities, what was most notable at the time was how different these men's backgrounds were, and this of course was The Times editorialist's point. There were peers, northern industrialists, London bankers, engineers, and artists. They came from different worlds, moved in different social circles, and, most importantly, operated in different markets.[88] While most of the commissioners were surely familiar with the others on the commission – many had been to school together, some had previously served together on committees, others had sat together in Parliament – this should in no way obscure the enormous differences in social standing between them. Even among the aristocrats, there was a deep divide between what was called the 'Grand Whiggery,' which included Russell, Granville, and Ellesmere, and the Baring–Labouchere wing.[89]

This varied group came together to plan the exhibition at a time of great political transition. The Great Exhibition coincided with the period in which the old Whig–Tory system was giving way to the gradual formation of the Liberal and Conservative parties and, it is argued here, played a significant role in helping to facilitate that shift by bringing together prospective liberals and by disseminating liberal values. While it is possible to trace an evolving liberalism at least from the 1830s (if not earlier), by most accounts a united Liberal party did not come into existence until some time after 1859.[90] The central event in this process was Peel's decision in 1846 to repeal the Corn Laws, which for thirty years had kept the price of grain artificially high to the benefit of landholders and the detriment of the increasing number of urban dwellers. Peel's bold move toward free trade, which cost him his political office though it increased his popular standing, splintered the Conservative party and created havoc with the party system. Following Peel's resignation and the formation of a new government under Russell, there were in effect three Parliamentary groups, none of which had enough votes to govern by itself: the Whigs (sometimes called Liberals), the Protectionists (sometimes called Conservatives or Tories) and the Peelites (sometimes called Conservatives, Liberal–Conservatives or Free-Traders). But, however one labels the various groups on the political scene, for nearly the entire period from 1846 to 1874 the political opposition in Parliament consisted of non-Peelite Conservatives.

The Royal Commission for the Great Exhibition was itself a microcosm of the various political forces – Whig, Radical, and Peelite – that would soon come to be known as Liberal, bringing together prospective liberals at a time shortly before they came to identify themselves in this way. The remarkable feat of the commission was to bridge the enormous gaps between the commissioners by temporarily uniting them around a common purpose, helping to forge a liberal coalition in the process. It joined together those who leaned towards free trade, but who otherwise appeared to have little in common.[91] It would be anachronistic to label many of the organizers of the Great Exhibition liberals; Peelite would be more appropriate for some, Whig or Radical for others. Many of them, nonetheless, were adherents of what would later be called liberalism, and would eventually identify themselves as liberals and join the Liberal party, a 'broad church' according to J. S. Mill.[92]

Moreover, the Great Exhibition itself was a force for the creation of the Liberal party, by disseminating liberal ideas both in its structure and organization and in its actual content. While it is extremely difficult to define liberalism, in the mid-nineteenth century British liberals, in general, believed in individualism, competition, free enterprise and free trade, education, and parliamentary reform. They regarded government as the harmonization of different and potentially incompatible classes and interest groups within the political nation; they were committed to the integration of all parts of the United Kingdom; they attempted to break free of landed influence and tended to emphasize that different social groups had common, rather than clashing, economic interests; they believed in the perfectibility of society; and they attempted to define Christianity in a broad and undogmatic manner that might unite, rather than fracture, the nation.[93] As subsequent chapters will document, not only did these ideas inform the organization and structure of the exhibition, but the commissioners and their assistants attempted to use the exhibition as a means of achieving these ends. Even before a Liberal party had been formed, the Great Exhibition gave coherence to the idea of liberalism.

Liberalism, however, was by no means an immutable concept, and the exhibition was an event that could – and did – take on a number of meanings; its symbolism had to be negotiated. The significance of the commission was that it imparted to the exhibition a certain image, that at least in part was based on who the commissioners were, where they came from, and what they stood for. What should be clear though from the outset is that the exhibition lacked any crude or fixed ideology. Rather, its organization reflects many different objectives. To the extent that there was a dominant aim, it was not so much to celebrate British industrial supremacy as to rectify deficiencies in industrialization, both the process and the product. What had begun not as a way 'to show the world that "we are the greatest," '[94] as one historian put it, but as a way to address the deficiencies in the design and the sales of British manufactures, would end as a paradigm for both the exercise and the display of liberal values in nineteenth-century Britain.

CHAPTER 2

Obstacles: Planning the Exhibition

THE ROYAL COMMISSION that Queen Victoria announced on 3 January 1850 succeeded famously. In just over a year, the commissioners and their assistants organized a display of over 100,000 exhibits in a building – built from the ground up in nine months – that was at the time the largest enclosed space on earth. The organizers solicited almost £80,000 in donations, held an international competition for the design of the exhibition building, secured guarantee funds of £250,000 to commence and complete construction of it, collected and organized the exhibits, publicized the event widely, and made arrangements that ultimately accommodated more than six million visits. The Great Exhibition was a phenomenal success, and accolades poured in from the day it opened, on May Day 1851.

The achievements of the Royal Commission were due in no small part to its superior organization and planning, and its adeptness at delegating authority to talented, capable assistants. The commission was neither directly nor constantly engaged in the preparations, at times meeting weekly, at other times only monthly. In general, it tried to remain above the fray surrounding particular disputes, and met mainly to resolve significant issues. As *The Times* put it, blending description and propaganda, it was 'placed at a calm and tranquil elevation over the whole din and bustle, and, like the Homeric gods, only occasionally condescending to look down upon that struggling scene of energy and enthusiasm.'[1]

Most of the issues relating to the exhibition were handled by sub-committees composed of members of the commission, along with 'several men of eminence in the particular pursuits most nearly connected with the subject of inquiry.' Thus the finance committee included, in addition to eight commissioners, A. Y. Spearman, 'a gentleman whose long connection with the Treasury had rendered him familiar with the practice of the government in financial matters,' and Samuel Morton Peto, one of the treasurers for the commission, 'whose extensive experience of contracts for great undertakings rendered him a most valuable and efficient adviser.'[2] This system made the most of the talent on the commission by involving those with particular interests, experiences, or areas of expertise, supplemented as needed by experts. The use of both commissioners and non-commissioners in the decision-making also pre-empted accusations of cronyism since, for example, few could question Peto's expertise in areas of finance.

The details of the exhibition were delegated to an executive committee, presided over first by Robert Stephenson, the famous railway engineer, and then by Lieutenant-Colonel William Reid, head of the Royal Military College, which met daily in offices in the Palace Yard. Working with the committee were two special commissioners, Lyon Playfair and Lieutenant-Colonel J. A. Lloyd, who acted as intermediaries between the Royal Commission and the more than 300 local committees, and a secretary, Matthew Digby Wyatt, who handled virtually all the day-to-day administrative details. The executive committee was responsible for soliciting and collecting contributions and exhibits, arranging the exhibits, regulating the admission of spectators, and providing for the safety of the building and its contents, along with anything else that came along. It also handled most of the correspondence, which amounted to almost 40,000 letters (incoming alone) by September 1851.[3] Although the Royal Commission has received most of the praise for organizing the exhibition, both at the time and by historians since, in fact the commission did little; most of the important work was handled by several competent, versatile young men. As a group they, like the commission itself, were interested in science, industry, commerce, and the arts, and they all had the ear and patronage of prominent and powerful individuals, particularly Albert and Peel.[4]

Despite capable men and a sophisticated organization, the road from January 1850 to May Day 1851 was not a smooth one. The formal announcement of the Royal Commission transformed the exhibition from a private Society of Arts affair to a public event. Although the Royal Commission was the necessary first step, it was only that. The early organizers – Cole, Scott Russell, Fuller, and a few others – had accomplished much since Whishaw's initial, tentative attempt at organizing an exhibition of industry five years earlier, but, as of January 1850 when the commission was announced, they were still a long way away, in terms of organization, from the opening, with only fifteen months in which to formulate and execute their plans for an international exhibition of industry. The Royal Commissioners and organizers had to produce a plan of action, and they had to sell their idea of the exhibition to the public. They also had to confront a series of problems, each of which imperilled the exhibition. First, they had to resolve the issue of funding, which meant terminating the contract with the Mundays. This in turn created organizational problems which threatened to undermine the exhibition from within. Finally, they had to find a suitable design and location for the building. The first and third of these became very public disputes, and are especially significant because their resolution helped impart to the exhibition its national character. What is important to bear in mind is that there were many points at which the entire enterprise could have failed, and that success came only on May Day 1851.

TERMINATING THE CONTRACT

The Royal Commission met for the first time at the Palace of Westminster on 11 January 1850. Heading the agenda was the contract between the Society of Arts and the Mundays, and the commissioners quickly decided to ask the Lords of the Treasury to terminate the contract based on a clause Cole had inserted just before the contract had been signed.[5] Important sectors of the press were vehemently against the private financing of a public – and national – exhibition. At the time the contract had been signed there was no other apparent way to fund the exhibition; the organizers needed money up front to get the preparations under way, and to put the plan before the public. But they seem not to have been entirely comfortable with the idea of the contract at any point, even though they acknowledged its necessity. They neglected, for example, to mention it at the large meeting at the

Mansion House on 17 October 1849, even though it would have been logical to present the full facts of the organization to the public at that time.[6] This became an issue because the organizers used that Mansion House meeting to make their first fund-raising appeal. When the press learned of the contract six weeks later, the organizers came across as having been deceitful, asking for public subscriptions on the one hand, while having sought private funding on the other.

The change of heart regarding the contract occurred because perceptions of the Great Exhibition changed dramatically between the time the Society of Arts signed the contract with the Mundays in the early fall of 1849, and late December 1849, after Charles Wentworth Dilke had made a tour of the manufacturing towns drumming up support for the exhibition. By the end of 1849 there had been substantial demonstrations of support for the idea of a national exhibition of industry. As it became clear that the exhibition was going to be a large and national event, the executive committee began to receive letters in favor of non-private funding. In early January the Mayor of Manchester requested an interview with Prince Albert to discuss the contract even before the commission was announced. When Albert turned him down, the Manchester delegation held a meeting to protest the haste with which they thought the contract had been signed and passed a resolution 'opposing any immediate ratification of the contract.'[7] And the *Literary Gazette* referred to the contract as 'Mundayan,' claiming that it would produce a Mundayan exposition with Mundayan prizes and profits.[8] This, combined with the declarations of support, financial and otherwise, following the Mansion House dinner meant that by mid-December the Mundays were no longer needed or wanted.

The opposition to the Society of Arts' contract with the Mundays revolved around several interrelated issues. The first was profits, and whether the Mundays would benefit financially from a project that was being funded by the public. The organizers were all too aware of the delicate nature of this matter. Back in November 1849 Fuller and Labouchere had traveled to Windsor to meet with Albert, who had inquired whether the contractors would make a substantial profit on their investment. Fuller said he estimated the Mundays' profit to be of the order of £100,000, whereupon Labouchere asked whether there was a way to curtail or limit the amount.[9] A week later, Cole and Albert discussed the same issue, whether the Mundays would agreed to 'a limitation of profits and on what terms.'[10] It was Prince Albert as much as anyone who led the charge against the contract. *The Times*, which had praised the signing of the contract as a step which transformed a vague idea into 'a real *bona fide* plan,' tried to reassure the public that their subscriptions would not just go straight into the Mundays' pockets: 'It is true that the exhibition has in a certain limited degree become the private venture of two capitalists, but their hypothetical profits are hedged round and affected with many provisions and restrictions.'[11]

But *The Times*' readers were not nearly so accommodating. One correspondent characterized the contract with the Mundays as 'one of those aleatory bargains which are only to be met with in the lottery office or the gambling table,' and said that this was 'a bargain, with which the august name and unbusiness character of Prince Albert ought never to have been mixed up.'[12] The *Patent Journal* took an even more critical approach, in an article titled 'The Exhibition of 1851; Is it to be made a "Job?"' It objected to the contract, especially after the 17 October meeting at the Mansion House had revealed how strongly those in attendance were in favor of raising funds by public subscription. It accused the organizers of being duplicitous, of holding a public meeting to obtain support even though a private arrangement had already been made, and shuddered at the thought of 'private capitalists . . . making a *profit* by the *National* Exhibition!' The journal objected to the 'spirit' of the agreement, which it saw as 'derogatory to the character of the nation.'[13] Broadsheets began to appear criticizing the plans, some signed by 'Thalaba,' an Arabian hero who fought the forces of evil (fig. 5).

This controversy over the contract suggests not only a persistent suspicion of jobbery, or corruption, but also some deep reservations about the potential consequences of commercial capitalism. 'When a man enters into any contract,' wrote W. B. Adams for the *Westminster Review* in 1851, 'and especially a public one, in a commercial country, if it be a losing one he is usually called a fool or a rogue; if a profitable one, he is hooted as a jobber.'[14] This comment reflects an aversion to or discomfort with any financial risk-taking, especially where public funds were concerned.

It is not clear, however, that opinions would have been any different had no public funds been involved. Had the contract been carried out, and the Mundays advanced the money for the exhibition and been repaid from admissions, the contract would

THE GREAT JOB
OF 1851.

FELLOW COUNTRYMEN!—workers, either with head or hands, who take an interest in securing for honest English industry its just reward—grant me, I pray, a few moments' attention while I inflate this great bubble of 1851, 'till it burst, and be resolved into its primitive *lixivium* of soap and water.

The scheme of an Exhibition of the Industry of all Nations, resisted by successive administrations, has, at length, been foisted upon the public by a court intrigue, carried on with some five or six members of the Society of Arts in the Adelphi,—of which society Prince Albert is president—who in Prince Albert's name, and under his especial patronage, have succeeded in launching this unwieldy project on the vast ocean of Great British gullibility, and, at the same time, have thrust themselves into lucrative appointments on a Royal Commission—ever a fertile source of jobbing and corruption. As yet, no trustworthy evidence has been brought forward to prove that such Exhibitions were ever beneficial to the arts, manufactures, or trade of any country.

In a state of transition, from an artificial, high-duty system, called protective, to a more sound and healthy one, we have not yet obtained free-trade. The duty on foreign corn has been repealed; the duty on slave sugar reduced, by canting and recanting Lord John Russell; but many important necessaries of life are still as heavily taxed; tea, some three hundred per cent; beer, paper, tobacco—almost the only luxury of the working man—twelve hundred per cent; the Press, now consequently become, with few exceptions, the organ of the Money Power—the window tax, it appears, are still raised; yet despite this onerous amount of taxation—which the chief promoters of this scheme are deeply interested in maintaining at the cost of the productive classes—it is proposed suddenly to drive the English artizan and mechanic—still an unenfranchised political cipher—into direct competition with all the nations of the world. Cheapness, mark me,—("tremendous sacrifice!" "nominal prices!")—is one of the qualifications of articles for exhibition, though cheap things will be found *dear enough at last*,—after the mischief has been done. If this forced introduction of continental prices for manufactures be found necessary to the Money Power, at all events, let the working classes *insist* upon being *first relieved* from the system of indirect taxation upon articles of consumption, which falls *directly* upon *them*, and put a stop to the Whig million loans to the landlords out of the surplus taxation from the people.

The productive classes will be the *first to suffer* by this forced reduction in the price of all manufactured commodities; the *difference* must be paid by the working man, by a *reduction* of his *wages*, unless relieved by a proportionate reduction of taxation. He requires untaxed raw material, untaxed necessaries of life, and the Whigs repeal the duty on Bricks! He asks—small blame to him—for UNIVERSAL SUFFRAGE, and a Royal Commission is issued to devise means for increasing the already fearful amount of competition, the devil-take-the-hindmost principle, against which he already finds it so difficult to contend. Who is to profit, I ask, by this reduction? The Money Power, now becoming omnipotent, unless the people secure to themselves their fair share of political influence. People of England, remember the railway mania! and tremble, when you reflect that political power in this country, is still monopolized by men who parcelled you out and sold you, like bullocks in Smithfield, to the highest bidder.

Not content with inviting foreigners to exhibit their wares duty free, the Royal Commission has offered them money premiums

to tempt them to compete with us, and has obtained considerable sums of money for that purpose—the foreigners not subscribing one farthing, and I confess myself unable to comprehend how the British artist, manufacturer, legitimate trader or mechanic is to benefit by a National Subscription, for the purpose of erecting sixteen acres of *shop fronts* in Hyde Park, three-fourths of which must be devoted to the wares of our foreign competitors. In these days of steam-boats and railways, the trader runs no risk of having his goods damaged on the journey, and the cost is insignificant. The foreigner pays no English rates, rents, nor taxes, and will exhibit at our expense, with a sure sale afterwards, and probable future *demand* for *his* goods. He may and probably will deprive the "legitimate trader," who has to pay English *rent, rates,* and *taxes,* of his regular customers, who have already and to a perceptible amount *stopped their orders,* "until the great Exhibition of 1851." When the Exhibition is over, to whom will the orders be given? Why to the foreigner, to be sure, and his foreign novelties—novelties to John Bull at least, however ancient they may be. BULL! you are a great bubble swallower: but if you allow yourself to be bamfoozled by this barefaced imposition, this *impudent job,* this conspiracy of *art-manufacturers*—who can't sell their trumpery wares, then I say, and I say it with the highest respect for your many virtues, that *you* are a greater fool than I took you for. Therefore, I say, brave BULL, take timely warning! First very widely extend the suffrage, and then cut down your "Budget, as it is," to what "it might be." When you have accomplished these important preliminaries; when you have emancipated yourself from the thraldom of the feudal Whigs of the soil; when you have returned a House of Commons *which shall represent the People;* and when you have established *public* repositories of fine art in all your large towns—then, but *not till then,* invite your foreign competitors to exhibit specimens of their handy work. But if you do not mind what you are about, my worthy friend, the foreigner will come over, win your prizes, carry off your regular customers, and laugh at you for your pains, as a silly gullible old fool. And you, my dear BULL, will *not* laugh, unless it be at your own folly.

None but exceeding flat fish will be caught by the cock and bull story of the enterprising Yankee speculators who are to purchase the whole Exhibition! From whom are they to purchase the Exhibition? What are they to purchase?—an Adelphian *idea* of an Exhibition—a *pendant* to the great sea serpent! Have *they* also got a sham capitalist contractor and paid patriotic *Executive Committeemen* at £800 a year? Are the Yankees so rich in Californian dust that they have no better use for it than to fling it in our eyes? or perhaps they might like to purchase the Exhibition with Pennsylvanian securities? Therefore, do not subscribe to the "great plan" of 1851! You will find that you have more serious work on hand than getting up shilling exhibitions for the *gobemouches* of Europe, and cannot afford to subscribe a large capital for the purpose of stimulating the manufactures of Germany and France at your own cost.

Having lately consulted that invaluable instrument called a *foolometer,* discovered according to Sydney Smith by a celebrated stump orator of his day, I am assured on this infallible authority, that the great British *genus* meant to subscribe no more money to be squabbled and scrambled for by a gang of rapacious speculators.

Your sincere friend and well-wisher,

THALABA.

N.B.—When read please to circulate this?

Practical Typ., 62, Piccadilly, corner of Albermarle Street.

5. An anti-exhibition broadsheet: 'The Great Job of 1851'.

still have been seen as a 'job,' because for most people a national exhibition meant one that should be funded through public subscription. The problem with the contract was not only that many Britons bristled at the notion of a private capitalist making a profit on a public, national event. It was that they also believed – and were increasingly encouraged by the commissioners and the press to believe – that they, and not the Mundays or the government, should fund the exhibition. John Tallis, author of one of the many unofficial guides to the Great Exhibition, wrote: 'The wishes of the people so evidently turned towards considering the exhibition entirely as a national and self-supporting institution.'[15] Although Tallis wrote his account after the exhibition opened (that is, after it had been successfully funded by public donations), thus raising the issue of how much he was merely justifying a course of action that had already been taken, there is more than enough evidence to suggest that educated, respectable society increasingly preferred an exhibition financed through voluntary public subscription.

So strident was the outcry against the contract that in early December the executive committee of the Society of Arts formally asked the Mundays if they would put a ceiling on their potential profits. The Mundays' representative, George Drew, understandably bristled at the suggestion, countering that perhaps the government or the Society of Arts might also like to put a floor on potential losses. Drew said that the Mundays sympathized with the desire of the Prince 'to protect to the utmost the public interests in this matter,' and fully admitted that the public perceived the undertaking in a very different light than it had back in July, but that the risk the Mundays took ought to be remembered. He offered to submit the dispute to arbitration at the conclusion of the exhibition to determine the Mundays' share of the profits, and this was the course which was ultimately adopted, after the Royal Commission officially terminated the contract.[16]

The controversy over the contract had a number of implications. First, and most importantly, it determined a strategy for funding the exhibition. The outcry over the prospect of a national event being funded by private capitalists who might potentially benefit from public funds forced the organizers and commissioners to make the exhibition a truly public and national undertaking. The opposition to the contract forced the organizers to appeal not to the government or to the wealthy few, but to people of all classes, a step which turned the fund-raising for the Great Exhibition into a tribute to the principle of voluntarism. It is important as well to recognize the notions of nationalism here, as the exhibition was transformed from a private and sectional to a public and national event.

It is also clear from this episode how Albert and Cole had at times to lead public opinion in order to push the preparations for the exhibition forward, while at other times they in effect had to succumb to the demands of the press and the public. There is no question that either Cole or Albert thought that inviting the Mundays to provide financial backing for the exhibition was the ideal solution; at the time they had little choice. But when the public – here meaning relatively wealthy men of commerce, finance, and industry, as well as the editors of the highbrow periodicals (an admittedly limited definition) – refused to sanction such an approach, the organizers astutely modified their approach in order to maintain support for the endeavor.

Finally, the cancellation of the contract with the Mundays caused a number of organizational problems within the executive committee, and between the Royal

Commissioners, the executive committee, and the Society of Arts. The decision to cancel the contract was relatively easy. The subsequent funding and marketing of the exhibition would prove more challenging, but first the commissioners had to get their own house in order.

RESTRUCTURING THE INTERNAL ORGANIZATION

The decision to cancel the contract not only unequivocally redefined the exhibition as a national, public event, it also forced the commissioners to re-evaluate their organization, which had already been a problem for months. Underlying a series of organizational difficulties and personal rivalries were real conflicts about how the exhibition should be organized, and who should do the organizing. Through the fall of 1849 the exhibition had been the province of the Society of Arts. The function of the Royal Commission, when it was appointed, had been merely to 'make full and diligent inquiry' into the best way of carrying out the exhibition, giving the Society of Arts quasi-official sanction. Needless to say, this arrangement had its problems. One organization had to be responsible for both policy-making and execution, and once appointed only the Royal Commission could be that body.[17] But, while the creation of a Royal Commission meant that it was solely responsible for the preparations for the exhibition, only a few of its members were capable of or indeed even interested in carrying out the necessary daily operations. For that aspect there was the executive committee, originally appointed by the Society of Arts, charged with carrying out the day-to-day tasks of organizing the exhibition. The committee consisted of Henry Cole, Charles Wentworth Dilke, Francis Fuller, Robert Stephenson, and George Drew. But the termination of the contract had two consequences for the personnel involved in the executive committee. First, one of its members, George Drew, had been appointed solely to represent the interests of the Mundays, so his presence was clearly superfluous. Moreover, since the exhibition no longer explicitly involved the Society of Arts, and the Royal Commission was now in charge of all the plans, the four remaining members of the executive committee offered to submit their resignations in the interest of giving the commissioners the opportunity to choose new executive officers.[18]

The tension was compounded by the fact that relations were very strained between Cole, on the executive committee, and Scott Russell, secretary of the Society of Arts.[19] Henry Cole wrote in his diary on 4 November 1849: '[Scott] Russell observed that someone had said I was a great jobber and wondered why he had connected me with the scheme! He rather stumbled out an explanation upon perceiving my indignation.' And, five weeks later: 'C. W. Dilke came out: thought there was evidently a feeling in [the] Executive Committee that he and I were working against Fuller and Russell.'[20] Cole was in fact unsparing in his dislike of Russell, and noted all criticism of him in his diary.[21] The conflict between Cole and Scott Russell centered on who should serve as secretary to the Royal Commission, and hence be in charge of the preparations. Cole must have been infuriated when, after leaving a meeting with Albert believing that his good friend Samuel Redgrave would be the secretary to the Royal Commission, he discovered instead that Scott Russell was going to serve as one of the secretaries, along with Stafford Northcote, with whom Cole had feuded over the schools of design.[22]

John Scott Russell was born in 1808 in the weavers' village of Parkhead, near Glasgow, the son of a parish school teacher. He matriculated at the University of Glasgow at the age of thirteen, already with a grounding in Latin, and graduated four years later, moving to Edinburgh, where he became a math teacher and supplemented his income by teaching at a mechanics' institute. Though his lectures were very popular, he turned to industrial design, developing first a steam engine which was adopted by the Scottish Steam Carriage Company for its Glasgow–Paisley line, and later ships, becoming, in the words of one historian, 'the most scientifically educated naval architect in Britain at this time.'[23] In the mid-1840s he moved to London, having been recruited by Charles Wentworth Dilke, who was editor of the *Athenaeum*, to edit the *Railway Chronicle*, and soon thereafter joined the Society of Arts. During these years Russell seems to have gotten along well with Cole, despite their different backgrounds. Their families became friends, and they walked, talked, drank, and dined together, often with Cole's contacts in the art world. It was in fact Scott Russell who enticed Cole to join the staff of the *Railway Chronicle*, and later got him a post at Charles Dickens' *Daily News* at a salary of £750 per year.[24] While the source of tension between Scott Russell and Cole is not entirely clear, there is no question that Scott Russell had a tendency to involve himself in too many things at one time – designing ships, serving as secretary of the Society of Arts, working at the *Railway Chronicle* and the *Daily News* – and that he was a fairly abrasive, and perhaps at times incompetent, man.[25] But it was not only that Cole and others held a low opinion of Russell; it was that they were also personal and political rivals.

Joining Scott Russell as secretary to the Royal Commission was Stafford North-cote, and Cole got along only marginally better with him. Northcote was born in Devonshire in 1818, and was educated at Eton and Balliol, showing, according to his biographer, no great proficiency in school.[26] He handled odd jobs while waiting for a seat in Parliament, the most important of which was serving as Gladstone's private secretary at the Board of Trade, where he assisted in the abolition of the Navigation Laws. Although Northcote was worried, following his appointment as one of the secretaries, that it was Granville who had pulled strings for him, Granville reassured him: 'You have made your own reputation with the members of the government.'[27] Northcote was concerned about Britain's neglect of popular education, and had advocated the repeal of the Corn Laws, claiming to be a free-trader. He said about himself: 'I am more of a Peelite than anything else,'[28] and thus, despite whatever he lacked in intellect and initiative, he was ideologically consistent with many of the principles underlying the Great Exhibition.

Ever the conciliator, Northcote tried hard to smooth over his differences with Cole. After his appointment as one of the secretaries to the Royal Commission he wrote to Cole, referring especially to their disagreement about reforming the schools of design: 'I will not say anything of past differences of opinion further than this, that I see no reason why it should prevent cordial co-operation now, and I hope we have buried the tomahawk on both sides.'[29] And despite continuing ideological differences, Northcote made a significant effort to keep relations between the two amicable. He wrote, regarding a paper that Cole had asked him to read, 'I am afraid your tendency still is, what I always thought it in the days of our old battles, to sacrifice efficiency to popularity,' but he nevertheless wished Cole success. On another occasion he pleaded with Cole to stay on and not resign from the executive committee.[30]

Relations were tense not only within the executive committee, but also between it and the Royal Commission. At issue was how the exhibition was to be planned and organized because, as Peel put it, 'The Royal Commission is much too cumbersome a body for the satisfactory dispatch of . . . business.'[31] Part of the problem stemmed from the question of whether the executive committee belonged to the Society of Arts, which had initially appointed it, or to the Royal Commission, which had incorporated the executive committee when it was formed.[32] Even more problematic was whether it should be the secretaries to the Royal Commission (Scott Russell and Northcote) or the members of the executive committee (Cole, Stephenson, Dilke, and Drew) who should be involved in the decision-making and have the responsibility of carrying out the orders of the commission, a dispute which General Charles Grey, Albert's secretary, tried valiantly but largely unsuccessfully to resolve.[33]

Yet another troublesome issue between the Royal Commission and the executive committee was whether the latter would be allowed to attend the commission's meetings. Cole wrote in his autobiography that he and Dilke 'were not summoned to attend the early meetings of the commission, and this we felt much impeded our work.'[34] Cole's notes of a meeting with Richard Cobden in early February indicate that Cobden – ever a supporter of Cole – thought that the executive committee 'must be part of the commission,' but Cobden's pull was obviously not strong enough. On 7 February Cole threatened that he would resign unless they were allowed to attend the meetings of the commission, and the next day he, Stephenson, and Dilke carried out their threat. It was Granville who pacified them and convinced them to stay with the project, although it would be another ten months before Cole would attend a meeting of the finance sub-committee.[35] Wrote Northcote of the month-long discussions: 'We have been in the hottest of water.'[36]

The Royal Commission finally reconstituted the executive committee on 12 February. The only ostensible change was that Colonel Reid had become the new chairman, replacing Robert Stephenson, who was promoted to the commission. George Drew and Francis Fuller withdrew unofficially from the preparations and were not replaced, leaving the executive committee to Cole and Dilke, with the 'genial' Reid as their chairman.[37] Reid's duties were, in Cole's words, 'chiefly to keep in order the various influences which . . . helped to produce the exhibition,' and Cole thought this 'a prudent and successful appointment.'[38] Reid saw himself as an ombudsman.[39] That he and Cole were in accord on their respective responsibilities no doubt helped to diffuse some of the tension in the organization. A month of reorganizing, however, had little immediate impact, and there were some on the commission who did not view Reid as approvingly as Cole did. Granville reported to Grey in early March that Peel had pulled him out of the House of Lords, 'seriously alarmed about the manner of conducting the business of the exhibition – that the commission was as a body unfit for work, [and] that Colonel Reid was inefficient.' Granville agreed that the business of the commission was not being carried out in the best of spirits, that Reid was disappointing, and that Scott Russell was a 'bad secretary' with a 'disagreeable' manner. He wrote that Albert was 'almost the only person who has considered the subject both as a whole, and in its details – the whole thing would fall to pieces if he left it to itself.' Granville suggested reducing the number of references in the press to the Royal Commission, and decreasing the amount of work sent to Scott Russell, who, said Granville, should be sent on a 'mission which would take a little time.'[40] In the end, Scott Russell's role in the planning was sharply reduced, as was Northcote's; in their place Edgar A. Bowring was appointed as acting secretary to the Royal Commission, and he seems to have done yeoman work.

Oddly, given the amount of credit historians have given Cole for his work in organizing the exhibition, and given the amount of work he himself claimed he performed, there were times when he clearly had little or nothing to do, as the following excerpts from his personal diaries suggest:

> 19 February 1850: Palace Yard [the offices of the executive committee]: Nothing whatever to do.
>
> 20 February: Executive Committee: Nothing to be done.
>
> 11 June: Showed Northcote proposed letter [of resignation] to Colonel Grey; he said I would not send it – I think you are in an awkward position – Lord Granville will find you something to do.[41]

While there is no question that Cole was a major presence in the planning and organization of the exhibition – Lyon Playfair himself wrote that 'The mainspring of the exhibition from first to last was Sir Henry Cole'[42] – there is also evidence to suggest that at critical junctures he was either excluded from or absented himself from the decision-making hierarchy.

There are a number of likely explanations for his exclusion from committee meetings and for his occasional inactivity. These include his conflicts with Scott Russell, which continued throughout the spring of 1850 as Cole outmaneuvered Scott Russell for power within the Society of Arts;[43] his long-running feud with Northcote over the schools of design; and his own determination to exercise control and not to be subordinate to anyone. The fact is that Cole irritated those he worked with. As one historian has noted, Cole 'gave the impression of cultivating his friends entirely for his own selfish ends.'[44] And H. T. Wood, long-time historian of the Royal Society of Arts, wrote, 'His best friends and admirers must have wished that he had had greater regard for the feelings of others, and that he had been content to attain his objects without thrusting aside and trampling down those who did not agree with him.'[45]

The most important reason for Cole's exclusion, however, was that, contrary to what he himself believed (and contrary to what most historians have written), he was in fact dispensable. During the times when he had little to do, the work of the exhibition was ably carried on by Charles Wentworth Dilke and Lyon Playfair. It is these two men, largely ignored in previous accounts of the exhibition, who were responsible for making it the organizational success that it was. As noted above, Dilke took responsibility for all the organizational and secretarial work, and Playfair handled most of the interactions with the local committees. To be fair, in the autumn of 1850 Cole worked especially hard on reforming the patent law to insure that manufacturers could send their wares to the exhibition confident that their ideas would not be stolen, and was throughout instrumental in handling questions of space and the arrangement of exhibits in the building.[46] But, with few exceptions, it was Dilke and Playfair who, beginning in February 1850, handled the day-to-day running of the exhibition effort. What was beyond all of their control, however, was the controversy over the exhibition building: where it should be located and what it should look like. The dispute over these issues nearly derailed the entire enterprise.

✳   ✳   ✳

PROVIDING A BUILDING

One of the first acts of the Royal Commission was to appoint a building committee. Representing the commission on this committee were Buccleuch, who had some interest in engineering; Ellesmere, a patron of the arts; Charles Barry, architect of the new Houses of Parliament; William Cubitt, the engineer; and Robert Stephenson, all from the commission. They were joined by I. K. Brunel (fig. 6), chief engineer to the Great Western Railway and the son of the builder of the Thames Tunnel; C. L. Donaldson, a writer and authority on architecture; and C. R. Cockerell, who had completed the Fitzwilliam Museum in Cambridge. Aside from Buccleuch and Ellesmere, the obligatory aristocrats, the committee consisted of three architects and three engineers.[47] Although it appeared to be a strong one, Buccleuch and Ellesmere rarely attended its meetings; Barry was embroiled in the controversial rebuilding of the Houses of Parliament; Donaldson was, in the words of one architectural historian, 'an undistinguished practitioner;'[48] and it was Brunel who designed the Royal Commission's building proposal that for a time turned much of the nation against the exhibition. As Henry Cole commented towards the end of his life:

> [The Committee] was too numerous and too strong to be workable. It again illustrated the old proverb of 'too many cooks'. Art and Science did not work together,

6. Robert Howett, *Isambard Kingdom Brunel* (1857). National Portrait Gallery, London.

and throughout were opposed to the very end. Any *one* of the six could have done the work well, acting on his sole responsibility. But the whole nearly wrecked the exhibition by dispute and delay.[49]

Although some on the committee were remarkably talented and accomplished, collectively it could hardly have done worse – organizationally or politically.

The building committee met for the first time on 5 February 1850, and took up the issue of where the building should be located. In hindsight it is inconceivable that the exhibition should have been held anywhere other than in Hyde Park, in the heart of London, but at the time there was rancorous debate about where it should be located. Albert and Cole had considered various sites, but agreed that Hyde Park would be best as early as July 1849.[50] It was sufficiently removed from the busiest parts of the city to minimize any interruption of commerce, yet not so far that it would be inconvenient. According to Albert, another advantage of the park was that it 'admitted of equal good access to high and low, rich and poor.'[51]

But, at the time of the first meeting of the building committee, there were general reservations that Hyde Park was too central, that London would become too crowded, and that it would be difficult to transport goods to the park. The committee again considered a number of alternative sites. Regent's Park was the most likely and popular alternative, on account of its proximity to the railway termini and the canals, but Battersea Park, Victoria Park, Primrose Hill, Wormwood Scrubs, and even the Isle of Dogs all came under discussion. Eventually the committee returned to Hyde Park, Albert's original proposal. It was the only location for which the commission had already obtained the Crown's permission and there was a section consisting of some twenty acres of flat, open land that appeared to be ideal. On 21 February the committee recommended Hyde Park to the commission, and three weeks later the commissioners published – in English, French, and German – their invitation calling for designs for the exhibition building.[52]

When the competition closed in mid-April, the commission had received 233 designs (plus twelve more which trickled in after the deadline, making 245 in all), which were then exhibited at the Institution of Civil Engineers on Great George Street in Westminster.[53] But in their report of 9 May the committee rejected all the plans that had been submitted, and instead produced one of their own, designed largely by Brunel. It called for a brick building four times the length of Westminster Abbey, with a dome 150 feet high and 200 feet in diameter (larger than St Paul's or even St Peter's in Rome) constructed of brick and covered in sheet metal (fig. 7).[54] Not surprisingly, the building committee's design caused among the public 'a storm of disapprobation, plentifully intermixed with ridicule' not only because the design was so widely considered to be ugly, but also because it seemed unfeasible, requiring some fifteen million bricks.[55] This public-relations gaffe occurred in large part because the building committee lacked politically astute participants, and was far-removed from the *Journal of Design* principles that were the driving force behind the exhibition.[56]

The plan offered by the committee sparked a broad and general opposition to the exhibition which focused on the use of Hyde Park: that there would be damage to the park; that there would be an influx of undesirables, both vagabonds from within Britain and republican conspirators and socialists from the continent; that it would be difficult to control traffic and the expected crowds; that there would be disastrous

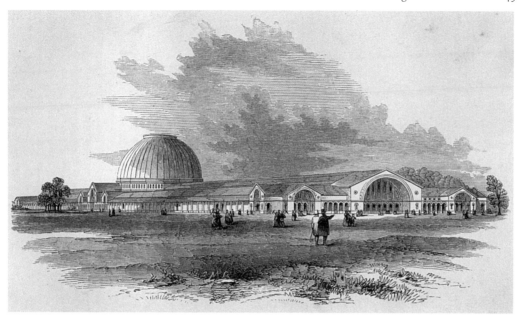

7. The building committee design for an exhibition building.

economic consequences for the City of London. As the pseudonymous author 'Greville' summed up the situation, everyone agreed that the building should not be in Hyde Park and that it should not be permanent. The building committee's proposal failed on both counts.[57] One writer to *The Times* objected to the Hyde Park location by asserting that it would be the latest in 'the long continued invasion' of John Bull's 'rights.' *The Times* itself, along with many other papers, came out against the commission's plan and the Hyde Park location.[58]

The outcry was taken up by Brougham in the House of Lords and Colonel Sibthorp in the House of Commons. Throughout the spring Brougham championed the opposition on the question of the site. He objected to the choice of Hyde Park, expressing his desire to protect 'one of the lungs' of the capital from being choked by a huge building, or 'a tubercle,' as he called it.[59] An even more vituperative attack came from Colonel Sibthorp (fig. 8), MP for Lincoln, whom one historian has characterized as 'a truculent figure with a fierce little beard and an accusing spy-glass . . . [who] clung obstinately, stubbornly and classically to all that was good and bad in the delectable past.'[60] For twenty-five years Sibthorp had stood against progress. He had been against Catholic emancipation, against Reform, against the repeal of the Corn Laws, against the granting of an allowance to Prince Albert on the ground that he was a foreigner, against the Public Libraries Act of 1850, and against the railways. Now he was against the exhibition.[61]

The widespread opposition to the construction in Hyde Park of a building that was clearly not temporary can be explained in part by the cultural significance of the park. The land that now comprises Hyde Park was owned by monasteries until Henry VIII dissolved them and took the grounds for hunting. As early as the 1560s the park served as a parade ground, and in the pre-Civil War era it was well known for its races. The House of Commons sold it in 1652, and it was around that time

8. Colonel Sibthorp. *Punch* (12 July 1851).

that it was first made available to the public, although John Evelyn complained in his diary that the new owner was charging an entrance fee. When the monarchy regained control of the lands in 1660 it had them enclosed and stocked with deer, turning Hyde Park into a place of fashion. William III purchased the lands in 1689, and his *Route du Roi*, corrupted by the English to 'Rod-dur-Ro,' soon became known as the 'Rotten Row,' which in 1851 would mark the northern edge of the Crystal Palace. During the eighteenth century Rotten Row, and its companion Ladies' Mile, became a promenade for London's respectable society; access was still very restricted.[62]

By the time Victoria succeeded to the throne in 1837, London was the place where, in summer, the landed class revived its friendships and acquaintances in style. From May to September there were musical soirées, garden parties, and balls, along with the races at Epsom and Ascot, which were not to be missed. Equally important were the regular morning rides or drives in Hyde Park, where society met and gossiped and planned future engagements. For respectable society, a ride on the Row became a daily social event, even though entrance to Rotten Row was no longer limited to the landed elites. By the 1830s, access was granted to prosperous businessmen, merchants, and their wives. It is something of a paradox that it was during the Victorian Age, renowned for its high moral code and social exclusivity, that Hyde Park became accessible to the *demi-monde* to an extent that would have been unthinkable a half-century before. It became a place where even prostitutes, if they dressed traditionally and rode well, were able to parade themselves. Especially important in opening up Hyde Park were the celebratory fairs held in conjunction with the coronations of George IV, William IV, and Victoria, where all social classes were represented.[63]

Those who fought against the exhibition most vehemently at this stage – the upper echelons of society, and particularly those who lived in Knightsbridge across from the park – wanted to keep the park as a playground for respectable society. When

Francis Fuller expressed some concern that Prince Albert's name was getting dragged through the mud, Albert's secretary Charles Grey responded that he was not particularly concerned by the outcry – although in this he was alone – because it came 'solely from the fashionable world.'[64] Henry Cole had in fact prepared a report on the number of houses near Hyde Park that would be affected by the exhibition building.[65] W. B. Adams, a writer for the *Westminster Review*, although veiling his opposition to the site behind the issue of access, also saw the exhibition building as an invasion of respectable society, as did *Punch*, which defended the exhibition as a joke on the elegant world which rode in Rotten Row.[66]

It is important to stress, however, that the opposition to the building committee's proposal was not solely based on class or residential status. Although the residents of Knightsbridge raised howls of protest, in the end the opposition in the spring of 1850 was as much in response to the brick building designed by Brunel as it was to the location itself. Charles Wood, Commissioner of Woods and Forests, intimated in a letter to Charles Grey in the midst of the dispute over the building and location that the opposition to the Hyde Park site was not entirely aristocratic. He implied that it was the fact that the building committee had designed a permanent building that was the problem.[67] The commission emerged victorious in part because it never wavered from its choice of Hyde Park as the site for the exhibition. That was the only site for which it had received approval from the Crown and the Lords of the Treasury, and the commission received support on this issue not only from the press (especially the *Economist*), but also from individuals and a number of the large northern manufacturing towns. All of these must have helped the commission remain firm in its choice.[68]

Throughout June there was widespread, if vague, opposition to the Hyde Park location, led by, though not limited to, Colonel Sibthorp. Sibthorp made a grouping of some ten elms that would have to be cut down to make room for the exhibition building his special concern, and raised the issue on some twelve different occasions (fig. 9).[69] He did have a legitimate gripe: The permission to take possession of the site granted to the Royal Commission by the Commissioner of Woods and Forests stipulated that no trees were to be cut down.[70] On one occasion Sibthorp told the House that these beautiful trees were to be cut down 'for one of the greatest humbugs, one of the greatest frauds, one of the greatest absurdities ever known ... all for the purpose of encouraging foreigners.'[71] Parliament began debating the site on 28 June 1850, but suspended debate until the following Monday, 1 July, after Labouchere pleaded with the House to withhold its judgment to give the commissioners time to reconsider. Gladstone seconded his motion for a delay, reassuring the House that 'If there is to be a dome as high as the Monument and twice the diameter of St Paul's, there is no reasonable apprehension that the building will be erected before Monday.'[72]

Just when it looked as though the situation could not possibly worsen, it did. On the morning of 29 June, Peel had a long discussion with his protégé Lyon Playfair on a variety of matters relating to the exhibition. At mid-day Peel attended a meeting of the commission, advising them on how to handle the outcry in Parliament. A few hours later, riding home, he was thrown from his horse. Four days later he was dead. Peel's death nearly dealt a fatal blow to the exhibition as well, for he was to have defended the choice of Hyde Park in Parliament. Cole wrote: 'The last words Peel said at the commission were, "That [Hyde Park] shall be [the] site or none."'[73]

ALBERT! SPARE THOSE TREES.

THE INDUSTRIOUS BOY.

"Please to Remember the Exposition."

By this time Albert was close to despairing of the entire plan (fig. 10). The press was indeed dragging his name through the mud, subscriptions were only trickling in, and the commissioners were on the verge of abandoning the exhibition altogether. Cole wrote in his diary, following a 4 July meeting with Albert, that the Prince Consort was prepared to give up on the exhibition if Hyde Park was not affirmed as the site.[74] Albert wrote to his brother Ernst:

> Unfortunately we are in deepest sorrow. A misfortune befell us from which we shall not so quickly recover. Peel is a loss for all Europe, a terrible loss for England, an irreparable one for the Crown and for us personally!! ...
> Now our Exhibition is to be driven from London; the patrons who are afraid, the Radicals who want to show their power over the crown property (the Parks), *The Times*, whose solicitor bought a house near Hyde Park, are abusing and insulting. This evening the decision is to be made. Peel, who had undertaken the defence, is no more, so we shall probably be defeated and have to give up the whole exhibition.[75]

Albert's and the commissioners' concern was the upcoming vote in Parliament, and according to Northcote the vote was very much in doubt, as was the commission's course of action if it gained only a narrow victory.[76] But good news came at the end of the same day, in the form of a letter from Lord John Russell to Prince Albert, from the House of Commons, reporting that the commissioners had won both votes, in each case by a comfortable majority.[77] The House – along with the nation – was still in mourning and shock following Peel's death. Lord John Russell had made a brief speech invoking Peel's memory, and the opposition forces were defeated. The preparations could proceed.

The debate over whether to permit the exhibition to take place in Hyde Park charts an important moment in the history of nineteenth-century Britain. The decision to place the exhibition building in the park challenged respectable society's two-part division of London: the fashionable, wealthy, and 'safe' West End and the

9. Colonel Sibthorp trying to prevent Prince Albert from cutting down the elms in Hyde Park to make room for the Crystal Palace. *Punch* (5 July 1851).

10. Prince Albert's Troubles. *Punch* (5 June 1850).

11. Henry Briggs, *Sir Joseph Paxton*. Devonshire Collection, Chatsworth.

commercial, poor, and 'dangerous' slums of the East End.[78] *The Times* and the West End inhabitants it represented reacted to this decision with fear and hostility, arguing that the West End would be polluted by all sorts of undesirables: Chartists, continental radicals, beggars, criminals, carriers of disease. Implicit in these cries of alarm was the idea that the identities of the middle classes and respectable society had to be protected from contamination. The organizers, in sum, took an enormous gamble, even more so coming only two years (almost to the day) after the great Chartist march. As we shall see, they also made extensive precautions to protect the park and its environs, but symbolically the decision to locate the exhibition in Hyde Park was an important one.

While the Parliamentary debate had been taking place, the building committee, still clinging to their unpopular and unfeasible design, had proceeded with their plans and begun to solicit tender offers. They eventually received nineteen bids, none of which fell below the £100,000 ceiling established by the commission, a limit which still vastly exceeded the amount that had been subscribed. After meeting with Playfair, Reid, Northcote, and Granville on 29 June, Cole left for Liverpool and Manchester to try to induce contractors to tender for a cheaper building. On 2 July, after having already been turned down by at least two firms, Cole took the mail train to Birmingham, where he went to see Fox & Henderson, the contracting firm in Smethwick. Charles Fox was away, but Henderson, wrote Cole, was prepared to tender for the building committee's plan. That evening Fox returned, and said that although the building committee's proposal would be impossible to construct in the time available, he would submit tender offers for it and two other proposals, one of which was Joseph Paxton's.[79] So along with the nineteen bids came a plan, from Fox & Henderson, 'of so peculiar a character as to require a special notice.'[80] But at the 11 July meeting of the building committee William Cubitt declared that the new plan did not appear to offer any savings over that proposed by the committee.[81]

The evolution of Paxton's plan is well known, and need be retold only briefly. Joseph Paxton in 1850 was the youthful landscape architect for the Duke of

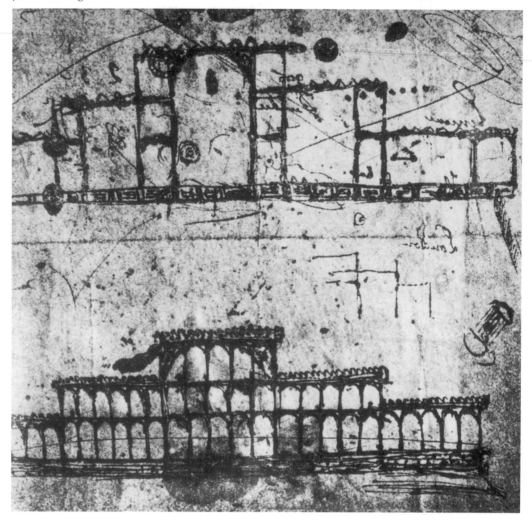

12. Paxton's blotting paper sketch of the Crystal Palace.

Devonshire, and also served as one of the directors of the Midland Railway (fig. 11). On 11 June he traveled to London for a business meeting with William Ellis MP, chairman of the Midland Railway. Together they went to the House of Commons, where Paxton and Ellis noted that they could barely hear the debate because of the poor acoustics in Barry's new building. Paxton said that Barry had botched that job, just as the commission was bungling the job of the exhibition. Although he had not seen the building committee's plans, he said that he had an idea of his own. Later that afternoon, at a meeting of the board of the Midland Railway, he drew a sketch of his plan on a piece of blotting paper (fig. 12), and showed it to Ellis. Ellis in turn passed it along to Cole, who agreed that if Paxton could produce a plan and an estimate of costs within a few days the commission might consider his proposal. The next day Albert granted Paxton an audience, after which Paxton hurried to see Fox & Henderson to ask them to make a tender offer for the exhibition building based on his plan. Although the next day was Sunday (and in fact the first Sunday on which the delivery of letters was forbidden by the new postal agreement), by using the electric telegraph and railway parcels Fox & Henderson were able to summon the great iron and glass manufacturers of the North to come to town the following day, Monday, to contribute their estimates. Within a week Fox & Henderson had calculated the cost of every pound of iron and inch of glass. At the same time Paxton, assisted by his Chatsworth staff, completed the proposal and all the working drawings. It took eight days.

On 20 June, on his way back to London, Paxton fortuitously ran into Robert Stephenson, showed him his plans, and received his support. Two days later – the same day the building committee's design was published – Paxton presented his plans to Granville (the Duke of Devonshire's nephew), who was also obviously impressed and passed his plan to the building committee.[82] On 24 June, Paxton had another interview with Prince Albert, this time with Fox and a representative from Chance Brothers, who had contracted with Fox to provide the glass. Paxton wrote after the meeting: 'I believe nothing can stand against my plans, *everybody* likes them.'[83] Paxton had many supporters. John Crace, the designer, took the liberty of writing a letter to Granville in which he noted that the opposition to the exhibition was due to the building committee's design being 'too massive and unsuited to the situation,' and asserted that Paxton's plan, which he had seen a week before, 'would conciliate or remove the popular objection.'[84] Peel was also an early convert to Paxton's plan, and would undoubtedly have pushed hard for him had he lived.[85]

What made possible the acceptance of Paxton's plan was that the building committee, in its advertisement for bids, had invited candidates to suggest improvements. This opened the door, once Fox & Henderson had submitted a bid, for them to push for Paxton's plan instead.[86] On 29 June, as part of Paxton's packaging of his proposal, he, Fox & Henderson, and Chance Brothers drew up an agreement among themselves by which Fox & Henderson would provide an estimate for the exhibition building according to Paxton's plans; Paxton would receive £2,500 if the offer was accepted; and Chance Brothers would supply the glass.[87] Only a few days later, Cole arrived at the offices of Fox & Henderson to secure a bid for the building committee's proposal. It was at this time that Paxton's plan could, in effect, be substituted for the original brick design.

The building committee was still stymied. Stephenson, after his chance meeting with Paxton on the train from Derby to London, had expressed his preference for Paxton's plan. Barry later claimed he had never approved of the committee's plan, though it is hard to believe that the plan could have made it out of the committee in the first place without his support, given his knowledge and stature. Brunel, although he went out of his way during these weeks to provide Paxton with information about the Hyde Park site, was determined that his own design should win.[88] While the committee was dithering, and with the 10 July deadline for tender offers approaching, Paxton went over the heads of the committee and had his plan published in the *Illustrated London News* to great acclaim on 6 July (fig. 13).[89] This was actually a step Paxton had planned at least two weeks earlier, following his meeting with Albert.[90] For all his humble beginnings, real and mythologized, by 1850 Paxton was astute, well connected, and politically aware. At the time of the Great Exhibition commentators generally described Paxton's plan as a *deus ex machina*, but in fact Paxton himself made it happen. He played the game, and played it well. Within days of publication he had the support of the public for his light, airy, novel, and temporary building.[91]

But, even once his design was published, it was hardly a foregone conclusion that

it would be adopted. He had many supporters, to be sure, although *The Times*, still sore over the defeat of the anti-Hyde Park motions in Parliament a few days earlier, called Paxton's plan a 'monstrous greenhouse,' and continued to criticize the preparations.[92] The final troublesome issue was cost. All of the plans received by the building committee, including Paxton's, cost considerably more than the total subscriptions up to that time. The commission had to find someone to assume the risk of the cost of the building – the very reason the Mundays had been brought on board in the first place, nearly a year before. Granville wrote to Albert that both he and Henry Labouchere were willing to put up £5,000 each if Overstone would contribute £1,000, but, for whatever reason, Overstone 'positively refused.'[93] Cole spoke with both Paxton and Fox about the possibility of their assuming the risk, but even before that idea could be pursued, he happened to pass by Samuel Morton Peto's office, where the two fell into conversation. They continued talking on their way to the Reform Club, where Peto offered to become guarantor of the building, volunteering to put up £50,000.[94]

It would not be overstating the case to assert that Peto's offer saved the exhibition, for two reasons. The first, which is well known is that Peto's offer brought in a flood of large contributions to what was eventually a £250,000 guarantee fund that enabled the commissioners to secure loans from the Bank of England to begin construction of the Crystal Palace.[95] What is less well known is that in a postscript to his 12 July 1850 letter to Grey, Peto wrote: 'Perhaps I might take the liberty of saying that I consider [that] the success of the exhibition would be considerably increased by the

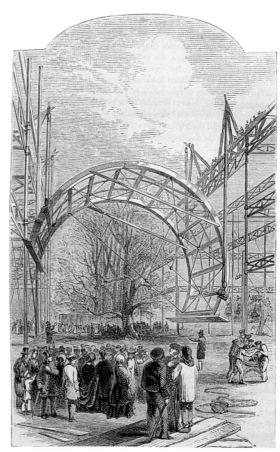

13. Paxton's original design for the Crystal Palace. *Illustrated London News* (6 July 1850).

14. Raising the transept over the trees. *Illustrated London News* (11 December 1850).

adoption of Mr Paxton's plan. . . .'[96] Although it is impossible to be sure in matters such as this, it is inconceivable that Peto's opinion – given his £50,000 offer – did not carry enormous weight with the commission, which had still not made up its mind to adopt Paxton's proposal. If this is the case, Peto's offer in effect determined the commissioners' decision for them. He simply made them an offer they could not refuse. With one stroke of his pen, Peto had chosen a design for the building and provided the funding for it at the same time.

In light of the succession of remarkable and even fortuitous events, it should not be forgotten how close the preparations came to collapsing during the second week of July. Paxton wrote to his wife, 'Nothing settled. . . . I have made up my mind to a disappointment but hope it may be otherwise. I am to be examined tomorrow, a great effort will be made for us but don't be bothered about it if we lose.'[97] Cole also described the tenuous situation, noting in his diary that Albert had remarked to him that 'He did not know where that man was who was to bring the thing together.' It was yet another stroke of bad luck that Stafford Northcote's father had just fallen seriously ill, causing Northcote to resign as secretary to the commission, just two weeks after Peel had died. Nevertheless, on 15 July, the commission met and officially adopted Paxton's plan and the exhibition was under way.[98] Paxton received numerous accolades. His daughter congratulated him that his plan had 'won the day and not 'bricks and mortar' that *The Times* writes about.'[99] A more humorous message came from his friend G. N. Brown: 'But who in fact ought to have been the successful candidate? Assuredly that person who like yourself, will take the most *panes*

15. The Crystal Palace from the north-east.

to construct the building.'[100] Not that any of this changed Paxton. His benefactor, the Duke of Devonshire, wrote in his diary of the *fête* that awaited Paxton upon his triumphant return to Chatsworth, and then added: 'Paxton quite [the] unaltered gardener.'[101]

A number of factors contributed to the commission's success in overcoming the opposition to their initial plan. Albert certainly displayed great patience and firmness, but he did not work alone. Paxton's design in the *Illustrated London News* captured the nation's imagination; Peel's death, although initially costly, roused emotional support in the House of Commons; and, at least according to the pseudonymous 'Greville,' 'a very liberal use was alleged to be made of the name of the Prince Consort' in order to get the Hyde Park site approved.[102] There would of course be other problems. Sibthorp continued to fulminate in Parliament for another few months, but his influence was largely negated by a stunning reversal in the press, which, led by *The Times*, began to support the exhibition almost as soon as Paxton's plan was officially adopted. Moreover, Paxton had thought up a brilliant solution to the problem of the trees: build the Crystal Palace over them by means of a transept, which would later be heralded as one of the outstanding features of the Crystal Palace (fig. 14). By mid-October Paxton was able to write home to the Duke of Devonshire: 'The glass palace is going very well, it begins to have the most imposing appearance, everyone who has seen it appears delighted and astonished.'[103] Just a few weeks later, in its 2 November 1850 issue, *Punch* christened the building 'the Crystal Palace' (fig. 15), elevating it to iconic status, and at the end of the year Albert sent off a note to Prince William of Prussia, saying, 'The exhibition is well forward.'[104]

The story of the planning and organization of the exhibition, however, is not yet finished. While the two very public debates over the contract with the Mundays and the location and design of the building were taking place, the commissioners and the executive committee in particular were working incredibly hard to sell the very idea of the exhibition to the public. Britons did not immediately support the idea, as the outcries over the contract and the building should have made clear. Resolving these disputes was only a stop-gap measure for the organizers, at best an exercise in damage control. Critical to the success of the exhibition would be the commission's ability to sell the plan to the public in a positive way, to promote and publicize the exhibition to the entire nation.

CHAPTER 3

Organization: Selling the Exhibition

T HERE WAS NOTHING PREORDAINED about the popularity of the exhibition. The initial pleas of the Royal Commission met with little enthusiasm, and for a long time the idea of the exhibition was quite unpopular. *Blackwood's* declared in September 1850: 'The fact is evident, that the nation is not responding to the call.'[1] And the *Edinburgh Review*, looking back over the preparations at the close of the exhibition, recalled that at the time the Royal Commission was issued,

> the prospects of the new-born corporation were far from dazzling. It is impossible to deny that there existed considerable zeal, and even much lively sympathy, in many quarters . . . [but] the design of the Royal Commission to organize local committees in every town, was not seconded by any great local enthusiasm. The chief difficulty, it would appear from the report of the first person dispatched upon this nation, 'is to find anybody that will listen to you at all on the subject'.[2]

For months subscriptions trickled in because Britons simply did not know what to make of the exhibition, or did not like what they heard.

The ultimate success of the exhibition was due to the novelty of the idea, the captivating design of the building, the lure of an international industrial competition, and the backing of the monarchy. It was also the result of the organizers' adroitness at defining for the public, and negotiating with the public, the meaning of the exhibition. They accomplished this through public meetings and speeches, posters, pamphlets, and a carefully orchestrated relationship with the press. But selling the exhibition meant not just imbuing it with meaning, but presenting a multiplicty of meanings, as the organizers continually shifted the focus of their appeal to fit their audience. They did so not as part of a conscious strategy, but out of political necessity, and in response to all sorts of unforeseen contingencies. In other words, giving meaning to the exhibition was less a statement of fact than a continuing process.

Promoting the exhibition also meant reaching out to the provincial towns. The Society of Arts and the Royal Commission conceived of the exhibition from the outset as a *national* event. By this they meant that it should ideally appeal to and represent not only all classes and political alignments, but also all regions within the United Kingdom.[3] A successful exhibition would require the provincial towns, as they were called, to provide financial support, to contribute exhibits, and to send visitors. The centerpiece of the commission's efforts to publicize and promote the exhibition in the provinces was an elaborate and comprehensive national organization. Building on the foundations laid by the Society of Arts, the executive committee oversaw the formation of more than 300 local committees throughout the United Kingdom which were ultimately responsible for gathering subscriptions, encouraging exhibitors, and, after the Great Exhibition opened, channeling visitors to the Crystal Palace. An analysis of the local committees and of the process by which the executive committee promoted the exhibition at the local, provincial level helps to explain how the exhibition became a national success, even as it delineates the limits of its appeal. Hence, the story of the exhibition needs to be told in relation to the provinces as much as to London.

What such an analysis reveals is that there was considerable local and regional variation. Although the organizers approached every town and community in a similar manner, the responses they received differed widely. It would be a mistake to assume that local politics and socio-economic conditions did not play a central role in the organization and promotion of the exhibition. The exhibition was most popular, and appeals on its behalf most successful, in prosperous, liberal, Dissenting, manufacturing, and commercial urban areas such as London, Manchester, Liverpool, Bradford, and Bath. Communities that were Tory, Anglican, and protectionist, such as Canterbury and Maidstone in Kent, or predominantly agricultural, such as Durham County, were almost uniformly recalcitrant despite the best efforts of the organizers. Economically distressed areas such as Tower Hamlets, or towns where there was a large radical working population such as Bury in Lancashire, posed additional problems, not the least of which was the organizers' fear of Chartist activity. The overall record of the organizers, it turns out, was mixed. There were many successes, but also notable failures. It is significant, though, that the organizers at least made an effort to reach out to all Britons, including, although again with varying degrees of success, those on the Celtic fringe, in Wales, Scotland, and Ireland.

There was, moreover, always a tension between metropolis and province.[4] As Colonel Phipps, Albert's secretary, wrote in 1849, 'The country committees should have some voice in the business as soon as the commission is established. But there must be a centre of action, and that centre must be London.'[5] At issue was just what voice the provinces would have. Bramley Moore of Liverpool wrote to Sir George Grey in November 1849 concerning the desirability of having representation from provincial towns such as Liverpool and Manchester on the executive committee. This would, he believed, 'secure the cordial co-operation of the provinces.' In a second letter a week later, he made his point even more directly: 'it must be borne in mind [that] the great contributions connected with machinery and mechanics must be supplied from the provincial towns and not by the metropolis.'[6] There was in the provinces considerable wariness of centralization, and the strain between metropolis and province would continue for the duration of the exhibition.[7]

But, for all the talk of securing the support of the provinces, the exhibition was organized from and depended on the financial support of the City of London.[8] The Lord Mayor made a telling comment at the large meeting at the Mansion House in October 1849, after the Society of Arts had already sought the support of the northern manufacturing towns. He said that 'although the concurrence of the City of London in this proposal is solicited last . . . we are asked to confirm the evidently general feeling of the country by our approval.'[9] The search for public support began in the manufacturing towns, but the search for money began in London.[10]

Exploring the relationship between metropolis and province reveals, however, that insofar as there may have been a divide between the supposedly separate worlds of London finance and commerce and provincial industry, the organizers were extremely adept at bridging it.[11] Although London provided an extraordinary array of exhibits, industrial and otherwise, fully half of the funds for the exhibition came from outside of London. Furthermore, it may not make sense to think of the relationship between London and the provinces solely as a century-long struggle between local and central control, demonstrating just how strong local interests were well into the nineteenth century.[12] Rather, a close look at the dynamic between the initiating tactics of the executive committee and the responses of the many local committees discloses striking levels of communication and cooperation between metropolis and province. While the commissioners went to great lengths to present 'their' view of the meaning and purpose of the exhibition, the provincial committees continually refined and expanded that vision to take into account local interests. There was, in short, a continuing dialogue between London and the provinces that suggests a dynamic, even dialectical, two-way relationship.

CONSTRUCTING THE EXHIBITION

The exhibition was throughout a protean event, its meaning diffuse and subjective. One of the most challenging tasks for the organizers was to find the language and ideas to promote the exhibition as widely as possible, which they accomplished primarily by means of a trio of meetings at the Mansion House in London. In London, particularly in the City, free trade was a controversial issue (fig. 16), regarded by many as the country's salvation but by others as a radical-inspired delusion. Despite the repeal of the Corn Laws in 1846 and the similarly protectionist Navigation Acts three years later, free trade continued to be politically divisive, and there remained in effect

16. The struggle between protectionism and free trade. *Punch* (25 January 1850).

A MEETING TO DISCUSS THE PRINCIPLES OF PROTECTION AND FREE TRADE.

a 'Protectionist Party' in Parliament until 1852. The repeal of the Corn Laws had been inextricably linked with the class politics of the 1840s, pitting in myth if less so in actuality the landed classes against northern industrialists and urban masses. For anti-Peelite Tories, free trade meant not only the abandonment of protection for agriculture, but a fundamental erosion of British power, based as it was on land, shipping, and the empire.[13] Recent scholarship suggests that there was a considerable diversity of opinion within the financial and commercial community, and two members of the Royal Commission with London ties – William Thompson and Thomas Baring – were prominent protectionists.[14] For an event such as the Great Exhibition, which was intended to appeal to as broad a spectrum of the political classes as possible, the free-trade label was fatal. But there was no mistaking the exhibition's origins in classical liberal economics, and, although the Royal Commission was bipartisan, its members were inclined towards free trade. It was important, then, for the Royal Commissioners to break the exhibition's association with free trade. While they promoted it on a variety of grounds, free trade, in the end, was the determining issue. Only insofar as the organizers could convince the press and the public – which at this stage really meant a very select group of wealthy and respectable gentry and men of commerce and finance – that the exhibition was *not* a tribute to free trade would they garner the necessary support for it.

The first of these Mansion House meetings, the one which had persuaded Albert to name the Royal Commission, was held on 17 October 1849 in order to announce the plans for the exhibition. Assembled in the Egyptian Hall were some twenty-seven members of the Society of Arts along with almost 400 merchants, bankers, MPs, and aldermen, who had been invited by the Society of Arts, using, with his permission, the mayor's name.[15] The mayor delivered the opening address, offering four grounds for supporting the exhibition: it would promote peace; it would increase commerce and benefit industry; it would show how much progress Britain had made, particularly in arts and manufactures; and it would confirm Britain's stature as the leading industrialized nation. He concluded by extolling the virtues of economic and industrial competition.[16]

Henry Cole followed the mayor, and advanced other reasons for supporting the exhibition. Most prominent among them was that the influx of visitors, 'some hundred thousand people to come flowing into London from all parts of the world by railways and steamboats to see the great exhibition,' would provide a boon to businesses of all sorts. There would be, he promised, 'a direct and obvious benefit from the exhibition.' For all the mayor's lofty talk of peace and progress, it was the lure of sales that constituted the core of Cole's appeal. Cole also asserted a very specific vision of British government in his discussion of how the exhibition was to be funded. He said that whereas in other countries projects of this kind had been carried out by governments, often through compulsory taxation, Cole thought they would all agree with him 'that the English people do much better for themselves than any government can do for them.' He characterized Britain as a country of entrepreneurs, in which the government kept out of its citizens' lives. In his view, it was this laissez-faire philosophy that had made Britain such a successful nation.

The longest and most significant speech of the meeting, however, came from Joseph Hume, the Scottish Radical MP and former Vice President of the Society of Arts. For several decades Hume had championed free trade and reform and attacked government spending. He was also a hero to industrial workers for his attempts to repeal the Combination Laws.[17] In his address he praised the virtues of 'individual exertion,' laissez-faire government, and free and open competition as the qualities that had brought to Britain its commercial success: 'Only let such a country as England be allowed to act for itself, every man free to apply his capital and industry as he found beneficial, and England might be left to compete with the whole world.'[18] Whereas other nations' economies were regulated and their industries subsidized, inhibiting investment, competition, and innovation, Britain was different. The thrust of his speech was to unite different partisan alignments by appealing to a shared suspicion of government. He offered an unabashed endorsement of laissez-faire government and free-trade economics.

Interestingly, the characterization of the exhibition provided by Cole and Hume at the first Mansion House meeting was not embraced by *The Times* the following day. Although the newspaper published a lengthy excerpt from Hume's address, its lead editorial praised the idea of the exhibition not as a tribute to laissez-faire economics and voluntarism, but as 'a good survey and estimate of our present industrial state,' and for its contribution to peace.[19] To be sure, in the minds of the classical liberal economists such as Smith and Ricardo, free trade and international peace were connected, but there is a clear difference in emphasis between Hume's speech and *The Times*' editorial. Only in passing did the paper mention that free trade and the reduction of tariff barriers had helped bring about the almost constant peace since 1815. At this early stage, the vision presented by *The Times* and that presented by the organizers of the exhibition overlapped, but were not identical.

The second Mansion House meeting took place on 25 January 1850, and was held principally to raise funds, which it did in abundance, with close to £10,000 being pledged that evening alone.[20] This meeting, like most promoting the exhibition, took the form of a series of speeches organized around resolutions: that the exhibition was 'in harmony with the public feeling;' that it was 'eminently calculated to improve manufactures and to aid in diffusing the principles of universal peace;' and that it should be funded not out of the public revenue but from voluntary subscriptions. If at the time of the first Mansion House meeting the meaning of the exhibition had been substantially oriented towards free trade, this was much less the case by the time of the second meeting, which focused more on the issue of peace. Thomas Baring, chairman of Lloyds, said that the planned exhibition was not only the product of forty years of peace between Britain and the rest of Europe, following the conclusion of the Napoleonic Wars, but also a tribute to what could be accomplished if national resources were not devoted to war or preparations for war. Affirming a belief consonant with a long line of liberal economic and political philosophy that included Smith, Paine, Mill, and Cobden, Baring also expressed the hope, reiterated by many others at the time, that the Great Exhibition would actually create peace by constructing new arenas in which nations could compete with each other, 'not with any feelings of hostility, which it was hoped were for ever extinguished, but with a noble sentiment of rivalry.' The exhibition was, in his words, 'a guarantee of the maintenance and continuance of peace.'

Nevertheless, the focus of the organizers' appeals remained diffuse.[21] William Cotton, the merchant, philanthropist, and one-time Governor of the Bank of England, explained that the exhibition was 'calculated to promote art and science, and encourage industry,' and that at the exhibition the nations of the world would 'meet together, not in war for the destruction of human life, but in a Christian and amicable contest to increase the comforts and enjoyments of life.' Baron Rothschild promised that the exhibition 'would have the effect of ensuring a great many orders' for British manufacturers. What differentiated this meeting from the previous one at the Mansion House was that there was no mention of the exhibition as a testament to free trade. Voluntarism was still in vogue as far as collecting subscriptions was concerned, and a general laissez-faire approach to government was still the basis for planning the exhibition, but unbridled free trade as an overarching economic philosophy was now seen as being still too controversial four years after the repeal of the Corn Laws for an event requiring national support. That the commissioners succeeded in promulgating their revised view of the exhibition may be inferred from an editorial published in the *Sun* the day after the second Mansion House meeting, which adopted the organizers' construction of the exhibition point for point, without mentioning free trade, despite the paper's free-trade leanings.[22]

By far the most celebratory of the three meetings at the Mansion House took place on 21 March 1850, and it openly identified Prince Albert with the project for the first time. Attending this 'grand banquet' were Albert and the Royal Commissioners, the chief officers of state, members of both Houses of Parliament, the Archbishop of Canterbury, foreign ambassadors, prominent residents of London, the heads of many large companies, and over one hundred mayors from England, Scotland, and Ireland, all in official dress. There was a lavish feast, the national anthem was played, there were toasts, and of course there were speeches (fig. 17).

17. The banquet at Mansion House, 21 March 1850. *Illustrated London News*, 23 March 1850.

Whereas the two earlier meetings at the Mansion House had promoted the exhibition on grounds that could be interpreted in party political terms, this third meeting was a celebration, a fête, with no attempt made to imbue the exhibition with any ideologically charged partisan overtones. Toward that end, the featured speaker was none other than Prince Albert, who for the first time presented in public his views of the exhibition and of the reasons for its creation:

> [W]e are living at a period of most wonderful transition, which tends rapidly to accomplish that great end – to which all history points – the realization of the unity of mankind. . . .
>
> The distances which separated the different nations and parts of the globe are rapidly vanishing before the achievements of modern invention. . . . The products of all quarters of the globe are placed at our disposal, and we have only to choose which is the best and the cheapest for our purposes, and the powers of production are intrusted to the stimulus of competition and capital.
>
> Gentlemen, the Exhibition of 1851 is to give us a true test of the point of development at which the whole of mankind has arrived in this great task, and a new starting point from which all nations will be able to direct their further exertions.[23]

He concluded with a line that would become part of the lore of the exhibition, as he spoke of 'peace, love and ready assistance, not only between individuals but between the nations of the earth.' Other speakers would promote the exhibition on a variety of grounds – though not at this particular meeting – but for Albert, at least in public, the Great Exhibition was about peace and progress. His speech was such a success that the Duchesses of Gloucester and Sutherland wrote to the Queen expressing their admiration.[24]

The central role given to Albert at this meeting was part of a broader strategy, developed by Henry Cole, to use the monarchy to promote the exhibition.[25] Whereas in 1849 Phipps had specifically ordered Cole to keep Albert's name out of the preparations so that his reputation would not be tarnished in case the event fell apart, by early 1850 their strategy had changed, and they were using the monarchy to sell the exhibition, calculating, it turns out correctly, that Britons would not refuse a plea for support from their Queen and her Prince. The *Scotsman*, for example, praised the participation of the monarchy in the exhibition as 'striking evidence' of how institutions, 'even those considered most stationary and obstructionist, have changed with the times and for the better.'[26] Not that this tactic was without its critics. *Fraser's*, for one, denounced the commissioners' appeal to loyalty, but in doing so confirmed that appealing to the patriotic sentiments of British men and women was an effective and well-used strategy.[27] Part of what made the exhibition popular was the organizers' success at turning Albert into an object of loyalty.[28]

The overly critical work of early-twentieth-century anti-Victorians such as Lytton Strachey and Arthur Ponsonby has left its mark on Albert's reputation. While it was inevitable that there should have been a reaction against the fawning memorials to 'Albert the Good' that followed his death in 1861, these grotesque portraits should not obscure his intelligence, commitment, and even popularity. There was, to be sure, significant opposition to Albert at the time of his marriage to Victoria, but this needs to be seen as political as much as personal. Victoria was politically inexperienced and naive. The only adviser she trusted was the Whig Prime Minister, Melbourne, and she, and Albert as a consequence, suffered from Tory criticism of her partisanship.

She was youthful and attractive, and Albert – also young, a foreigner, and Victoria's cousin – was not generally regarded as an appropriate husband for the Queen of England. Nor was there any clear role for Albert: he was not given access to Victoria's meetings with Melbourne, he was initially quite ignorant of British politics, and his stature was diminished after Sibthorp and the Tories reduced his annuity in the late 1830s. There were also rumors that Albert was Roman Catholic, or at least had Papist leanings, and he was mocked by London society for his earnestness and ineffectuality.[29]

It is also quite possible that Albert's central role in promoting the exhibition was a means of promoting himself. He was finally given an opportunity for public service when Peel appointed him chairman of the Fine Arts Commission, but his reputation languished in the 1840s as a result of his involvement in the repeal of the Corn Laws and Victoria's opposition to the Ten Hour Bill, which he thought would help alleviate the 'condition of England question.' Albert had made his first appearance in the House of Commons during the debate over the Corn Laws, and came under attack from the Tories for showing the alleged impartiality of the Crown to be a sham. Although free trade triumphed in 1846, Albert, at least in the short term, was one of its victims.[30] An international exhibition, particularly after the Society of Arts had found substantial support for the idea throughout Britain, was an ideal opportunity for Albert to put himself in front of the nation in a favorable light.

There is considerable evidence, in fact, that the Great Exhibition did indeed greatly strengthen Albert's ties to the middle classes. In George Douglas Campbell's memory Albert's labors on behalf of the exhibition 'were the first transactions which spread widely among the middle classes some knowledge of this remarkable man.'[31] The links between Albert, the Crystal Palace, the royal family, and middle-class values were made explicit in Franz Xavier Winterhalter's *The First of May, 1851* (fig. 18). It commemorates the Duke of Wellington's visit to Buckingham Palace to give his godson, Prince Arthur, a gift to celebrate his first birthday. The infant in return presents Wellington, hero of Waterloo and the embodiment of courage, with a nosegay. The Crystal Palace, which opened that day, can be seen in the distance, highlighted by rays of sun, and Albert appears to be turning toward it with satisfaction. If the Iron Duke symbolized past victories, the Crystal Palace was a portent of future glories. The portrait is an allegory of national pride and achievement with the family as its center.[32] It represents the beginning of the apotheosis of Prince Albert.

The most important speech at the March Mansion House meeting, however, came not from Albert but from Lord Stanley, the leader of the Tory opposition and an avowed protectionist, who declared:

> I know of no reason why my humble name should have been selected . . . unless it were to give a practical demonstration here, as we give a practical demonstration in the commission, that men of different political opinions, men of the most opposite views (*loud cheers*), can and always will work, and co-operate cordially and harmoniously together, for objects which all alike conceive to promote the public good.[33]

In short, the exhibition was for everyone regardless of political affiliation, and the presence of over one hundred mayors underscored that fact. Stanley's appeal stayed away from any party political issues, such as free trade, that might have reduced and

18. Francis Xavier Winterhalter, *The First of May, 1851* (1851). The Royal Collection.

limited, rather than broadened, support for the exhibition. As long as he did not delve into specifics, his vague ideal of the 'public good' could supersede party loyalties. The significance of his speech was that it turned what six months earlier had been a paean to free trade into a bipartisan event that virtually the entire nation could accept, and his claim that the exhibition was 'not a party question . . . not a political question,' as the Rev. Dr Morris put it at a meeting in Marylebone in early May 1850, would be reiterated by other speakers again and again at local meetings.[34]

Despite Stanley's pronouncements that the exhibition was not a partisan event, and despite the organizers' efforts to eliminate references to free trade, the day after the third Mansion House meeting the Peelite *Morning Chronicle* happily christened it *'the inaugural festival of free trade.'* Unfortunately for the organizers, this phrase reverberated throughout the Tory press. Fervent opposition to the exhibition poured in from the protectionist right, especially from *Blackwood's*.[35] W. E. Aytoun fired a battery of criticisms against the exhibition in the September 1850 issue: that it was 'an expensive toy' and 'a European bazaar;' that there was not enough time to put it together; that the building would take up too much space; that workers would have neither the means nor the funds to visit the exhibition.[36] But the *Blackburn Standard* saw through *Blackwood's* denigration of the exhibition, rightly perceiving that free trade was the journal's bugbear. The *Standard* countered that two-thirds of Aytoun's article was 'devoted to strictures . . . on the errors and wrongs of free trade,' and had nothing to do with the exhibition itself. The *Standard* defended the exhibition as having 'been kept most scrupulously . . . from all taint of political or party design.'[37]

John Bull, the weekly propaganda machine of the Tories, came out in support of the exhibition following the third Mansion House meeting, but with some misgivings, especially one that the event was being used for 'party purposes,' meaning free trade:

> If the project had been put forth in that sense, and for that purpose, instead of being received with cordial approbation throughout the kingdom, it would have been scouted as a piece of political charlatanry; and to this low and discreditable level it will infallibly sink down, unless the attempt so to represent it be at once discountenanced as it deserves to be. The free-traders have no right to filch the popularity which the scheme of His Royal Highness has most justly gained for itself, and to inflict upon it in return the unpopularity with which they themselves are no less justly overwhelmed.[38]

Although the journal was otherwise supportive of Albert and the exhibition, *John Bull*'s attacks against the free trade aspect of Great Exhibition became increasingly vitriolic. By June it had labelled the exhibition 'THE FREE TRADE FESTIVAL' in its headlines. The paper claimed that the exhibition was being coopted 'by a set of designing schemers,' who sought to use the event to boost the cause of free trade.[39]

There is no question that many of the organizers believed fervently in the efficacy of free trade, nor that the exhibition was at least in part an attempt to lessen international trade barriers. When Stanley gave his speech, he was attempting to convince his audience that the exhibition was something other than what it was. And he was by no means the only organizer to engage in such a tactic. At a meeting in Marylebone in May, two months later, Richard Cobden found himself avoiding the term 'free trade' altogether, referring instead to his commitment to 'commercial freedom,' a palatable euphemism. He reassured those in attendance that he 'would not be a party to any scheme' which was likely to bring to London a vast influx of goods from around the world which would be sold at the expense of local merchants and shopkeepers. He stated emphatically: 'That is not the object of the exposition.'[40] These are surprising words coming from the leader of the free-trade movement. That Cobden was willing at least temporarily to jettison his free-trade philosophy and to sound protectionist in order to appeal to local merchants demonstrates the lengths the commissioners went to in order to promote the exhibition.

The *Britannia*, a nationalistic, protectionist paper, saw right through the smokescreen thrown up by the organizers. It characterized the exhibition as a 'Free-trade Jubilee, brought to an apparently successful issue under false pretences.'[41] And as an example the *Britannia* needed to look no further than an article in the *Economist* a month after the third Mansion House meeting, which, taking its cues from Stanley and Cobden, also tried this tactic of removing free trade as one of the defining characteristics of the exhibition. 'Someone named it inappropriately the Festival of Free Trade,' declared the *Economist* hyperbolically. 'It is much better called by the *Westminster Review*, "The Practical Peace Congress."'[42] This statement, coming from an indefatigable booster of free-trade economics, is quite a concession. The exhibition symbolized many things; peace and free trade were two of them. But calling it a 'peace congress' boosted its popularity, whereas labeling it a 'festival of free trade' elicited howls of protest from the protectionist opposition. Although critics of the exhibition continued to denigrate and dismiss it as a 'festival of free trade,' from the official point of view, free trade was not to be used as a promotional tool, and was rarely mentioned by promoters of the exhibition after the first Mansion House meeting.

Because free trade was so controversial, the organizers had to find other grounds on which to promote the exhibition. These were distilled by Lord Stanley in his Mansion House address, when he claimed that the exhibition would 'bring into harmonious concord the nations of the world' and give 'encouragement . . . to the industry of all nations,' and they were reiterated almost verbatim by Prince Albert in a memorandum a month after the exhibition.[43] This characterization of the exhibition, that it would foster peace and industrial progress, was adopted and repeated throughout the press.[44] But, if the Mansion House meetings succeeded in reducing the idea behind the exhibition to a palatable core, peace and progress remained vague and general terms that could be modified in a variety of ways, and so at the local level the organizers employed a myriad of arguments in order to appeal to a diversity of political views and socio-economic backgrounds.

Soon after the formation of the commission, Matthew Digby Wyatt, in his capacity as secretary to the executive committee, issued a list of 'suggested resolutions' that was sent out in advance of local meetings, delineating what the executive committee thought should be discussed. These guidelines offered four reasons to support the exhibition: because it would benefit all areas of the economy, including the arts, agriculture, manufactures, and trade; because it would benefit all classes, 'whether as producers, distributors or consumers', and especially workers; because it would promote peace; and because it had the backing of the monarchy.[45] The organizers, in essence, publicized and promoted the exhibition as a great panacea. But although Wyatt offered suggestions and provided a general outline of the content of the meetings, he was of course unable to limit what was said at the hundreds of local meetings. The meetings all followed the same general format, but each also took on its own individual, local character. There were several speeches, usually outlining the origins, preparations, and likely benefits of the exhibition, which were then followed by various resolutions, expressing the support of those in attendance and providing for the formation of a local committee. It does not appear that there was ordinarily any free discussion, although occasionally meetings served as a means of countering opposition to the exhibition. In many instances, local organizers adopted almost word for word the language used by the commissioners at the Mansion House meetings and in their circulars. But local meetings provided an opportunity to elaborate and refine the commission's suggested interpretation of the exhibition. Local committees used the meetings to imbue it with meanings that would promote the exhibition in a given area, or to a specific social or economic or religious group. It was not so much that these meetings changed what the commissioners claimed the exhibition represented as that the commissioners had left a lot of room for maneuver in defining the meaning of the exhibition.

In Kensington, for example, a retailing area within the greater London metropolis, the lure was sales.[46] The parade of speakers offered a number of reasons to support the exhibition, most of which came directly from Wyatt's list of suggested resolutions, but more significant than the lofty expressions of peace, progress, and social harmony was that Thomas Milner Gibson urged those in attendance to support the exhibition because it was in their personal, financial self-interest to do so. Although he acknowledged that some would call his reasoning 'common-place and low,' Milner Gibson claimed the exhibition would bring over one million people to the metropolis, and calculated that, if each visitor spent only £1, this would be 'a practical result.' His speech is also interesting because he did not shy away from the free-trade issue, as the Royal Commissioners had at the second and third Mansion House meetings. On the contrary, he said that in certain sectors British inferiority was due not to any defect in ability, 'but rather to the injurious influence which excise regulations have had.' Milner Gibson suggested that when different exhibits were placed side by side at the exhibition, people would realize how pernicious excise tax regulations were, and he repeated an oft-cited example concerning the glass industry, which had languished under heavy excise taxes but had begun to recover since their repeal. At this local meeting, Milner Gibson was able to express his support for free trade, presumably without fear of turning people against the exhibition. In contrast, when Richard Cobden had presented the same argument to a different audience at the meeting in Marylebone, he had bent over backwards to avoid anything that might connote free trade. Here, then, were two speakers, both of whom believed in free trade, offering the same reason to support the exhibition, yet one drew cheers for supporting the lifting of trade restrictions, while the other drew cheers for reassuring the audience that they would not be swamped by foreign goods.

A meeting held in Woolwich on 4 June 1850 promoted the exhibition on very different grounds, focusing not on retailing and sales but on mercantilism and the overseas empire. It was in Woolwich that Henry VIII had established a Royal Dockyard in 1512 for his new navy, and more than 300 years later the meeting there would certainly have drawn those interested in commerce and shipping. The principal speaker was David Williams Wire, the under-sheriff for London (and later Lord Mayor). After covering all the usual points, at times to the point of hyperbole, Wire presented a rosy vision of the empire as an institution of mercantile exchange that was driving not only the British but the entire world economy. Every time there had been a threat to British commerce, he said, the British had found new routes and new markets by 'sending their sons to distant lands,' and that as a result Britain was 'becoming the emporium of the commercial, and the mistress of the entire world.' He extolled the British for their perseverance and adaptability, but, more importantly, he offered a defense of the empire itself, describing it as a central British institution. He defended it on commercial grounds: that by colonizing or, in his words, 'civilizing' foreign lands and peoples, the British were essentially creating for themselves new markets for British goods, a process that would be furthered by the exhibition.[47] So in retailing areas the lure was sales; in shipping areas the appeal was based on commerce and empire.

In certain areas the organizers promoted the exhibition by emphasizing its benefits for workers and its ameliorative effect on class relations. In Kensington, another of the speakers was George Godwin, a Brompton architect and editor of the *Builder* from 1844 onwards, who had worked zealously to improve the living conditions of the poor. He spoke about the impetus the exhibition would give to industry by educating workers and creating 'artistic operatives,' and the benefits that would accrue to working men and women who would soon have within reach 'what once were luxuries enjoyed only by the few.' There was also a speech from a self-described 'working man,' Mr Dunford, who spoke about 'the dignity of labour' and 'the industry and talent of the working men of England.' He urged all workers to 'come forward with their sixpences.' It is impossible to know whether Mr Dunford was a plant, or, if legitimate, how many 'working men' there were in attendance. Perhaps there were actually workers present; perhaps the organizers of the meeting antici- pated that there would be some, and that workers would be more likely to support an appeal that came from someone of their own background; or perhaps the organizers wanted the middle classes in attendance to believe that workers were supportive of the exhibition and that the commission was doing what it could to involve them. Dunford's speech, in any case, was probably reassuring to his social superiors, who in all likelihood would have seen him not as a threatening Chartist, but as an intelligent, well-spoken, and presumably respectably dressed artisan.

Confirmation of this, perhaps, came from the Duchess of Sutherland, who attended the meeting and afterwards wrote to the Queen about the 'most interesting mixture of people – several manufacturers speaking.'[48] Hers is a significant letter because it demonstrates that women were present at local meetings, even if they did not give speeches. And while there is no evidence that the organizers oriented their appeal to women in any obvious fashion, wealthy London women nevertheless found ways to support the exhibition. The Duchess was so 'delighted' – her word – by the meeting that she invited a number of her friends to Stafford House 'to consider the best means of forwarding the objects of the Exhibition' (fig. 19). The committee included the wives of a number of the men behind the exhibition – Countess Granville, Lady John Russell, Lady Mary Stanley – as well as several other aristocrats. They collected subscriptions, and within a few weeks had raised an astounding £975.[49] Women,

19. Meeting of the Ladies' Committee at Stafford House. *Illustrated London News* (9 March 1850).

especially wealthy women, had a role in the preparations for the exhibition, but it was largely hidden from view.

Godwin's and Dunford's speeches presented an image of workers as industrious patriots, equally willing to produce goods for consumption as to fight in wars. They portrayed British society as harmonious, devoid of any struggle between labor and capital. And, with their emphasis on moral character and the elevation and cultivation of taste, they represented an attempt to incorporate the working classes into the imagined socio-economic order idealized by the middle classes, and embodied in the schools of design and mechanics' institutes.[50] It is unlikely that there were many workers at the Kensington meeting. Rather, this entire portion of the meeting was devoted to making the middle classes feel more secure about the working classes, by presenting middle-class paternalism as innocent beneficence, and by characterizing the working classes as unthreatening.

Promoting the exhibition, however, required more than simply giving speeches; it also necessitated a carefully orchestrated relationship with the press, and, with the exception of the free-trade issue, the organizers were extremely adept at using the press to promote the exhibition. There were a number of technological developments during the 1830s which contributed to the mass publication and circulation of newspapers and periodicals. The invention of the high-speed press, the use of cheaper paper, and new printing techniques lowered the costs of production. The spread of railways eased distribution. Publishers realized that if they cut the price of their publications they could both reach a wider audience and increase profits. And there was a general increase in literacy, especially among the skilled workers, small shopkeepers, clerks, and domestic servants, that resulted in a new mass audience for printed matter by the second quarter of the nineteenth century.[51]

The executive committee took advantage of these changes. It made sure, for example, that its preparations for the exhibition were widely advertised, and its choice of London papers covered a fair proportion of the political spectrum, from the *Morning Post*, the 'organ of the traditional ruling classes,' to *The Times*, already the paper of record and oriented towards the mercantile and industrial classes, to the *Chronicle*, more Whig–liberal and Peelite in orientation.[52] It is worth noting, though, that the organizers excluded the Radical and religious press, and that although the *Post*, which was ultra-Protestant, was included, *John Bull*, also ultra-Protestant but oriented towards the lower-middle classes, was not. They were also careful about leaks to the press regarding the commission's preparations, and expended much energy trying to convert the press to their point of view.[53] As early as the summer of 1849 Henry Cole went to see the editor of *The Times*, and afterwards wrote in his diary, 'He quite approved of the exhibition.'[54] *The Times* was by far the most important newspaper, and securing its support was critical to the success of the exhibition. Wrote the cynical and anonymous author of *Stone the First at the Great Glass House*, which sold for a sixpence and was one of many anonymous books and pamphlets written in 1850–1 about the exhibition: '*The Times* averred that the Great Exhibition was a Great Thing; and the world believed it.'[55]

The organizers also kept a watchful eye on how the exhibition was being reported. Matthew Digby Wyatt arranged to have each London daily send him five copies of any issue that contained a report on the exhibition, one for him, one for Phipps and Albert, and the others to be distributed among the members of the committee or added to the commission's archives.[56] The executive committee was understandably concerned with the press's portrayal of the exhibition. In the midst of the turmoil over the design of the exhibition building, when *The Times* had temporarily retreated from its earlier support and was thundering about how the proposed exhibition building would ruin Hyde Park and lessen the value of the houses opposite, Granville complained to Grey, 'I do not know why *The Times* seems determined not to insert a good article on the exhibition.'[57] Keeping a tight control over information, and maintaining a close scrutiny of the press, was instrumental to the commission's efforts to present to the nation its vision of the exhibition.

On the whole, the press embraced, and often actively promoted, the exhibition. Some papers and journals adopted the commission's characterization of the meaning of the exhibition in its entirety. An anonymous author in the *Westminster Review*, for example, summed up the objectives of the exhibition as follows, in April 1850: 'To promote brotherhood amongst mankind; to make all cognizant of what each can do for others; to diminish human drudgery by mechanism; to promote art of the higher kind; to show how clothing may be best made by machines, without hand-craftry.'[58] In other words, to encourage peace, industry, and art. Especially support-ive of the commissioners and their plans were the *Daily News* (the editor of which was Charles Wentworth Dilke, father of the Dilke on the executive committee), the *Economist*, and the *Sun*, all three liberal in politics and defending free trade in com-merce and voluntarism in matters of religion.[59]

The organizers were also (probably unwittingly) assisted in their efforts to trans-form and transmit the ideology of the exhibition by a number of popular writers during the year preceding the opening of the exhibition. Henry Mayhew, in his playful *1851; or, the Adventures of Mr. and Mrs. Sandboys*, picked up on Wyatt's second resolution, that the exhibition was 'especially calculated to promote the welfare of the working classes by offering examples of excellence and stimulating production,' in writing that the exhibition was 'the first attempt to dignify and refine toil.' It would, he continued, 'diffuse a high standard of excellence among our oper-atives, and thus . . . raise the artistic qualities of labour, so that men, no longer working with their fingers alone, shall find that which is now mere drudgery con-verted into a delight, their intellects expanded, their natures softened, and their pur-suits ennobled by the process.'[60] And S. P. Newcombe advanced the theme of peace – the third of Wyatt's suggested resolutions – in his children's book, *Little Henry's Holiday at the Great Exhibition*: 'There was a brotherly feeling beaming from the faces of all. . . . For the first time since the world was made, men of all nations were *working* together in one great act of peace.'[61]

The success of the organizers in promulgating their vision of the exhibition emerges as well from the remarkable degree to which the language used by the organizers was adopted by the press and by ordinary Britons. That is, in their own private writings, individuals characterized the exhibition in the very same terms that were employed at local committee meetings and reiterated in the press. This was noticeably so regarding the expected relationship between the exhibition and inter-national peace. In a letter to the Duke of Wellington, for example, Hugh McCorquo-dale referred to the Crystal Palace as the 'Temple of Peace,' a phrase that surfaced again and again in the press.[62] And John Tod, an otherwise anonymous engineer from Scotland, wrote in his private diary that at the exhibition international rivalry and hostility were displaced by honest competition and that nations discovered that they were not so different from one another and 'eagerly embraced the opportunity of mutually assisting, comforting, encouraging, and improving one another.'[63] It is certainly possible that Tod was able to perceive a lessening of international hostility at the Crystal Palace; more likely, however, is that he was repeating a phrase or theme that he had read or heard voiced over and over again. These comments are indicative of the extent to which the Royal Commissioners and the executive committee succeeded in shaping and responding to public opinion regarding the meaning of the exhibition.

Many of the papers that were less supportive of the Great Exhibition were Tory and protectionist, such as the *Herald* and *Britannia*. The *Morning Herald* was a staunchly protectionist 'family paper' that had been a supporter of Peel until his adoption of free trade in 1846, at which point it became one of his foremost opponents. The *Herald* was critical of the exhibition on free-trade grounds, but only until late October 1850, when construction of the Crystal Palace began with the effect of increasing public support for the exhibition, at which point the paper muted most of its criticism. The *Britannia*, another Conservative and Protestant weekly, provided minimal coverage of the preparations, with little enthusiasm.[64] With the exception of *Blackwood's* and *John Bull*, Tory-leaning mainstream journals tended less to oppose the exhibition outright than to minimize their coverage of it.

Radical and Chartist papers also found fault with the exhibition. The propagandistic quality of the local meetings was not lost on the *Mechanics' Magazine*, which offered a blistering criticism of several of the London meetings in early 1850, complaining that 'public meetings' were 'not places for the calm and dispassionate discussion of any question whatever,' and merely illustrated 'the blind servility with which high and low amongst us, are ever ready to follow in the train of rank and fashion.'[65] *Reynolds's Newspaper* derided the exhibition as a 'monster bubble' and a 'gigantic humbug,' and urged workers to withhold their support for a plan that had originated in ignorance, was progressing with recklessness, and would terminate in nothing but disappointment and commercial distress.[66] These criticisms by the Radical press indicate both the extent of the success and the limits of the commissioners' appeals: no matter how protean it was, the exhibition was not infinitely elastic. Despite all their contortions, the organizers were unable to overcome the opposition of the protectionist press on the one hand, and the Radical Chartist press on the other, although, as we shall see, this did not halt the stampede of British men and women of all classes to the exhibition once it was open.

The organizers were successful in promoting the exhibition because, like all good salesmen, they tempered their sales pitch to fit their audience, and Wyatt's brilliantly conceived organizational structure allowed for a maximum of both central guidance and local variation. But it is important to recognize that many of the 'meanings' offered by the organizers were in fact contradictory. The broadening of free trade could not coexist with assurances that British markets would not be flooded by foreign goods; likewise, the pursuit of peace and the extension of Britain's imperial ambitions were also antithetical. Thus the meaning of the exhibition, far from being 'clear,' as several historians have written, was rife with contradictions.[67] This was especially true in the provinces.

✳   ✳   ✳

ORGANIZATIONAL STRUCTURE AND TACTICS

At its very first meeting in early January 1850, the Royal Commission directed the executive committee to issue a circular to the mayors of all the towns in the United Kingdom announcing that the Queen had created a royal commission to arrange the exhibition, and requesting that, if no local committee had yet been formed, the mayor establish one. The executive committee issued similar circulars to the chambers of commerce and to the royal agricultural societies.[68] The organizers were appealing, then, to political, financial, commercial, industrial, and agricultural power bases. As Grey wrote to Cole in mid-1850, regarding the executive committee's efforts to organize local committees and reach out to the provinces, 'This is the right way to organize the country.'[69]

In all likelihood, Grey meant that remark in at least two different ways. Just as it was evident that the national exhibition could not succeed without the support of the provinces, the creation of local committees also enabled the Royal Commission and the executive committee to regulate who supported the exhibition, and how they did so. Henry Cole noted in his diary that 'Reid objected to too much popular agitation – it would and had compromised the Prince somewhat – The action must be through the local committees or not at all.'[70] That is, the local committees were a means of control, of excluding certain groups – Chartists, for example – that would not have been palatable to the landed and business interests that were investing heavily in the exhibition.

Heading the organization effort was Matthew Digby Wyatt, secretary to the executive committee, who deluged the local committees with circulars and forms. He sent out copies of a speech by Lord Stanley supporting the exhibition, which had been printed on placards, requesting that they be 'stuck up in the market place . . . on *market* days.' He produced a memorandum which pointed out 'how every village or hamlet in the United Kingdom has an opportunity of taking its part in the forthcoming exhibition.' And he oversaw the production of posters advertising the exhibition which specifically targeted railway companies and railway stations. In short, Wyatt engineered and implemented an elaborate and comprehensive publicity campaign.[71]

But promoting the exhibition required more than simply giving speeches, putting up posters, or utilizing the press. So important was the local aspect of the exhibition that the commission appointed two special commissioners to communicate with the provincial communities: Lyon Playfair and Lieutenant-Colonel J. A. Lloyd. They were enlisted because, as of the spring of 1850, the organization of the exhibition was in trouble: the controversy over the Mundays' contract had already raged on for months, and Colonel Sibthorp was fulminating about the trees in Hyde Park. At the local level the 'industrial classes,' meaning in this case manufacturers, were withholding their support, which made the government particularly anxious since Albert had already firmly committed himself to the project. Playfair had two meetings with Albert at which the Prince Consort explained the difficulties facing the commission, and then he and Lloyd were set to work.[72]

Both Playfair and Lloyd were well educated, well traveled, and well connected. Both had backgrounds in science: Playfair had earned his doctorate in chemistry, and had worked as the manager of a calico-manufacturing firm before being appointed an honorary professor of chemistry at the Royal Institution in Manchester; Lloyd had served as captain of the engineers for Simon Bolivar, the liberator of Colombia, before becoming a Fellow of the Royal Society, an associate of the Institute of Civil Engineers, and a scientist for the Admiralty. Playfair had studied at St Andrews, Glasgow, and Edinburgh, and thus brought to the organizational efforts his Scottish connections; he had also made a business trip to Calcutta. Lloyd, having spent much of his time overseas in South America, contributed to the commission his knowledge of that vital and foreign part of the world. Both men, then, had imperial and not just British connections. Playfair especially was socially and politically well connected, having previously been appointed by Peel to a royal commission charged with inquiring into the state of large towns and populous districts, on which he met a number of men who would later be associated with the Great Exhibition, including Buccleuch, Robert Stephenson, and Thomas Cubitt. Both were industrious and energetic, and brought to the exhibition great breadth of knowledge and experience.[73]

The two of them built on the rudimentary system of communicating with the provinces that the executive committee had inherited from the Society of Arts, the centerpiece of which was the local committees, of which there were 297 by the time the commissioners published their *First Report* to the Queen (map 2). The formation of these committees had begun quietly during the summer of 1849 when Cole and Fuller made their initial tour of the northern manufacturing towns, and the recruiting effort continued more earnestly in the autumn, after the first Mansion House meeting in October.[74] There were two points of connection between the executive committee and the local committees. One was the 'local commissioners,' appointed by the executive committee. Many towns, however, refused to deal with these outsiders. The *Manchester Guardian*, for example, objected to the fact that the local commissioners would in effect be the 'ministerial agents or servants of the commission in London, rather than the *bona fide* representatives of the local committee, and the district for which they may be appointed.'[75] Here again is evidence of the tension between metropolis and province, and in particular resentment on the part of provincial towns, especially a proud northern capital like Manchester, over control from London.

The other channel of communication between the executive committee and the local committees was through the local secretaries. These were chosen by the local committees themselves, to represent local interests to the executive committee and the Royal Commission. Although the mayors received most of the credit, it was these locally appointed secretaries who handled most of the vital, day-to-day tasks. They were, according to one journal, 'the working bees of the hive,' and shouldered much of the responsibility for canvassing, collecting money, and making the arrangements necessary for selecting the exhibits.[76] The willingness of the Royal Commission and the executive committee to work with local representatives illustrates their flexibility and the extent to which they realized the importance of involving the provinces.

Two conditions were essential to gaining a town's support: a competent and supportive local committee, and a personal visit by one of the deputies from the executive committee. J. A. Lloyd, in a July 1850 memorandum, stressed the importance of the former, urging that 'great pains should be taken in the selection' of local committees and commissioners.[77] A variety of organizational problems could beset a local committee. One was when the leading citizens of a town involved themselves in the committee even if they were not enthusiastic about the exhibition, or not

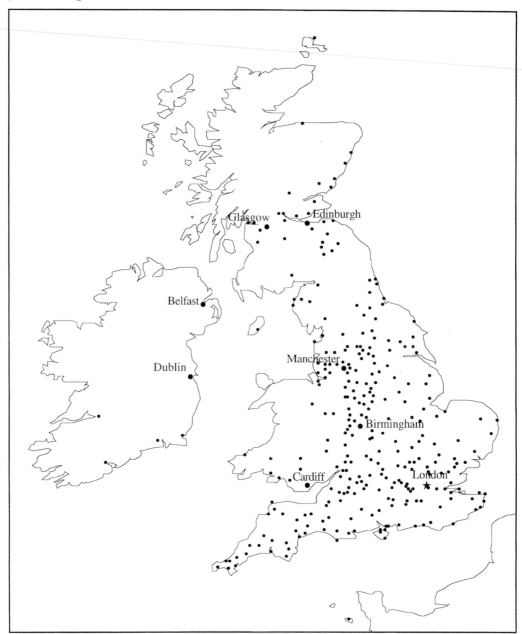

Map 2. Local Committees.

willing to devote their energies to promoting it. A second potential problem was that town notables might refuse to get involved altogether, which usually caused other citizens to withhold their support. In either case, the results were disastrous for the organizers of the exhibition, at least until they could either reorganize the committee or persuade those concerned that the exhibition was worth supporting.[78]

Just as the constitution of the local committee was important, so too was a personal visit by Playfair or Lloyd or one of the other deputies from the executive committee. Almost as soon as Playfair and Lloyd had been appointed special commissioners they headed for the provinces: Playfair traveled north, Lloyd south.

Their job was to promote and publicize the exhibition in every town on an individual, case-by-case basis, appealing to national glory, local pride, and commercial well-being, whatever worked. There is little doubt that the visits paid to the towns succeeded in turning the tide of both indifference and opposition. Integral to the efforts of the special commissioners was the dissemination of information, persuading towns and committees that the exhibition would benefit them. In Dover, for example, Lloyd found apathy and slow subscriptions, but when he told the committee of the benefits likely to arise from tourism, they became energized and the mayor and local committee agreed personally to canvass the town and call a public meeting.[79] Where people were ignorant of the particulars of the exhibition, they were generally apathetic, but where they were provided with information, few refused their support.

Playfair was particularly successful in convincing recalcitrant towns or committees to support the exhibition, although not surprisingly the towns of the North on which he was concentrating were, on the whole, more inclined to support an industrial exhibition than southern towns. Playfair considered the sudden turnaround of Sheffield following his visit there such a success that he wanted to draw Albert's attention to it as an instructive example. A year or so before Playfair's visit, a meeting had been held there to receive Captain Ibbetson of the Society of Arts, with the mayor presiding, where 'all the leading merchants and manufacturers of the town and several of the principal gentry were present.' Not in attendance, but having sent letters of support, were several peers and the local Member of Parliament. At that meeting, the organizers marketed the exhibition by suggesting that consumers on the continent no longer perceived Sheffield to be as dominant in cutlery as it once had been, implying that it should participate in the exhibition in order to prove that its cutlery was still of superior caliber.[80] Apparently this appeal was insufficient to produce offers of support for the exhibition, because in October 1850 Playfair had to return. He spent five days in Sheffield, meeting principally with Nelson Overend, the chief magistrate, and Younger Mitchell, a teacher at the school of design. Playfair reported that on one occasion he met with them and others for eighteen hours straight. During his stay the number of exhibits rose from 150 to 296, and the amount of exhibition space requested increased from 5,000 to 13,700 square feet. Playfair also noted that a committee of forty artisans decided to divide the town into districts and visited and instructed 'the manufacturers as to the favourable efforts which the exhibition would have upon industry,' which was in Playfair's opinion 'a most remarkable feature.' He concluded: 'From a thorough failure Sheffield has become a complete success.'[81] Playfair had similarly successful experiences in numerous other towns, but only after a considerable investment of time and hard work.[82] Soliciting support for the exhibition, then, was done individually, town by town. Wyatt and the executive committee did what they could from London, but the exhibition succeeded because the organizers found the right blend of centralization and decentralization.

One of the most successful, if symbolic, tactics used to garner support and create a sense of belonging was the circulation of little red leather books, in which promoters and subscribers could sign their names. The organizers used these books to appeal to civic pride and individual vanity. The cover, which contained the royal seal, was embossed with gold, and read, 'Promoters of the Great Exhibition of Industry of All Nations to be held in 1851 under the Presidency of His Royal Highness Prince Albert.' The books contained an official-looking letter of authorization signed by

Prince Albert and extracts of the 30 June 1849 meeting at Buckingham Palace and the 14 July 1849 meeting at Osborne.[83] Playfair and Lloyd took copies of the red book on their trips to the provinces, and it became a major feature of their presentations and an important means of gathering support. In Macclesfield, for example, there had been a well-attended and promising meeting in April 1850, but at that meeting Hepworth Dixon had promised that the red book with the royal seal would be sent for subscriptions. According to Playfair, who visited the town two months later, the manufacturers were 'highly indignant that this red book was never sent,' and refused to subscribe their names in anything less brilliant. Playfair promised to get one, although he was unable to promise one with the royal arms. This seemed to be a satisfactory compromise, but he perceived much apathy in Macclesfield, and warned the commission not to expect much from that town.[84] It took another visit in August, this time by Lloyd, before Macclesfield generated any subscriptions.[85] While hardly the determining feature, symbolic items such as the red book played an important role in providing contributors with a sense of status and recognition. The red book turned support for the Great Exhibition into a matter of civic, local, and national honor.

One strategy the executive committee tried unsuccessfully was to use paid lecturers to travel to the towns, provide details about the exhibition, speak on its behalf, and aid in the formation of a local committee.[86] According to Lloyd, however, these lecturers were ineffective because, being paid, they were 'looked on with suspicion.' It was better, Lloyd wrote, to have an official from the executive committee speak gratis, or to have trustworthy locals give a speech.[87] The use of lecturers ended up being a public-relations disaster. *Blackwood's*, in September 1850, bitterly objected to 'the system of itinerant lecturing and peripatetic persuasion.' The magazine asserted that, however distinguished and qualified the lecturers were, dispatching them to extol the advantages of the exhibition was 'inconsistent with the dignity of a great national undertaking,' and implied that there was 'no spontaneous movement on the part of the British nation' to support the exhibition.[88]

The hired deputies were also difficult to control. As Henry Cole noted of one, 'he had been engaged several times in public disputes and was known as an impetuous and injudicious man.'[89] There was bickering among the deputies about their compensation, and even a case of mistaken identity. Apparently an impostor by the name of 'Warren,' posing as a royal commissioner, held a large meeting at the Coventry Mechanics' Institute on 24 May 1850. He had selected one hundred working-class men, and at a meeting they had chosen a chairman and committee to be independent of the regular local committee. When Lloyd finally had a chance to speak with some of the artisans who had met with 'Warren,' they said that they believed he had 'some connection with Vincent the Chartist.'[90] Issues of authority and identity were recurring problems, and it was for this reason that the official deputies from the executive committee carried with them letters of introduction and authorization signed by Prince Albert.[91] There is no question that the organizing authorities were concerned about assemblies of working-class men, who were accordingly largely excluded from the regular local meetings.

Although the organizational effort on behalf of the exhibition was essentially the same in every town, each town responded differently: different people, different industries, different concerns. As Herbert Byng Hall wrote of his trip through the west of England, 'How strange and varied are the sentiments expressed.'[92] Some

Britons eulogized the idea, some derided it, others remained reserved. It is instructive, then, to look at the specifics of individual cases. What is remarkable about the exhibition, and the efforts of those who organized it, is that it appealed to so many different communities and individuals, though there remained substantial pockets of opposition and apathy.

THE PROVINCIAL RESPONSE

There were a variety of elements that determined how a given town or region responded to the appeals of the executive committee. Foremost among them were the state of the economy, political alignments, and social divisions. Although the organizational structure was the same everywhere, the responses of cities, towns, and local communities to the appeals of the Royal Commission varied considerably. Table 1 (p. 76), which lists the number of subscribers, the amount subscribed, and subscriptions per capita for selected local committees, illustrates the enormous range of responses. The Great Exhibition, then, was not uniformly embraced through the British Isles. Rather, the picture one gets is of substantial pockets of resistance, and in a number of cases outright opposition, even though most areas ended up supporting the endeavor.

If any town was likely to support the Great Exhibition, it was Manchester, where, in the words of one historian, 'the "din of machinery" was the music of economic progress.'[93] Although in the eighteenth century cotton had created Manchester, by the middle of the nineteenth century it was much more than a 'metropolis of manufacturers.' It had a diverse economy and was the trade center of an entire region, commercially linked with the whole world. Its local government was dominated by merchants, lawyers, bankers, and a 'shopocracy' which in Cobden's opinion had been instrumental in the struggle to incorporate Manchester as a borough in 1837–8. It was a city of producers and consumers, of industrialists and commercial merchants and capitalists, who for a span of three decades in the mid-nineteenth century shared an ideological commitment to free trade, symbolized by their support of the Anti-Corn Law League and their construction of the Manchester Free Trade Hall, perhaps the only city hall dedicated not to a person but to a proposition.[94] Manchester was also a city with a tradition of support for culture and the arts, particularly after 1820, when the Royal Manchester Institution and the Mechanics' Institute began to hold financially successful and well-attended exhibitions of works of art and industry.[95]

In Manchester, the first large meeting to promote the exhibition took place in November 1849 in the mayor's parlor at the town hall. As in most places, it was 'of a private character,' which meant that admission was by invitation not advertisement; this excluded any social undesirables. The deputies from the Society of Arts had asked to meet with 'the chief members of any chambers of commerce, agricultural associations, literary or scientific bodies, and generally such individuals as should seem, from their position, most likely to become interested in this matter.' Thus from the outset the issue of participation in the planning of the exhibition was left largely to the local communities, although within the general parameters established in London. In attendance were, according to the *Manchester Guardian*, 200 'influential

Table 1: Subscriptions Raised by Selected Local Committees[96]

City	Population	Number of subscribers	Subscription £	Subscription per capita £	Average subscription £
Bath	54,248		200	0.004	
Belfast	99,660		582	0.006	
Birmingham	232,841		897	0.004	
Bolton	61,171	1,006	726	0.012	0.72
Bradford	103,778		1,605	0.015	
Bristol	137,328	143	778	0.006	5.51
Bury	31,262	11	84	0.003	7.60
Cambridge Univ.	1,212	47	139	0.115	2.96
Cambridge Town	26,603	102	187	0.007	1.83
Canterbury	18,398	100	79	0.004	0.79
Cardiff	18,294		96	0.005	
Chatham	28,424		75	0.003	
Cork	86,485		50	0.001	
Derby	40,609		342	0.008	
Dublin	254,850	69	406	0.002	5.88
Dundee	78,829		203	0.003	
Durham	13,168	181	171	0.013	0.94
Edinburgh	66,734		909	0.014	
Glasgow	333,657	238	2,666	0.008	11.20
Leeds	172,270		2,030	0.012	
Leicester	60,584	120	200	0.003	1.67
Liverpool	376,063	387	758	0.002	1.96
London (City)	127,869		26,632	0.208	
Maidstone	20,730		74	0.004	
Manchester	303,382		4,548	0.015	
Marylebone	370,957	614	1,258	0.003	2.05
Merthyr Tydfil	63,080		207	0.003	
Oldham	52,820	11	90	0.002	8.18
Oxford	27,973		200	0.007	
Preston	69,493	67	302	0.004	4.51
Rochester	14,938		13	0.008	
Sheffield	135,310		845	0.006	
Swansea	31,461		156	0.005	
Tower Hamlets	510,727		315	0.001	
Westminster	241,611		7,681	0.032	

merchants, manufacturers and bankers.' There were representatives from all the major industrial interests – cotton, machinery, silk, and general manufactures – along with clergy, prominent public figures and magistrates, local nobility, and other 'leading inhabitants,' not only from Manchester proper but from the neighboring towns of Bury, Bolton, Salford, Oldham, and Stockport.[97] The theory behind the meetings was that if the leading figures of the community – financial, social, religious – could be persuaded to support the ideas underlying the exhibition, then more widespread local support would follow. In this regard meetings like this one were generally successful. They drew together not only those who had a genuine interest in a particular project, but also habitual attenders of public meetings who had organizational experience even if little interest in the subject at hand.[98] Many of those at the first meeting in Manchester became substantial donors, local organizers, and exhibitors as well.

The speakers offered a number of reasons for supporting the exhibition, though none appealed more to civic and local pride than the mayor, John Potter:

When we considered the great extent of the adaptations of machinery to the arts in Manchester, when we looked upon the number of eminent names amongst us, as engineers, when we looked upon our enormous cotton manufacture, in all its varieties and beauties of form, when we also recollected the importance of the rising and increasing silk trade which existed amongst us, and the magnificent damasks which were produced in Manchester . . . we must at least acknowledge at once, that there were a vast variety of articles which we could contribute to this great exhibition, and that the community in which we lived must be essentially benefited by their exhibition.[99]

He stated that the exhibition would benefit all mankind, and had 'the support of all classes of the community.' As evidence Potter noted that 103 individuals and firms had already written their names in the red book as promoters and subscribers. Henry Cole then provided some details about the organizers' plans, before representatives of the local elite offered their own resolutions. The Lord Bishop of Manchester said that the Great Exhibition would be beneficial by lowering the prices of goods and raw materials, by increasing markets, and hence by increasing employment. He also suggested that the exhibition would bring people together, thus making the exhibition 'a grand and important step in social progress.' Alderman William Neild, who had served as mayor of Manchester in the early 1840s, extolled the virtues of competition and claimed that since the time of King Alfred there had been no monarch 'so much beloved' as Queen Victoria. And John Bright anticipated that the exhibition would not only show other nations the British way of life, but would glorify the virtues of labor and industry.[100] While there is no evidence that the speeches were doled out as favors in return for large financial contributions to the exhibition fund, there was, unsurprisingly, a linkage between the two: those most likely to be involved in town politics were those who also had money, and who were also likely to be offered positions of prominence at a meeting to organize an event such as the exhibition.[101]

The organizational effort in Manchester on behalf of the exhibition was a testament to the power – both financial and ideological – of what might be called the Unitarian commercial middle class in that city. Research has shown that five Unitarian families provided late-eighteenth- and early-nineteenth-century Manchester with a considerable share of its leading commercial, scientific, professional, and literary men: the Heywoods, Philipses, Henrys, Potters, and Gregs.[102] Members of all five were early and large contributors to the exhibition subscription fund.[103] As a group, these families were liberal in politics, tolerant where Dissenting religion was concerned, committed to education and the improvement of the working classes, and respectful of scientific thought. The Gregs and Heywoods had helped establish the Statistical Society in 1833, and the Potters, Gregs, Philipses, and Heywoods were all prominent members of the Anti-Corn Law League. Additionally, many of the exhibition's early supporters in Manchester had been involved in the formation of the Mechanics' Institute and the Commercial Association.[104] In contrast, of the so-called 'Tory elite,'[105] only two men – Samuel Jones Loyd and William Entwisle, who were cousins and business partners – were large contributors to or prominent supporters of the exhibition effort. The exhibition was not a partisan political event, and the organizers fought hard against it being labeled as such, but there is no question that certain political groups (Liberals, free-traders, men of commerce and industry) were more likely to support the exhibition than others (Tories, protectionists, men of agriculture).

The Manchester committee is an example of local organization *par excellence*. The first meeting, as noted above, was well attended, and resulted in a committee that although not exactly representative of the community, in that it was dominated by the liberal elite, nonetheless drew on local talent and included enough Tories to make it plausible to claim political representativeness. Its sub-committee for subscriptions raised more than £4,700 in just under six months, of which £4,150 went to the Royal Commission in London, the rest being used to defray the cost of supplies and publicity. The local secretaries solicited exhibits that were representative of the area and looked out for the interests of local exhibitors.[106]

There was, however, occasional tension between Manchester and London. One principal area of concern was that the exhibition would be of greater commercial benefit to London than to the provinces. One resident of Manchester, in a letter written early in 1850 to Francis Fuller, expressed doubts about whether the exhibition would produce for Manchester 'a single additional customer.' He wrote that as a consequence 'A want of enthusiasm was prevalent,' and that the support that existed was thin, noting that the £3,300 raised at that point had come from only forty people. He recommended that an appeal to patriotism – 'That England had challenged the rest of the world and that they should support it' – would be more successful than trying to persuade the merchants of Manchester that the exhibition was in their commercial interest.[107] Although in certain areas of London deputies from the Royal Commission held out the possibility of a financial windfall of up to £2 million,[108] needless to say this benefit to the capital was not a very effective argument in the provinces. The Royal Commission had to find other grounds on which to promote the exhibition in the provinces, which it did in no small part by leaving the promotion of the exhibition to the local committees, though always guided by London.

In Manchester, then, the commissioners had everything working in their favor: a booming industrial economy and a strong, liberal, middle class that supported free trade. But rarely were conditions so propitious, and Leeds and Bradford, two West Riding textile towns, are cases in point. In the eighteenth century Leeds had been one of the most important centers for woolen and worsted manufacturing in the West Riding area. During the first half of the nineteenth century, however, it lost much of its worsted industry to Bradford. Leeds had retained its importance as a producer of woolens, although this was an industry in which machinery had made substantially fewer inroads.[109] Partly as a consequence, by the time of the exhibition Leeds was a town of many trades, a commercial center with a mixed industrial base, whereas Bradford remained essentially a textiles town.[110] Bradford was one of the 'shock cities' of the Industrial Revolution and, in the words of one historian, 'regarded itself and was generally regarded as a byword for progress.'[111] Its population exploded from a mere 6,000 in 1801 to more than 52,000 a half-century later, an increase of more than 800 percent. Leeds had also grown in population, but not nearly so quickly, and observers at the time perceived in Leeds a conservatism and lethargy compared to Bradford; it was not until 1851, long after most other large towns, that the citizens of Leeds formed a chamber of commerce, one of the more notable local consequences of the Great Exhibition.[112]

There were also important socio-political differences between the two towns. According to one study, by 1851 the foundations of a mid-Victorian, middle-class, liberal consensus had emerged in Bradford. Liberal–entrepreneurial and voluntarist ideologies had come to predominate, and with them a middle class, especially in the face of the decline of the traditional landed elites and the disarray of the working classes.[113] By contrast, in Leeds there were greater social, political, and economic divisions, despite the absence of an obvious two- or three-class social structure. There was also continual conflict between Whig/Nonconformists and Tory/Anglicans, and middle-class unity was at best partial and intermittent.[114]

Differences in population and industry and in political accommodations meant that Leeds and Bradford responded to the exhibition in different ways. Bradford approached it with great confidence, proud of its prowess and supremacy in making cheap worsted fabrics. Its business and industrial leaders enthusiastically supported the formation of their local committee, boldly asserting that the exhibition would confirm Bradford's already established reputation. Fifty-five of the fifty-seven exhibitors from Bradford were connected with worsted manufacturing. The mayor seemed unconcerned by the prospect of competition with French worsted materials, and it became Bradford's pride that its subscribers contributed more per head to the exhibition fund than those of any other town in England, and that its subscriptions per capita ranked near the top as well.[115]

In Leeds, at least as far as the woolen industry was concerned, the exhibition presented 'an opportunity to refute accusations of backwardness.' The West Riding woolen industry had been hit hard by foreign competition, and John Gott for one saw the exhibition 'as a possible remedy for trade depression.'[116] Martin Cawood, secretary to the Leeds local committee, made the contrast between the two cities starkly in a letter to the *Leeds Mercury* just before the exhibition opened. He noted that whereas Leeds and most of the West Riding towns were content with exhibit counters of 'plain deal covered with crimson or blue cloth, oak, maple, or mahogany oil-cased paper' on which to display their goods, the Bradford exhibitors had 'gone to much greater expense,' and were planning to use '1,500 feet of plate glass to protect and show off their goods.' And the *Leeds Mercury* itself summed up the competition between Leeds and Bradford after the opening, commenting that there was 'nothing in the whole building more absolutely plain than the Leeds woollen department,' while, on the other side of the aisle, 'Bradford had taken prodigious pains . . . and with brilliant effect, to give their goods every advantage.'[117] As far as the wool textile industry was concerned, Bradford was on the rise and Leeds on the decline, and the exhibition made that divergence painfully clear.

But Leeds was not exclusively a wool textile town by any means. In fact, the production of textiles occupied only 34 percent of those employed in the city.[118] Leeds had such a varied economy that many local industries and interests stood to gain by the exhibition. The woolen industry aside, Leeds was extremely supportive. Only London, Manchester, and Glasgow exceeded Leeds' total contribution of £2,030, and Leeds' status near the top holds even when subscriptions are considered in proportion to population.

It was not surprising that the northern industrial cities supported the exhibition, albeit with different levels of enthusiasm. What is more notable is how the organizers were able to garner support in less industrial areas, such as Liverpool and Bath. In Liverpool, the organizers ran into trouble because a number of Liverpudlians opposed the exhibition on outright political grounds, believing the exhibition to be part of 'a free trade movement.' The town also exhibited a high level of discontent with government in general, and residents connected the exhibition with the government. Moreover, many inhabitants did not see how the exhibition would further their interests because Liverpool was not a manufacturing town, and they were of the opinion that there was no need for them to subscribe because admission receipts would be ample enough to cover costs. When Playfair visited the city in May 1850, he found 'much hostility to the exhibition . . . and no zeal,' a finding consistent with Liverpool's reticence in supporting the exhibition that dated all the way back to the first meeting held there in November 1849. Town authorities and civic leaders predicted that it would be impossible for the commission to get Liverpool to support the exhibition, and they gave Playfair no encouragement.[119]

Critical to Playfair's efforts in Liverpool, aside from the usual spate of meetings, was securing the backing of the *Liverpool Mercury*. He met with Mrs Egerton Smith, the proprietor and editor, who became enthusiastic about the Great Exhibition, 'and through her columns, the public were vigorously assailed.'[120] The *Mail*, Tory and High Church, saw great potential for disaster in the exhibition of 1851, but in the weekly circulation wars it took only third place behind the *Mercury* and the *Journal*, the two Liberal papers.[121] Mrs Smith virtually shamed the city into supporting the exhibition: 'The time has now come for Liverpool to redeem its part of the pledge. . . . There is perhaps no town in the kingdom more interested, both directly and indirectly, in the prosperity of this movement than Liverpool.' The *Mercury* pointed out that the Great Exhibition was not just for producers, it was for merchants and traders and retailers.[122] And Liverpool's two main exhibits at the Crystal Palace – a forty-foot-long scale model of the Liverpool docks that cost the town £1,000 and a large case of imports which were intended to form the basis of 'a museum of commercial activity' when they were returned to Liverpool after the exhibition – testified to the centrality of commerce at the Great Exhibition, along with industry.[123] Playfair was also able to secure a political reconciliation of free-traders and protectionists: The local committee decided that 'the principal men, in parties consisting of one ultra-protectionist, and one liberal each,' would canvass the wards to try to eliminate the 'political prejudice' regarding the exhibition and to foster support. By the time Playfair moved on to his next stop, he believed he had 'thoroughly awakened' the town of Liverpool.[124]

Bath provides an interesting comparison, because it was also not an industrial town. But it could compete in the fine-arts category, and one organizer even suggested that, were it to exhibit a model of the city as well, Bath might attract thousands of tourists. This is somewhat ironic, because the Great Exhibition actually had an adverse effect on the Bath economy by drawing tourists away from its spas and into London instead.[125] Bath received the usual visits from the executive committee, but ultimately the organizers' success there hinged on local socio-economic conditions. The organizers were successful in part because they convinced local businessmen – who manufactured principally luxury goods – that they were less likely to be hurt by imports than some other cities. They also benefitted from the general lack of class antagonism in Bath and from cooperation between the town's various social groups as they increasingly oriented their appeal to the working classes.[126] To further this end, the committee announced that it would deposit a book in the British Museum which recorded each donor's name, 'without distinction between peer and peasant.'[127] Judging from the number of excursion trains that departed from Bath after the exhibition opened to the public, the committee was quite successful in this appeal.[128] Finally, the organizers drew on local patriotic sentiments, creating an impression of national consensus around the event. One circular from the Bath committee called upon 'fellow-citizens and neighbours' to aid the exhibition because it was presided over by the Prince and sanctioned by the Queen. Bath successfully contributed to the exhibition even though it was not an industrial city.

What the examples of Manchester, Leeds, Bradford, Liverpool, and Bath illustrate is that economics played a critical role in how likely a town was to support the exhibition. Bradford, a one-industry town where business was booming, was full of confidence and eager to show off its wealth and manufacturing prowess. In Leeds, the economy was diverse and strong overall, except for the woolen industry. Consequently, Leeds was able to provide a significant level of support for the exhibition, but not from the woolen sector. As for Bath and Liverpool, neither was an industrial center, yet both became major supporters, in each case largely because of their economic structures: Bath's economy, based on luxury goods and tourism, was largely immune to imports; Liverpool's focused on commerce, so that once the organizers had convinced townspeople that they stood to gain from the exhibition, enthusiastic support came quickly. Politics too played an important role, in that none of these towns was particularly Tory or protectionist. In all five cases, local visits and a superior organizational structure were the essential building blocks, and in all five cases the exhibition spoke to specific local concerns.

OPPOSITION AND FAILURE

Most towns were in the end supportive, even enthusiastic. There were, however, a number of places where the organizers' appeals were ignored or rejected, or where, for a variety of reasons, the organizational effort was unsuccessful. There is no question, for example, that overall the executive committee's strategy and tactics worked most effectively in urban areas. But this was not uniformly the case. The executive committee had little success, for example, in Tower Hamlets, a section of London which in 1850 consisted of some 400,000 inhabitants in twenty-six parishes, sharing no center or interest, and having no unifying body to organize a local meeting. Charles Booth would later describe the people living in the area as 'the most destitute population in England.'[129] The middle class constituted only about 8 percent of the total population, unemployment was probably at least 15 percent, and most residents were poor artisans, street sellers, and minimum-wage laborers.[130] Most were neither willing nor able to attend a daytime meeting. Were a meeting to be held in the evening, wrote one of the deputies for the executive committee, residents would have too far to travel, and the meeting room would be 'filled with the worst population of the borough – Chartists and others who would probably disturb the proceedings and give a character little to be desired to the meeting . . . [and] move to carry some absurd or mischievous resolution.' Moreover, the region was divided between those in parishes which had an interest in shipping, and those in Spitalfields and Bethnal Green which generally consisted of weavers, who were strongly opposed to free trade and thus predisposed against the exhibition.[131] Tower Hamlets subscribed only £315, one of the lowest amounts on a per-capita basis.[132]

Despite all these obstacles, the executive committee hoped that the residents of the Hamlets would contribute to the exhibition and made sure to include them in its organizational efforts. They were not especially successful, but what mattered to them was less the amount of money raised in the Hamlets than the simple fact of their inclusion in the preparation for the exhibition. The case of Tower Hamlets reveals the organizers searching for respectable artisans and workers, being careful not to run the risk of exposing the exhibition to Chartists and other social undesirables.

The executive committee experienced difficulties too in the agricultural regions. Although the organizers went to considerable lengths to garner the support of farmers and agriculturalists, Cole discerned early on that agriculture was a problematic sector, and that 'In the agricultural districts especially we must be very quiet.'[133] In the county of Durham, Lord Londonderry took great pains to promote the exhibition on behalf of the Royal Commission, but with little success. Londonderry wrote letters to both the Duke of Cleveland, who was very powerful in the county, and to Mr Burdon, chairman of the Quarter Sessions, seeking their support and participation. Cleveland's opinion was 'decidedly against' taking steps to convene a meeting in Durham because it was 'purely agricultural:' 'At a period like the present when distress here is so deeply and widely spread amongst all classes in this county, the time appears to be ill chosen, for asking the county from its impoverished resources, to draw its purse strings, to contribute to what for it individually would be of no possible advantage.'[134] As for Burdon, he reported that he had not heard much conversation on the subject of the exhibition, nor did he think that it would excite much interest in the county. Rather, he thought it 'more likely to interest towns and manufacturing districts, than such as afford rural and mining occupations,' as was the case locally. Londonderry concluded that in light of these comments, combined with 'the peculiar ecclesiastical and mining interests in Durham' and the lack of a 'really great landed proprietor' other than Cleveland, any efforts on his part would be a failure. He urged the executive committee to focus its attentions either on the city of Durham or on Northumberland, where the Duke of Northumberland had considerable influence.[135]

The problem in the agricultural and mining districts was not only ideological – that is, opposition to free trade – but also practical. Many residents in agricultural areas were unclear about what they could exhibit, and in general, where exhibits were few, subscriptions were low as well.[136] Moreover, the organizers were quite simply unable to make it clear to farmers how the exhibition would benefit them. As *Punch* joked in 1851:

> I hears a vast deal, and I s'pose I shall moor,
> About that famous dimond the gurt Koh-i-Noor,
> That's wuth nigh a million, as folks do relate;
> But what's that with wheat down below thirty-eight?
>
> There's minerals, and physic, and chymical drugs,
> There's tapestry, and floor-cloth, and carpets, and rugs,
> And there's porcelain and crockery, so fine and so grand;
> But all that wun't afford no relief to the land.[137]

Speakers from the executive committee tried to link the exhibition with the annual meeting of the Agricultural Society of England, which would take place in Hyde Park and which they claimed would comprise 'a fifth grand division' of exhibits, but there was great resistance to mechanization, and the free-trade associations of the exhibition proved to be an insurmountable barrier.[138]

Social relations were another factor that frequently hampered the efforts of the organizers. In Preston, there was what Lloyd referred to as 'a slight misunderstanding between the operatives and the higher classes.' Workers had complained that they felt 'kept back,' and that the avowal of the local committee 'that they [the working classes] would not be answerable for the funds subscribed' had created feelings of resentment and exclusion. They said that they had been 'left ignorant and uninstructed in regard to the advantages to them of the exhibition.' Although it is impossible to be sure, based on the evidence from other towns it is likely that the local committee had deliberately excluded the working classes from the preparations for fear of radicalism, but were now paying the consequences. The deputation of workers that met with Lloyd added that 'they must be clearly told their own interest . . . honouring their industry, heightening their future prospects.' This last comment underscores the importance of promoting the exhibition on specific grounds that were carefully targeted to the audience in question, something the Royal Commission and executive committee were generally able to do very successfully. Lloyd did his best to reassure the envoys that the exhibition was in their interest, and the deputation acknowledged that they had received pamphlets which made explicit the goals and expected benefits of the exhibition, but had simply not read them. In the end, Lloyd was able to work out a solution, proposed by the mayor, whereby the workers would select four or five delegates to become members of the local committee, thus giving them a sense of inclusion. As a result of Lloyd's careful work, Preston managed to raise more than £300 for the subscription fund, a respectable showing.[139]

In their effort to organize the provinces the organizers consistently refused to acknowledge the importance of politics. Time and again Playfair and Lloyd, when they had difficulty with a town or region, explained the lack of interest in the exhibition in terms of organizational issues. In Bury, for example, a Lancashire town near Manchester with a population of about 30,000 people, Lloyd discovered that as of late July 1850 only paltry amounts had been subscribed. He attributed the problem to 'apathy and want of good will' on the committee itself, which he said was 'unfortunately constituted – the secretary being a most inefficient one and the chairman (a cotton spinner) who does not care for exhibiting.' The town excused its low subscriptions because of obligations to the town hall, schools, and agricultural meetings, but Lloyd noted that they had just decided to subscribe £2,000 for a monument.[140] A more likely explanation is that there was lingering suspicion of London stemming from the Corn Laws. Similarly, Rochester and Chatham, in Kent, were 'both miserable places as far as the exhibition is concerned.' Lloyd blamed the lack of support for the exhibition on 'the constitution of the local committee' and 'people of higher caste and standing not coming forward more prominently.'[141] What Lloyd did not mention was that both of these towns were agricultural, High Church Anglican, and protectionist, and thus it was for political reasons as much as any other that the 'people of higher caste and standing' were reluctant to support the exhibition early on. Ultimately all three towns subscribed small amounts: £84 from Bury, £9 from Rochester, and £75 from Chatham; all three were at or near the bottom in terms of per-capita contributions. Moreover, Bury raised only £3 after Lloyd's visit.[142] Whereas in most towns a visit from Lloyd or Playfair invigorated local efforts, in these towns that simply did not happen. No amount of organization could overcome outright partisan opposition.

The organizers also had mixed success in the so-called Celtic fringe, which they certainly recognized as important to involve in the exhibition, although they seem to have had no explicit policy regarding these regions.[143] They were most successful in

Scotland, where, during the summer of 1850, Lyon Playfair, who had extensive Scottish connections, made a successful fund-raising trip to the major towns. He found enthusiastic attitudes toward the exhibition in Edinburgh, especially among workers and artisans in the iron and furniture trades. Although one large meeting of the working classes began inauspiciously, with a few Chartists 'making much noise,' Playfair wrote afterwards that he had 'thoroughly converted the whole meeting.' When the resolution was offered that the exhibition was calculated to be of great use to the working classes, only three hands were raised in opposition. Later in the summer Playfair summarized: 'Edinburgh is doing well on the whole. Among the higher classes there is still much dislike of the exhibition, but the lower and middle classes are very favourable.' He did not indicate the source of these class differences, but they seem to have made little difference, as Edinburgh ranked in the top ten in total amount raised out of the more than 300 towns that formed local committees in support of the exhibition.[144] In Glasgow, where Playfair traveled in July, he found the citizens quite inactive, but when he mentioned the support the exhibition had in other towns he effectively shamed the citizens of Glasgow into backing and contributing to the event. In the end Playfair grossly underestimated the amount of Glasgow's contribution: Glasgow ranked fourth in total subscriptions, with £2,666, and first in subscriptions per subscriber.[145] By the time the exhibition opened, all of the major Scottish towns had sent representative exhibits to the Crystal Palace, a reflection of the fairly prosperous, industrial, and urban-based nature of the economy.[146]

The organizers were much less active in Wales, although they did have some of their publicity material printed in Welsh.[147] In Cardiff and Swansea there were a number of promoters early on, men who had evinced enough interest in the exhibition to attend a meeting and sign their name, but this did not translate into large amounts of money for the exhibition, and on a per-capita basis both towns ended up well down in the list of rankings. Only Merthyr Tydfil raised a significant amount of money for the subscription fund. Wales contributed extensively only in the first category of exhibits, the raw materials, especially coal and iron, which reflects both the strengths and limitations of the Welsh economy during this era. Agriculture, not industry, was the largest single sector in the Welsh economy throughout the nineteenth century, followed by mining, and Wales remained largely rural.[148]

Predictably, the Conservative *Cardiff and Merthyr Guardian* was lukewarm in its coverage of the exhibition, while the Liberal *Cambrian*, in Swansea, was more effusive, but in both there is evidence of tension between England and Wales. The *Cardiff and Merthyr Guardian* declared at one point that Richard Cobden was trying to prove 'that *we*, – i.e., the whole population of England – are better off under free trade than protection,' leaving it very ambiguous whether the paper in fact saw Wales as part of Britain (and was using the terms England and Britain interchangeably, as many did in the mid-nineteenth century), or whether it was bristling at Cobden's notion that Wales might be part of a broader 'we.'[149] Likewise, the *Cambrian* reported in early 1850 that 'England is now formally committed to her trial of industrial strength with other nations; and, that the issue might be complete, it is desirable that her champions as well as her rivals everywhere be got into immediate training.' In the previous sentence, however, the paper noted that the Royal Commission would appoint local commissioners in all parts of the 'United Kingdom.'[150] Again, it is unclear whether the writer used these terms interchangeably, or whether he perceived the exhibition to be 'English,' with Wales, as part of the United Kingdom, left to play a supporting role.

20. The great protection meeting in the Rotunda, Dublin. *Illustrated London News* (26 January 1850).

Ireland's showing at the exhibition was even poorer, especially in manufactured goods, which were limited to watches, jewelry, and tweeds. Only Belfast, Dublin, and Cork contributed more than a few items, and out of 13,000 exhibitors from the British Isles, fewer than 300 were Irish.[151] On the whole, the exhibition seems to have passed Ireland by. Although Cole had visited Dublin as part of his first tour of the manufacturing regions in 1849, the *Nation*, published in Dublin, did not print a single article about the exhibition until 24 May 1851, nor did the paper take any notice of its closing. The Irish Tenant League was of much greater importance.[152] Not that this should be surprising: Despite having joined the Union fifty years earlier, Ireland was predominantly Catholic at a time when anti-Catholic sentiments were strong; its economy was largely rural and agricultural and had been devastated by the famine; and its industry had suffered under free trade. Much of Ireland was fiercely protectionist, as evidenced by the large protectionist meeting held in Dublin in January 1850 (fig. 20), perhaps timed to coincide with the second Mansion House meeting in London. Linen was the most successful industry, and as such made up a substantial portion of Ireland's contribution to the exhibition, but even in this industry growth was minuscule in Ireland compared to that in Lancashire.[153]

The Great Exhibition revealed markedly different levels of integration between Scotland, Wales, Ireland, and England. Not the least of these differences were varying levels of industrialization: The proportion of employed males engaged in non-agricultural occupations as of 1851 was between 50 and 60 percent in England, Scotland, and Wales, but less than one-third in Ireland.[154] As with the English towns, local conditions made an enormous difference in how these regions responded to and participated in the exhibition. Wales, Scotland, and Ireland were all more rural and less industrial and had lower concentrations of wealth than England. Scotland, the most developed of the three, had the most to offer the exhibition by way of money and exhibits, and the organizers' efforts reflected these economic realities. More broadly, there was a clear sense in 1851 that Scotland was very much a part of Britain: except for the Highlands, Scotland shared with England virtually the same language, religion, level of literacy, and ideal of Parliamentary democracy. Railroads connected Glasgow and Edinburgh with London, and Scotland's universities were among the best in the world. Wales was more distant, but within reach, and once the organizers convinced the Welsh that the exhibition included raw materials such as coal, as well as manufactures, it became clear how Wales could participate along with the rest of Great Britain. But Ireland, at least as far as the exhibition was concerned, was much further removed. Map 2 illustrates dramatically how sparse the local committees were in Wales and Ireland, and how popular the exhibition was, by contrast, in Scotland, particularly along its industrial belt. Apparently in these rural areas the organizers largely abandoned their recruiting and fund-raising efforts, deciding to concentrate their attentions elsewhere.

CONFLICT AND CONSENSUS

Foremost among the characteristics that made a high level of popularity for the exhibition probable in a given geographical area was the extent to which the local economy was based on industry and commerce, as opposed to agriculture. Where the economy was largely agricultural, the population tended to be diffuse and incomes generally low, meaning few people were likely to subscribe. Because the exhibition was billed as an industrial exhibition, the executive committee had to work hard to convince people that it had room for agricultural implements and samples of raw materials. Moreover, both the wealthy landowners whose incomes derived from the produce of the land and the farmers who worked the land were overwhelmingly protectionist, and hence unlikely to support what they perceived to be a free-trade fair. Where the economy was industrial and commercial, there was usually a high concentration of either wealthy gentry or at least comfortably middle-class businessmen who might, as was profoundly the case in Manchester, share many of the values the exhibition embodied. There also tended to be more talent available to form and run an effective local committee, in many cases drawing from the leadership of pre-existing organizations such as mechanics' institutes and commercial associations. Dense population also made it easier for the deputies from the executive committee to pay a visit and meet with people and explain the objects of the exhibition, visits which were critical in earning the support of the provinces. Also important was the support of the 'higher classes,' either the local gentry or the wealthy, respectable middle class in the case of more urban areas; those lower on the social ladder tended to emulate their superiors.

The executive committee succeeded in rousing the provinces for several additional reasons. They approached each town at both the community and the individual level. Invitations to meetings went out to representatives of local organizations such as mechanics' institutes, chambers of commerce, and literary and philosophical societies, as well as to prominent industrial, civil, and religious leaders.[155] And the organizers were deft at harmonizing their own concern for industrial design and international peace with the more local interests of provincial towns, individuals, and institutions. It was not that the provincial towns did not share the lofty aims of Cole and the men of the Society of Arts, as some historians have suggested.[156] Rather, local committees had to be instructed as to how local and national interests could converge in the Great Exhibition; how, for example, economic progress and international peace could mutually reinforce each other. The keys to success in both areas were the creation of well-balanced, supportive, efficient local committees, forceful personal visits, and a sophisticated publicity campaign. Where these were lacking the organizers generally met with apathy and opposition.

In the end, though, protectionism was a key element in determining how supportive of the exhibition a community would be. There is a remarkable correlation between those towns and regions throughout the United Kingdom that returned Whig–Liberal or Peelite MPs in the 1847 and 1852 elections, and those that supported the exhibition. Looking at four towns and a London borough that were especially supportive of the exhibition (Manchester, Bradford, Sheffield, Bath, and Westminster), nineteen of the twenty MPs returned in those two elections were Whig–Liberal or Peelite. By contrast, in four towns or regions that expressed reluctance to support the exhibition (Liverpool, Canterbury, Maidstone, and Rochester), only six of sixteen MPs returned were Whig–Liberal or Peelite, and three of them lost their seats from 1847 to 1852. This high level of correlation is apparent in Scotland and Wales as well. Glasgow and Edinburgh, both very interested in the exhibition, returned Liberal MPs for both seats in both elections. Merthyr Tydfil, which was also enthusiastic about the exhibition, returned Whig–Liberal MPs in 1847 and 1852. Swansea on the other hand, in Glamorganshire, returned two Whig–Liberals and two Protectionists, and was much less forthcoming in its support.

The organizers' achievement was that this liberal, Peelite, free-trade enterprise that was largely English, not British, nevertheless came to be seen as a non-partisan national event. They built a remarkably comprehensive national organization that included Scotland and Wales (if not Ireland), and were able to construct the exhibition as an event with many faces, largely concealing its English and free-trade components in the process. Selling the exhibition was less a matter of converting hostile opposition than it was one of careful maneuvering in mine-filled terrain, and the organizers were remarkably adept at fostering consensus and appealing to local interests, primarily through their vigilant courtship of the press and their skillful use of public meetings. These meetings served a variety of purposes: they were held to raise money, to solicit exhibits, to encourage people to attend, and to counter whatever reservations people might have about the plan. Most importantly, these meetings gave meaning to the exhibition. By presenting the exhibition from multiple points of view and changing the meaning of the exhibition to fit the audience, the organizers allowed their audiences to change the meaning of the exhibition.

One way to understand the exhibition, adopting a functionalist approach, is to see it as a collective and spontaneous affirmation of the ideas and values that give a society meaning and which need to be reaffirmed at regular intervals in mass events such as

Victoria's Coronation, her Diamond Jubilee, or the Festival of Britain. Alternatively, one could regard the exhibition 'not as the embodiment of shared consensus, but as propaganda on behalf of a particular value system.'[157] Different contemporary groups may have viewed the event in different ways; underneath the consensual surface there may have been tensions and divisions.

The Great Exhibition is best viewed adopting a combination of these perspectives. There is no question that the exhibition was organized, at almost all levels, by elites who at times had very clear objectives: to improve taste, to inculcate an ethic of hard work, to foster social harmony. Indeed, every celebration that was a part of the exhibition – the local meetings, the opening itself – was a tribute to the existing social order, even while there were obvious disagreements about the meaning of the event and who it should include. But it is also true that, once given the opportunity, an extraordinary number of British men and women supported the exhibition. Moreover, those disagreements that existed were more often about the form the exhibition should take and its meaning than whether the event itself should occur. In short, there was both conflict and compromise.

The exhibition was organized in two directions: from the top down, and from the bottom up. That is, the organizers articulated certain broad themes, but then time and again appealed to the provinces for feedback. There was a continual symbiotic relationship. The same was true of the organizers' relationship with the press, which it would seem both constructed and reflected public opinion. It is clear that the Great Exhibition was not a 'spontaneous outburst,' that it had to be publicized and promoted in order for it to succeed. But neither can it be dismissed as pure propaganda, if only because its messages were so varied and subject to change.

PART II MEANING

21. The western (British) nave of the Crystal Palace.

CHAPTER 4

Commerce and Culture

IT IS A DAUNTING TASK even to describe, much less to draw conclusions about, the objects displayed in the Crystal Palace (fig. 21). As John Tallis, author of one of the many guides to the exhibition, wrote:

> One of the distinguishing characteristics of the Great Exhibition is its vast comprehensiveness. Nothing was too stupendous, too rare, too costly for its acquisition; nothing too minute or apparently too insignificant for its consideration. Every possible invention and appliance for the service of man found a place with its embracing limits; every realization of human genius, every effort of human industry might be contemplated therein, from the most consummate elaboration of the profoundest intellect, to the simplest contrivance of uneducated thought.[1]

There were more than 100,000 exhibits, sent in by almost 14,000 individual and corporate exhibitors, selected by hundreds of committees from Britain, its colonies and dependencies, and numerous other countries. In the words of the American Benjamin Silliman, the Crystal Palace was a 'vast storehouse of the nations,'[2] the alphabetized list of exhibits stretching from 'Absynthium,' provided by a Sardinian, to 'Zithers,' sent in by two Viennese manufacturers.[3]

The problem faced by the historian who would analyze these exhibits is not only that there were so many of them, but that they were there for so many different reasons and to fulfill so many different functions. According to the publicity notice of a meeting in Manchester to promote the exhibition, the objectives of the exhibition were 'to bring together specimens of industry and ingenuity of all nations;' 'to encourage the communication of knowledge and the free interchange of ideas and to promote friendly intercourse amongst the different nations of the earth;' 'to furnish a stimulus to talent and enterprise;' to provide opportunities for improvement to 'manufacturers, artisans and mechanics' who could use the exhibition to compare 'productions of genius and skill' from around the world; to provide 'a stimulus' to British industry and trade; to provide an opportunity for the artisan to display the results of his 'ingenuity and industry' alongside those of the largest manufacturers; to teach 'the necessity of united action' between 'skill and capital;' and to promote social and international harmony 'which cannot fail to advance the improvement of the human race.'[4] It is not surprising that it took 100,000 objects to meet these disparate goals.

* * *

CONTENTS AND CLASSIFICATION

The British exhibits were chosen through a decentralized and at times unregulated process that allowed the organizers to involve all the local committees, towns, and regions in Britain, while at the same time retaining for themselves the power to make final decisions. Reid, Playfair, and the other organizers in London provided the general outline for the exhibits and guided the selection process, but responsibility for the selection and arrangement of the exhibits fell largely to the local committees. These had considerable discretion in determining the principles upon which the selection of exhibits would be made, the selection itself, and how space within the Crystal Palace would be allotted, within certain general confines.[5]

The localization of the selection process opened up the exhibition to almost any work of industry or commerce broadly construed. Although the organizers had a keen awareness of who was and was not participating, at least among the famous manufacturers, and at times had to plead with potential exhibitors to send their goods, in the end all Reid and Playfair could do was leave matters to the local committees and hope for the best. This meant that the exhibition was open to a broad spectrum of exhibitors; that it was inclusive rather than exclusive; and that it could encompass the full range of commercial possibilities. Much of what ended up in the Crystal Palace, therefore, was beyond the control of the organizers. Merchants, manufacturers, and municipalities all had their own agendas, and the exhibition reflected these as well.

With such a decentralized process there had to be some system of classification, some way of imposing order on 'the works of industry of all nations.'[6] Part of the lore of the exhibition is that it was Prince Albert who conceptualized the first classification system, a tripartite division embracing 'the raw materials of industry; the manufactures made from them; and the art used to adorn them.' But the classification of exhibits was hardly an easy task or a foregone conclusion. It was worked on by a number of scientists over a period of months before Lyon Playfair finalized the thirty-part system of classification that was eventually adopted to organize the exhibits (table 2 opposite).[7]

The British exhibits were divided into four sections, covering thirty classes. Foreign exhibits, which were selected by committees established by exhibiting countries, fell outside this classification scheme. What stands out, first, is that the classification of exhibits replicated and privileged the manufacturing process. Raw materials (lumps of coal, bales of cotton) were taken by heavy machinery (steam engines, hydraulic presses, power looms) to manufacture works of industry (clothing, furniture, cutlery, anything one might find in the home or office). The problem with regarding the classification system as symbolically representing the manufacturing process is that Class XXX, the fine arts, does not fit. Additionally, several of the classes in the machinery section covered machines that were not used for industrial production, for example lighthouses and sewer systems in Class VII, ships and guns in Class VIII, and clocks and pianos in Class X. In other words, the manufacturing process was important, but not to the exclusion of other objectives. The same can be said of mechanization: it too was an important part of the manufacturing process, one possible approach, but no more than that. Raw materials could be molded by craftsmen without any assistance from machinery just as they could be molded by machines with hardly any human labor involved.

Table 2: Classification of Exhibits

1	Raw Materials	
	I	Mining and Quarrying, Metallurgy and Mineral Products
	II	Chemical and Pharmaceutical Processes and Products
	III	Substances used as Food
	IV	Vegetable and Animal Substances
2	Machinery	
	V	Machines for Direct Use (carriages, railway)
	VI	Manufacturing Machines and Tools
	VII	Mechanical, Engineering, Architectural and Building Contrivances
	VIII	Naval Architecture, Military Engineering, Ordnance, Armour
	IX	Agricultural and Horticultural Machines and Implements
	X	Philosophical Instruments and Miscellaneous Contrivances
3	Manufactures	
	XI	Cotton
	XII	Woollen and Worsted
	XIII	Silk and Velvet
	XIV	Manufactures from Flax and Hemp
	XV	Mixed Fabrics, including shawls
	XVI	Leather (including saddlery and harnesses), Skins, Fur, Hair
	XVII	Paper, Printing, Bookbinding
	XVIII	Woven, Spun, Felted and Laid Fabrics
	XIX	Tapestry, Lace and Embroidery
	XX	Articles of Clothing for immediate, personal or domestic use
	XXI	Cutlery, Edge Tools and Hand Tools, and Surgical Instruments
	XXII	General Hardware
	XXIII	Works in Precious Metals, Jewellery and all articles of luxury
	XXIV	Glass
	XXV	Ceramic Manufacture, China, Porcelain and Earthenware
	XXVI	Decorative Furniture, Paper Hangings and Papier Mâché
	XXVII	Manufactures in Mineral Substances, used for building or decorations
	XXVIII	Manufactures from Animal or Vegetable Substances
	XXIX	Miscellaneous Manufactures and Small Wares
4	Fine Arts	
	XXX	Fine Arts, Sculpture, Models and the Plastic Arts generally, Mosaics and Enamels, illustrative of the taste and skill displayed in such applications of human industry

The thirty-part classification system that the commission finally adopted, although it seems logical and unified, had to appeal to several different constituencies and incorporated elements from a variety of different systems. In fact, for the Great Exhibition four separate classification systems were woven together into this single overarching structure. The first reflected Albert's interest in organizing all knowledge, in providing a taxonomy of all things. The second sought to meet the demands of the scientist. The third, the three-part division of raw materials, machinery, and manufactures, was a means of instruction that traced and illustrated the manufacturing or production process. And the fourth divided finished goods into separate departments in order to represent them to consumers in the most convenient way possible. The classification scheme adopted for the Great Exhibition is obviously different from the alphabetical system adopted by the *Encyclopaedia Britannica*, or the philosophical order used in the Enlightenment *Encyclopédie* edited by Denis Diderot and Jean D'Alembert between 1751 and 1772. It is a testament to the power and status of commerce that everything in the world could be organized along commercial lines, and it was also the first classification system ever attempted of industrial work.[8]

The embodiment of the classification system for the Great Exhibition was the *Official Descriptive and Illustrated Catalogue*, the standard reference book for the exhibition, published in three volumes by Spicer Brothers and W. Clowes and Sons. Lavishly illustrated and containing nearly 1,500 pages, the *Official Catalogue* was published in five parts beginning in May 1851. Because only the first part had been completed for the opening of the exhibition, a smaller, condensed, one-volume shilling edition of 320 pages was also available.[9] The *Official Catalogue* listed, in numerous cases described, and in many instances illustrated every item exhibited in the Crystal Palace. It was the ultimate guide to and compendium of the exhibits. The compilers had sent out forms to the exhibitors which, once they were returned, were read, revised, and corrected by 'scientific gentlemen' to eliminate inaccuracies.[10] More than just 'a lasting memorial of the splendid collection' as the editor's preface promised, it had, as 'a book of reference to the philosopher, merchant and manufacturer,' an unabashedly educational purpose.[11] Almost a century earlier, d'Alembert had said of the *Encyclopédie* that its intent was not only to supply a certain body of knowledge, but to change the way people thought.[12] This would be an equally apt assessment of the *Official Catalogue*. All collections shape the world, and the collection that was the Great Exhibition was no exception. Rather than emphasizing any one aspect, it encouraged not only Britons but manufacturers and producers and suppliers around the world to think in the most inclusive way possible about production and commerce.

If there was one theme that united the exhibits and the organizers' objectives it was education in the broadest sense: educating producers about new materials and processes, educating consumers about new products, and educating a substantial portion of British society about the value of industry, commerce, and mechanization, and the importance of art and taste.[13] Industrialization in Britain was neither accidental nor spontaneous, and could have taken on any number of different forms.[14] The organizers of the exhibition had in mind a certain idea of what industry and industrialization should look like, and the Great Exhibition was the physical embodiment of that vision. It promulgated an image of industrialization that was inclusive rather than exclusive, and that was private and firm-based more than it was public and state-supported.

Symbolic of this rather vague and muddled approach was the layout of exhibits inside the Crystal Palace (fig. 22). Their physical arrangement did not in fact parallel the neat classification devised by the organizers. Because the power source for the machinery was in the north-west corner, all the heavy machinery was placed along the north side. And because of structural considerations, the lighter goods were placed in the galleries. The raw materials were located in the south, and the manufactured goods in the center. In other words, the raw materials and produce – the

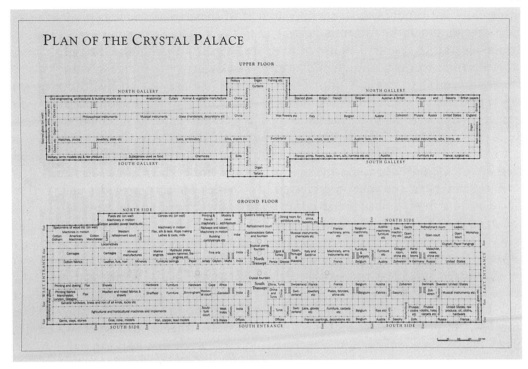

22. Floor plan of the Crystal Palace. Victoria and Albert Museum, London.

least attractive and least interesting portions of the display – were disposed at the side, while articles belonging to the superior manufacturers were brought prominently in view by being arranged all along the center of the building, where their richness and splendor of color and form could be shown to the greatest advantage. The placement of the exhibits, then, conflicted with one of the purposes of the exhibition, which was to educate the populace about industrialization. There was no way to walk the exhibits in the order in which they were meant to be seen; that would have entailed crisscrossing the Crystal Palace back and forth, over and over again.

Moreover, the arrangement of the exhibits emphasized the fact that the Great Exhibition was not just an exhibition of works of industry, it was a spectacle.[15] The layout made little sense from the perspective of educating people about the *process* of industrialization, but made perfect sense for a nation that wanted to educate its citizens about the *products* of industrialization. The Great Exhibition edifyingly juxtaposed the public technology of work (locomotives and steel hammers) with the private accoutrements of domesticity (furniture, utensils, and clothing), and, inside, the effect of the structure and the more than 100,000 exhibits was overwhelming. Visitors, one after another, expressed the feeling of being bewildered and astonished not only by the building, but by the quantity of goods inside it. Many accounts describe visitors aimlessly walking the vast cluttered interior space, lost among the products of the world, ultimately leaving after a few hours, exhausted, never having even made it beyond the nave.[16] One writer referred to the 'state of mental helplessness' before the embarrassment of riches.[17]

A brief analysis of the meaning of the word 'industry' at the time of the exhibition reveals just how inclusive the organizers were, and just how many options, or paths, were available. At the time of the Great Exhibition, 'industry' had two primary meanings: sustained effort, hard work, or diligence; and an institution or set of institutions for production or trade. The first of these two meanings predominated from the middle of the fifteenth century until the middle of the nineteenth century. In the eighteenth century, 'house of industry' meant a workhouse, literally a place where people worked hard, a public institution where the indigent were fed and forced to work. It was not until the 1840s that industry as an institution began to replace industry as a human quality.[18] Only in modern common parlance does industry refer to thundering machines or a largely mechanized production process, as in 'heavy industry.' Thus when *The Times* christened the Crystal Palace 'The Temple of Industry,' it was using the term as a celebration less of a mechanized, factory-oriented production process than of hard work.[19]

A console table and mirror exhibited by Charles McLean provides an excellent illustration of how industry and effort were praised, even at the expense of other values such as sales and artistic merit (fig. 23). After the local committee for London had rejected his piece of furniture, McLean appealed the decision to the Royal Commission claiming that the table and mirror were 'by far the largest in London,' and would greatly ornament the Crystal Palace. Matthew Digby Wyatt read McLean's letter and reported to the commission that the sideboard was 'in point of taste heavy and somewhat too florid,' but the gilding was 'magnificent,' and the 'getting up' was 'most spirited,' having cost McLean some £2,000. In other words, what was special about the table and mirror was the effort and hard work that McLean had put into it. In the end, the commissioners decided that since McLean agreed that the counter of the console table could be used to display other exhibits, they would grant the space he was requesting. In fact, they placed his mirror in the nave of the Crystal Palace, one of the most prominent and desirable locations.[20]

There was also an abundance of didactic literature connecting the Great Exhibition and hard work. In his *Fireside Facts*, S. P. Newcombe tried to impress upon his readers that although it was Paxton and Fox who were knighted, it was the working man who was the true nobleman. 'Indeed,' Newcombe continued, 'the working-men are the only noblemen. He who can, and will not work, is a *base*-man; no matter how he may be born.'[21] And one of the more popular attractions inside the Crystal Palace were the beehives, 'exceedingly curious little palaces of industry,' according to John Tallis.[22] One anonymous author asserted that the most significant aspect of the exhibition was 'its bearing on industry; its representation of the working bees of the world's hive.'[23] Work was undoubtedly one of the most important Victorian values celebrated by the Great Exhibition: Thomas Carlyle wrote of the 'perennial noble-ness, and even sacredness, in Work' in *Past and Present* (1843), contrasting it with 'Idleness,' in which there was 'perpetual despair.'[24] While scholars have closely asso-ciated work with the middle class – it was only through hard work that the engines of capitalism could keep turning – and consequently seen the discourse of labor as an attempt to inculcate middle-class values among the working classes, the political value of work should not be underestimated. Invoking the ethic of hard work rep-resented an implicit critique of the 'non-working' aristocracy.[25] Of course, one of the great ironies of the exhibition was that it affirmed the importance of the very duties that many of the spectators were temporarily neglecting.

Focusing on industry in its more modern meaning also obscures the importance of commerce as one of the central themes of the exhibition. Henry Cole began his 'Introduction' to the *Official Descriptive and Illustrated Catalogue* with a declara-tion: 'The activity of the present day chiefly develops itself in commercial industry,

23. Console table and
mirror, by Charles
McLean.

and it is in accordance with the spirit of the age that the nations of the world have
now collected together their choicest productions.'[26] Significantly, Cole did not limit
'productions' to goods manufactured by machines; he left the term broad and
undefined, because in 1851 there were all sorts of 'productions:' hand-crafted, home-
made, cooperative, forged, molded, cast, carved (by hand or with a machine),
machine-made, and mass-produced. Mechanization, to paraphrase Siegfried Giedion,
had not yet taken command.[27] The handicraftsman was just as much a man of
industry as the operator of a machine in a textile factory, which explains why objects
that were the product of exceptional craftsmanship stood side by side with objects
that were the product of machines. At the time of the exhibition, machines and labor
coexisted.

Industrialization as molded by the exhibition did not mean a choice between art
and industry, between quality and quantity, or between commerce and culture. The

very idea of 'arts manufactures,' one of the fundamental ideological building blocks of the exhibition, constituted an essential element in the construction of industrialization. Like the exhibition itself, this formulation of industrialization had to be packaged and promoted. The Great Exhibition was more than simply a sign of industrialization. It was a vehicle through which the industrialization of British society took place. This is not to say that the exhibition caused the industrialization of British society in an economic sense; it did not. Rather, it was part of an attempt to transform Britain culturally, to forge a society that was receptive to a certain form of industrialization. Through the Great Exhibition the organizers sought to construct an industrialized market society that was broad-based, innovative, and tasteful; in short, a society that was built on both commerce and culture.

The Great Exhibition [. . .]. It was about improving the producti[. . .] by expanding markets and trade, and t[. . .] raw materials ([. . .] [t]heme perfectly. There was no reason fo[. . .] including other data to introduce them to producers, and to connect supplie[. . .] with manufacturers. [. . .] the thirty-part classification system, c[. . .][produ]ction and the source of British power [. . .] [ma]terials in 1851 did not consist simply [. . .] [manu]facturing. As Robert Ellis explained i[. . .] [pr]oducts in the *Official Catalogue*, raw [. . .] [the]se substances which 'human industry is [. . .] [va]ried forms of manufactured articles,' an[. . .] [s]ource of 'manufacturing power.'[29] In other words, there were two equally important approaches to production: man-made and machine-made. This fundamental division has been described as that between the advanced organic economy, which was characteristic of early modern England and was limited in size by the productivity of the land, and the mineral-based energy economy, which was brought about by the Industrial Revolution, and which escaped the problem of the fixed supply of land by featuring new inorganic materials such as iron, pottery, and glass. The fact that these two economic orders so clearly coexisted at the time of the Great Exhibition supports the view that the 'massive restructuring of the economy' was by no means fully accomplished by 1851.[30]

Behind many of the displays of raw materials lay a genuinely educational purpose. Toward this end, the editors of the *Official Catalogue* attempted to convert the many different, changing, and local terms used in international trade 'into the precise and enduring expressions of science.' In the seventeenth century the physicist Robert Boyle had predicted that important results were likely to arise from 'the naturalist's insight into trades.' In consciously attempting to put Boyle's program into practice by using both commercial and scientific names for goods, particularly in Classes I–IV, the editors sought to make the *Catalogue* useful for both the 'naturalist' and the 'commercial man.'[31] The editors, then, were working to classify and standardize all things, and as a result to improve commerce. The collation of information about Britain's

24. Raw materials outside the west entrance to the Crystal Palace.

colonies, which were the sources for many of the raw materials exhibited, had the additional effect of servicing the empire by establishing a cultural technology of rule based on language and terminology.[32] More broadly, the Great Exhibition reflects the widespread mid-nineteenth century impulse, embodied in Darwin, Lyell, and George Eliot's Edward Casaubon, to classify and taxonomize as a means of coping with massive changes in society and knowledge.

The exhibitors and annotators also took great pains to describe and illustrate in detail how certain raw materials had been discovered, how they were extracted, and what their uses were. The executive committee had found it especially challenging to generate design for the raw materials section, so Playfair encouraged potential exhibitors to design illustrations of the manufacturing, mining, or extraction process, arguing that the general public, which might overlook a product such as a lump of coal, might take more interest if they could follow, by means of charts or illustrations, the process by which it was made.[33] As a result there were all sorts of graphs, maps, and models, such as W. Wilson Sanders' exhibit of 700 specimens of wood from around the world, arranged geographically, with scientific and local name, weight per cubic foot, and principal uses.[34]

Here, and throughout the exhibition, the emphasis was on what made Britain best, what made a region best, what made a firm or process best. A Dudley mining establishment which exhibited a collection of iron ores illustrating the general iron-making resources of Great Britain discussed in its catalogue entry 'the principal causes of the advantages possessed by Great Britain in the manufacture of iron.' The display, and the accompanying charts and maps in the *Official Catalogue*, noted that almost one-third of Great Britain's gross production of iron came from Wales, and nearly that much again from Scotland, once again emphasizing the integration of all parts of the United Kingdom.[35]

A number of displays also sought to make industry seem less destructive and threatening, even salutary. One of the exhibitors in Class I was the Duke of Buccleuch, a Royal Commissioner, who exhibited a model of the furnaces and pots employed in his mines used for separating silver from lead ore. In the annotation that followed, the eminent German chemist Justus Liebig wrote:

> the results of this arrangement are most apparent, and beneficial to the surrounding neighbourhood. Formerly, the noxious fumes passing from the shafts of the furnaces, poisoned the neighbourhood; the heather was burnt up, vegetation destroyed, and no animal could graze, or bird feed near the spot. Now, the heather is seen in luxuriance close around the establishment, the sheep graze within a stone's throw of the chimney's base, and game on all sides take shelter.[36]

Comments such as this sought not only to demonstrate the Duke's benevolence, but to educate those in attendance about the benefits of industrialization, teaching them that industry was not incompatible with the rural ideal.[37]

One of the most monumental tasks facing the commissioners was to organize the British colonies, dominions, and dependencies and make them part of the exhibition, and, fittingly, the imperial displays at the Great Exhibition were located at the very center of the Crystal Palace. The list of contributors was impressive, and included, as the *Official Catalogue* referred to them, 'British Possessions in Asia' (India and Ceylon), Europe (Malta, Gibraltar, and the Channel Islands), Africa (Cape of Good Hope, Mauritius, the Seychelles), the Americas (Canada, the Caribbean islands such as Barbados, the Bahamas, Bermuda, and Grenada), and Australasia (Australia and New Zealand).

The contributions of the East India Company, the chairman of which sat on the Royal Commission, formed the centerpiece of the imperial display. Henry Cole's plan, ably implemented by Professor J. Forbes Royle, who had conducted the negotiations with the East India Company, was to present India, and by extension the empire, as a vast treasure-trove of untapped wealth and resources. The Indian Court was stocked with fine finished products, but the underlying purpose of the display was quite clearly to introduce manufacturers to new materials. In this Cole and Royle were in conflict with some of the leading industrial design reformers such as Owen Jones, Matthew Digby Wyatt, and Richard Redgrave, who, according to one historian, 'looked to Indian ornamental design to provide inspiration and to infuse new life into the moribund industrial arts in Britain.'[38] Royle wrote, in his introduction to the Indian section in the *Official Catalogue*, that the goal of the Indian exhibits was 'at once to interest the public and to give such confidence to the manufacturer as to induce him to submit them to trial.' For Royle it was axiomatic that India would benefit from this arrangement. In his eyes, the exhibition was to benefit all countries with 'little-known products possessed of valuable properties, and procurable in large quantities at a cheap rate, if a demand could be created for them.'[39] In other words, to discover, develop, and create a demand for new raw materials, thus expanding the entire commercial and manufacturing system.

Similarly, the exhibits from 'Australasia' – New South Wales, South Australia, and Tasmania (known in 1851 as Van Diemen's Land) – introduced visitors to the variety of goods these territories offered, presenting a vision of Australia transformed from a penal colony into an economically vital component of the empire of the future.[40] While the scale and scope of the exhibits were really quite limited, the *Official Catalogue* promoted Australia as 'the most extensive wool-producing country in the world,' and praised it for the growing value of its exports to Britain.[41] It was significant, but not surprising, that the *Official Catalogue* and the numerous guide-books downplayed the inclusion of colonial handicrafts. What mattered, for Britain and for other countries with colonial or imperial ambitions, was to find new sources of raw materials and, later on, new markets for their manufactured goods.

The exhibition turned the empire into a cog in the manufacturing process.[42] The introduction to the exhibits from Africa in the *Official Catalogue* implied that Africa was useful to Britain only for its raw materials. Likewise with Canada, which sent two 'trophies' – tribute, in effect – one consisting of timber (fig. 25), the other of furs organized by the Hudson Bay Company.[43] Nowhere could visitors discern the reality of exchange, the inner workings and costs of the international trading system that revolved around Britain, unless they looked carefully in the *Illustrated London News*, which blindly depicted 'the ingenuity which our Great Exhibition has called into action in far-distant lands' (fig. 26). In this engraving, Bengali ivory workers are making miniature elephant carvings for the exhibition, using as their model the char-coal sketches that cover the walls. The workshop is supervised by a British army officer.[44] There was a disjuncture between the symbolic meanings generated by the exhibition and the material conditions of commodity capitalism and geopolitical power, as the negative side of imperialism – the oppression, subjugation, and strip-ping of natural resources – was hidden behind the cornucopia of riches inside the Crystal Palace.

The exhibition also domesticated the empire. Through maps and charts, visitors learned what 'belonged' to them. As one observer enthused in the *Art Union*, the East India Company exhibits had the effect of 'impressing every visitor with the importance of such possessions to Great Britain.'[45] The very language used by the organizers in the catalogue – 'British possessions' – suggested a degree of control and coherence that was surely lacking at the administrative level.[46] Moreover, a number of colonial exhibits suggested, iconographically, a high level of integration between the metropole and the periphery. A Tasmanian furniture maker, for example,

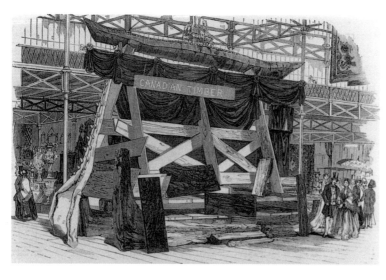

25. The 'Canadian Timber Trophy'. *Illustrated London News*, (21 June 1851).

26. Imperial exploitation: Bengalis carving ivory for the Great Exhibition. *Illustrated London News* (26 April 1851).

exhibited a chair on the back of which was a shield, supported by a kangaroo and an emu, and surmounted by an English rose; on one side was a Scottish thistle, on the other an Irish shamrock.[47] In objects such as this, far-flung territories became as much a part of the British empire as the home territories. As the Governor of the Cape pointed out in a letter to the Royal Commission, this would afford instruction for those who might emigrate as to what they would find, as well as making manufacturers aware of potential markets and stimulating British investment in the colonies.[48]

The Royal Commission for 1851 comprised of exactly the sort of men who have been termed 'gentlemanly capitalists,' that combination of landowning elites with a strong interest in commerce, along with a new class of merchants, financiers, and businessmen.[49] It was this alliance of land and money that sought and profited from the empire. If one views the exhibition not just as a display of industry, but as an economic event of much greater scope that forged all sorts of connections between the public and private sectors, between the metropolis and the provinces, between aristocrats, manufacturers, bankers, shippers, and workers, and especially between Britain and its burgeoning empire, then the imperatives behind the exhibition become much clearer, as do its imperial resonances.

For those who were not 'gentlemanly capitalists' and for whom the lure of increased trade and profits might not have had such an immediate appeal, the exhibition glorified the empire, conveying the rich diversity and fascination of different imperial territories. It did so by, metaphorically, taking visitors to places they had never seen, and in all likelihood would never be able to. At the exhibition, British men and women could 'go' to India, to see the infamous Koh-i-noor Diamond or a howdah on an elephant (even if it was stuffed), or to Tunis, to see exotic goods from the 'East' (figs 27 and 28). The exhibition turned the Crystal Palace into, in the words of so many visitors, a fairyland, a tour around the world.

The Crystal Palace, like the British Museum and India House, presented and represented British-controlled territories throughout the world in such a way as to project an image of wealth and control. The display at the exhibition was so successful that the following year the Royal Society of Arts proposed an Indian Exhibition, to be held in 1853, jointly with the East India Company. Their purpose was to develop more fully 'the immense natural resources of the Indian Empire, as a means of making the arts and manufactures of India better known in Europe, and

27. John Nash, stuffed elephant and howdah from India.

28. The 'Tunis Court'.

with a view of suggesting new subjects of industry, which may at the same time prove beneficial to both England [sic] and India.'[50] Indeed, the number of visitors to the India Museum doubled in 1851 over the previous year, suggesting that the imperial display did in fact boost interest in India.[51] The exhibition had succeeded in promoting Britain's imperial presence by putting the empire on display, introducing British men and women – consumers and producers, and, most important, future supporters and defenders of the very idea of 'empire' – to the concept. For Britons who would otherwise have had little or no connection with the empire, the exhibition made clear that it was an important component of British wealth, power, and prestige.

MACHINERY

A second category of exhibits that had an overtly educational purpose was the machinery, Classes V–X in the classification scheme. It is important to emphasize here that the organizers of the exhibition defined 'machinery' broadly to include much more than merely those machines that produced or manufactured goods; only one of the five classes under the general heading of machinery contained manufacturing machines (Class VI). Thus 'machinery' did not necessarily mean enormous, loud, steam-powered machines for large-scale manufacture, but rather any implement used in production. This included mechanical looms (used in the production of cloth), scales (used in the 'production' or measurement of weight), and simple plows and hoes (used in the production of food). Again, this is evidence of the organizers expanding rather than restricting the impression people had of the process of production, promulgating a vision of industrialization that was fundamentally inclusive of the many different approaches to production that co-existed in mid-Victorian Britain.

Nevertheless, it was Classes V and VI, the heavy machinery, that visitors and commentators generally deemed the most significant, even if scientists' interests lay elsewhere. They were two of the largest classes in the classification scheme, and constituted, according to the *Official Catalogue*, 'the most direct representation of one of the principal sources of the industrial success and prosperity of Great Britain.'[52] It was these exhibits that received the longest and most detailed descriptions and illustrations in the *Catalogue*.[53] A number of them were 'in motion,' powered by insulated steam pipes beneath the floor boards which connected to a small engine house at the north-west corner of the exhibition building. The machines in this section of the building were partitioned from the rest to contain the noise and dust emitted by their rumbling and clanging. *The Times* described the machinery in motion as 'the most wonderful and important part of the whole collection,' and gushed about 'the varied display of beautiful machines.'[54] They provided, in the words of the *Official Catalogue*, 'an overwhelming impression of speed and power.'[55]

This section was also one of the most popular. As Robert Askrill wrote in *The Yorkshire Visitors' Guide to the Great Exhibition*, 'The collection of machinery excites far deeper interest than anything else exhibited,' and Henry Mayhew described how on the shilling days visitors pressed two and three deep to watch the machinery in motion; it seems to have appealed to all ages, sexes, and classes.[56] It appears likely that the appeal was not only education and instruction, but also novelty, and perhaps even entertainment. In other words, the organizers intended for the exhibition to be one thing, but in reality it became something quite different. There was no incompatibility here between what was planned and what was spontaneous, but there was certainly a difference.

The highlight of this class was Hibbert, Platt and Son's cotton machinery, which was assigned the first number in the catalogue in this class, and had a five-page description and two full-page plates devoted to it. A series of fifteen machines in one room demonstrated in great detail the cotton-spinning process, as cotton was opened, carded, doubled, spun, warped, and woven, all before the eyes of the visitors, who were kept at a safe distance from the machinery by an iron railing (fig. 29). The entry in the *Official Catalogue* described the function of each particular machine and discussed its role in the larger process, but visitors to the exhibition would have received similar information by means of written cards and human attendants. The goal was not only to educate and explain to people how cotton was manufactured, but to introduce them to the benefits of machines and mechanized production. Presumably exhibitors also wanted manufacturers to order new machines having seen their wonders demonstrated, again highlighting the difference between organizers' and manufacturers' intentions. But in either case the exhibition was like a science museum, or, as John Tallis put it, 'a veritable acting industrial encyclopaedia.'[57] This was especially the case for men of science, many of whom attempted to purchase scientific exhibits following the exhibition.[58]

29. Hibbert, Platt and Son's cotton machines. *Illustrated London News* (23 August 1851).

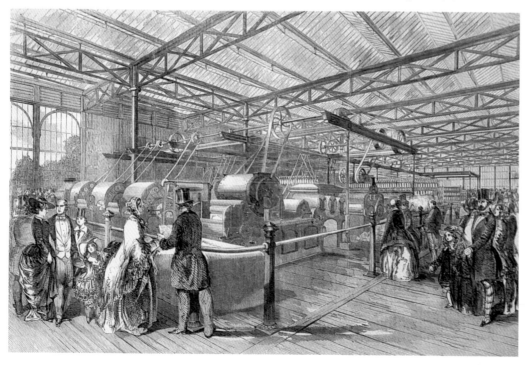

Progress was everywhere as the machinery promised new forms, new designs, new mechanisms, new results. The machines were, in the words of one commentator, 'the epitome of man's industrial progress – of his untiring efforts to release himself from his material bondage.'[59] Many exhibitors and commentators stressed that machines saved time and labor costs. Machines not only fulfilled functions formerly accomplished by direct human labor, but executed those processes better and more consistently. A cigarette machine, for example, could perform fourteen different operations, and make 80–100 cigarettes per minute 'neater than those made by hand.'[60] John Tallis claimed that machinery 'relieved the sons of labour from their severest toil,' by substituting 'iron and steam for bone and muscle.' And although he acknowledged that the short-term results of the introduction of machinery were often detrimental to the working classes, he (and many others) believed that in the long run it would prove beneficial both to the working classes and to the broader economic health of the nation.[61] Regarding a model of a 'patent steam travelling crane' for lifting and removing heavy weights at railway depots, timber yards, factories, and foundries sent in by McNicholl & Vernon of Liverpool, the annotator of the *Catalogue* calculated that 'In addition to the immense saving in time that is effected by these machines, the saving in wages of labour is very great.' One boy, at ten shillings per week, could with this machine complete the same amount of work that previously took six men.[62] The annotator did not, however, discuss what would happen to the five men who were put out of work. It is ironic that the very exhibition that celebrated the working man also showed how to replace him.

Machines also performed a broader social function. According to Robert Askrill, by lessening the price of goods they provided 'countless comforts and enjoyments to the masses,' who otherwise would have themselves toiled away as machines, trying to eke out a meagre existence.[63] Askrill and the anonymous author of *A Guide to the Great Exhibition; containing a description of every principal object of interest*, shared the (perhaps overly optimistic) view that machinery was bringing together the educated and the uneducated, the high and the low, in mutual respect, to the advantage of both; in short, that it had a leveling effect on class hierarchies, that it might even help alleviate class divisions and antagonisms.[64]

One way of making the machines palatable, even comforting, was to portray machine technology not simply as utilitarian, but as a source of aesthetic satisfaction, to fuse beauty and utility. Queen Victoria herself referred to the 'beautiful machinery,'[65] and a correspondent for *Scientific American* gushed while standing in front of the British locomotives, 'Oh how I like to look upon those mighty iron arms heaving up and down or moving backwards and forwards at every heave of the steam giant's breast.'[66] Anthropomorphizing the machinery was one way for Victorians to express their sense of awe at its thundering, clattering, and wheezing inside the Crystal Palace. Machines, therefore, were not only utilitarian, they were aesthetically pleasing.

It should be clear that, although the Crystal Palace took on many functions and meanings, it was certainly a place of instruction, a school of industry. It taught scientists about new philosophical instruments, manufacturers about new materials, and the broader population about industry. For the shilling visitors in particular, according to Henry Mayhew, the Crystal Palace served as a giant schoolhouse, 'more of a school than a show,' especially with some 1,750 attendants, both male and female, who stood by to explain and demonstrate the various machines and processes on

30. Attendant demonstrating de la Rue's envelope machine.

display (fig. 30).[67] Many school directors wrote to the executive committee requesting free admission for their students, and by the end of the summer 493 schools had sent some 35,000 schoolchildren to the exhibition.[68] There were also lectures in London by members of the University of Oxford on topics relating to the exhibition such as metallurgy, chemistry, and iron manufactures.[69]

Emphasizing education at the Crystal Palace reveals much about the novelty of industry and machines in mid-Victorian Britain. Industrialization and mechanization were so unfamiliar, in fact, that Lieutenant-Colonel Reid, secretary to the executive committee, had to explain to General Charles Grey, Albert's personal secretary, about steam power and how it worked in factories and workshops when the organizers were deciding whether to install steam pipes beneath the floor of the Crystal Palace in order to power the machinery.[70] Engravings from the time of the exhibition depict men and women crowding around machines, enthralled by what they were witnessing, perhaps for the first time. The Crystal Palace was designed to showcase mechanization of all kinds, to educate those in attendance about the power and uses of technology.

The importance of introducing visitors to machinery and mechanization, or 'industry,' is underscored by the comments of several writers that there were ambivalent attitudes on the part of the British towards industrialization and machinery. James Ward, in *The World in its Workshops*, found 'here and there, it is true, a lingering prejudice or so;' similarly, John Tallis wrote, 'we have not altogether overcome our prejudice to whirring wheels and hissing boilers,' though he added that 'the majority of thinking men have long ago come to the conclusion that steam and iron ought to, and eventually will, do the positive labour of the world.'[71] More broadly, Lyon Playfair noted a lack of societal recognition for success in industry and manufacturing. Most Britons in 1851 would have recognized only three primary professions: church, law, and medicine, and perhaps the army as well. 'Industry,' wrote Playfair, 'to which this country owes her success among nations, has never been raised to the rank of a profession. For her sons there are no honours, no recognized social position.'[72] This comment recalls the famous case of Daniel Doyce, the inventor in Charles Dickens' *Little Dorrit*, whose industriousness was held up time and again by the Patent Office. Frustrated, he finally left England for the continent where he found the employment and honor that had been denied him back home. Whether or not the Great Exhibition was the 'highwater mark' of industrial values, it is clear that industry and industrialization were not yet taken for granted at the time of the exhibition, and in that respect the exhibition was designed to serve an important educational function.[73]

MANUFACTURES

There was no category that better illustrated the educational purpose of the exhibition and the interrelatedness of commerce and culture than the finished manufactures, Classes XI–XXIX in the *Official Catalogue*. In addition to educating producers about new materials, and manufacturers, artisans, and laborers about machines, the exhibition also attempted to turn Britain into a society that produced and consumed in a tasteful way. The finished manufactures reflected the organizers' desire to shape an emerging commercial and industrial society in a particular fashion. The commissioners were concerned about the social and cultural implications of an industrializing society, about the disappearance of craftsmanship and a perceived loss of taste, so they emphasized arts manufactures. The exhibition was a means of influencing the manufacturing process to include design and taste, and not just profit. The organizers were educating those in attendance about a certain type of commercial society that comprised both arts (culture) and manufactures (commerce). But there were all sorts of other worries that were reflected in the manufactures displayed in the Crystal Palace. Many of the organizers were concerned about social and urban problems, those left behind in an industrializing society, so they exhibited low-income housing and inventions for invalids. They were worried that the British economy was becoming stagnant, and so they gave priority to those items that were new and improved, or multi-purpose. It is important to realize, then, that the Great Exhibition represents the physical embodiment of a particular formulation of commercial and industrial society: what it should look like, where it should go.

It is also important to recognize that the exhibition did not *only* embody the aims of its organizers. It also reflected the interests of numerous individuals and groups within mid-nineteenth-century British society. The prime example here is that, despite the best efforts of the organizers to keep the exhibition from becoming a commercial event where goods could be bought and sold, it became, in the end, just that. There were at times conflicts between the organizers – who had an interest in the long-term improvement of the British economy and who were concerned about expanding the process of production and improving taste – and merchants, tradesmen, and manufacturers who in many cases viewed the exhibition as an opportunity to bolster short-term profits. James Nasmyth, of the Bridgewater Foundry near Manchester, warned that the commissioners were seriously overestimating the desire of manufacturers to send heavy machinery, given the high cost of transportation and superintendents for the machines.[74] Art critics, too, had their own agenda, one that focused almost exclusively on craftsmanship even to the detriment of sales. What is remarkable about the exhibition is that it had room, literally, for all sorts of different approaches to production and consumption. It is important, therefore, to note the differences between how the organizers conceived of the exhibition and the form it ultimately took.

In manufactures Britain was truly 'the workshop of the world,' and it was this section that the *Official Catalogue* proclaimed 'the most important department of commercial activity.'[75] The exhibition was, in the words of one contemporary, 'an enormous pantechnicon,' a warehouse of consumer goods (fig. 31).[76] The entire exhibition was about possibilities, about opening up people's minds and presenting them with new ideas. Many things were exhibited as often as not simply to demonstrate that something could be made, that a given substance was useful. It was about expanding the process of production, making it more inclusive, opening doors to new materials, new products, new methods, new markets. The humorous *House that Albert Built* poked fun at the minimal requirements for inclusion in the exhibition:

31. Goods for the home.

> Open the house was, to wares of all sorts;
>   The only conditions enforced –
>   Some little utility,
>   Some little ability;
>   The only exceptions made –
>   Liquids that gladden,
>   Liquids that madden.

The exhibition was a celebration of British ingenuity. There is no better evidence for this than the number of objects at the Great Exhibition that were clearly never intended to be sold. Among the sofas, tables, clothes, and clocks there were a number of 'absurdities,' 'productions of dreaming insufficiency.' One of these 'absurdities' was Dunin's 'Man of Steel,' an expanding mannequin constructed of some 7,000 individual pieces, which received one of the Council Medals, of which only about 150 were given. Tallis called this invention 'so puzzling in nature' that the inventor 'must have taken his degree in the academy of Laputa,' a reference to Swift's *Gulliver's Travels*. Other 'absurdities' included an artificial silver nose, a vase made of mutton-fat and lard, an 'ostracide' (a machine for opening oysters), and a 'silent alarum bedstead' which, instead of sounding an alarm, tipped the sleeper into a cold-water bath.[77]

A few trends emerge from the superabundance of objects on display in Classes XI–XXIX. There was, not surprisingly, great emphasis on manufactures being new or improved, and being the largest or smallest, strongest, fastest, best, or most economical. A second trend at the Great Exhibition, related to the culture of the new, was multi-purpose objects. This was especially true of the furniture, the best example of which was Taylor & Sons' furniture for a steamship's or yacht's cabin, which consisted of a couch which could double as a bed, stuffed with a 'patent cork fibre' for buoyancy, connected to two cabinets, one of which formed 'a self-acting washing-stand, and containing requisites for the dressing-room and toilette,' the other 'forming a patent portable water-closet,' all of which was 'immediately convertible into a floating life-preserver' and, if kept together, would form a life-raft (fig. 32).[78]

32. Multi-purpose steamship furniture, by Taylor & Sons.

33. Prince Albert's model working-class home. *Illustrated London News* (14 June 1851).

Many items exhibited had social purposes. There was a striking amount of furniture for invalids, but chief among the exhibits with social purposes were Prince Albert's model working-class houses, designed by Henry Roberts and exhibited by the Society for Improving the Condition of the Labouring Classes (of which Albert was President). These were located outside the Crystal Palace, near the south-east corner of the building (fig. 33).[79] They housed four families, two on each floor, had open staircases, freely circulating air (by means of 'ventilating bricks,' perforated glass, and sliding screens), an interior toilet, and high ceilings. They also contained three separate bedrooms – a master bedroom, and one each for the boys and girls – which was, according to one of the publicity brochures for the houses, 'so essential to morality and decency.'[80] The *Official Catalogue* promoted the houses on the basis of their 'dryness, warmth, durability, security from fire, deadening of sound, and economy of construction.'

In many respects, Albert's working-class houses were the quintessential Victorian invention, and embodied many of the values that were central to the exhibition such as order, economy, social welfare, and profits. Albert regarded the construction of these working-class homes as the first step toward 'improving' the quality of life of the working classes. Providing them with cheerful and comfortable homes would result in improved health, sobriety, and domestic peace, especially in conjunction with education and employment opportunities.[81] Toward this end the cottages were separate from the exhibition, and free and open to the public, so that more people would be able to look at them. 'It is the humbler classes themselves who chiefly require to be educated in more correct notions of what cleanliness and domestic comfort render necessary,' *The Times* condescended, 'and if they once thoroughly appreciated the sanitary defects of their present habitations their feelings and opinions would largely control the plans of those who usually build for them.'[82] By using design to foster certain broadly conceived social and economic goals, the houses represented the conjunction of a practical response to an environmental problem, a sense of social awareness, and a passion for instruction and improvement. They represented a reaction to the troubled 1840s and a response to recent government inquiries into poor housing and health among the working classes. Just as importantly, however, they were a means of making money. A brochure produced by the Society for Improving the Condition of the Labouring Classes calculated that the houses would offer investors a 7 percent return.[83] In the end, the houses proved extremely popular, drawing more than 250,000 visitors, and within two weeks after the close of the exhibition construction had begun on two groups of houses based on Albert's and Roberts' model.[84]

A number of manufactured goods were allegorical, expressing nationalistic or patriotic themes. An eighty-blade sportsman's knife manufactured by Joseph Rodgers & Sons of Sheffield (fig. 34) had a gold inlaid handle representing, among other things, the exhibition building, Osborne, Windsor Castle, and the Britannia Bridge, a tubular railway bridge designed by Robert Stephenson spanning some 1,500 feet across the Menai Straits in Wales between Bangor and Anglesey, which had been completed in 1850 and was hailed as one of the world's great engineering feats.[85] Watherston & Brogden designed a vase which depicted Britannia flanked by Scotia and Hibernia, surrounded by four heads representing the four quarters of the globe (fig. 35).[86] Below the figures were festoons of diamonds representing the rose, thistle, and shamrock. Surrounding the body of the vase were reliefs depicting Britons, Romans, Saxons, and Normans, and the Battle of Hastings. Beneath were famous British historical

34. An eighty-blade sportsman's knife, by Joseph Rogers & Sons.

35. Patriotic vase, by Watherston and Brogden.

figures such as Nelson, Wellington, Milton, Shakespeare, Newton, and Watt being crowned with laurel wreaths. On the lower part of the vase were figures symbolizing Truth, Prudence, Industry, and Fortitude. These objects created and diffused a national image: that England, Wales, Scotland, and Ireland together constituted one nation; that Britain's greatness rested on the ideas and successes of its heroes.

The manufactures at the Crystal Palace also reflected the importance the organizers placed on finding a way to combine commerce and culture, arts and manufactures, taste and profits, and it was here that the British system of production came under severe criticism. Many of the decorative household goods were mercilessly deprecated by art critics who attended the exhibition. The young William Morris, for example, found the Crystal Palace and the exhibits inside 'wonderfully ugly,' though this should be tempered by the subsequent revelation in his essay 'How I Became a Socialist' that 'the leading passion of my life has been and is hatred of modern civilization.'[87] But the foremost critic was Ralph Nicholson Wornum, after 1854 the Keeper and secretary of the National Gallery. His essay, 'The Exhibition as a Lesson in Taste,' which won a prize from the *Art Journal* and was widely quoted by critics (and by historians since), criticized both manufactures and manufacturers for their superficiality, incongruity of style, and ornamentation. Wornum wrote that 'the paramount impression conveyed to the critical mind must be a general want of education in taste.' He was critical because, as he saw it, there was nothing new in the exhibition in terms of ornamental design; it was all imitative. He complained that all he could find were copies of old ideas, 'old things in an old taste.' Manufacturers, rather than applying design to some useful purpose, used ornamentation as an end in itself, subordinating form and function and thus destroying the integrity of the object.[88]

In his essay Wornum drew on the design theories of two prominent art critics: Augustus Welby Pugin and John Ruskin. Pugin's *Contrasts* (1836) provided a graphic satire of contemporary life and architecture, professing to demonstrate in pairs of contrasted pictures the superiority not only of Gothic architecture to modern Classic, but of medieval to modern society. In *The True Principles of Pointed or Christian Architecture* (1841), he described and illustrated the growing confusion of ornamentation and design. 'It is impossible to enumerate half the absurdities of modern metalworkers,' he wrote, 'but all these proceed from the false notion of *disguising* instead of *beautifying* articles of utility.'[89] According to Pugin, beautiful forms were based on utility, a principle Cole and Redgrave had adopted in their *Journal of Design*, even if they did not embrace Pugin's love of the Gothic style. In *The Seven Lamps of Architecture* (1849), Ruskin had emphasized natural objects and subject (or meaning) rather than the arrangement of lines or colors, and rejected all non-natural shapes. He saw sculpture and painting as the only 'fine arts;' he regarded architecture as mere building and construction; and he saw no promise in new materials such as iron or glass. For Ruskin, the exhibits were antithetical to everything he believed.

There was no question that Britain could produce enormous quantities of goods. The question was: Were they aesthetically appealing? If Wornum, Pugin, and Ruskin represented one side of the debate, James Nasmyth, the Manchester manufacturer referred to earlier, expressed the opposite in a letter to the executive committee which reveals much about the tension in the Victorian economy between quality and quantity. He wrote that British manufacturers did not require exhibitions to demonstrate their superiority, for the surplus of exports over imports did just that. 'We go for quantity and fair average excellence rather than for *perfection*,' he continued, 'in search after which many on the continent become poor or never rise to wealth.' The harsh lesson of 1851, Nasmyth suspected, was that British manufacturers would be 'beat by the foreigners in many articles in respect to abstract perfection,' but that Britain would thrive as a prosperous manufacturing and commercial nation in spite of it. 'Quantity is what England will ever be supreme in,' he concluded. 'Economic production is our forte and ever will be.'[90] It is possible that Nasmyth was expressing a sense of cultural inferiority; more likely his letter merely confirms that Britain and the continental countries were at different stages of industrialization.[91] In Britain, the focus was on quantity and utility, on making products for as many people as possible; sales were the bottom line, and British manufacturers had realized that selling cheaper goods to a large portion of the population would produce higher profits than selling a few high-priced goods. On the continent, the focus was still on handcrafted goods, on products for the wealthy. Nasmyth's letter therefore goes a long way towards explaining why some manufacturers were reluctant to support the exhibition. It would appear from the letter that the organizers and manufacturers were often at cross-purposes. The organizers – principally Henry Cole and Prince Albert – wanted to make the exhibition about 'arts manufactures,' that is, aesthetically appealing goods, but many manufacturers could not have cared less, as long as their products sold.

The organizers' interest in improving standards of taste is exemplified by their inclusion of the fine arts, Class XXX in the classification scheme. The exhibits in this area illustrated the very problem faced by Cole and the other organizers: How to wed works of art and industry. Where, in an industrial exhibition, should the fine arts be placed? Given that the exhibition was about industry and not the fine arts, the *Official Catalogue* strictly limited the fine arts class to 'Those departments of art which are . . . connected with mechanical processes.' Paintings, as works of art, were excluded, but were admissible insofar as they exhibited any improvements in colors. But, even once admitted, they were to be regarded 'not so much as examples of the skill of the artist, as of that of the preparer of colors.'[92] Not surprisingly, many of the fine arts exhibits were criticized, although some of the sculptures included in Class XXX were among the most popular exhibits.[93] The fine arts were an anomaly in the exhibition. The theory behind their inclusion made sense: that designers would study the fine arts, improve their taste, and incorporate the principles they learned in new arts manufactures. It is unclear, however, whether this process ever took place, or whether the 'fine arts' were in any way finer or more principled than the manufactures.

At the heart of all the criticism of the exhibits were ambivalent, even negative attitudes toward industrialization, mechanization, and the division of labor, all of which could result in objects being assembled piecemeal by uneducated workers who had no training in broader issues of design.[94] The underlying issue in the assessments of the exhibits by Wornum, Pugin, Ruskin, and others, always present but rarely voiced, was not so much the aesthetic design of the finished products *per se* as how they were manufactured. Victorians had a love–hate relationship with technology, fetishizing it on the one hand, critical of its effects on consumer goods on the other. Critics of design were essentially critics of the division of labor, and their critiques were at heart a lament for craftsmanship. Although their discussions were devoted to how exhibits looked, the real issue was how they were made.[95]

In *An Inquiry into the Nature and Causes of the Wealth of Nations* (1776), Adam Smith had described how productivity came most readily from a division of labor. He pointed out that a division of labor fostered increased dexterity on the part of the worker, saved valuable time, and led to the invention of machines which facilitated and reduced labor, all of which increased productivity. When this took place at the societal level, he claimed, wealth expanded to include all ranks of people. Smith was also aware, however, of the consequences of the division of labor, that it forced workers to perform a single task repeatedly, reducing their capacity for inventiveness and creativity.[96] The Great Exhibition of 1851 focused national attention on both the positive and negative consequences of Smith's formulation of the economy. On the one hand, the exhibition was a celebration of British production, of how much Britain could produce, and for such a large portion of the population. On the other hand, it served as an opportunity to criticize that very same production process for creating untrained workers who could only manufacture poor-quality goods with little aesthetic appeal. Much of the criticism, therefore, was nostalgia for an idealized old world of craftsmanship that had supposedly been lost (if indeed it had ever existed). The Great Exhibition was a debate about quantity versus quality, a forum for two different and competing visions of Britain's national identity and economic future.

Serving both as a utopian view of the future and as a lament for a largely imaginary past was the Medieval Court, set within the manufactures (fig. 36). So as to prevent too great a uniformity in the exhibition, and to diminish the enormous labor of the executive committee, the Royal Commission had allotted to different exhibitors 'courts' in which they could display their goods in the manner they

36. Pugin's Medieval Court in the Gothic Revival style.

thought most suitable, subject to general regulations. These included a set of four rooms for the Austrians, Hibbert, Platt and Sons' cotton machinery, and Pugin's Medieval Court.[97] Designed and organized by Pugin in conjunction with several other Birmingham design and manufacturing firms, the Medieval Court contained hand-crafted furniture in the Gothic style.[98] On one side, the Court was hung with ecclesiastical ornaments, including a giant cross that became the touchstone for anti-Catholic sentiments (see Chapter 6); on the other side it was a virtual storehouse of domestic furniture. In the center was a motley collection of stoves, pots, sofas, and tables.[99] The Medieval Court was a return to pre-modern methods of production, and a preview of the team-oriented craftsmanship that would characterize William Morris' Arts and Crafts productions. It is a testament to the organizers' desire for inclusiveness that such an anomaly could exist within the Crystal Palace.

Although it was popular, and a tribute to craftsmanship, most contemporaries dismissed the Medieval Court as backward and outdated, antithetical to progress. Tallis found the Court 'a little too theatric in effect,' and called the 'pious' sentiments that once inspired such decorative work 'lifeless . . . in a more enlightened age.'[100] The author of an article in the *Eclectic Review* drew the contrast between the Medieval Court and 'progress' even more starkly by denigrating the Court as 'felicitous copyism.' He contrasted the Medieval Court with a locomotive which, because its 'external form' was shaped by 'intrinsic necessities' – form follows function – was aesthetically superior to those decorative objects whose purpose was masked. He wrote of 'the power, the eloquence, the fitness, the simple outlines and harmonious combinations' of the locomotive, the product of utility, compared to 'the poor meretricious make-believe' of Pugin's Gothic furniture, 'with its false outlines [and] incongruous ornament.'[101]

Mid-century design critics and reformers such as Cole, Ruskin, Pugin, and Wornum claimed that machines were having a deleterious effect on production by diminishing the role of craftsmen, by separating design and production, and by creating the possibility of cheap imitations.[102] This was an issue of national concern that had predated the exhibition by at least two decades, and continued to rage well after the exhibition closed.[103] What the mid-century critics did not discern was that the division of labor had nothing to do with mechanization. Mechanization exacerbated the problems associated with the division of labor, but at the time Adam Smith popularized that phrase neither mechanization nor machines (at least not in the more modern form) had existed. Specialization of design and production took place long before the introduction of machines; machines initially had little direct influence on design, and the extent of mechanization was far less at the time of the Great Exhibition than historians have generally acknowledged.[104] This suggests that the issue was not mechanization, as both contemporaries and historians have suggested, but the division of labor.

The design critique, however, was taken very seriously at the time. It had already led to three Parliamentary select committees, the establishment of the government schools of design, the institution of patent protection for designs, and the various exhibitions that took place during the 1840s.[105] All of these attempted in one way or another to revive craftsmanship. The subdivision of labor meant that 'artisans' had become 'mechanics,' uneducated in broader principles of design; hence the schools of design. The public had lost its sense of aesthetics; hence the exhibition that would put British quantity side by side with continental quality. What critics of design either did not see or refused to admit was that the problem had its roots in the very system of capitalist production that depended for its success on the division of labor.

There were, additionally, many at the time of the Great Exhibition who saw the benefits industrialization and mechanization offered, and cared little that their fire screen was machine-made and not hand-crafted, especially if it cost less.[106] Although modern art critics have vilified Victorian designers and manufacturers for what they call excessive ornamentation, for many Victorians simply being able to ornament the surface of a dresser was a remarkable and wonderful change.[107] Moreover, many Victorians liked the exhibits outright. In his Ode for the opening of the exhibition, Tennyson wrote of 'All of beauty, all of use / That one fair planet can produce.'[108] Equally impressed was the artist Henrietta Ward, who wrote in her autobiography that 'The exhibition revolutionized the home surroundings of the people. Tasteful table decorations, flower-decked tables, and light and elegant silver succeeded the cumbersome plate of the Georgian period.' She remembered lovely hand- and machine-made carpets, and recalled mosaic table tops and pottery 'which roused a feeling for envious possession.'[109] For Ward, as indeed for Queen Victoria, the exhibits were splendid, and most of those who attended the exhibition lavished on them their attention and admiration.[110]

The arts manufactures on display at the Great Exhibition are evidence both of the manufacturing process at its beginnings and of a path not taken. Ruskin's view, that ornamentation was valuable only insofar as it preserved the integrity of an object, that commerce and culture were antithetical, emerged victorious in critical culture. He also asserted that the right question to ask regarding all ornament was whether it was done with enjoyment. With this as his starting point, Ruskin condemned all machine-made ornamentation on social grounds.[111] Pugin did so on aesthetic grounds, that machine-made ornamentation was deceitful. The views of Ruskin and Pugin would see their fruition in the work of William Morris and the Arts and Crafts style, which challenged the ornate and elaborate manufactures that had been so praised and denigrated in 1851.[112] Morris fused Pugin's aesthetic critique and Ruskin's social critique. Seeking to restore aesthetic values to craftsmanship, Morris forever banished the exhibits of 1851 to the dustbin of history. But if Morris solved the design critique, and if he was more honest about the social critique – that the problem was the very nature of capitalist society, by which he meant the division of labor – he was unable to do anything about it. There was a conflict between Morris' theory of the unity of labor and the actual practice of his firm.[113] The subdivision of labor was permanent. What was not permanent was a division between commerce and culture.

The manufactured goods sought to educate those in attendance, producers and consumers alike, about the importance of good taste. They forced contemporaries to confront the question that for Cole underlay the entire exhibition: was it possible to wed art and manufactures? Cole believed that it was, and toward that end had founded Summerly's Arts Manufactures, his own design firm which had taken a prize at one of the Society of Arts' exhibitions, and the *Journal of Design*, which sought to promote the idea that good design meant good business. At one extreme, among those who disagreed with him, were art critics such as Wornum and Pugin for whom the emphasis on taste was really a smokescreen for a much deeper issue, the division of labor and its effect on production. At the other extreme were men such as Nasmyth who questioned the relevance of this issue in the first place, claiming that, as long as British goods sold, design simply did not matter. At the time of the exhibition, it would have been impossible to know which of these approaches to production and consumption would prevail. What the organizers had done was to set these different approaches side by side, and let observers choose between them. The manufactures on display in the Crystal Palace, therefore, promoted a debate about Britain's economic future, and by extension about how its national identity should be shaped.

THE COMMERCIALIZATION OF THE CRYSTAL PALACE

There is no better evidence of the organizers' desire to improve taste and production than their decision not to allow prices on exhibits, which clearly reflected their interest in hosting a competition that would benefit production and international commerce over the long term, rather than merely offering a sales opportunity to merchants and manufacturers. The exhibition was not to feature goods as marketable commodities, but rather to perfect the manufacturing process. If commerce flourished as a result, so much the better.[114] The prohibition on prices was also a compromise to appease London tradesmen and protectionists who were concerned about foreign manufacturers selling their products below cost in order to secure market share and boost business. Albert's secretary Colonel Phipps wrote that pricing exhibits 'would have changed the exhibition into a vast bazaar to the great detriment of the London tradesmen.'[115] The two reasons were often blurred, however, because protectionists frequently used the more high-minded objection as a cover for their true reasons. In March 1850, for example, the chairman of the Westminster local committee reported that subscriptions were low because there was a prevailing idea that the exhibition was 'likely to assume the character of a commercial speculation, that exhibitors will have facilities afforded them of carrying on a system of sale.' This would, in his opinion, prevent the exhibition from being 'an honourable competition among all nations.'[116]

Few decisions aroused more opposition than the prohibition on pricing exhibits. A West Riding manufacturer wrote to *The Times* expressing his disagreement with the commissioners' decision on the ground that many articles were being exhibited because of the economy of their production. He argued that there were items no one would think of exhibiting were it not for the low price at which they could be sold, and that, if a manufacturer could produce for a sixpence what another manufacturer could only produce for a shilling, that fact should be noted. Mass production was one of the areas in which Britain clearly led the rest of the world, but manufacturers had no way of demonstrating this strength without prices. He warned that the consequence of the commissioners' decision would be that there was 'no use sending anything which is not either novel or curious,'[117] which explains why there were so many useless one-of-a-kind items.

The debate over pricing reveals two very different approaches to the exhibition and to the kinds of objects appropriate for display. The *Economist* editorialized before the exhibition opened: 'We take it for granted that only things will be exhibited which are supposed to be useful, agreeable, or convenient. The bulk will be made to sell. Things that are of no use, whatever time and trouble they may have cost their makers, should find little place in such an exhibition. It is not to be a cabinet of curiosities, or a museum of wonders.'[118] At a meeting in Sheffield to promote the exhibition, one of the local commissioners for that city said 'that the exhibition should be considered as a stern reality, not as a mere display of curiosities.' He emphasized utility, stressing that all exhibits should be of the kind that could be 'manufactured in the regular course of business.' His view, like the *Economist*'s, was that the exhibition was for staple goods that were made to be sold.[119]

A year later, however, after it had opened, the *Economist* acknowledged that the reality of the exhibition was quite different from what it had anticipated. It noted that in several departments exhibits were marked 'article disposed of,' meaning that it had been sold; 'to that extent,' the *Economist* opined, 'the show has become a market.' But it was not 'a market where the world's wants can be supplied,' nor was it even 'a guide to the merchant.' In the *Economist*'s assessment, the exhibition was more for the inventor and the philosopher than the trader.[120] In short, the Crystal Palace represented the playing out of different visions regarding the exhibition, whether it was to be an industrial exhibition with an educational purpose or more of a trade fair with overtly commercial connotations.

These two views paralleled the two most common ways of expressing the value of goods or commodities. One, the symbolic, or the labor theory of value, focused on the amount of labor put into manufacturing a given product, which gave rise to the over-ornamented arts manufactures and the moral-laden statuary. The other, the monetary, or the exchange theory of value, focused only on supply and demand, on what price the market would bear, regardless of how much it cost to manufacture the article. The old, pre-industrial economy, nominally based on craftsmanship, had expressed value in terms of labor. The new economy, still emerging but very present by 1851, already based on a division of labor and soon to be based on mass production, expressed val[...] The exhibition represented an attempt to join the two ec[...] of [...]ste and design. The tentative and unsat[...] answer it provided was [...] consumerism was acceptable as long as it was ta[...] the [...] hibition, [...] moral issue, a means of justifying the n[...]

Arguing agains[...] [...]lic economy which emphasized value [...] facturers who countered that the abil[...] [...]ensively, so that they could be sold che[...] [...]oth thrift and industriousness. If they[...] [...]they could then place their mass-produ[...] [...] moral equivalents of the more expens[...] [...]rs wanted to use the exhibition to imp[...] [...]etailers used the exhibition as a vehic[...]

The man wh[...] the symbolic and the monetary econo[...] [...]e calculator. He used the commission's decision to p[...] as a platform to criticize the symbolic, moral, and outdated economy represented by the exhibition. In *The Exposition of 1851* he ridiculed the litany of reasons given by the commissioners, and by moralistic shopkeepers, for not pricing goods, principally 'that the public, being unable to judge of the article, will be guided too much by the cheapness of its money price, neglecting its other qualities, and will thus be induced to purchase worthless things.'[121] He countered by boldly asserting that 'The price in money is the *most important element* in every bargain.' In the end, the commissioners attempted a compromise at the exhibition, which was to prohibit prices (thus partially upholding the older, moral, symbolic economy), but to allow the juries to take into account price as a consideration in their awarding of prizes.

Market forces, however, obliterated their weak attempt to preserve the older economy and to placate those who refused to change. There were, it turned out, a number of ways around the prohibition on prices. Exhibitors were free to employ attendants to explain exhibits, and, although these agents were forbidden to invite visitors to purchase the goods on display, the Royal Commission did not prevent them from handing visitors, at their request, 'an explanation of the merits and prices of articles exhibited.'[122] In the eighteenth century Josiah Wedgwood had revolutionized retailing by opening showrooms with samples of his wares on display, but with no stock for sale. The showroom passed on customers' orders to the factory, which made the product and then shipped directly to the customer.[123] It is likely that the exhibition worked in this manner, as hundreds if not thousands of exhibitors produced advertising cards, price sheets, brochures, and posters which they made available to visitors interested in their displays.[124] And so the exhibition became in reality a trade fair. Although it may have disappointed many London tradesmen who had extravagantly hoped for a boom in business, it remunerated many exhibitors who were able to use the exhibition to secure orders for their products.[125]

Moreover, despite the best efforts of the Royal Commission to prevent the Great Exhibition from becoming a giant emporium, it became just that after it closed to the public. Following the closing ceremony, the Crystal Palace was open for a few additional days to exhibitors, some 30,000–40,000 of whom entered on 14 October. Within a few minutes after the building opened at noon, according to the *Express*, 'the interior resembled a bazaar, so brisk and general was the trade going on.'[126] The Crystal Palace was indeed a shopping mall and a department store, dispersing its goods throughout the world (fig. 37).[127] But this is true not so much because it turned the goods on display into commodities, or because 'it largely excluded the articles common to everyday life,'[128] as one historian has suggested, but for just the opposite reason: because the Crystal Palace was stuffed with everyday goods for the middle classes, such as cutlery, chairs, mirrors, clothes, curtains. And the goods displayed did not just cater to middle-class taste, they helped form that taste, educating people not only about what to consume, but to consume in the first place.[129] The Great Exhibition taught British men and women to want things and to buy things, new things and better things.[130] While it does not represent the birth of a consumer society, it may well represent its coming of age, as it put side by side the most dissimilar objects. And while this can hardly be considered to be the organizers' intention, the commercialization of the Crystal Palace suggests once again how multifaceted the exhibition was.

*   *   *

37. George Cruikshank, 'The Dispersion of the Works of All Nations from the Great Exhibition of 1851'.

THE CONSTRUCTION OF AN INDUSTRIALIZED SOCIETY

The organizers of the exhibition held a remarkably sophisticated view of the British economy. They defined the production process broadly to include raw materials, hand-crafted as well as machine-made goods, and scientific and electronic inventions. They addressed British competitiveness, especially vis-à-vis France, in the manufacture of finished goods, where taste and design (the quality side of the quality versus quantity debate, or the culture side of the commerce versus culture debate) were important issues.[131] And, as noted in Chapter 3, the commissioners went out of their way to solicit the support of bankers and financiers for the exhibition. City of London residents and businesses not only subscribed more per capita than any other region, they contributed almost one-third of the total amount raised before the exhibition opened. Men of finance such as Samuel Jones Loyd, Thomas Baring, Samuel Morton Peto, and Baron Rothschild were early and large contributors, as was the Bank of England. And in cities such as Manchester, bankers were among the largest contributors and the most prominent participants in the organization of the exhibition.[132] In short, the organizers were remarkably adept at bridging what has been described as 'the distance between land, finance and the upper reaches of the service sector on the one side, and mechanical industry on the other.'[133] They accomplished this by means of their inclusive vision of the economy and their ability to indicate the various sorts of connections that needed to take place in order for the economy to flourish.

The organizers also understood the economy's mixed character, that it was working well in certain areas but not in others. From the start, the exhibition made apparent Britain's precarious position despite its widely acknowledged status as the most powerful and progressive nation. In some ways mid-nineteenth-century Britain truly was 'the workshop of the world,' producing about two-thirds of the world's coal and more than half of its iron and cotton cloth.[134] But the Industrial Revolution occurred slowly, affecting different regions at different times, and did not become firmly entrenched throughout British society until the second half of the nineteenth century.[135] And while Britain was clearly pre-eminent in raw materials, machinery, and quantity of manufactures, this was emphatically not the case with the design of many of its manufactures. In matters of ornamentation and in the design of household goods Britain consistently ranked well below its continental competitors. It lagged behind the French in silks and silverwork, and behind both the French and the Germans in woodcarving and printed cottons.[136] In short, the exhibition confirmed what British manufacturers had suspected for at least a decade, which was that their products were not standing up well to foreign competition. Only if one took into account 'beauty, economy, and utility combined' did Britain have 'no competitors.'[137] Britain came out on top in the production of general hardware and glass, and was producing the highest-quality steel, but when McCormick's reaper, from America, handily defeated the British entries in a contest, cutting an astounding twenty acres per day, *The Times* granted that it was 'the most valuable contribution from abroad to the stock of our previous knowledge.'[138]

There were also concerns about Britain's proficiency in mechanization and science. A number of economic historians have differentiated between the 'first' and 'second' industrial revolutions in Britain.[139] During the first phase of industrialization, 'the important inventions were simple, the products of skill, practical experience and a readiness to try anything new and see whether it worked.' Science and esoteric knowledge played little part. Sources of power such as water and coal and primary raw materials such as iron, were familiar and widely available in Britain, which helps explain its status as the pre-eminent industrial nation of the mid-nineteenth century. By contrast, the key components of the 'second' Industrial Revolution were the mechanization of machine-making, which depended on standardization, and the growth and increasing importance of science, particularly electrical and chemical knowledge.[140] Despite their early start and awesome material advantages, if the Great Exhibition provides an accurate picture, the British had already lost their dominance in the area of mechanization. The leading products in this area – Singer's sewing machine and Colt's revolver – were both American.[141]

As for science, with all the focus on heavy machinery in motion, British commentators missed much. Analysts almost uniformly failed to grasp the significance of hydraulic machinery. Robert Hunt, who edited a synopsis of the *Official Catalogue*, described Fromont's turbine as nothing more than an efficient horizontal water wheel.[142] And the only application of electricity generally thought to be of importance was the electric telegraph, widely regarded as one of the machines with the most potential. Dr Lardner, a *Times* correspondent, fantasized about a 'never-ceasing interchange of news over the entire extent of that network of wires which has overspread the country,' and foresaw a communications revolution: 'When this mode of intercommunication shall be available to the public in all parts of Europe, great changes in the social and commercial relations of the centres of commerce and population must be witnessed.'[143] Yet in retrospect one of the most important machines was Robert Stanton's electromagnetic engine, even though the *Official Catalogue* did not deem it either important enough or of general enough interest to merit a lengthy entry.[144] At the time of the Great Exhibition, electric machines were classified as 'philosophical instruments,' in Class X. Engineers regarded electric devices with contempt, as playthings. Isambard Kingdom Brunel, in the midst of rebuilding Paddington Station, told Scott Russell that he wished to see excluded from the exhibition 'any mentions of *electric machines* which as yet can be considered only toys.' In contrast, Brunel considered his own giant steam engines 'useful.'[145]

The disdain for electrical machines other than the telegraph points to a fairly widespread antipathy to science. Two decades before the exhibition, Charles Babbage had published his *Reflections on the Decline of Science in England and Some of its Causes* (1830). Already by that time, according to Babbage, Britain was 'much below other nations' in the more difficult and abstract sciences. He found it shocking that a country so 'distinguished for its mechanical and manufacturing ingenuity' should be so indifferent to the technical aspects that provided the foundations for its success. The decline of science, he claimed, was caused in part by an educational system which neglected science because its pursuit did not 'constitute a distinct profession' in Britain as it did in many other countries. Babbage cited a lack of support for science in the government, among the general population, and especially among 'the higher classes.'[146]

Nor was Babbage alone in his assessment. Soon after the exhibition Lyon Playfair raised a warning cry about British production and attitudes toward science with what have turned out to be some remarkably astute and prescient observations:

A rapid transition is taking place in industry; the raw material, formerly our capital advantage over other nations, is gradually being equalized in price, and made available to all by the improvements in locomotion: industry must in [the] future be supported, not by a competition of local advantages, but by a competition of intellect. All European nations, except England, have recognized this fact.

That is, Britain would be unable to retain its premier status as a result of its strength in raw materials and production alone. British manufacturers were already looking overseas for designers, a trend which Playfair thought would be disastrous in the future. According to Playfair, in schools outside Britain students were taught the scientific principles involved in manufacturing, and workers received 'intellectual training' which had a noticeable effect on manufactures. He was warning that Britain's uneducated workers would soon hold the country's back in the face of its more skilled competitors. The core problem was that British education was 'utterly unsuited to the wants of the age' in its emphasis on classical languages and literature, a system he suggested that was more suited to 'fabricate literati' than to further 'exact science.' Playfair found it lamentable that Oxford and Cambridge did so little to encourage the sciences. He urged the creation of an industrial university, and insisted that instruction in the sciences form 'an important part' of the education of British schoolchildren.[147]

The analysis of the state of British science offered by Playfair and Babbage had a sound basis in the exhibition. Even though Britain won sixteen of thirty-one council medals awarded in Class X (scientific instruments), with France its nearest rival taking home nine, there was little ground for complacency. Three of Britain's medals were for photography, and four for the electric telegraph. Of the nine other medals, three went to inventors unconnected with industry, and four went to one-of-a-kind oddities such as Dunin's expanding figure. The most successful of the British scientific instruments were the microscopes, which won two medals. In contrast, seven of the nine French medals were for instruments with clear commercial applications: barometers, an air pump, a heliostat (an instrument in which a mirror is automatically moved so that it reflects sunlight in a constant direction), and theodolites (surveying instruments). In astronomy, navigation, chemistry, and meteorology the jury was consistently underwhelmed by the British offerings. The results of the competition in this all-important class suggested that Britain's lead in developing scientific instruments was slipping. Its rivals, while perhaps not yet surpassing Britain, were catching up quickly owing to superior educational systems, and it was for this very reason that the organizers established the Department of Science and Art – the Department of Education after 1856 – following the exhibition.[148]

Lyon Playfair recognized all of this, and issued a strong warning about Britain's competitiveness: 'Do not let us nourish our national vanity by fondly congratulating ourselves that, as we were successful, we had little to fear.' He admonished:

It is a grave matter of reflection, whether the exhibition did not show very clearly and distinctly that the rate of industrial advance of many European nations, even of those who were obviously in our rear, was greater than our own; and if it were so, as I believe it to have been, it does not require much acumen to perceive that in a long race the fastest-sailing ships will win, even though they are for a time behind. . . . The Roman empire fell rapidly, because, nourishing its national vanity, it refused the lessons of defeat and construed them into victory.[149]

Playfair could not have understood the situation better had he actually seen the future.

The purpose of the exhibition, therefore, was to provide for a national assessment that would lead to the transformation of the British economy.[150] This goal, of evaluating and improving Britain's economic position, was accomplished by setting up the exhibition as a giant international competition, pitting the British exhibits against their foreign competitors'. Even as the exhibition became a means of glorifying and extolling Britain – its economy, its government, its work ethic – it was at heart an attempt to evaluate and improve, through education and example, certain perceived deficiencies in British production and consumption. The organizers' vision, realized through the Great Exhibition, was to speak to two relevant problems facing mid-nineteenth-century British commercial society: the need to connect finance and industry, and the need to counter foreign competition.

The organizers sought to shape the process of industrialization in patently liberal ways. They attempted to make it inclusive of all forms of production, both large-scale, quantity-oriented mass-production, and small-scale, artisan- or workshop-based specialized production.[151] They attempted to inculcate an ethic of taste, art, and culture to go along with more brazenly commercial manufactures. And they attempted to foster an ethic of bottom-up, private, firm-based production rather than a top-down, mercantilist, government-directed form of manufacturing. They saw before them a multiplicity of production processes and possibilities, and used the Great Exhibition to demonstrate, evaluate, and choose between them. This is especially apparent in the multiple definitions of industry that were in vogue at the time, that industry was not defined narrowly as large-scale mass production, but rather as people making things in a variety of ways. It is also apparent in the organizers' emphasis on exhibits being 'new' or 'improved,' and in the classification system, designed as it was to foster scientific development and innovation. The Great Exhibition did not prove that one form of production was better than another, or that mass production would win out. Rather, it revealed choices that people had. The emphasis, as with free trade, was on process, not outcome.

The exhibition, in short, was an industrial divide, when people were attempting to choose which path to take, and debating the merits of those paths.[152] As we have seen, the exhibition represented an uneasy and unsatisfactory alliance between two visions of the economy: the older, symbolic, labor-based economy favored by Ruskin, Wornum, and Morris; and the newer, market-oriented, monetary economy preferred by Babbage, Nasmyth, large northern manufacturers, and most consumers. Cole and Albert were caught in the middle, standing at a crossroads. *The Times* certainly recognized that Britain's path to industrialization was one of the very serious questions posed by the Great Exhibition when it asked: 'In what direction as an industrial community should we henceforth travel, and by what means should we proceed?' Should Britain emphasize 'the costly and the beautiful,' or the unpretentious and the utilitarian? At a turning point between what *The Times* called the Old World and the New World, the paper inquired whether Britain should raise its manufactures to continental and oriental standards of taste or struggle to reduce prices and reach a greater portion of the population; in short, quantity versus quality. Until 1851, most British manufacturers had concentrated on the former. Rather unsatisfactorily, *The Times* urged both approaches, claiming that the recently created design schools, the juries' reports, new patent laws, and publicity given to new machinery, materials, and processes as a result of the exhibition would all enable Britain to continue to produce utilitarian goods, but with greater aesthetic value.[153] Through the Great Exhibition, the organizers – liberal aristocrats and men of commerce and science with an interest in modernization – sought to construct a certain kind of market society. They sought to refashion British society so as to embrace both commerce and culture. The fact that it is now almost a truism that these two concepts are antithetical should not obscure the moment at which a certain group of Britons saw them as complementary.

The picture presented by the Great Exhibition, it turns out, is a rather schizophrenic one that does not fit easily into preconceived notions of British decline. There is no doubt that in 1851 Britain was the world's single Great Power, economically and militarily. But the Great Exhibition revealed, for the astute observer, signs of underlying weaknesses, the beginnings of the erosion of Britain's economic preeminence upon which its military and imperial strength rested. While British industries were increasing their output in absolute terms, their relative share of world production was steadily falling.[154] Already by the time of the exhibition Britain was losing customers, at least at home where consumers tended to prefer the foreign-made goods that flooded the country after the relaxation of tariffs during the 1840s. More importantly, there were warning signs that, in matters of science and education especially, Britain was not developing with an eye towards the future. This is not to suggest that it was not the leading *industrial* power in 1851, for it clearly was. Rather, what is suggested here is that other countries were already challenging Britain's broader *economic* supremacy.

Britain's relative economic decline after the mid-nineteenth century may be a lot more understandable if it is allowed to encompass more than just coal and textiles. In fact decline may not be the best way of describing the post-1851 British economy.[155] The tendency of historians to concentrate on manufacturing in their explanations of decline has been misleading, because most of the largest businesses in Victorian Britain were in the service sector.[156] In other words, if one takes a broader view of the British economy in 1851 at the time of the exhibition, if one does not focus predominantly on coal and textiles, then one avoids the teleology of British decline. In fact, change and diversification, rather than (industrial) decline, become the more important issue.

An analysis of the Great Exhibition, then, may help resolve some of the issues and apparent contradictions in the now voluminous debate over British economic decline. It leaves standing the overall argument of those works that emphasize the centrality of industry by confirming that in capital-intensive industries that drew on largely unskilled labor Britain was clearly ahead of all other countries at the time of the exhibition. And in those terms alone, Britain declined, relatively, after about 1870. It also leaves standing those analyses that emphasize the importance of finance and services. While it was difficult for these sectors to 'exhibit' at the Crystal Palace, they were critical to the exhibition's financial success. In fact, the exhibition provided a model of how finance and industry could connect. The exhibition lends credence to those who have argued that Britain declined because it failed to make the switch from the first to the second Industrial Revolution; that inability to innovate was already taking place by 1851.[157] Finally, the exhibition supports the contention that Britain never really declined at all because its economy has always been diverse, successful in some areas, less successful in others. This was exactly the view taken by the commissioners for 1851.

Insofar as Britain has experienced decline since 1851, in either absolute or relative terms, it is essential not to view this as inevitable. The Great Exhibition offered Britons the opportunity to improve various commercial, industrial, and educational deficiencies. It provided a model for the improvement of the British economy: connecting finance and industry, introducing new materials and techniques, expanding the process of production, broadening the base of consumption. But, in a patently liberal way, the exhibition did not tell Britons what lessons they should derive from it. The fact is, the exhibition was too big, too amorphous, too decentralized for its lessons to be clear.

The exhibition's significance is that it defined Britain as an industrial nation. While this was taken for granted for years, it seems that this point needs to be re-emphasized. For all the claims about how important finance and commerce were – and they were growing in all areas of Britain – it was not until 1911 that services caught up with manufacturing in their share of employment in Britain.[158] Note, however, that industry in 1851 meant something different than what is ordinarily taken to be the case. It meant hand-crafted as much as machine-made goods. It meant small-scale as much as large-scale production. And it meant finding a balance of both arts and manufactures, of commerce and culture.

CHAPTER 5

Integration and Segregation

JOHN TALLIS, author of one of the many popular guides to the Great Exhibition, claimed that at the Crystal Palace 'all social distinctions were for the moment merged in the general feeling of pride and admiration at the wondrous result of science and labour exhibited in the Palace of Glass. Never before in England had there been so free and general a mixture of classes as under that roof.'[1] Yet Tallis also described how industrialists and factory workers scrutinized the latest machinery, women examined the cloths and handicrafts, and fashionable society virtually ignored the exhibits altogether, preferring instead to remain in the transept of the Crystal Palace 'to see and be seen.'[2] Tallis' comments, which were echoed by many of his contemporaries, encapsulate some of the ways in which the Great Exhibition and the Crystal Palace served both to integrate and to segregate Victorian society along social, regional, occupational, and gender lines. The organizers of the Great Exhibition sought to bring together all sectors of British society under one roof. Yet, at the same time, the arrangement of exhibits, admission prices, patterns of attendance, and latent fears of the working classes reflected and reinforced hierarchies and divisions within Victorian society.

THE COMMISSION AND THE WORKING CLASSES

During the first few days of the exhibition, the Crystal Palace was, according to *The Times*, 'in the hands of the wealthy and the gently and nobly born.'[3] The Royal Commissioners had insured that this would be the case by elaborately structuring the price of admission, which for the first three weeks never fell below five shillings. In mid-May *The Times* reported that whereas the nave was often filled, though not inconveniently so, the 'more remote parts' were not being visited in large numbers, with some areas remaining almost empty throughout the day. All of this changed when the Crystal Palace was thrown open to the shilling visitors on 26 May.

Most people expected the worst. *The Times* cautioned that 'when the masses take possession of the interior it will be well nigh impossible to see anything,' and suggested that those readers with a spare five shillings who wished to see the interior should attend before 'King Mob enters.'[4] The paper expected the five-shilling visitors to stay away after 26 May when 'the aristocratic element retires from the scene' and 'an entirely new class of visitors' appeared, 'a fresh order of spectators.'[5] John Tallis described how 'many an old lady and timorous gentleman anticipated nothing but riot and disorder.'[6] Writers raised the specter of Chartism, revolution, and even famine. The *Economist* was one of the few journals that tried to lessen such fears, reassuring its readers that visitors would come 'for the enlightened purpose of gaining and imparting instruction and improvement,' and would be, 'as the rule, orderly, well-conducted men, given to run about and see everything that is to be seen, and not given to low debauchery.'[7]

The years that preceded the exhibition were a time of tremendous fear among the middle and upper classes of the working classes. Between the French Revolutions of 1789 and 1848, the tension in Britain between Disraeli's 'Two Nations' was, as one historian has put it, 'almost constantly at the breaking point,' and fear of social crisis or revolution was never absent from the official mind of government.[8] Even liberals such as Thomas Babington Macaulay, who supported Reform in 1832, regarded universal suffrage with 'dread and aversion' because it was 'incompatible with property, and . . . consequently incompatible with civilization.'[9] Moreover, despite the disorganized and divided nature of the Chartist movement, and its political as opposed to social or class orientation, the Charter – essentially a declaration of rights – read like a declaration of revolution.[10] On the heels of the Irish Chartist Feargus O'Connor's election to Parliament in 1847, the commercial crisis following the bad wheat and potato harvests of 1846–7, and the Paris Revolution in February 1848, the propertied classes feared for their state in April 1848. Although the government, remembering the Peterloo massacre of 1819 and the negative consequences of creating martyrs, exercised great restraint in dealing with the Chartist gathering on Kennington Common, the mob in April 1848 – estimated at around 25,000 – produced virtual middle-class hysteria.[11] This fear of the working-class mob was not without its justifications, coming as it did on the heels of more than a century of public disturbances in London and these anxieties led to ambivalent attitudes on the part of the organizers and promoters of the exhibition toward the working classes during the preparations for the Great Exhibition.[12]

Throughout the planning of the exhibition, the Royal Commission also experienced pressures from competing constituencies on the issue of how and to what extent to involve the working classes. In October 1850, soon after construction of the exhibition building began, Charles Dickens expressed to Henry Cole his belief that the commission should not wait three weeks after the opening of the exhibition before allowing the shilling visitors into the Crystal Palace, as was rumored to be the plan. At the same time, however, Granville, who had just returned from the continent, reported to Cole that 'the upper classes abroad thought we should have a revolution in '51.'[13]

The more progressive planners envisioned the exhibition as an opportunity to publicize not only the material progress of the industrial age, but the contributions of industrial workers to these advances. From the outset, Prince Albert, who for years had expressed an interest in the condition of the working classes, and who in 1844 had become President of the Society to Improve the Condition of the Working Classes, acknowledged that their involvement was critical to the success of the exhibition.[14] At his suggestion, Samuel Wilberforce, the Bishop of Oxford, delivered an important address at the first meeting of the Westminster local committee, 'On the Dignity of Labour.' Wilberforce asserted that the exhibition 'sets forth in its true light the dignity of the working classes – and it tends to make other people feel the dignity which attaches to the producers of these things.' He was confident that the many recent mechanical and industrial inventions would help 'ameliorate the condition of the lower classes of the people, and to bring within their reach advantages which had previously been restricted to the richer grades of society.'[15] Wilberforce used the exhibition to preach what has been called 'the gospel of work.'[16]

A few days after the Westminster meeting, Wilberforce received a letter from Colonel Phipps, Prince Albert's secretary, thanking him for his speech, which Albert considered '*by far the best* that was delivered upon that occasion.' Phipps wrote that Albert intended to have the speech printed for circulation among the working classes, and that he expected 'the dignity of labour' to become 'a proud and valuable watchword,' as indeed it did. Charles Knight employed Wilberforce's phrase in an article in Dickens' *Household Words*, Lady Emmeline Stuart Wortley adopted his sentiments in her popular poem 'Honour to Labour,' and the Earl of Carlisle reinforced the overall theme at the third Mansion House dinner, when he proposed his after-dinner toast to 'the working men of the United Kingdom,' who were expected to produce many of the goods on display and who would form a considerable portion of those in attendance at the exhibition.[17]

Albert also decided that a committee, which would include some working men, should be formed to promote the interests of the working classes at the exhibition and to interest them in it. Cole became the secretary of the committee, which Wilberforce agreed to join at Phipps' invitation.[18] Other prominent members of the Central Working Classes Committee (CWCC) included Charles Dickens, Arnold Thackeray, Dr Southwood Smith, Robert Chambers, and John Forster, editor of the *Daily News*. There were several Protestant clergymen, four Members of Parliament, and three former Chartists – Henry Vincent, Francis Place, and William Lovett – as well as the controversial Rev. Sidney Godolphin Osborne, known for his many letters to *The Times* under the initials 'S.G.O.'[19] Among those who declined to serve were John Bright, allegedly because of too many engagements, and Thomas Carlyle, who, while believing that the exhibition would offer 'something useful for the working people,' preferred not to serve on committees.[20] Given the elite composition of the Royal Commission, the CWCC must have appeared quite radical.

Indeed, when the CWCC asked the Royal Commission in early May to sanction its efforts to ensure working-class visits to the exhibition, it received an outright refusal. This failure reveals the extent of the fear – what William Lovett referred to afterwards as the 'aristocratic prejudice' – felt by several of the commissioners for the more radical segments of the working classes, especially those with Chartist sympathies. Reid had been worried that Prince Albert would end up being placed at the head of a 'democratic movement' with the possibility of a 'great agitation of the "working classes,"' and Lord Stanley had objected to the composition of the CWCC, particularly the inclusion of 'S.G.O.,' threatening to resign if the commission granted it official recognition.[21] Henry Cole, on the other hand, astutely noted that 'if the Chartists had not been named, the efficacy of the Committee with the Working Classes would have been greatly impaired. . . .' He concluded, 'The Working Classes may have erroneous leaders, but it must not be forgotten that they are leaders.'[22] Left with no other recourse, the CWCC dissolved itself after being in existence for barely one month. Charles Dickens, who proposed the dissolution, argued that without official recognition, the CWCC would be unable either to render efficiently the services it sought to perform or to command the confidence of the working classes.[23]

The brief life of the CWCC illuminates not just the organizational difficulties facing the commission, which included retaining control over those who were promoting the exhibition under its auspices, but, more profoundly, issues of trust. Henry Vincent, one of the members of the committee and, in Cole's words, 'a leader among the Chartists,' had by all accounts become an advocate of the exhibition, but when he reported to Cole that workers in the North were 'hanging back and suspicious,' Cole countered that wherever he had been he had not found this to be the case, and that he had had 'no difficulty in gaining their confidence and good will.' Vincent pleaded with Cole to insure that there be some committee appointed that would have the working classes as their primary concern. '[D]on't let the working classes imagine,' he added, 'that they are not worth having one.' As proof that workers would support the exhibition, Vincent reported that, when lecturing in Newbury the previous night, he had spoken for ten minutes about the exhibition to the thousand people who were there, and as a result they had resolved to form a committee for the town forthwith.[24] One reason for the organizers' rejection of Vincent may have been the difficulty of knowing whether he might also have been using the exhibition to increase Chartist support. The inclusion of Chartists in the preparations proved to be an intolerable proposition for the Royal Commission, even if that meant sacrificing certain sectors of the working classes.

Among the problems facing historians who would analyze the commission's dealings with the working classes are the many and varied uses of 'labor' and 'work' that existed at the time of the Great Exhibition. The exhibition was conceived, planned, and described as a 'Jubilee of Toil,' 'a Festival of the Workingman,' and a 'Festival of Labour.'[25] But the term 'labor' in 1851 referred as much to the work done by leaders of industry and independent artisans as to that done by an industrial proletariat; that is, it was defined broadly, meaning anyone who was not idle. This included, in addition to those who put in a day's work for a day's pay (the traditional working classes), owners of factories, for example.[26] On the Royal Commission, then, representing labor (in the 1851 meaning of the word) were John Gott, Thomas Field Gibson, Thomas Bazley, and Richard Cobden, all industrial magnates or representatives of their local industries. On the other hand, 'labor' also meant the work done by the builders who were erecting the Crystal Palace at the relatively comfortable daily wage of 3s–5s, who were well publicized as 'decently clad, honest-looking men, many of them with much intelligence in their faces,' busily at work, reassuring the nation (fig. 38).[27]

Two poems, both written in conjunction with the exhibition, illustrate how differently observers perceived workers and the relationship between the exhibition and labor. Whereas Martin Tupper wrote in his poem 'The Great Exhibition of 1851' that 'The triumph of the artisan has come about at length,/and kings and princes flock to praise his comeliness and strength,'[28] John Critchley Prince saw things quite differently in *Household Words*:

> But what to me are these inspiring changes,
> That gorgeous show, that spectacle sublime?
> My labour, leagued with poverty, estranges
> Me from this mental marvel of our time.
> I cannot share the triumph and the pageant,
> I, a poor toiler at the whirling wheel,
> The slave, not servant, of a ponderous agent,
> With bounding steam-pulse, and with arms of steel.[29]

38. Workers building the Crystal Palace. *Illustrated London News* (7 December 1850).

What these contradictory views reveal are deep fissures within Victorian society. They also speak to a very complicated social structure, especially at the lower levels. Martin Tupper's 'artisan' should not be confused with John Critchley Prince's 'poor toiler at the whirling wheel,' although these two characterizations could be as much about politics as about social description. As a result of what is called the 'linguistic turn,' some scholars now argue that the history of class is less the history of conflict between wage laborers and industrial capitalists than the history of the language people used, since words provided the essential source of both individual and collective identity.[30] The ambiguity surrounding the outreach efforts of the Royal Commission – that is, who they were attempting to reach and what they meant by 'working classes' – stems in large part from the ambiguity of the terminology about class, and all the evidence suggests that the organizers' ideas, as well as those of almost all contemporary observers, were equally blurred.

It is also important to recognize the malleability of a slogan such as 'the dignity of labor,' because not all of those who deployed it were as favorably disposed to the exhibition as Wilberforce. G. Julian Harney, a Chartist who signed many of his articles in the radical press 'L'Ami du Peuple,' dismissed the exhibits as 'plunder, wrung from the people of all lands, by their conquerors, the men of blood, privilege, and capital.'[31] In so doing, he was asserting that all the rhetoric about 'the dignity of labor' was a way of cloaking the real exploitation on display in the Crystal Palace. But even as he criticized the formulation of the exhibition, he perceived its ideal to be a worthy goal:

I can imagine a *fete* worthy of an Industrial Exhibition, in which the people at large should participate. I can imagine artists and artisans, workers from the field, and the factory, the mine, and ship summoned to take part in a Federation of Labour, – combining Industry, Art, and Science. . . . I can imagine a rich array of material wealth, which would testify to the enjoyment, as well as skill and industry of the workers, of which the profit and the glory would be theirs, untouched by useless distribution and *exploiting* capitalists. Lastly, I can imagine that such a

fete – such an Exhibition – will be only when the working classes shall first have
... substituted for the rule of masters, and royalty of a degenerated monarchy, –
'the supremacy of Labour, and the Sovereignty of the Nation'.[32]

Harney's vision demonstrates the use of a phrase alluding to 'the dignity of labor' for
developing a sense of political identity antithetical to that offered by the organizers.
It also raises the possibility that 'the dignity of labor,' like respectability, was poly-
valent, meaning that seemingly contradictory constructions of its meaning could
coexist within a single forum such as the exhibition.[33] Respectability had different
meanings for different groups in different contexts, as, for example, skilled workers
adapted middle-class ideals of respectability and independence to artisanal traditions
of collectivity and freedom.[34] Moreover, 'the coercive power of discourse' can 'be
resisted by presenting alternative definitions and appropriating key concepts.'[35] If the
scholarly literature on respectability provides any insight, it suggests that workers
may have been able to cling to Harney's construction of 'the dignity of labor,' while
flocking to the exhibition nonetheless, interpreting it in their own terms, and
adapting it to their own lives. Similarly, Henry Vincent might well have been able to
promote the exhibition to workers, even as he was using the exhibition to promote
his own Radical agenda.

Of course, there was a certain hollowness behind 'dignity of labor' discourse.
Inscribed on the prize medals given to the exhibitors was the phrase, 'Pulcher et ille
labor palma decorare laborem' (To reward labor with a palm branch is also a beautiful act), but the medals were in most cases presented not to the workers who actually produced the exhibits, but to the entrepreneurs who stood to gain the most by
their sale. Moreover, the medals were written in a language that could be read and
understood only by the educated elite. *Punch*, ever critical of the established order,
perceived that what was missing from the event was the display of the 'industrious'
at work (fig. 39).[36] But, the humorous magazine noted, 'as needlewomen cannot be
starved, nor tailors "sweated", nor miners blown up, amongst a multitude of people,
with any degree of safety, it is suggested that paintings of our various artisans labouring in their usual vocations, should accompany the display of substances and fabrics

39. Workers on display. **SPECIMENS FROM MR. PUNCH'S INDUSTRIAL EXHIBITION OF 1850.**
Punch (13 April 1851). (TO BE IMPROVED IN 1851).

which we owe to the labourers of ingenuity of respective classes.'[37] This observation implied, not too subtly, that the Great Exhibition was celebrating the labor of honest workers in order to hide the real conditions in which labor was performed within the mid-nineteenth century capitalist system.

The refusal of the Royal Commission to sanction the CWCC presented several problems. According to Granville, Albert 'felt himself somewhat committed' by having asked the Bishop of Oxford to form the committee in the first place, and thought 'it would be disadvantageous to the commission to reject the claims of the working classes.'[38] Henry Vincent provided an even more dire assessment of the implications of the failure of the CWCC when he said at its last meeting that 'the working classes regarded the exhibition as a movement to wean them from politics.'[39] Although historians should be wary of taking Vincent's comments on this issue at face value, given his political orientation and his own personal interest in serving as a mediary between the organizers and the working classes, there is no question that the organizers of the exhibition sought to inculcate in the working classes certain values, and included them in the planning only within certain official structures.

The Royal Commission's disavowal of the CWCC also left it without a means of incorporating workers in the preparations. Charles Grey emphasized that the organizers needed to find 'some new machinery' to involve the working classes in the exhibition, as they 'must not be allowed to think . . . that there is any indifference on the part of H.R.H. to their interests.' He added that there was 'no aspect of the exhibition in which Albert took a greater interest.'[40] Robert Peel, who thought that Lord Stanley had been right in refusing to sanction the committee and that it would be imprudent for the commission to retrace its steps, urged that the Royal Commission itself 'should through the local committees take the necessary steps for the protection of the working classes.'[41] This course of action was endorsed by J. A. Lloyd, who had traveled throughout the provinces and had tried to organize working-class support for the exhibition. He warned:

> So long as the co-operation of the working classes is under perfectly manageable control and thoroughly and entirely subordinate to the mayors and local committees, much *kindly* feeling will only result and nothing but good will come of it. But, a very little oversight and a very little mismanagement may cause great mischief and erect into sudden importance a vast power, which may not be reducible again to its proper limits after the exhibition shall have passed away.
>
> Hitherto I have been successful in bringing this impatience for independent action into a proper channel and subordinate to the *apparent* wishes of the mayor and authorities, and consequently within proper bounds. How long such success might last with me, is extremely problematical.[42]

To a considerable degree, this was the course that the commission and the executive committee pursued. They approached the working classes through the medium of the local committees, by sending publicity material to mechanics' institutes, by specifically targeting the workers in their descriptions of the likely benefits of the exhibition and by openly seeking their donations.

But again it should be emphasized that the royal commissioners were reaching out primarily, in Lloyd's words, to 'the most intelligent and *trustworthy* of the better class of operatives or manufacturers.'[43] They focused not on the 'ragged classes,' but on respectable, articulate, working artisans, what historians have sometimes called the labor aristocracy, or the artisan elite.[44] The placards they put up in mechanics' institutes, for example, which mentioned the contributions of the exhibition to world peace but dwelled to a far greater extent on its educational aspects – that it would provide workers 'with an unlimited supply of new ideas . . . in the most compressed, compendious, distinct, model-defined and ocular form' – were clearly oriented towards skilled artisans, inventors, entrepreneurs, and manufacturers with small workshops.[45] And in Southampton, when the first subscription list was made public, it listed separately a number of donations – from clerks, draftsmen, workmen, and servants – to illustrate the 'co-operation of [the] working classes.'[46] Obviously these occupations reflect only one segment of those who would have been considered workers.

Nevertheless, some of the local committees went to great lengths to involve workers in their preparations. At a meeting in Aberdeen, those present resolved that a committee of twelve, to be named by the workers in attendance, would be added to the local committee. In Bolton, the local committee created a separate subscription fund called 'The Operative Fund,' to assist artisans in perfecting items for display at the exhibition. And in Leeds the local committee issued an address to the foremen of the mills, requesting that they do their utmost to interest their workers. One result was that John Gott's employees subscribed more than £78, one of many instances in which workers contributed to the Great Exhibition fund.[47] It would be inaccurate, however, to suggest that workers supported the exhibition only because the executive committee and the many local committees convinced them to do so. Sections of the working classes were encouraged to support and attend the exhibition in spite of the organizers' fears, but many others did so of their own accord.[48] The workmen of the Carriage and Harness Manufactory in Derby, for example, 'without solicitation,' reported *The Times* glowingly, subscribed slightly more than £5 to the Derby exhibition fund.[49]

The Industrial Revolution was a gradual process that was by no means complete by 1851, and had produced neither a self-conscious working class nor a homogeneous bourgeoisie by that time.[50] The dominance of handicrafts in the British economy until at least the late nineteenth century was certainly apparent at the Great Exhibition. The very panes of glass used for the Crystal Palace, all 300,000 of them, were blown by hand, and most of the goods on display were the products not of machines, but of craftsmen.[51] Because of the prevalence of artisanal as opposed to large mechanized factory production at the time of the exhibition, it was not uncommon to find a 'community of interest of masters and workers,' as each invested skills – labor, working capital, organizational ability – in a shared enterprise that on many occasions linked them together against aristocrats, merchant capitalists, and financiers. It is important not to view workers' and employers' interests as inherently and inevitably antithetical and oppositional, because they were frequently cooperative and coterminous.[52] For employers and workers alike, the Great Exhibition offered the promise of a more democratic society as well as the knowledge by which to improve and expand production.

Certain arrangements concerning the working classes, however, were not devolved to the local committees. While the Royal Commission and the executive committee seemed comfortable ceding to the local committees responsibility for generating support (both financial and otherwise), this was not the case with preparing for the influx of workers from the North into London during the exhibition. It made perfect sense, of course, not to have the provincial local committees making decisions that would affect the metropolis, but this would be too superficial an explanation for why the executive committee retained responsibility for certain aspects of the preparations and not for others. The fact remains that, with memories of Chartism and the Revolutions of 1848 still very much on people's minds, security was a serious and touchy issue. The Royal Commission asked Alexander Redgrave of the Home Office to join Colonel William Reid, chairman of the executive committee, in examining issues relating to the conveyance of the working classes to London, as well as problems that might arise from the influx of working-class visitors from the provinces into London.

Redgrave looked into three issues regarding working-class attendance at the exhibition: inexpensive and convenient transportation to London; 'respectable and reasonable' lodgings while in London; and access to public sights. According to the memorandum he submitted at the end of July, his objective was 'that such arrangements should in themselves conduce to the maintenance of good order and regularity *without the appearance of any ostensible precautions*, and that they should offer such facilities as will induce the working classes to follow, for their own advantage, the course pointed out.'[53] Redgrave was hardly alone in expressing such sentiments. Richard Askrill, author of *The Yorkshire Visitors' Guide to the Great Exhibition* (1851), a twopenny publication directed at the working classes, warned that 'While in London the working classes should not fritter away their time and money in seeing panoramas and shows, and paltry theatres.'[54] Just as certain liberal, reformist, anti-establishment Whigs whose genuine idealism concealed more paternalistic purposes believed, for example, that the British Museum and Westminster Abbey were 'valuable cultural resources' which the government should manage with a view towards social and moral improvement of the working classes, Redgrave and many on the commission saw the exhibition in a similar manner.[55]

Redgrave's report, which he submitted in December 1850, suggested that the Royal Commission should sanction activities for the working classes, provide them with ample means of participating in 'intellectual amusements,' and assist them in 'putting their holiday to good account.' Redgrave anticipated that, while it was the exhibition which would draw working people to London, it would not be the only attraction they would see there. It was in the commission's best interest, then, to offer artisans facilities for gratifying their 'curiosities' that would lessen the likelihood of them being 'led into some of the hundred amusements which will tempt the stranger in London, calculated to excite rather than improve, to debase instead of elevate.' Toward this end, Redgrave recommended that the Royal Commission approach the directors of the British Museum, the National Gallery, the East India Company, Sir John Soane's Museum, Kew Gardens, and the Board of Ordinance for the Tower of London, about opening hours and whether admission fees might be reduced upon production of a railway excursion ticket, all in the interest of providing rational recreation for the working classes.[56]

Although Redgrave convinced the commission 'that it would be unnecessary and undesirable that they should interfere with the natural course of private arrangements,' its involvement in planning for the influx of the working classes into London was in fact rather more ambiguous. Through the executive committee, the commission communicated with the railway companies about reducing fares for those attending the exhibition, contacted the police and museum directors about visiting hours and admission prices for working-class excursionists, and organized a registry for the listing of lodgings.[57] Here, as in so many other instances concerning the exhibition, the official rhetoric was of letting private enterprise and entrepreneurship provide whatever was needed; the reality, as we shall see, was at least in part state planning and involvement.

EXCURSION TRAVEL

One of the most remarkable features of the Great Exhibition was the number of people who attended. There were more than six million paid entrances to the Crystal Palace during the exhibition which, allowing for foreign and repeat visits, may have represented as much as one-fifth of the population of Britain.[58] Almost all of those who did not live in London traveled there via the railways, and this massive movement of people marked the beginning of a revolution in leisure. That so many Britons journeyed to London, and that so many found lodgings while they were there, is a tribute to the organizational efforts of the executive and local committees. But it would be wrong to suggest that their goal was simply to bring as many people as possible to London to see the exhibition. The organizers permitted and emphasized localism and individual initiative, but always within certain general confines. The exhibition's success depended in large part on the number of people who went, but a wariness of workers and crowds and foreigners was always present in the organizers' decisions. Nor were they alone in their fears: The railway directors and the owners of lodging houses were just as skittish about the potential unrest of working-class mobs.

The process of getting to London, at least for many of the working and middle classes who lived outside of the metropolitan area, began with local subscription clubs. These were usually created by the local committees, though private companies and civic organizations also participated. Those wishing to attend the exhibition would join the subscription club nearest to where they lived, and subscribe a small, fixed amount per week, sometimes for up to a year, in order to save enough to make the journey. The money was most commonly invested by the club officers in a local savings bank, together with any donations that wealthier members of the community might have offered. In Liverpool, for example, subscriptions of at least one shilling had to be paid weekly, for a minimum of three months, at either the Savings Bank or one of five District Provident Societies, beginning in January 1851. The club needed a minimum of 250 people, to whom the organizers promised a fare of not more than 15s 6d for a seven- or fourteen-day trip to begin some time after the price of admission to the exhibition was reduced to one shilling. The club emphasized that it was enrolling members of 'both sexes.' The officers would then negotiate with the local railway or steamship company for a reduced fare for the group and purchase the tickets. A club might also organize accommodation in London, or at least provide information about where and how to find lodgings; some provided excursionists with spending money as well.[59]

Prominent among those arranging excursions to the Great Exhibition were working men's associations and mechanics' institutes. The membership of these sorts

of organizations suggests that those who took advantage of the subscription associations created for the exhibition were predominantly respectable, regularly employed
workers and skilled artisans. Through savings banks and friendly societies, many of
them had already acquired the idea of regular saving on a small scale.[60] Although there
is a seemingly endless debate among historians over how the Industrial Revolution
affected living standards, it is clear that by 1851 many skilled workers were able to
afford the excursion to London, especially as fares during the summer fell to as low
as 5s–10s from the northern manufacturing towns.[61]

The local subscription clubs were of critical importance in helping to ensure the
success of the Great Exhibition. Although many working men and women were
familiar with, even if not yet accustomed to, day-excursions by rail in 1851, this was
emphatically not the case with lengthy journeys across the country, sometimes lasting
two full days. Such a prospect must have been more than a little forbidding. John
Tod, a Lasswade engineer, traveled by train for almost twenty-four hours with his
family to see the exhibition. He wrote, as they approached the Scotland/England
border around midnight: 'We are driving like a swallow, over real English soil and
breathing pure English air, but thought, where is that noisy steam friend taking me.
I am shot through the air with something like the speed of a cannon bullet into a
country of which I had seen nothing and knew almost as little, and it is in the dead
of night.'[62] The subscription clubs helped overcome these fears by providing information about the journey, lodgings, and meals, and by making many of the necessary arrangements.

For those who did not join subscription clubs there were railway agents, who
arranged special package deals for would-be excursionists. Thomas Cook was the
most famous of these, and he and his son traveled indefatigably through the towns
of Yorkshire and the Midlands, publicizing his excursions in conjunction with the
Midland Railway. One of his most successful tactics was to engage bands to play
outside mills and factories on Saturday nights to attract the attention of recently paid
workers, to whom Cook would then sell tickets. He also arranged lodgings.[63] In all
likelihood Cook was inspired not only by a desire to make money, but also by
Albert's idealism. He told his prospective excursionists that they should regard the
exhibition 'not as a show or a place of amusement, but [as] a great school of science,
of art, of industry, of peace and universal brotherhood.'[64] The exhibition may also
have appealed to Cook, a former Baptist preacher who believed fervently in temper-
ance, at least in part because all intoxicating liquors were banned from the Crystal
Palace.[65] By the time the exhibition closed, he had been responsible for sending
165,000 people to London on the Midland Railway, or some 3 percent of the total
who went to the exhibition.[66]

Although most of the arrangements, and all of the collection of money, were
handled locally, the executive committee was substantially involved in the campaign
to bring the working classes to London by rail. In mid-September 1850, Colonel Reid
met with the directors of the major railway companies to discuss at what fares they
could convey the working classes to London, as well as 'how the artisans should be
brought up, so as to maintain good order in the Capital.'[67] During the next few
months, the railway directors decided with the executive committee to convey only
those people who had subscribed to clubs, once again revealing the presence of grave
concerns about the possibility of radical activity emanating from large, unregulated
working-class groups.[68] The agreement was intended to stimulate the formation of

subscription clubs, by implying that only members would be able to enjoy reduced fares. In return for these reductions, the railway companies would gain the advantage of knowing how many passengers to expect. It was also a means of exercising control over the working classes, by forcing them into organizations that could be regulated and monitored. It was not until February 1851 that a joint committee of the London & North Western Railway and the Midland Railway agreed that passengers not in clubs would be eligible for the reduced fares, but little was done to publicize this decision, and none of the other major companies seems to have followed suit, or even to have given much consideration to the issue.[69]

Much of the reluctance on the part of the railway companies to make concessions to the organizers of the Great Exhibition was due to the fact that the directors vastly underestimated the number of people likely to travel to London to see it. Despite the increase in regularly scheduled third-class and excursion traffic during the 1840s, the railway companies did not anticipate the large number of people from the working and middle classes who were prepared to travel to London to visit an industrial exhibition.[70] *Herepath's Railway and Commercial Journal* was among those that urged caution in expanding or purchasing new stock to meet the anticipated demand to get to the Great Exhibition.[71]

If during the month of May the railways had little impact on the exhibition (and vice versa), with most of the passengers coming from the middle and upper classes, once the Crystal Palace was opened up to the shilling visitors after 26 May, business began to boom.[72] The heaviest traffic and the stiffest competition was in Yorkshire and the manufacturing districts, and fares on most lines plummeted.[73] Although it is difficult to assess just how many people traveled to London on excursion trains to see the Great Exhibition in 1851, various estimates put the figure at somewhere between 750,000 and 1,000,000, which constituted, in the words of one historian, 'the largest movement of population ever to have taken place in Britain.'[74] So extraordinary was the mass exodus of people from the industrial North that George Cruikshank sketched its consequences for both Manchester and London in Henry Mayhew's *1851; or, The Adventures of Mr. and Mrs. Sandboys . . .* (figs. 40 and 41). In the case of the former, the streets are deserted, with shops closed and signs reading,

40. George Cruikshank, 'Manchester in 1851'.   41. George Cruikshank, 'London in 1851'.

Map 3. The railway network in 1852.

'Gone for the summer.' In the case of London, the impact of the influx of visitors is equally obvious.

Without the railways, people from outside London could not possibly have visited the Great Exhibition in the large numbers that they did. Maps 1 and 3 illustrate the extent of the railway network in Britain in 1840 and in 1852, suggesting that the Great Exhibition was in fact the first event that was able to attract people from all over the nation. They demonstrate the increasing geographic integration of Britain during the decade preceding the exhibition, and the saturation of the industrial Midlands around Birmingham, Derby, and Manchester. There is also a high correlation between the areas served by the railways and the locations of the local committees (see Map 2). The joint absence of railways lines and local committees is especially apparent in Scotland (except in the area between Glasgow, Edinburgh, Perth, and Dundee), Wales (except for the south coast between Cardiff and Swansea), and Northumberland.

There is no question that the Great Exhibition and the railways benefitted each other in a symbiotic relationship, and in ways much more significant than merely short-term profits or increases in passenger traffic.[75] Although railway excursions had been organized as early as the 1830s, the Great Exhibition transformed the excursion from 'a thrilling novelty into an established part of Victorian life.'[76] It was the catalyst of a revolution in how people spent their leisure time.[77] The Great Exhibition also raised the standing of the railways in people's minds, and proved, despite much controversy over passengers and fares, most of which was hidden from the public, that the railway system could function as a working unit.[78] There is also no denying that the fortunes of the Great Exhibition rested on the railways, and that it succeeded and made such an impression because of them. Without them, it has been said, the project would have been 'inconceivable.'[79]

* * *

LODGINGS

Providing lodgings was another of those areas where the Royal Commission sought to strike a balance between central planning and a more laissez-faire approach. Underlying the organizers' discussions were, once again, outright fear of the masses that were expected to pour into London during the summer of 1851, fear that was tempered by either a desire among some to ensure the visitors' moral well-being, or by unabashed commercial greed.

In early 1851, the Royal Commission decided after months of inquiries that it would be best to leave the matter of lodgings to the exertions of the visitors themselves, since any action on the part of the organizers would 'interfere with [the] many praiseworthy undertakings of private individuals.'[80] Ironically, this decision followed on the heels of the report presented by Alexander Redgrave five weeks earlier, in which he had determined that it would be 'necessary to take a more decided step in regard to "accommodation for the working classes visiting the exhibition."' He had discovered that only a few people had set up large working-class lodgings because the scheme was so speculative, and proposed an alternative plan of registering prospective lodgers near the railway termini, and having guides at stations to assist the working classes when they arrived and accompany them to vacant lodgings.[81]

In the interim, what had taken place was that two registers of accommodation had been created. The first of these was organized by Matthew Digby Wyatt, who proposed that the executive committee collect listings free of charge from people 'of good character,' who had to permit authorized inspection of the lodgings for rent. Accommodation for married couples and families, single men, and single women were all to be kept separate, and 'in no case' could single men and single women be housed at the same premises. Moreover, in the case of women's lodgings, the superintendent had to be a married woman.[82] All the evidence suggests, however, that few landlords made use of this service.

The other major listing service was organized by the publisher John Cassell, who was genuinely committed to the welfare of the working classes, though he also exploited the exhibition to the fullest. Cassell's first concern was about solving a social problem, though if he turned a profit and publicized his *Working Man's Friend*, so much the better. He realized early on that the working classes would take a lively interest in the exhibition, and hailed the event as a movement that could benefit them. He wrote in the *Working Man's Friend*, a publication read in many factories:

> Here, instead of *monarchs*, we shall have *artisans* commanding the wonder of the world. It will be the triumph of industry, and the coronation of labour. It will be seen that mechanics and labourers hold the sceptre over the material world, and that they have swayed it to bless their species. . . . It has been customary for the masses to do homage to the rich and the titled; but England, in 1851, shall introduce on the stage a new drama, in which princes and nobles shall do honour to the sons and daughters of toil, and thus at length pay a debt which has been accumulating for ages.[83]

Cassell canvassed his friends in the House of Commons, secured fifteen patrons there including one of the Royal Commissioners, and then announced the preparation of an artisan lodging-house register. He printed 100,000 forms for distribution to London housekeepers; took an office on Catherine Street, just off the Strand near

Covent Garden; and hired a registrar and staff to send out canvassers, process appli-cations, and digest the reports of the district inspectors who would ensure the respectability of the houses. The cost of registration of any lodging was 2s 6d, of which 1s 6d had to be paid to the Board of Inland Revenue as advertisement duty. All the rooms for rent were offered under a uniform tariff of charges: 1s 3d for a single bed per night, including boot cleaning; 2s for a double bed and boot cleaning; 9d for a breakfast of tea or coffee and bread and butter, or 1s for a breakfast that included meat. Armed with this information, Cassell published a 'general register' of houses and apartments, as well as a 'classified catalogue' of places belonging to indi-viduals connected with religious communities. The register was sent out upon receipt of six penny-postage stamps.[84]

John Cassell also published exhibition-related reading material for the working classes. For those who could neither visit London nor afford the *Illustrated London News* at 6d per week, Cassell planned a cheap but 'monumental' record of the occa-sion. *The Illustrated Exhibitor, a Tribute to the World's Industrial Exhibition* was designed to fill four volumes, but was published weekly at 2d a part, or monthly at 8d. Cassell's outlay seems to have been considerable, but the inaugural issue sold out in a day and had to be reprinted. By the end of the first month he was claiming sales of 100,000 copies.[85] Richard Cobden, for one, applauded his good friend's efforts to publicize the exhibition among the working classes, and felt sure that the executive committee would provide him with any information he needed.[86] Clearly there was money to be made from the working classes at the exhibition, for those who were able to overcome their fears or feelings of condescension toward them.

There was, then, no formal, comprehensive plan to provide lodgings for the working classes in London, just as there had been no centralized scheme to get them to London. Instead, the commissioners tried to stimulate private enterprise, though within some general parameters they had established.[87] Certainly the most notable speculative venture was the '"monster" establishment for the reception of the working classes' designed by Thomas Harrison of Renalgh Road, Pimlico, near the Pimlico pier where steamboats arrived from the city every ten minutes. His boarding house occupied two acres, could accommodate 1,000 people per night in private cubicles, and offered all sorts of amenities for about 1s 6d. Care was also pro-vided for those who 'in the joyousness of their hearts, and their unaccustomed liberty,' drank too much.[88] But, for all the publicity that Harrison's boarding house received,[89] the building was rarely more than one-quarter full, and in October, just after the exhibition closed, Harrison appealed to Prince Albert for compensation because he was 'ruined.' Harrison had originally used his building as a depository for furniture and merchandise, and had asked Owen Jones to recommend to exhibitors that they use his warehouse for their empty boxes during the exhibition, a plan that would have involved no outlay on his part. Jones had replied that what the executive committee really needed was a place with sleeping accommodation that was well ven-tilated and close to Hyde Park. Harrison, having in his own words 'a very high opinion of the great undertaking,' and wanting to do his part to further the cause, converted his warehouse into a lodging house, getting contractors to work on credit with the promise that he would pay the workmen from his receipts after the exhibi-tion. The result, he wrote, was 'disappointment and ruin.'[90] Not surprisingly, the finance committee denied his request for protection from creditors, and refused to provide him with any remuneration.[91]

In all likelihood most people found places to stay through less organized means. One such person was Josiah Chater, a young Cambridge bookkeeper and accountant who later became one of the founders of the Cambridge Young Men's Christian Association (YMCA). In his quest for lodgings Chater let his fiancée and her sister stay with friends, while he went to a large 'working man's home' which could accommodate 200 men in ships' bunks. It was not to his liking, however, and there were no private rooms available. After walking around London for a while longer, Chater and his brother decided to stay at the home of someone they had met on the street, a ship broker, for a few shillings a night.[92] Others benefitted from their employers: Lord Willoughby D'Eresby rented a house in London in order to accommodate the tenants on his estate who might want to visit the exhibition.[93]

Some never found lodgings at all. The *Illustrated London News* reported the story of one man from Peterborough who traveled to London intending to spend the night, but seemed not to know how to search for lodgings, so he returned home, some eighty miles away, arriving about midnight. Since he had not completed his tour of the exhibition, he simply returned to London the following day in order to do so.[94] Others had to make do with lodgings that were well below their standards. George Cruikshank parodied this occurrence – or perhaps excursionists' worries that such a thing might occur – in his sketch, 'Looking for Lodgings,' part of Henry Mayhew's *1851; or, The Adventures of Mr. and Mrs. Sandboys...* (fig. 42). The illustration depicts a respectably dressed middle-class family descending into a dimly lit cellar which contains only one bed, a hammock hanging from the ceiling. 'This is all I have,' says the housekeeper, having let all her other rooms.[95]

Driving the mad rush to provide lodgings before the opening of the exhibition was not just the lure of profits, but continuing middle-class fear of the masses. Clergymen in particular took a 'zealous' interest in the 'health' and 'morals' of the working classes.[96] Their concern was that people who did not find housing would become squatters and vagrants, dirtying the city, spreading disease, and committing crimes. The *Journal of the Exhibition* reported in November 1850 that many housekeepers were beginning to frame rules and regulations for the working classes. One housekeeper required lodgers to pay a week in advance; not to be in the bedrooms past 10 a.m. or before 9 p.m. except in case of illness; and not to deface the walls. Liquor, gambling, card playing, quarreling, and profane or abusive language were all

42. George Cruikshank, 'Looking for lodgings'.

prohibited, and tenants had to observe habits of cleanliness.[97] But inside the Crystal Palace, as well as outside, although people feared the worst, nothing but order prevailed. For all the planning, both private and on the part of the executive committee, in the end voluntarism on an individual basis provided for everyone.

ADMISSION PRICES

Fears of the working classes were especially obvious in the deliberations over how to structure the price of tickets for admission to the Great Exhibition. As John Tallis succinctly put it at the time, no doubt with considerable understatement, admission prices were fixed with 'a good deal of discussion.'[98] The Royal Commission again faced pressure from many different quarters, and was itself probably divided. Both Dickens and Macaulay favored letting in the shilling visitors as soon as possible, even on the opening day, but Francis Fuller reported to Granville a 'growing feeling in the minds of the gentry, bankers, merchants and first class tradesmen that without some security in the shape of high prices of admission on certain days the crowds will be so tremendous as to render the discomfort – if not the danger – extremely great. The ladies also are unanimous on this point.'[99] Most of those consulted by the commission or the executive committee proposed a multi-tiered structuring of admission fees starting at one shilling.

Joseph Paxton threw the discussion over admission prices into disarray when, on 23 January 1851, timed perfectly to coincide with the commission's meeting on this very subject, he proposed in an open letter to Lord John Russell in *The Times* that there be free admission. He argued that it would be more 'practicable . . . and more in harmony with the enlarged and enlightened purpose of the exhibition,' and suggested that admission be charged for the first two weeks, and that one day a week after that (Wednesdays) 'be reserved for the higher classes . . . who may prefer to pay for the exclusive privilege of admission, rather than encounter the inconvenience of a crowd.' He advocated making up the deficit with a Parliamentary grant, which he thought would be a small price to pay given that, in his estimation, the exhibition would produce some £2 million in revenue for the nation.[100]

The editor of *The Times*, however, no doubt knowing that a suggestion such as this from a folk hero like Paxton would greatly embarrass the Royal Commissioners, informed the commission of Paxton's letter before publishing it. Granville retorted to Gray, 'Paxton's head has been turned by the events of the last six months, and it is not surprising that they should have had that effect upon a self-educated man.' If ever proof was needed of the limits of social mobility in mid-Victorian England, Granville's deprecating comment should provide it. With time of the essence, Granville and the editor of *The Times* arranged matters so that the edition containing Paxton's letter also included an editorial calling it impractical, and potentially too dangerous, to provide free admission.[101]

This was a debate, then, between two very different visions of the exhibition, the nation, and the nature and purpose of government. Paxton, eager to include the working-classes, saw the admission fee as a tax on knowledge, affecting those who wished to partake of the 'beneficial influence' of the exhibition. To charge people would diminish what he saw as the 'liberal' and 'cosmopolitan spirit' of the exhibition. He wanted the exhibition free for the workers whose industry he thought it was intended to celebrate, and believed it proper for the government to encourage their inclusion. *The Times* and at least some members of the Royal Commission, on the other hand, were unable to overcome their memories of Peterloo and Kennington Common and their fears of the mob. Not only were they not as willing as Paxton to include the working classes in their vision of the nation, they held a very different conception of government as well. *The Times* argued that a Parliamentary grant would in effect be a tax on everyone, including those who would never see the exhibition (and hence not as fair as taxing only those who attended the exhibition). For *The Times* and the Royal Commission, the purpose of government was emphatically not to subsidize the poor, at least not without certain limits.

Paxton's proposal came under blistering attack in *The Times* and elsewhere. One author opposed his plan not out of 'fears . . . for the conduct of any who entered the building' – though many others opposed his plan on these very grounds – but because it would have made the exhibition dependent on government funding rather than self-supporting, and hence 'contrary to British habits of public action.'[102] A 'local commissioner' complained that no suggestion was so likely 'to defeat the great ends of the exhibition' and 'degrade it to the level of a gratuitous show,' because under a system of free admission people would go to the Crystal Palace 'with no other object than to pass the day or gape away a vacant hour,' and they would obstruct the many who would go to observe and gain instruction, 'the very object of the exhibition.'[103]

When the commission met, it decided to issue season tickets at £3 3s 'for a gentleman,' and £2 2s 'for a lady.' Only those with season tickets would be permitted inside the Crystal Palace on opening day. On the second and third days the fee was to be £1. On the fourth day the charge was to drop to 5s, where it would remain until 26 May, when the admission price would be 1s from Monday to Thursday, 2s 6d on Fridays, and 5s on Saturdays. The commission also agreed that children under the age of thirteen should be admitted at half price.[104] It was, perhaps, an imperfect solution, but one designed to meet the needs and ameliorate the fears of most Britons.

During the course of the exhibition, the commission twice reduced the price of tickets: On 31 July the prices of a season ticket fell to £1 10s and £1 for men and women respectively, and on 9 August the price of admission on Saturday was reduced to 2s 6d. Surprisingly, given its earlier resistance to making the exhibition more accessible to workers, *The Times* supported this reduction, arguing, 'The exhibition will hardly have fulfilled its objects if the labouring classes do not appear there in larger proportions than is at present the case.'[105] But, the paper added, hedging, there were some difficulties in reducing admission prices, stemming from the increasing popularity of the exhibition 'among the middle and upper classes,' the implication being that, as long as these 'higher' classes were still attending the exhibition in large numbers, it was inadvisable to allow in many more working class visitors. As *The Times* flatly asserted a few days after the reduction, it was simply not practical for the commissioners to admit 'a larger proportion of the humbler classes.'[106] Snobbery, class disdain, and fears of a working-class mob did not die easily.

Letters expressing fear and opposition to the pricing plan deluged the commission throughout the spring, even after the opening of the exhibition. One London resident, whose views were not at all atypical, estimated that there would be two million visitors, and that the capacity of the building was only 50,000. Assuming that it would take six days to see the exhibition in its entirety, and given the number of days the exhibition was scheduled to remain open, the building would have to hold twice as many people as it was capable of. He concluded, 'the assemblage would become a *crowd*,' and said that the object of the commission should be 'to ensure the maximum of receipts and the *minimum of visitors*.'[107] Other London residents wrote in fearing outright conspiracy. A man named Thomas who lived on the Strand and had published a few issues of a periodical called the *Protestant*, was convinced that the Catholic Church was planning a 'political movement' which sought 'to establish political power under the guise of a demand for extended religious toleration.' Thomas was concerned for the safety of the building, and for the people and exhibits inside it. He was adamant that there should be no free admissions, and urged that the commissioners construct a railing around the Crystal Palace to protect 'so fragile a structure.' He also thought that there should be separate days for the admission of Britons and non-Britons.[108]

Other London residents expressed more carefully thought-out reasons for modifying the admission prices one way or the other. A group of 120 Westminster tradesmen, mostly from Regent Street and Bond Street, presented their local committee with a petition asking that the beginning of the shilling days be delayed until 1 July, except for Whitsuntide (the week beginning 8 June). While they said that they wanted all classes and people of all nations to attend the Great Exhibition, they could not 'shut their eyes to the very great influx of the operative classes' who were likely to come to London to see the exhibition, 'and the consequent likelihood of the higher orders quitting it,' which they believed would have dire commercial consequences because May and June were their two most profitable months. Anything shortening 'the season' would be 'injurious . . . and ruinous' to many local businessmen.[109]

The commission also heard from those complaining that the price of admission was too high but, not surprisingly, in much smaller numbers. 'A clerk' wrote to *The Times*, 'mortified' to find that the Saturday price was five shillings, because many of the London clerks and warehouse workers labored a half-day on Saturday, making it the only day during the week when they could visit the exhibition without losing work. Paying five shillings for a ticket was well beyond their reach.[110]

The Royal Commission had decided that one shilling was the sum that would allow the respectable artisan into the exhibition, and keep the riffraff out. To put this in perspective, skilled laborers at the Crystal Palace were paid on average 28s a week.[111] The shilling barrier – and the commissioners' behavior overall – suggests that they saw the divisions within society as between those who were 'respectable' and those who were not.[112] But it is also important to appreciate that in all likelihood the commissioners had little idea of just who they were including and who they were excluding when they fixed the price of admission at one shilling.[113] The admission fee was not the result of any precise social analysis, but in all likelihood a guess based on a number of assumptions about the make-up of society. It was, to borrow a phrase from the passage of the Reform Bill of 1867, a leap in the dark.

✻   ✻   ✻

THE SHILLING DAYS

When the Crystal Palace was opened to the masses on 26 May, the first of the shilling days, London was in a state of armed readiness. As the American William Drew, on holiday in England, observed, 'A well clad army of police is stationed all over the city.... You cannot go ten rods without finding a policeman.'[114] As far back as November 1850, the executive committee had begun organizing the police force for the exhibition. The Police Commissioner, Richard Mayne, had filed a report calling for an extra 1,000 officers, and the Duke of Wellington expressed to Granville his belief that 15,000 men would be required.[115] The executive committee discussed swearing in the sappers (the military engineers) as special constables, but Reid advised against it because they were seen as too militaristic; he wanted them to support, rather than be a part of, the police force. He suggested instead that the commission consider appointing as special constables the attendants caring for the exhibits, given that they already had an interest in the safety of the property in the building and in the maintenance of order. Reid also thought that the Police Commissioner's estimate of the number of policemen required was greatly exaggerated, and that any disturbances would take place not at the exhibition, but at other meeting places. Rather than sending a large police force to the Crystal Palace, Reid wanted to hold them in reserve, ready to be distributed wherever they were needed.[116]

As 26 May drew nearer, the metropolitan police force recommended closing the doors of the Crystal Palace when the number of people inside reached 50,000, and suggested that all visitors follow a certain path to keep people moving and reduce confusion.[117] Both of these recommendations were ignored, but Police Commissioner Mayne nevertheless had over 600 policemen in the building on the first two-shilling days, including some from the Belgian police force; the average number of police on duty in the Crystal Palace throughout the exhibition ranged from 300 to 400. Mayne had also installed a signal on the roof of the Crystal Palace to alert the police stationed at the park gates when the building was full so that they could restrict access to the park.[118]

For all the wonders of the Great Exhibition, what astonished and impressed observers most at the time was how little trouble there was. According to *Fraser's Magazine*, people feared that 'London was to be overrun, sacked, and pillaged.' The reality, according to the magazine after the close of the exhibition, was quite different: 'No circumstance connected with the "getting up" and management of the affair is more remarkable than the conduct of the people.'[119] All the fears of a working-class mob went unrealized. *The Times* reported on 27 May, that 'to the amazement of almost everyone' the Crystal Palace was not nearly as crowded as people had expected – or feared.[120] Macaulay was surprised as well: 'Today the exhibition opens at a shilling. It seems to be the fate of this extraordinary show to confound all predictions, favourable and unfavourable. Fewer people went on the shilling day than on the five-shilling day.'[121] In fact, there were fewer people in the Crystal Palace on Monday, 26 May, than on any previous day. 'The multitude seems to have been afraid of one another,' reported the *Economist*, 'and comparatively very few went.' There were slightly more people at the exhibition the next day, but they were no less decorous. The numbers increased during the course of the week; ironically, on Friday, when the price of admission increased, there were 55,000 people in attendance, the most of any day that week.[122] Clearly Britons had stayed away out of fear, trickling back to the exhibition only as their fears proved unfounded. It may also have been that they chose to stay away in the interest of self-image, preferring to see themselves as respectable five-shilling visitors rather than as the disreputable shilling visitors envisaged by the press. The *Economist* concluded: 'At the close of the first week of shilling days, we can say that no more orderly people ever existed than the multitude of London.'[123] The Royal Commission itself thought that everything had proceeded splendidly, and Alexander Redgrave, who had been so apprehensive before the exhibition, wrote that the visits of the working classes were 'most gratifying.'[124]

Although Britons may have stayed away from the Great Exhibition during the first few shilling days, they poured into the Crystal Palace during the summer of 1851, surpassing all estimates.[125] According to the Registrar-General, the movement of some four million people was 'a greater and more general movement of population than has ever before been witnessed, in the times of which there are authentic records.'[126] In general, the number of people in the building on the shilling days ranged from 45,000 to 60,000; from 18,000 to 30,000 on Fridays; and around 6,000 on Saturdays, in addition to a steady flow of 2,000–4,000 season ticket holders per day after 1 July.[127] The greatest number of people on a single day was 109,915 on Tuesday, 7 October; the most in the building at any given time was 92,000, on the same day. It is important to remember, as *The Times* did at the time, that these extraordinary figures illustrate popular movements that only a few years earlier 'would have been pronounced on the highest authority most dangerous to the safety of the state.'[128] By the end of the summer, when more than 100,000 people per day flocked to the Crystal Palace, the building had truly become, in the words of its architect Joseph Paxton, 'The People's Palace.'[129]

The only event that even approached becoming an incident occurred on 7 October, when the Duke of Wellington arrived and was quickly recognized and cheered by the crowds. Those in attendance who could not see the Duke heard the rumble, became alarmed, and cried out that the building was collapsing. The crowd began to panic, there was a huge rush for the doors, and it was all the police could do to carry the Duke to safety.[130]

Admissions were low during May and early June for a variety of reasons: the relatively high price of tickets (at least until 26 May); the need to wait until the excursion trains began (originally they were not scheduled to begin until 1 July); and references in newspapers to the ongoing arrival of new exhibits, which may have created the impression that the exhibition was not yet complete and that visitors might be better off waiting. But by mid-June Britons from all over were arriving in London to see the exhibition. Many writers told the story of an elderly woman, variously described as being either eighty-four or one hundred years old, who made the trip from Penzance, in Cornwall (fig. 43).[131] Whereas in early May the *Journal of the Exhibition* reported that 'As yet the influx of visitors into London is small,' by the end of the summer the sidewalks along Piccadilly and from Hyde Park Corner up Sloane Street to Knightsbridge were 'swarming with dense black columns of pedestrians, all wending their way to the Crystal Palace.'[132]

Was the Great Exhibition affordable to the working classes? The attendance figures for the exhibition suggest that it was, but the record is somewhat ambiguous. The press made great use of public-interest stories, and gave much publicity to workers who took the night trains from Yorkshire, spent the day at the exhibition, and returned home that night, ready for work the following morning, thus losing only a

43. Mary Callinack from Penzance. *Illustrated London News* (25 October 1851).

day's wages. Special admiration went to those who took sandwiches and spent nothing beyond the shilling for admission.[133] These stories created the impression of workers with little free time, and even less spending money, able to manage only a brief and frugal visit to London, unable to afford accommodation, and often unable to bring their families. But this would be an incomplete picture, because there is considerable evidence that many people did stay in London and make more than one visit to the exhibition.[134]

An illustration from the *Illustrated London News* (fig. 44) provides some evidence

44. Agricultural workers at the Great Exhibition. *Illustrated London News* (19 July 1851).

that the working poor attended the exhibition, although these agricultural laborers are depicted as well behaved, and are clearly not of the 'riffraff' or the 'dangerous classes;' agricultural workers were generally regarded as more deferential than urban laborers.[135] More than one paper reported on the number of watches being pawned so that workers could scrape together the money they needed to attend the exhibition.[136] But given that by far the greatest cost was rail travel to London, the shilling fee would seem negligible. On the other hand, *Punch* parodied the frantic saving that no doubt took place, in its fictional account of a young worker who said, in mid-October 1851: 'Lor! – Ex'bition closed; and I within three halfpence of the shilling! – Blow it!'[137] In mid-August *The Times* reported not for the first time on the small number of working-class visitors who had attended. The paper inferred that, since there was no reason to believe that the exhibition was unpopular among the working classes, the price of admission must not 'lie well and easily within their means.'[138] And Richard Cobden was surprised when, on the Saturday before the exhibition closed with the price of admission at 2s 6d, the crowd was not as large as on the shilling days. 'It is curious to see,' wrote Cobden to his friend Julie Salis-Schwabe, 'how eighteen pence will prove an obstacle to people, even when they are stimulated by the greatest desire to see a place, which must be closed for ever in a few hours.'[139] Even the Tory-leaning *Times* perceived in late September 'a strong leaning towards respectability, or we should rather say selectiveness,' in the prices of admission.[140] Maybe, then, the Crystal Palace was more exclusive than historians have suggested.[141]

If this is so, what made the exhibition affordable to some workers, despite the steep price of admission and the large amounts they had to save to make the excursion from the northern towns, was that so many companies and employers paid for their workers to attend it. In this area, as in so many others, the Great Exhibition was a tribute to the spirit of voluntarism and philanthropy, bolstered by cooperation between workers and employers, and perhaps tempered by an occasional desire to exercise social control. Banks, insurance companies, railway companies, and private firms both large and small helped their employees get to the Great Exhibition.[142] The London brewery Truman, Hanbury, Buxton & Co. gave 300 men a two-day holiday and a half-crown each day to cover expenses.[143] And a group of London booksellers agreed to give their assistants a holiday and the necessary expenses to see the exhibition.[144] Firms outside of London were just as giving, despite the added expense. According to *The Times*, this 'liberal spirit' illustrated the 'cordial co-operation' in Britain between employers and employees.[145]

Some employers had an obvious personal interest in the exhibition. At Baring's Bank, where one of the senior partners, Thomas Baring, was a Royal Commissioner and another, Joshua Bates, had subscribed £500, the staff were provided with season tickets at the bank's expense.[146] Other employers were rather more self-interested. One of the largest carpet firms in Wilton sent more than a hundred workers to London, all expenses paid; the firm had a number of carpets on display at the exhibition and wanted its workers to see what they, and no doubt their rivals, had produced. Arguably this would have boosted worker morale and given them a sense of accomplishment.[147] The Admiralty also provided leave to a number of its dock-workers who were asked to report on any new machines or processes that might be of value in their work. It stressed, however, that it would be very displeased to learn that any of its men had devoted time to any object other than that of visiting the exhibition.[148]

There were also many occasions when employers provided assistance to a group of employees who had already begun saving for the exhibition. It was not uncommon for factories to contribute as a unit to local subscription clubs, and many workers formed their own organizations using such clubs as models, subscribing funds out of their weekly pay-packets. In Leeds some of the largest mills had such associations. The officers of these clubs were elected by the workers themselves, but they could often rely on the cooperation and assistance of their employers. In Nottingham the employers in the lace firms offered a week's holiday if their employees wished to take it to attend the exhibition.[149] Such cooperation provided obvious advantages to both sides, and is one indication of the extent to which the classes worked together to make the exhibition a success. There were of course fears on both sides, and some of the comments offered by employers on their motivation for paying for their workers to attend the exhibition are certainly suggestive of rather patronizing attitudes. Many employers at the time, however, seemed to have been moved by a genuine spirit of charity and of wanting to improve living standards for those in their employ.

INTEGRATION AND SEGREGATION

The number of people who attended the Great Exhibition outstripped all expectations and, as John Tallis wrote, 'The exceeding popularity of the exhibition eventually became its greatest wonder.'[150] Most prognosticators had anticipated that there would be social segregation at the Crystal Palace: that the five-shilling visitors would stay away after 26 May when 'an entirely new class of visitors' appeared on the scene. The reality, however, was of social integration, as the Crystal Palace brought together all classes under one roof. *The Times* reported that on one of the first shilling days there was, mingling among the 37,000 shilling spectators, a considerable portion of so-called respectable society. Whereas on 26–27 May there were few season ticket holders, and then mostly men, by the 28th 'they flocked in without reserve.' *The Times* wrote of the 'fraternization of the great and the humble,' of 'high-born ladies' venturing 'amidst the thronging masses.'[151] This at a time when the mingling was mainly between the middle and the upper classes; the working classes had barely begun to arrive.[152]

In fact, observers were as struck by the social mixing that took place between the upper and middle classes, before 26 May, as they were by that which occurred between those two classes together and the working classes, after the shilling days began. *Punch* printed a cartoon soon after the exhibition opened showing 'Her Majesty, as She Appeared on the FIRST of MAY, Surrounded by "Horrible Conspirators and Assassins"' (fig. 45). The people surrounding the Queen, however, are clearly not workers; they are well-dressed, respectable middle-class sorts, with bonnets and top-hats. Nevertheless, to mix with royalty was a rare and significant occurrence. The Duke of Devonshire wrote to his nephew in India about the time he was gazing at one of the statues in the nave, when he was 'accosted' by a small woman. 'Ma'am,' he said, and '*Ecco*! It was the Queen,' who attended the exhibition frequently during the month of May, walking among the workmen and exhibitors. She

HER MAJESTY, as She Appeared on the FIRST of MAY,
Surrounded by "Horrible Conspirators and Assassins."

45. The Queen and her subjects. *Punch* (3 May 1851).

THE POUND AND THE SHILLING.

"Whoever Thought of Meeting You Here?"

46. The classes and the masses. *Punch* (14 June 1851).

was very popular, according to the Duke; Albert, he said, looked 'stupefied.'[153] The appearance of the Queen was always exciting and made heads turn. She was attended by no bodyguard as she toured the building, conversing with her companions and making small talk with the stall attendants whose exhibits interested her. William Drew found her subjects to be 'decorous and polite' toward her, with no 'rushing or crowding.'[154]

Punch, ever the astute social observer, captured the integrative function of the Crystal Palace in 'The Pound and the Shilling: "Whoever Thought of Meeting You Here?"' (fig. 46). John Leech's engraving depicts the Duke of Wellington and some well-dressed ladies, face to face with a working man in a stocking cap and his children, whose clothes are tattered and patched. The caption can be read two ways: 'Whoever thought of meeting *you* here,' suggesting that the social classes in Victorian England were generally segregated and that respectable society had assumed the Crystal Palace to be part of their domain; or, 'Whoever thought of meeting you *here*,' meaning that there were places where the classes mingled, but that respectable society did not consider the Crystal Palace to be one of them. Either way, the meaning of the drawing is clear: there was substantial social mixing at the Great Exhibition.

Although there had been some mingling of the classes at various festivals prior to 1851, in a society characterized for centuries by social segregation the Great Exhibition became one of the few occasions and places – and a form of social space – where all classes could coexist. The *Economist* referred to 'all classes meeting and sharing a common enjoyment.'[155] Everyone could exhibit, from the Queen to the poorest quilt-maker. Moreover, the classes began to see themselves as related and interdependent. Farmers and merchants might be at odds over national economic policy, but popular songs such as 'Trade and Spade' recognized their mutual dependence.[156] The factory owner and the consumer alike were beginning to recognize the value of skilled labor in producing the wealth of the nation.

Not that observers had any trouble categorizing those in attendance by either manners or appearance. The Society for Promoting Christian Knowledge, which published a book on *The Industry of Nations, as exemplified in the Great Exhibition of 1851*, observed that the various classes and groups of people could be 'recognized without difficulty,' the Londoners distinguishable by their fine clothes and pale skin, the visitors from the country by their 'ruggy health' and expressions of amazement at the wonders of the world.[157] *The Times* referred to those with 'humble dress and faces brown with exposure to the sun, and hands blackened by toil.'[158] And the American Benjamin Silliman was able to pick out the working classes, not only by their appearance, which he wrote was tidy and plain, but by their manners, which he thought were less deferential than they had been at other times.[159] By bringing the classes into closer proximity, the Crystal Palace also reinforced and made more apparent class differences.

Not surprisingly, people differed in their perceptions of the differences between the classes. Most observers were amazed at how well behaved the lower classes were, and how little crime there was at the exhibition, sharing the view of *The Times*, which described the masses as 'well dressed, orderly and sedate, earnestly engaged in examining all that interests them, not quarrelsome or obstinate, but playing with manifest propriety and good temperament the important part assigned to them at this gathering.'[160] On the other hand, Gideon Mantell, a crotchety old surgeon and geologist, was extremely deprecating of the lower orders after attending the exhibition on 8 October:

> Went again to the exhibition; the crowd tremendous; at the time I entered 97,000 [*sic*] persons were in the building: in the course of the day nearly 110,000 – one hundred and ten thousand! Vulgar, ignorant, country people: many dirty women with their infants were sitting on the seats giving suck with their breasts uncovered, beneath the lovely female figures of the sculptor. Oh! how I wished I had the power to petrify the living, and animate the marble.[161]

During the last week of the exhibition when there was an enormous last-minute rush to attend, the working classes invaded the nave, previously the refuge of respectable society, and sat at the edge of Osler's crystal fountain to eat their picnic lunches and nurse their babies.[162] *Punch* mocked this affront to bourgeois sensibilities with the line, 'One touch of nature makes the whole world kin!' in its cartoon, 'Dinner-Time in the Crystal Palace' (fig. 47).[163] There were separate spaces for different classes, but the Great Exhibition also forced the classes into unprecedented degrees of proximity to one another. Nevertheless, even together, the classes were still different, and prejudices were deeply rooted.

DINNER-TIME AT THE CRYSTAL PALACE.

47. Flaunting bourgeois norms: working-class mothers nurse their children in the nave. *Punch* (5 July 1851).

John Tallis even perceived a difference in the way the classes looked at exhibits, between the five-shilling visitors who were leisured, almost uninterested, and the shilling visitors, rushing about and attentive.[164] The classes may have mingled and mixed, but in a fundamental way they remained separate. He speculated that for the great number of people in the nave, as opposed to the galleries, the aesthetics of the place were the chief attraction: 'To these it was first and foremost a lounge and a panorama.' These people supposedly cared little for the details which occurred beyond the reach of the eye, and which did not form a striking part of the 'specta-cle' – his word. But the visitors from the country, from the workshops and the farms, seemed to have a different object, or purpose, in mind. Appearing to Tallis to be less sensitive to the grace and beauty of the building and the statues in the nave, they set themselves more resolutely to study the particular exhibits which for them had prac-tical interest.[165] One consequence of the influx of shilling visitors was that the more remote areas of the Crystal Palace received attention, not so much because the nave was crowded, *The Times* speculated, but because the working classes were more inter-ested in exhibits of machinery and manufactures than the finery in the nave.[166] As *Punch* derisively commented:

> The 'superior classes' must begin to look about them, if they would retain the epithet assigned to them; for there is no doubt which class has shown itself to be the superior, in the view taken of the Great Exhibition.
>
> The high-paying portion of the public go to look at each other, and to be looked at, while the shilling visitors go to gain instruction from what they see; and the result is, they are far better behaved than the well-dressed promenaders who push each other about, and stare each other out of countenance on the days of the high price of admission.[167]

Punch should not always be taken entirely at face value, but the picture that emerges is that in the Crystal Palace the classes kept to themselves and behaved differently from one another, despite the fact that they were all mixing under one roof.

At any museum or exhibition, people always look at what interests them most. The fact that a Victorian industrial worker concentrated on different exhibits than a well-to-do London banker revealed class differences as well as differences in personal preferences, occupation, religion, or location of residence. Each class, and every group, found its own space within the Crystal Palace. The Devonshire farmer, perhaps impatient with the Medieval Court or the marble statues, was seen diligently studying the latest hints and improvements in ploughs and spades. The Lancashire mechanic was observed looking intently at the new inventions exhibited by London machinists. And, of course, the upper classes congregated in the nave to see and be seen, surrounded by the statues and the Koh-i-noor Diamond and the fine arts, as far away from industry and the masses as they could be.[168] Space within the Crystal Palace was also divided along gender lines, with areas apparently of more interest for men such as the agricultural machinery, and others seemingly more attractive for women, such as the bolts of cloth (figs 48 and 49).[169]

What all of this suggests is that the Great Exhibition contained something for everyone, but not the same thing. Different classes went to the Great Exhibition for different reasons, to see different things, and, as a consequence, carved out different spaces for themselves within the building. Most people at the time were amazed that there was such a mixing of classes without major disruption in the still tense

48. Agricultural machinery: exhibits for men.

49. Bradford Court: exhibits for women.

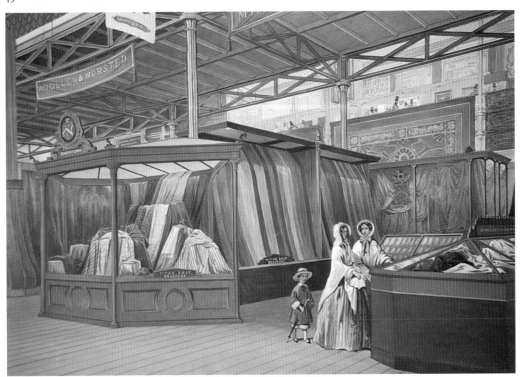

post-1848 atmosphere. It should be remembered, however, that people continued to segregate themselves. Palmerston, for example, chose to attend the exhibition only on Saturdays when the price of admission was high and the number of working-class visitors was low.[170] The evidence suggests that the Crystal Palace replicated class divisions within Victorian society even as it forced the classes to mingle to a perhaps unprecedented degree.

This nexus of integration and segregation reflects some of the social changes within mid-Victorian society. In the pre-industrial world there was spatial integration of people and activities; people were differentiated by their appearance. In contemporary society, there is spatial segregation of people and activities, which serves to differentiate people who are otherwise homogeneous in terms of appearance.[171] What we can see in the Crystal Palace is confusion, created by the process of transformation from one ordering system to another. The Crystal Palace, as much as it put people in their place, and as much as people put themselves in certain places, mixed up the places in which people felt comfortable.

By the end of the summer, *The Times* remarked, 'the people have now become the exhibition.' In the presence of the enormous number of people that were congregating in the Crystal Palace, the works of industry on display were no longer the premier attraction.[172] Rather, of primary interest for most contemporaries was that all classes and ranks were attending and participating equally in an event. The high mixed with the low. Right up until 26 May, the organizers of the exhibition had, along with many ordinary citizens and observers, feared the working classes. By the end of that first shilling day, many of those fears had vanished. They would, of course, resurface, but for a brief period the Great Exhibition had opened up the possibility of a British national identity based as much on social integration as on social segregation. The organizers' achievement was their ability to put together an event that was criticized by the Tories for fomenting revolution, and by Radicals for exploiting workers, yet appealed to an enormous segment of the populace nonetheless. They succeeded in turning an event that could be dismissed by either side as partisan into a festival with truly national appeal.

Even more, the Great Exhibition showed Britain to be a nation with a high degree of social cohesiveness.[173] People unquestionably felt part of the same society, but also seemed well aware that it was divided into groups that could not converge. On the surface, the exhibition displayed what was, as many historians have suggested, a 'profound caesura' of class politics in mid-Victorian England;[174] certainly many observers at the time perceived a lessening of class antagonisms. But underneath the nostrums about social harmony there were very clear class divisions, and, for many British men and women, irreconcilable ones. They were ambiguous, and changeable, and by and large non-confrontational, but there were differences nonetheless. What was remarkable about the Great Exhibition was that, despite these obvious class distinctions, it challenged established norms about social and physical boundaries. There was, in a sense, both integration and segregation. In the end, the most telling remark came from Macaulay, who confidently stated that at the time of the Great Exhibition, only three years after the revolutions of 1848, the idea of class revolution was as preposterous as the chance of the moon falling out of the sky.[175] The Great Exhibition revealed Britain to be a nation that, despite profound divisions, held together.

CHAPTER 6

Nationalism and Internationalism

'THE HAPPY FAMILY IN HYDE PARK' (fig. 50), a John Tenniel cartoon that appeared in *Punch* two months after the exhibition opened, seems to represent the amity and togetherness of the human community. Prince Albert is standing outside the Crystal Palace, bringing to the attention of some well-dressed ladies and gentlemen the fact that representatives from all nations have congregated inside, where they are happily dancing, talking, and celebrating their collective participation in the great peace congress being held in Hyde Park. As was so often the case, *Punch* had captured the public mood, highlighting the internationalist, peaceful orientation of the exhibition.

But when was *Punch* ever not poking fun at someone or something? A closer reading of this illustration reveals its irony, suggesting the opposite of what it appears and mocking the very theme it seems to be espousing. Lest the reader miss this point, the 'Punch' character, in the lower left-hand corner, is smiling wryly, even knowingly, as if to remind the reader not to miss the deeper meaning of the image. To look closely at Tenniel's drawing is to notice that those in the foreground are Europeans, while those in the background, separated behind the glass windows of the Crystal Palace, are exotic foreigners: a Chinese, an American Indian, a Turk wearing a turban, and a bushy-haired Russian. They are alien 'others,' on display as in a museum case or a circus cage, engaged in a bizarre and perhaps primitive dance. The British and Europeans, looking in, are separated from, and literally defined by, those they are looking at. They are civilized; the 'others' are wild, almost Bacchanalian. Rather than suggesting the happy union of peoples of all nations, that all people are one, Tenniel's caricature ridicules the strange rituals of foreigners, revealing an undercurrent of nationalism, even racism. This drawing, then, captures the complex interrelationship between nationalism and internationalism at the Great Exhibition.

These two seemingly contradictory ideologies were present from the outset. As discussed in Chapter 1, while Albert had no doubt but that the exhibition should be international in scope, those in attendance at the first planning meeting decided to emphasize the exhibition's benefits to British industry in particular.[1] In other words, although the exhibition originated from internationalist sentiments, it could and would be presented and interpreted in nationalistic terms.[2] Nationalism and internationalism formed the two columns upon which the exhibition was built.

And, for many at the time of the exhibition, nationalism and internationalism were by no means mutually exclusive; they were complementary, not contradictory. The irony and incongruity of instruments of war and peace sitting side by side was certainly not lost on either *Punch* (fig. 51) or Henry Sutherland Edwards:

> What strange contradictions were seen in each place;
> For instance, to go into one single case,

50. Nationalism and internationalism at the Great Exhibition: John Tenniel, *Punch* (19 July 1851).

THE HAPPY FAMILY IN HYDE PARK.

51. Armaments at the Great Peace Festival. *Punch* (5 July 1851).

PEACE!--A SKETCH FROM THE CRYSTAL PALACE.

In her surgical instruments France had rewards,
While she also gained prizes for muskets and swords.
To promoters of death the same medals they give
As to those who enable sick mortals to live.[3]

Others, however, such as E. A. Moriarty in the *Edinburgh Review*, suggested that the many improvements in projectiles and firearms were 'all steps in the path of peace,' because they increased the distance between combatants.[4] Peace meant deterrence not disarmament. Even as they rejoiced to see warships from the United States and Turkey used to carry goods to the exhibition – Thackeray wrote in his 'May Day Ode' of 'Symbols of peace, their vessel rides' – Britons were not at all disturbed to see their own steamer *Singapore*, laden with troops bound for South Africa, leave from the same harbor.[5] As one author wrote, 'There was to be seen for some time in apparently friendly conversation, the Iron Duke and the Lancashire cotton spinner – Wellington and Cobden – the man of war and the apostle of peace!'[6] At the Great Exhibition, Cobden and Wellington each had a place.

COBDENITE INTERNATIONALISM AND PALMERSTONIAN NATIONALISM

The overarching tenor of the Great Exhibition was pacifist internationalism. Prince Albert had set the tone when at the Mansion House meeting in March 1850 he spoke of 'peace, love, and ready assistance, not only between individuals but between the nations of the earth.'[7] And the commissioners stated definitively in one of their publicity brochures, 'The exhibition of 1851 will fulfil the prophecy of the sacred volume, and hasten the period "when men shall beat their swords into ploughshares, and their spears into pruning-hooks." It is a stage forward in that millennium which announces "peace and goodwill towards men!"'[8]

To a considerable degree the organizers were successful in promulgating their vision of the exhibition as a festival of peace. Numerous writers followed their lead and asserted that international peace and understanding were at hand, reiterating their sentiments, at times repeating their words verbatim. John Tallis, in his guidebook to the Crystal Palace, observed that 'Peace was on every lip,' and the anonymous author of *The Royal Exchange and the Palace of Industry* stated that 'The Palace of Industry was the Temple of Peace.'[9] One especially prominent theme was that all people and all nations constituted a single family. The anonymous author of a children's book wrote that the exhibition would bring the nations of the world together 'in love and trade, like one great family.'[10] Another author wrote, in his guide to the Crystal Palace, that the exhibition 'will do much to teach the politicians, merchants, manufacturers and labourers of different nations, that the whole commercial world constitutes one vast community, in which the true interests, advancement and well-being of the people are as mutual and as much bound together as those of the people of any one nation.'[11] In short, there were ties that bound the human community together that superseded national loyalties and prejudices. In 1851, the Great Exhibition stood as a symbol of international brotherhood and mutual dependence that in the eyes of many would usher in an era of peace between nations.

Many of these expressions of peace contained a hopeful, predictive quality. 'Besides the incalculable influence it [the Great Exhibition] must exercise on the taste, skill, knowledge, and commerce of the world,' wrote one anonymous author, 'it will probably go far towards the suppression of wars.'[12] But a number of these utterances also had a retrospective aspect. Commentators, including those at the highest levels of government such as Lord John Russell, saw the exhibition as the offspring of almost forty years of peace between Britain and the rest of Europe, a tribute to what could be accomplished if natural resources were not devoted to war or preparations for war. Russell noted that thirty-five years earlier Europe was emerging from a dreadful, costly conflict, during which nations had exhibited 'the virtues of war – hardihood, enterprise, and fortitude.' Now, he hoped, nations would see the benefits of peace. In Russell's eyes, the Great Exhibition was both a product and a cause of peace.[13]

What informed these statements was the hope that the exhibition would create peace, or at least reduce the likelihood of war, by constructing new arenas in which nations could compete with each other, and by encouraging commercial, linguistic, and scientific ties among them. James Ward described in no uncertain terms how commerce would replace and eliminate the need for war. 'In lieu of fabricating weapons for mutual destruction,' he wrote, 'mankind seem tacitly agreed to rival each other in the manufacture of commodities essentially requisite for their mutual advantage,' a process that had, according to Ward, been occurring for a quarter-century. He continued: 'It is simply a transfer of skill and industry – from bullets of lead to bales of cotton.'[14]

Others added that this process would be facilitated by the turn to free trade. Through its celebration of industry and economic competition, the Great Exhibition would foster prosperity, international understanding, and commercial relations that would, over the long term, eliminate war. In the words of the *Economist*:

> Free Trade and they [the friends of peace] are close allies, and would bind all nations in bonds of amity. Without peace, the law that permits unrestrained intercourse would be a dead letter – without Free Trade, peace would have none of the intercourse of friendship. As Free Traders, therefore, we share the hopes of the members of the Peace Congress, and strive ardently for objects similar to those which attract them together.[15]

In the decades following the conclusion of the Napoleonic Wars, there were essentially two views of free trade among continental European nations. Large countries with strong central administrations which could hope to nurture industry within their own borders, and which suffered in the face of British industrial might and imposed tariffs on imports, generally opposed free trade; and smaller countries, which in general could not rely on home markets and needed to export, tended to support it. On the whole, the smaller and more liberal areas (Switzerland, the Rhineland, Westphalia, and Saxony) fared better economically than the larger, more protectionist countries (Spain, Austria, Russia, and France except for Alsace). The Zollverein, or German customs union, established in 1834, was the best example of the benefits of economic integration, and was held up by many at the time of the exhibition as a model to be followed.[16]

This view, that free trade would foster peace, formed one of the core beliefs of the Manchester School, that loose conglomeration of businessmen, pacifists, utilitarians, and Radicals who, with the *Economist* as their collective mouthpiece, advocated free

trade and laissez-faire economics.[17] Disillusioned with the aristocratic Whig government of the late 1830s, a number of Manchester industrialists headed by George
Wilson and Richard Cobden concluded that their political and economic future, as
well as the economic future of the nation, lay in the abolition of the Corn Laws,
which had been a symbol of aristocratic misrule since their imposition in 1815. This
was a patently anti-aristocratic argument: Cobden and Bright especially believed that
war, conquest, and taxation for war nurtured the old oligarchies. The Manchester
School was instrumental in the Anti-Corn Law League and the repeal of the Corn
Laws in 1846. Manchesterism also held that free trade would foster economic integration, which would in turn not only make the nations of Europe richer and develop
their full economic potential but would lessen the likelihood of major wars between
them. Historians have long recognized that the liberal economic philosophy of the
Anti-Corn Law League and the Manchester School was grounded in, and was, in
many respects, the outcome of, the teachings of classical economists such as Adam
Smith and David Ricardo, who argued against mercantilism and in favor of a reduced
role for the government in economic matters. It also drew on the ideas of Jeremy
Bentham, especially his 'Plan for a Universal and Perpetual Peace,' one of the essays
in *Principles of International Law*.[18] Bentham's plan would be adopted almost point
by point by Henry Cole in a speech at the Society of Arts 'On the International
Results of the Exhibition.' Of the ideological links between the exhibition and the
Manchester School there can be little doubt.

   If there was any single person who represented internationalism at the time of the
Great Exhibition, it was Richard Cobden.[19] For him, the Great Exhibition provided
a unique opportunity to promote his internationalist beliefs, beliefs he largely shared
with Prince Albert. Cobden stated his position clearly and succinctly at a public
meeting in Birmingham:

> We shall by that means [the exhibition] break down the barriers that have sepa-
> rated the people of different nations, and witness the universal republic; the year
> 1851 will be a memorable one, indeed: it will witness a triumph of industry, instead
> of a triumph of arms. We shall not witness the reception of the allied sovereigns
> after some fearful conflict, men bowing their heads in submission; but, instead,
> thousands and tens of thousands will cross the channel . . . with the fullest con-
> viction that war, rather than a national aggrandizement, has been the curse, and the
> evil which has retarded the progress of liberty and of virtue; and we shall show to
> them that the people of England . . . are ready to sign a treaty of amity with all the
> nations on the face of the earth.[20]

Cobden's phrase about thousands crossing the Channel must have terrified those in
attendance, but they could only have been reassured – if not inspired – by his talk of
'a triumph of industry.' His speech unquestionably constitutes a ringing endorsement
of the internationalist philosophy of the Manchester School; he was, after all, its
leading figure.[21]

   Cobden's nemesis during these mid-century years was Lord Palmerston, Foreign
Secretary in the Whig governments of Grey (1830–4), Melbourne (1835–41), and
Russell (1846–51).[22] As most historians have acknowledged, it is impossible to understand the course and development of British foreign policy in the nineteenth century
without accounting for Palmerston.[23] The cornerstone of Palmerston's foreign policy

was the national interest: 'We have no eternal allies, we have no perpetual enemies,' he said in 1848. 'Our interests are eternal and perpetual, and those interests it is our duty to follow.'[24] In short, Palmerston's foreign policy rested on foundations that could not have been more different from Cobden's. Even as the internationalists celebrated the liberal revolutions of 1848, Palmerston fretted over how to prevent revolution from turning into international war.

The central event in the battle between Cobden and Palmerston for the heart and mind of John Bull was the Don Pacifico affair of 1850, in which David Pacifico, a Jew born in Gibraltar but living in Athens, claimed the protection of the British government after an anti-Semitic mob ransacked his house in 1847. After efforts by the British Foreign Office to secure redress proved futile, the Royal Navy in early 1850 blockaded Greek ports and seized several merchant vessels, with Palmerston defending the action against the protests of almost all other European nations.[25] The importance of the Don Pacifico affair was less the diplomatic resolution than the actions Palmerston took and the debate over those actions in Parliament in mid-June. Four former or future prime ministers attacked Palmerston during the Parliamentary debate, disturbed by his bald nationalism, interventionism, disregard for the rights of other peoples, and, most importantly, his offensiveness to other powers that endangered European stability and hence Britain's low tax rates. But on the second evening, in a speech lasting well into the night, Palmerston provided a reply that appealed not only to the intellect of his listeners, but to their emotions and nationalistic impulses: '[As] the Roman, in days of old, held himself free from indignity when he could say *Civis Romanus sum*, so also a British subject, in whatever land he may be, shall feel confident that the watchful eye and the strong arm of England, will protect him against injustice and wrong.'[26] While he acknowledged that recourse should first be sought in accordance with the laws of the nation involved, he maintained that, in the absence of justice, the British government should be prepared to intervene. His speech was a *tour de force*, and even Prince Albert, who could not have admired Palmerston less, called it a 'masterpiece.'[27] Although the debate continued for two more days, Palmerston's appeal to British pride and patriotism had already carried the House, despite Cobden's objections.[28]

Palmerston's speech did not change the course of British foreign policy, which remained mainly non-interventionist in continental Europe (as distinct from the empire) until 1914, but his defence of gunboat diplomacy rekindled Britons' nationalistic and interventionist impulses, especially as it came on the heels of the French invasion scare of 1847 and the revolutions of 1848. Palmerston had touched the heart, as opposed to the mind, of John Bull. Cobden and the Manchester School had forgotten the words of Thomas Malthus, who had said that nations, like people, are at times governed less by interest than by passion. In contrast, Palmerston knew that Don Pacifico mattered little and would soon be forgotten. What was important were principles. In his speech Palmerston had convinced the nation that his policy was neither Whig nor Tory, but British.[29] From 1850 to 1865, Palmerston's nationalism occupied a central position in the British popular politics.[30]

While the Don Pacifico affair was as much a defeat for Cobden as it was a victory for Palmerston, Cobden and Palmerston did not always disagree.[31] They shared a belief, for example, that free trade suited the moral temper and commercial supremacy of Britain. Before attending Cambridge, Palmerston had studied Smith at Edinburgh, where he became convinced of the material benefits of free trade. In the debate on the Corn Laws he had even stressed the contribution free trade would make to inter-national relations, speaking of 'the exchange of commodities . . . accompanied by the extension and diffusion of knowledge – by the interchange of mutual benefits engen-dering mutual kind feelings – multiplying and confirming friendly relations.' He also spoke of repudiating the Corn Laws so that 'commerce may go freely forth, leading civilization with one hand, and peace with the other, to render mankind happier, wiser, better.'[32] But Palmerston, unlike Cobden, would never let free trade come before what he perceived to be the national interest. In fact, he despised the political arguments of the Manchester Men.[33]

The Don Pacifico affair exposed a fervently nationalistic and patriotic side of the British. Not that this came as a surprise to Cobden – only a disappointment. In a 1847 letter to John Bright, Cobden had written of 'the pugnacious, energetic, self-sufficient, foreigner-despising, and pitying character of the noble insular creature John Bull.'[34] Cobden, Albert, Cole, and the other internationalists did their best at the time of the Great Exhibition to reform these attitudes, but they made few inroads. For every internationalist article in the *Westminster Review* or *Edinburgh Review*, there was a counterpoint in *Blackwood's*, *John Bull*, or any of a number of popular books. And although *The Times*, the *Daily News*, and the *Morning Chronicle* all expressed internationalist sentiments, as the *Punch* illustration of 'The Happy Family in Hyde Park' makes clear, fervent nationalism always lay near the surface.

The consequences of Palmerston's Don Pacifico speech were many, some of which have been noted above. The whole episode took on added significance because it occurred when the exhibition looked as though it would fall apart over the design of the building and the opposition to having a permanent structure in Hyde Park. While it may have been coincidental, it was surely important that at a crucial moment in the planning of the exhibition, when subscriptions and popular support were at a low, Britons found an outlet for their nationalistic sentiments. The Great Exhibition, despite its internationalist origins and overtones, became a supremely nationalistic event.

NATIONAL IDENTITY AND THE 'OTHER'

Nationalism is a slippery concept with a multiplicity of meanings, but what we know from studies of nationalism and national identity is that every society forms an image of itself and of its citizens in order to maintain a coherent identity.[35] Since bound-aries of national belonging are constantly being redrawn, we need to regard society as a locale in which there is a continuous contest between adherents of different ideas about what constitutes the national identity. This having been said, there are certain occasions which can serve as focal points for discussions about national identity. Fairs and festivals have long been considered such opportunities, and the Great Exhibition of 1851, the first international industrial exhibition and the first world's fair, was no exception.[36] The Great Exhibition served as an opportunity for British writers and politicians to assert and reaffirm those elements that they considered integral to British national identity, to extol the qualities, beliefs, and values they saw as central to the British state.

The anonymous *Exhibition Lay*, one of countless celebratory poems published and sold for a shilling a copy at the time of the exhibition, glorified the host nation with these lines:

> Bless England, Lord! guide Thou her ways,
>   Let People, Prince and Queen
> Remember what our England is,
>   and what she long hath been.
> A land where Freedom's eye unbent
>   hath met Oppression's frown
> Where Freedom's hand hath dared to strike
>   the foul oppression down.
> Where liberty our birthright is –
>   no empty vaunting name;
> A thousand years of patient growth
>   may well endear its claim.[37]

The author, then, lauded Britain for its monarchy, for its long history, and for its pursuit of freedom, liberty, and progress. But it is worth noting the use of 'England' here rather than 'Britain;' although the words were often interchangeable, at the time of the exhibition there was a tension between these two concepts that always left in doubt just which nation the writer was describing.[38]

James Ward (who also published under the pseudonym 'Philoponos') described Britain as follows:

> We are – with our great national advantages, our unbounded supply of coals and of all the useful metals, the energetic and never-tiring industry of our population, the enterprising spirit of our Anglo-Saxon blood, our peculiar climate which renders bodily and mental activity a condition of healthy existence, and our insular position, so pre-eminently favourable to commerce – we are, by these and other great national advantages, and for an indefinite term continue to be, the great manufacturing and mercantile nation of the world.[39]

To Ward, Britons were hard-working and entrepreneurial, different from – and superior to – all other nations in large part because they lived on an island. F. W. N. Bayley (the author and first editor of the *Illustrated London News*) also emphasized the importance of commerce when he wrote that the exhibition asked all nations to 'be a part of Britain, and shake hands with commerce. . . . Once on British soil,' Bayley added, in a bald assertion of commercialism, 'your wares we sell.'[40] 'What is the leading characteristic of the present time in England?' asked William Johnston, in his assessment of *England as It Is*. 'I answer, its industrialism – its wealth-seeking spirit.' But this characterization, like so many others, was still hotly contested. Johnson continued, 'This spirit is at war with the sentimental, the romantic, and the delicate in thought and feeling.'[41]

Freedom was another of the attributes appropriated by Britons for themselves at the time of the exhibition. Witness Joseph Turner, who wrote a celebratory poem to commemorate the Great Exhibition:

Hence are we set on high amid the nations,
To us they trust their best and brightest things,
Hence to us standing on the sure foundations,
Free Truth, free Thought, free Word, such glory clings.[42]

And Caroline Gascoyne, in her *Recollections and Tales of the Crystal Palace*, wrote:

Away with chains! – Britannia's flag unfurled,
Speaks Peace and Freedom to th'assembled world!
Where'er her banner floats – or sounds her name,
Distant or near, her power is still the same –
The power of Justice, Liberty, and Right,
Calm in their force, majestic in their might!

And none who sought her shores, by power opprest,
Have failed to find there, Freedom, Peace, and Rest.[43]

In other words, Britain was seen as industrial and commercial, its people energetic and enterprising, its social and political system based on freedom, liberty, and justice.

The poems and prose of Ward, Johnston, Gascoyne, Turner, and others constitute what might be called 'essentialist' expressions of national identity, meaning that they are non-oppositional expressions of self-understanding. National identity, however, is rarely formed in a vacuum. It is as one scholar has written, 'contingent and relational . . . defined by the social or territorial boundaries drawn to distinguish the collective self and its implicit negation, the other.' In other words, it is constructed referentially, in comparison with and frequently in opposition to other national identities. Moreover national identities of this sort often depend less on objective differences than on 'the subjective experience of difference.'[44]

At the time of the Great Exhibition, writers regularly expressed these differences, real or perceived, as blatant assertions of imagined and immutable national characteristics. *The World's Fair; or, Children's Prize Gift Book* celebrated the English for their 'industry and perseverance.' In contrast, Indians were poor and simple; Turks were 'a fine and handsome race of people, and very grave and sensible, except when they are angry, when they grow raging and furious;' and Italians were beggars and bandits, and not particularly industrious, even though their country had fertile soil and a good climate. Germans were thoughtful, romantic, and well educated; the Dutch industrious and cleanly.[45] In general, northern Europeans were held in the highest regard, followed by southern Europeans, with Russians, Asians, Africans, and American Indians bringing up the rear. Racial and ethnic groups that were perceived as exotic or different, and nations that were not Westernized or industrialized, were considered lowest in the hierarchy.

Always implicit, if not explicit, in descriptions of countries and their exhibits – real or imagined – was that Britain was different. *Britannia*, in its analysis of the German contributions, discussed the powder-barrels and muskets, swords and bayonets, and artillery which constituted 'Germany's preparations for the great peace exhibition.' That is, the Germans were militaristic; the British peace-loving.[46] Several commentators criticized Turkey, China, Italy, and Austria, which exhibited 'little or nothing adapted to the support and comfort of the masses,' for being too 'rich and aristo-cratic,' in contrast to 'those nations which are more free [and] have proportionally more articles on exhibition that are of service to the common people.'[47] Similarly, a broadsheet titled *The Productions of All Nations about to appear at the Great Exhibition of 1851* contained a caricature of Russian tsar Nicholas the Great pulling a barrel labeled 'elbow grease from 30,000,000 serfs.' In comparison, Britannia exhibited 'a chartered free press,' to eradicate vices, to redress social ills, and to disseminate 'knowledge, liberty, and truth.'[48]

As Freud observed in his *Civilization and its Discontents*, it is frequently those communities or nations that are closest to each other, culturally or geographically, that engage in feuds and ridicule, exhibiting what he called the 'narcissism of minor differences.'[49] Participants in this sort of conflict are essentially similar people who exaggerate what separates them in a desperate search for identity. In the case of Britain at the time of the exhibition, the two closest nations, culturally and territorially, were America and France, often referred to as 'Brother Jonathan' and 'Our Gallic Neighbours.'

America came under severe and almost universal criticism for not having abandoned slavery, and was one of the foils, or counter-examples, used by Britons most frequently to assert their love of freedom and liberty. *Punch*, in its discussion of the American exhibits, wrote contemptuously that the only noteworthy example of American manufacture was a slave, referring to Hiram Powers' statue of a Greek slave (fig. 52). 'We have the Greek Captive in dead stone,' wrote *Punch*. 'Why not the Virginian slave in living ebony?'[50] A John Tenniel cartoon depicting a saddened, half-dressed African woman in chains, in the same pose as Powers' *Greek Slave*, made the same point visually (fig. 53).[51] Soon after the exhibition, an anonymous book was published called *Chaff; or, The Yankee and Nigger at the Exhibition*. In the two-act farce, set in London at the time of the Great Exhibition, Silas Washington Doodle, a major in the United States army, shoots Gumbo Jumbo, a black man, for having dared to sleep in the same room as a native, free-born citizen of the United States. One of the other lodgers at the boarding house then inquires of Doodle why Hiram Powers sculpted a Greek slave when he had so many models (that is, African slaves) at home to study.[52]

On the other hand, writers commended America for keeping industry free of governmental interference. William Drew praised the American exhibits for their durability, usefulness, and inexpensiveness, which he claimed was the result of 'Brother Jonathan' being 'the freest boy on earth.' Drew saw some similarities in this respect in Britain, where 'the free principle preponderates.'[53] And at one of the local meetings to promote the exhibition, Colonel Reid warned that the exhibits from America might disappoint because, 'having free institutions like ourselves, their government has not the power, like the centralized governments of Europe, to take the entire arrangement and selection of articles to be sent over.'[54] In point of fact the exhibits from America did not 'adequately represent their capabilities,' and the American display was so modest that France took over some of the unused space.[55] Nevertheless, these comments indicate that there were instances where Britons affirmed their cultural ties to America.

America was by no means the only country used by British writers in this oppositional, contrasting fashion. They used France to illustrate how in Britain government was democratic and the economy (at least in theory) based on laissez-faire

52. Hiram Powers, *Greek Slave* (1843). Corcoran Gallery of Art, Washington.

53. John Tenniel, 'Virginian slave'. *Punch* (7 June 1851).

principles and private enterprise. Robert Stephenson wrote: 'Had the project been tried in France, it would have been carried through with far less difficulty, as it would have had the advantage of the power and purse of the government, which being utterly impossible with our habits of public action, is absolutely necessary to make the proposition popular.'[56] Britons were especially proud that the funds for the Crystal Palace were collected from public subscription, and not by raising taxes. Henry Mayhew expressed the view of many when he wrote, 'And well may the nation be proud of its Crystal Palace. No other people in the world could have raised such a building – without one shilling being drawn from the national resources.'[57] As for France's exhibits, *The Times* noted that France had not yet eliminated government patronage and support from the manufacturing process. The paper pointed out that in Britain, unlike the continental states, there was in industrial production hardly a trace of governmental influence. Instead, there was an independent manufacturing system in which private enterprise, private capital, and utilitarianism predominated.[58]

So powerful were these generalizations – not just about France and America but also about Russia, Germany, Austria, and Italy – that they made any kind of rigorous analysis of foreign exhibits difficult. The displays of foreign goods received considerable attention in the press, but rarely did they present, for contemporary observers, positive – or even representative – portrayals of other nations and peoples. For the most part foreign goods were deemed valuable only insofar as they fitted the organizers' commercial vision. Visitors, of course, would have learned enormously from the display of foreign goods at the exhibition, but much more dominant in the public discourse were stereotypes about national characteristics.

One perceived difference between Britain and other nations that arose on many occasions was religion. Since Henry VIII there had existed in Britain a xenophobic, nationalistic, anti-Catholic spirit that continued to serve as one of the sources of Britain's stability in the nineteenth century.[59] It also distinctly colored the Great Exhibition, which served as a vehicle for many Britons to affirm both their Christian and their Protestant identity. For the author of *The Palace of Glass and the Gathering of the People*, published by the Religious Tract Society, the exhibition implied 'greatness.' And the causes of such greatness? The character of the Anglo-Saxon race, Britain's physical climate, its island insularity, its forms of government, and 'above all . . . the result of Christianity.'[60] In the hierarchy of nations imposed by the physical layout of exhibits in the Crystal Palace, a bond of Christianity united the Christian and 'civilized' nations of the West against the 'barbaric' nations of Africa and the East.

Britons tended to define themselves not only by their Christianity, but more specifically by their Protestantism, and, not surprisingly, British Protestantism was set in opposition to (usually papal, but occasionally Irish) Catholicism. The Rev. Thomas Aveling claimed that Britain's greatness, prosperity and superiority were due, 'especially and most pre-eminently, to the religion of the land – the Protestant Christianity of the Bible.' He explained that Protestant Christianity – as opposed to Popery – had taught Britons to think for themselves, encouraged the spread of education, provided principles for social interactions, and created a spirit of peace and friendship.[61] The *Protestant Magazine* offered a historical comparison between the Anglo-Protestant and Roman Catholic cultures, representing Protestant England as free, prosperous, peaceful, and happy, whereas 'Popish Rome' was oppressed, declining, and tyrannized.[62]

Within the Crystal Palace itself, Pugin's Medieval Court became a touchstone for anti-Catholic feelings because of the giant cross that was to be included in the display. In March, the evangelical Arthur Kinnaird noticed the Great Rood from the screen at St Edmund's College, Ware, raised up high above the Medieval Court, and complained to Lord Ashley, who, concerned that 'a Popish chapel was being erected inside the exhibition,' relayed his fears to Lord John Russell and Prince Albert. 'The only thing that has been brought into this court is a Cross, not a Crucifix,' Granville declared reassuringly. Pugin acquiesced when Granville informed him that the cross could not remain there at a height which was inconsistent with regulations, and assured him that it had been positioned by a foreman who was only trying to save room. While one wall would be hung with ecclesiastical ornaments, Granville was now confident that the mix of 'domestic furniture' such as stoves, sofas, and tables would lend the court 'a sufficiently secular character.'[63] Nevertheless *The Times* received a flood of letters, one of which opposed the cross as an 'insult to the religion of the country,' and Granville wrote of 'the Protestant alarm' caused by the inclusion of the cross, despite his efforts to mediate the situation. He added that 'the bigotry was so tremendous that they were anxious to keep as quiet as possible,' and implored *The Times* not to raise a 'No Popery' cry.[64]

But this vision of Britain as a Protestant nation was hardly an uncontested one at the time of the Great Exhibition. The very inclusion of the cross suggests the improved position of Catholicism by the mid-nineteenth century, and indeed, for Pugin and his followers, Catholicism was the very essence of English culture: one style meant one faith. Pugin's writings promoted his belief that there was only one true style for a Christian England – the Gothic. While the Gothic had been in vogue since Horace Walpole and had been widely practiced since before Pugin was born, it was he who put belief into it. He was a Catholic, and, for him, Gothic architecture, Catholic architecture, and English architecture were synonymous.[65]

The furor over Pugin's Medieval Court must be seen in the context of the increased prominence, both real and imagined, of Catholicism in mid-nineteenth-century Britain. Notwithstanding the long history of anti-Catholicism in Britain, the anti-Catholic attitudes and cries of 'No Popery' that accompanied the preparations for the exhibition were very much a product of the early Victorian years: of the enormous and rapid increase in Irish (Catholic) immigration, and of Pope Pius IX's act of 'Papal Aggression' in 1850, whereby the Papacy decided to restore the administrative structure of bishops and diocese which the English Catholic Church had not had since the Reformation, causing an outburst of anti-Catholic sentiment and providing the impetus for the Ecclesiastical Titles Act of 1851, which imposed a fine on any bishop of a non-Anglican Church who took a territorial title.[66] All of this occurred at a time when many in Britain perceived the status and primacy of Protestantism in Britain to be vulnerable. The Religious Census of 1851, for example, which indicated that slightly fewer than half of those surveyed on Census Sunday attended Church of England services, shattered any illusions Britons might have held about Anglican hegemony, although just as worrisome for contemporaries was that only half of those canvassed attended church at all.[67] Even though the results of the census would not be published until 1852, there had already been disconcerting signs that the Anglican Church was losing its power and authority, especially among the working classes. There were also concerns resulting from the conversions of Pusey and Newman to Catholicism, anxiety that arose less from the number of conversions than from their highly visible nature and the social status of the converts.[68]

The resurgence of Catholicism during the early Victorian years cannot be separated from the Oxford Movement (or Tractarianism, as it was sometimes called), Young England, and the Pre-Raphaelite Brotherhood, whose first public exhibitions of paintings coincided with the preparations for the Great Exhibition. All three movements were, at heart, nostalgic escapes from a disagreeable present to an agreeable but imaginary past: the Oxford Movement rejected the Protestant element in Anglicanism in favor of its pre-Reformation Catholic tradition; Young England, that group of Conservatives who opposed Peel, sought to resuscitate a mythically benevolent feudal system, romanticized in Disraeli's *Coningsby* (1844); and the Pre-Raphaelites, though as uncertain in their faith as most Victorians, were nonetheless convinced that aesthetic renewal involved the revival of a specifically Christian and medieval art. Despite William Holman Hunt's Protestant affiliation, the Pre-Raphaelite Brotherhood contributed to fears of popish plots when Dante Gabriel Rossetti (who was Italian, and thus suspect for that reason) and John Everett Millais both exhibited at the Royal Academy paintings with Tractarian overtones in 1850.[69]

The whole contemporaneous medieval revival, which reached its apogee in the famous Eglinton tournament in 1839 (when a group of young Tories, inspired by Walter Scott's *Ivanhoe*, donned armour and re-enacted a medieval joust to symbolize aristocratic unity), was part of the same phenomenon. It rejected both the ideals and the reality of industrialization and questioned the very idea of progress put forward by Albert at his Mansion House address.[70] Thomas Carlyle, in *Past and Present* (1843), had written that an ideal society could be achieved only within the context of tradition. The Future, he argued, was not dissevered from the Past, but based continuously upon it. He offered a vision of 'Englishness' that was rooted in an idealization of tradition and a rejection of change, an ideal that was shared by both Tory and Radical leaders, as well as by the participants in the Oxford Movement, Young England, the Pre-Raphaelite Brotherhood, and the Gothic Revival.

Not that the battle lines were always so clear. Ruskin, otherwise a defender and promoter of the Gothic Revival, approved of the Pre-Raphaelites' naturalism but distrusted their 'Romanist and Tractarian tendencies.'[71] And Prince Albert, while clearly a proponent of material and industrial progress, was nonetheless the very embodiment of medieval chivalry in the modern gentleman. A jewel cabinet made for Victoria by Elkington and Company and exhibited at the Crystal Palace shows, in miniature, Albert in armor and Victoria wearing medieval or perhaps Tudor dress (fig. 54).[72] The fact remains that the Great Exhibition was rife with contradictions, and those who organized and participated in it were motivated both by their antipathy to industrialization – their conviction that it had ruined craftsmanship – and by their celebration of it.

Moreover, as the skirmish over Pugin's Medieval Court suggests, the very nature of British national identity was a hotly contested issue at the Great Exhibition, and this was especially true with regard to religious matters. While Britain was almost entirely Christian (there was a tiny Jewish minority), there was very little consensus about what that meant. Some mid-Victorians calling themselves Christians (for example, Mormons and Unitarians) were denied the right to do so by others, and even after Catholic emancipation in 1829 many Christians continued to maintain that Britain was a Protestant state, as they did at the Great Exhibition.

And, finally, directly related to the Catholic question, was the Irish question. As one historian has written, 'it was not always clear where the politics of popery ended and those of Paddy began.'[73] The 1851 census in England and Wales counted about 750,000 Irish-born Catholics, and, although this amounted to only 4.5 percent of the population, this represented an enormous increase from the 420,000 present only a decade earlier. Most were unskilled and semi-skilled laborers from rural and illiterate backgrounds; they generally lived in the poorer sections of urban areas, and were concentrated in London, western Scotland, and the cities of Lancashire and Yorkshire. Although there were many divisions within the Irish community, in the eyes of British Protestants they were poor, ignorant, alien, and, most importantly, different, clinging to their own separate identity.[74]

A number of significant trends, then, came together at the time of the Great

54. Jewel cabinet, by Louis Gruner for Elkington and Company (1851). The Royal Collection.

Exhibition. These include the enormous increase in Irish (Catholic) immigration; the series of highly visible conversions to Catholicism; the Pope's act of Papal Aggression; and the virulent nationalism that followed the Don Pacifico affair. Anti-Catholicism provided a vehicle for Britons to express many of the same features of British national identity as the Great Exhibition: liberty, freedom, democracy.[75] Opposing Catholicism was also a means for Britons to profess their belief in the efficacy of progress, as Protestants disparaged Catholicism as a check on economic and social progress. They also contrasted Ireland's backwardness, despite its supposedly superior natural resources, with Scotland's prosperity; likewise within Ireland itself, comparing the Catholic south to Protestant Ulster. Writers cited Spain and Italy – Catholic countries – as examples of fallen empires, the implication always being that Protestant Britain would be different.[76] As several historians have argued, anti-Catholicism was instrumental in the development of British national identity, was integral to the idea of a free nation, and provided an umbrella for Whigs and Tories, Anglicans and Dissenters, aristocrats and workers.[77] Protestants carefully defined and categorized the 'popish' enemy, and in the process defined themselves.

If Britons used those nations that were closest, culturally and/or geographically, against which to define themselves, British writers also used those countries and peoples that were most different. Thomas Onwhyn's *Mr. and Mrs. Brown's Visit to*

London to see the Great Exhibition of All Nations. How they were astonished at its wonders, inconvenienced by the crowds, and frightened out of their wits, by the Foreigners, was merciless in its contempt for exotic foreigners. In the Crystal Palace the Browns encounter a Russian, called 'Don Cossack,' who has bushy hair, is dressed in military garb, and carries a sword (fig. 55); bedouin, 'dark gentlemen in their bed-clothes,' who carry spears; and a Turk with a goatee, a plumed hat, and a dagger in his belt. After the Browns flee the exhibition they are nearly suffocated by a cloud of tobacco smoke, the result of foreigners "puffing in all directions." Especially deprecating in an anthropological sense is Onwhyn's caricature of a group from the 'Cannibal Islands' at an outdoor restaurant, sitting at a picnic table beneath a sign that reads 'Soup à la Hottentot.' They have dark skin, bare feet, and monkey-like faces; one holds a knife and is threatening to eat the Browns' child (fig. 56). They are depicted as animalistic, cannibalistic savages, the exact opposite of how the British liked to see themselves.

Perhaps the most revealing and interesting characterization of 'otherness' at the time of the exhibition is the satirical *Authentic Account of the Chinese Commission, which was sent to report on the Great Exhibition; wherein the opinion of China is shown as not corresponding at all with our own* by Henry Sutherland Edwards (fig. 57). Pretending to view British culture from the outside, the 'report,' a long rhyming poem, tells the following story.

55. Russophobia: 'Don Cossack'.

A good natured Don Cossack, takes notice of Anna Maria, much to her terror Some Negroes exhibit their ivories to little Johnny.

They go to have some refreshment ...a party from the Cannibal Islands after eyeing little Johnny, in a mysterious manner, offer a price for him.

56. The savage other: 'Cannibal Islanders'.

The Chinese Emperor has heard about the Great Exhibition and wants to know more about it, so he decides to send Congou, who has killed his grandmother, mother, wife, and daughter. As the Emperor explains:

> I could not thrust forth from our much favoured clime
> A man who had never committed a crime.
> When I send one in barbarous countries to pine,
> It's because he's not fit to be strangled in mine.

However, the Emperor is unsure whether Congou is the right person to represent China abroad. He becomes desperate, and 'as the Emperor felt in no better condition,/he determined to call in and kill a physician,' clearly a warning about the arbitrary nature of despotic power. Brought before the Emperor is Sing-Song, a physician and philosopher, full of integrity, who tries to evade certain death by suggesting that he accompany Congou to London so that the Emperor might obtain a more balanced picture of the exhibition. The Emperor agrees, so off Congou and Sing-Song go, charged with reporting on 'the plan, which the Western barbarians of Europe suggest,/for collecting all things which they think they make best.'

While Sing-Song, representing the rational, enlightened, unprejudiced perspective, respects the artistic and scientific achievements of Western civilization, and starts to enjoy life in London, Congou stubbornly continues to wear his blinders, unable and unwilling to understand the strange habits he encounters. He hates the whole exhibition:

> The opening, in short, was as dull as could be;
> There was no execution whatever to see;
> There was no one impaled, and the use of the saw
> Is not even mentioned in Englishman's law.

It would be hard for a reader to miss the pointed criticism of the Chinese embodied in this comment.

When Congou and Sing-Song return to China, each offers his report to the Emperor. Sing-Song's is balanced. Although he complains that the uses of opium are not fully understood, he praises the British for the electric telegraph and railway locomotion, and says that they can be proud of the exhibition. He concedes that there is visible progress in the West. He is the scientist who feels bound to tell the truth. Congou, on the other hand, expresses his utter contempt for Western civilization. In doing so, in characterizing the British as barbaric, he is, of course, revealing how barbaric the British perceived the Chinese to be:

> The organs and pianos, which made such a noise
> Compared with our tam-tams, are nothing but toys.
> Excepting the objects from China in short,
> There was nothing worth naming in any report.

In fact, most observers at the time agreed that the Chinese pavilion was one of the most disappointing; most of the exhibits were collected not by the Chinese, but by the East India Company. Congou continued:

> The classes called upper, appeared not to know
> That the nails of their fingers they ought to let grow.
> Altogether this England showed nothing worth showing,
> And the English knew nothing at all that's worth knowing.
> The best things in London I saw all along,
> Were some lanterns, and tam-tams, a junk and a gong.
> Wisdom ceases with us, and, howe'er they may try,
> The barbarians will be but barbarians for aye!

For this assessment Congou was made a Mandarin, while Sing-Song was to be executed for taking such a 'one-sided view.'

This story, and the accompanying illustrations depicting the Chinese in a stereotyped manner with pronounced Mongol features, exaggerated moustaches, and

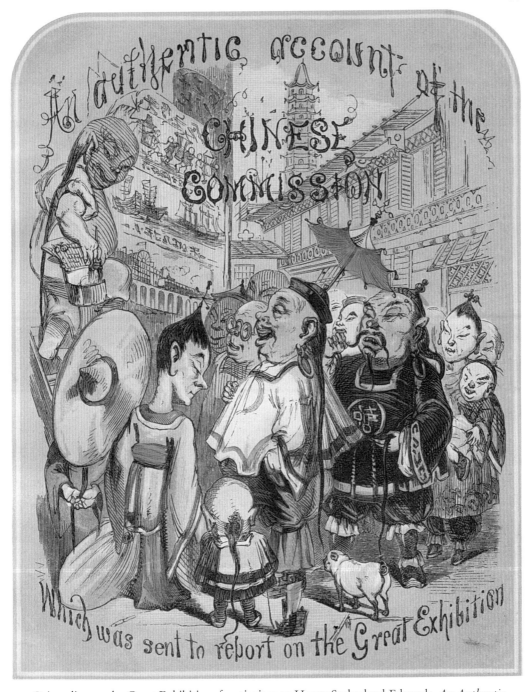

57. Orientalism at the Great Exhibition: frontispiece to Henry Sutherland Edwards, *An Authentic Account of the Chinese Commission, which was sent to report on the Great Exhibition.*

pigtails, makes obvious the extent of British prejudice and hostility toward alien, non-Christian civilizations. In Edwards' depiction – which is hardly unique – the Chinese are devoid of a sense of justice. They rehabilitate the murderer and hang the enlightened scientist. They are bloodthirsty and inhumane, and are subject to an uncontrollable despot who is stupid, cruel, and arbitrary in his exercise of power. There is no question that this sort of stereotyping, though by no means new, had a profound impact on the British. John Tod, the Lasswade engineer, recorded in his diary that he saw in the Chinese pavilion a Chinese man, 'not at all a beauty to our eyes,' with 'coarse' features. In the Tunisian section he saw 'several tall, fat, dark looking fellows, Turks jabbering away, in their oriental dress.' Tod also wrote of a black man he saw in the American section whose 'eyes and teeth were fearful,' and who butchered the English language.[78] Edwards' story illustrates what has been called 'the problematics of alterity,' the difficulties humans have in dealing with and understanding alien others.[79] On the one hand, Sing-Song the philosopher represents a projection of the Western European *philosophe*; he has lost most of his Chinese otherness. On the other hand, most of the story clearly represents differences that are characterized as inferiorities and value judgments.

The point of such a story, however, may have been less about denigrating the Chinese than it was about constructing a certain image of what it meant to be British, although these were both undoubtedly part of the same orientalist impulse. Edwards' *Authentic Account of the Chinese Commission* can quite profitably be read as a masked expression of British identity. The value of costumes is that they represent an inversion of one's own nature. By impersonating an 'other,' a person exposes essential features in his or her self.[80] Edwards' story, then, becomes a 'symbolic reversal for expressive purposes.'[81] By exposing or describing the negative – the Chinese – Edwards has celebrated and clarified the positive – the British. After all, if the British were the opposite of Sing-Song and the Chinese Emperor, then they were rational, unprejudiced, just, open-minded, non-violent, and believers in material progress. This is not to make any claims that the British were in fact 'liberal,' only that this was the way they wished to represent themselves.

The exact reason or occasion for the writing of Edwards' story is unknown, but it is quite possible that he was prompted, or inspired, by the sudden appearance of He-Sing, an alleged Chinese mandarin, into the procession at the opening of the Crystal Palace (fig. 58). Among the foreign officials congregating in the nave before the appearance of the Queen was a mysterious Chinese man, clothed in satin, silent, but seemingly at ease. The sight of him shaking hands with the Duke of Wellington led observers to believe that he was a man of some importance, although China had sent no official representative to the exhibition. Then suddenly, during the singing of the Hallelujah chorus, this 'live importation from the Celestial empire,' in the words of *The Times*, pushed his way through the crowd to the front of the throne and began to bow repeatedly to the Queen. Since no one knew who he was, but not wanting to offend, he was included in the procession that toured the Crystal Palace. It turns out that He-Sing was no Mandarin, but instead the proprietor of a Chinese junk moored at a pier in the Thames. There, advertising himself as 'the Acting Imperial Representative of China,' he and his crew exhibited a 'Museum of Curiosities' and gave nightly performances of Chinese swordplay. He had been trying by means of a publicity stunt to attract sightseers to tour his boat at a shilling per person.[82]

Edwards' *Authentic Account of the Chinese Commission* reveals the process by which Britons defined themselves against, or in comparison to, other nations and peoples. In *Orientalism*, Edward Said made clear how 'the Orient has helped to define Europe (or the West) as its contrasting image, idea, personality, experience.' He argued that 'European culture gained in strength and identity by setting itself off against the Orient as a sort of surrogate and even underground self.'[83] Although by 'Orient' Said was referring to the Middle East, he could, at least in this instance, have

58. H. C. Selous, *The Opening of the Great Exhibition* (1851–2). Victoria and Albert Museum, London.

just as accurately been describing British attitudes toward East Asia. 'There is no more effective way of bonding together the disparate sections of restless peoples,' Eric Hobsbawm has written, 'than to unite them against outsiders.'[84] This is not to imply that at the time of the Great Exhibition a sense of what it meant to be British superseded or expunged other ties or identities. As we have seen, local, class, and party divisions remained strong. What the nationalist sentiments expressed around the occasion of the exhibition suggest is that, even if only for a brief period, many Britons were able to subsume their allegiances to class, region, factory, or community, and rally around the flag hoisted above the Crystal Palace.[85] Nor would it be accurate to say that this was a universal, shared, or uncontested vision. Only that a substantial number of British men and women had a sense of what they shared with each other and, perhaps more importantly, what differentiated them from the people of other nations.

FEAR OF FOREIGNERS

There is something paradoxical about the many depictions and descriptions of foreigners at the Great Exhibition. Visual sources leave the historian with the impression that foreigners flooded London during the summer of 1851 – from Africa and Asia and America as much as from Europe. In sketch after sketch of the opening of the exhibition, or of the streets of London, there they are: the Mandarin with slanted eyes and Fu Manchu moustache; the Turk with pantaloons and a saber; the American Indian chief with feathers in his hair and a blanket draped across his shoulders. It all seems improbable in an age when it took weeks to sail from New York to London, to say nothing of the journey from Peking or the African jungle.

Yet many Londoners perceived there to be an unusually large number of foreigners in town.[86] The artist Henrietta Ward remembered in her *Memories of Ninety Years*:

> From every part of the globe came representatives, many gorgeous in oriental robes. Dusky Indian Princes with turbans and jewels on their foreheads; sallow-faced Chinese Mandarins in silken embroidered dress; sedate little Japanese potentates with inscrutable faces; broad-faced, woolly-headed African Chiefs wearing bright colours; travellers from America, Australia, Canada and other countries, mingling with Russians, Poles, Frenchmen, Italians and Austrians.[87]

And the American Benjamin Silliman described how, as he walked through the streets of London, he could hear half the languages of Europe, and some of the Far East.[88] Add these recollections to the many caricatures and drawings of foreigners cited earlier, and the historian is left with a picture of London awash with visitors from exotic lands.

A comment by the author of a pamphlet for the Society for the Promotion of Christian Knowledge suggests, however, that things might not have been as they seemed. This author granted that he was having difficulty spotting foreigners, but explained that, rather than wearing 'national costume' that would have differentiated them from Britons, foreigners were instead adopting 'the unobtrusive style of English dress,' thus avoiding 'undesirable publicity.'[89] Presumably most foreigners visiting London were wealthy and therefore more likely to wear a generalized 'Western' attire rather than national costumes. It is possible that foreigners in London were abandoning their indigenous dress for less conspicuous fashions; if so, the illustrators who drew the opening ceremony got it all wrong: they drew foreigners in their native dress. It is more likely, however, that this author was having difficulty spotting foreigners because there were so few of them. His perception may reveal more about his expectations of the number of foreigners who were going to be in London than it does about how many actually made the trip. It may also reveal much about how Britons viewed the few foreigners whom they saw.

For centuries British dislike and distrust of foreigners had waxed and waned, but during the nineteenth century they were remarkably tolerant of political refugees. Many refugees worked in specialist occupations, and thus did not compete with the British for jobs, and the principle of asylum was part of the general liberal canon of beliefs that predominated during the mid-century years.[90] Nevertheless, fear of foreigners – and of the crowds, disturbances, and crime that were expected to be the likely consequences – were rampant during the months preceding the opening of the exhibition (fig. 59). Many of the fears expressed were colored by memories of 1848. The Home Office received hundreds of letters, both signed and anonymous, such as the following:

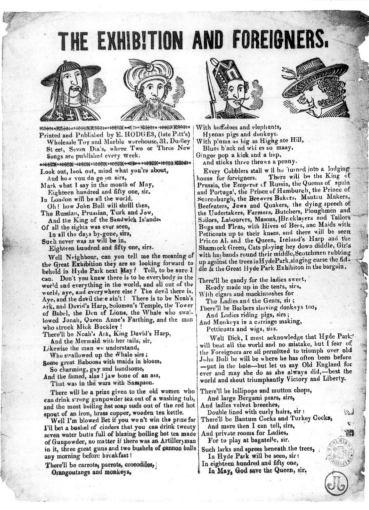

59. Xenophobic broadsheet.

Woe to *England*. All the *French Socialists* it is understood are coming over to the *Exhibition*!!!! It will be *well* if *London* is not destroyed by *Fire*!!!! The *Pope* has *successfully* thrown the *Apple of Discord amongst us*!!!![91]

The popular press covered and no doubt inflamed these fears. *John Bull* started worrying almost six months before the opening about the influx of foreigners whose moral and religious standards it believed were below the British, and foretold problems of sanitation and overcrowding. The paper warned: 'evil is before us.'[92] The *Express* reported that some expected the first of May to 'usher in a revolution,' and that others were looking suspiciously at any foreigner 'to trace, if possible, under his jaunty, careless manner, the sinister aspect of the spy and the conspirator.' There were all sorts of rumors, including reports of demagogues holding secret Sunday meetings.[93]

A number of Britons expressed their fears to the Duke of Wellington, still considered the savior and protector of the nation. One correspondent thought the exhibition would attract 'vast multitudes of strangers, many of whom cannot be said to be very favourably disposed to our country or liberties, or religion.' Anticipating more than one million foreigners, he suggested that the navy be kept afloat, patrolling in particular near the coast of Ireland.[94] Hugh McCorquodale wrote a sixteen-page letter to Wellington, outlining the dangers he feared would result from the influx of foreigners and offering an eighteen-point plan of action. His concern was that foreigners would turn Albert's 'magnificent conception' into '*a modern Babel*,' and made reference to 10 April 1848, 'When the Chartist hubbub . . . drove our citizens to their wits' end, and frightened London from its prosperity.' His proposed countermeasures included plans to cordon off London; barracking troops at places like Gray's Inn and Lincoln's Inn, hidden from view in virtual forts; augmenting the police fourfold; arranging for a church bell signal to remove omnibuses from the streets as in 1848 so that they would not be used as barricades 'after the fashion of our Gallic neighbours;' and keeping a watchful eye on societies with foreigners which might use the 'neutral ground' of the Crystal Palace 'for plotting.'[95]

Wellington relayed these fears, as well as his own, in a series of letters to the Prime Minister, Lord John Russell. 'I think that we ought to be prepared,' he wrote, 'for a campaign commencing on the 1st of May and enduring 'till the end of August at least, possibly 'till the end of September!' Wellington did not doubt that there would be an assembly 'of all the mischievous spirits, and *Hommes d'Actions* as they are called, in Europe.'[96] He and Russell even discussed seeking the assistance of the French police in order to identify 'red republicans' who might come to England to create some sort of disturbance, and to learn riot-control tactics. Francis Cavendish, the great-nephew of the fifth Duke of Devonshire, who spent seventeen years in the Foreign Office as private secretary to Lord John Russell and Lord Clarendon, noted in his diary that Wellington insisted on there being seven infantry regiments in London during the summer of 1851, as a safety measure in light of the eight million foreigners who were expected.[97]

The press generally gave little credence to rumors that foreigners might foment revolution during the exhibition, with the exceptions of *John Bull* and the *Morning Post*.[98] *The Times* sought to calm the public: 'People must surely be unconscionable alarmists to persuade themselves . . . that Englishmen would submit to be driven by foreigners when they would not even be led of themselves.' *The Times* also pointed out, revealing its antipathy towards the Irish, that given the considerable experience of the metropolitan police in dragging 'frantic Irishmen from a fifth storey to the station house,' continental revolutionaries should not pose a problem.[99] Charles Dickens mocked those who predicted revolution as 'Nervous old ladies, dyspeptic half-pay officers, suspicious quidnuncs, plot-dreading diplomatists, and grudging rate-payers' who foolishly believed that foreigners would take over the country while the police pretended to be asleep.[100] *Punch* was equally scornful of the 'bigoted Englishman, belonging to the fine old John Bull school,' who expected 'nothing less than the Plague' from the presence in London of foreigners 'with long moustachios, long beard[s] . . . long hair and dirty habits.'[101]

All reassurances aside, foreign governments were equally concerned. William Temple, Palmerston's brother and British Ambassador to the Kingdom of the Two Sicilies, reported to Palmerston that the King of Naples disapproved of his subjects either sending goods to or visiting the exhibition, being of the opinion 'that the exhibition would afford a pretext for the assembling of all the violent republicans in Europe, and that the Neapolitans by mixing in such society would run great risk of having their minds tainted with revolutionary doctrines.' Similar expressions came from St Petersburg, Vienna, and Paris.[102] King Frederick William IV of Prussia wrote to Albert about the possibility of a revolution or uprising, after receiving a letter from Ernest Augustus, King of Hanover and one of Victoria's uncles, who had heard that Albert and his ministers were 'beginning to jabber with anxiety about this rubbishy exhibition.' Ernest Augustus wrote of 'the infamies, plots and *menées* of the excommunicated of all lands, who are now in London.' Albert tried to be reassuring:

> As regards England, I can only assure Your Majesty that we here fear neither risings nor murderous attacks, and that, although many political refugees from every country live and perhaps conspire here, they behave peaceably living in great poverty. They have realized from their own observations and experience that the British people have nothing in common with their feelings, and that London is perhaps the worst *terrain* for their schemes.

He also tried to dispel the rumor that the court had decided to quit London during the exhibition.[103]

These expressions of fear reflected more than simply worries about a repeat of 1848. Popular writers published tracts whipping up anti-foreigner hysteria by raising the specter of plagues and epidemics as well. In *The Philosopher's Mite to the Great Exhibition*, which created something of a panic, 'Dr Collier' claimed that throughout British history the worst epidemics had followed and were traceable to sudden and large influxes of foreigners. J. C. H. Freund countered in *A Small Contribution to the Great Exhibition of 1851* that not all large gatherings spread disease, and that the number of 'demoralized and depraved characters' at the exhibition would be few. Nevertheless, even Freund urged the government to demand that foreigners bring medical certificates, that boats not accept passengers who seemed contagious, and that foreigners be examined for contagious diseases upon their arrival.[104] Insofar as ideas of contagion serve a demarcating function, they are essential to a society's search for order and identity. Transgressions against a society's standards of health and cleanliness, such as leprosy, syphilis, or AIDS, whether voluntary or not, powerfully threaten the order of that society.[105] In the works of 'Dr Collier' and Freund, fears of foreigners manifested themselves in concerns over the diseases they would bring into Britain, that they would literally infect British society.

Punch brilliantly captured the widespread fear of the dirt and disease foreigners would bring with them in 'A Hint to the Commissioners,' by John Leech (fig. 60). Three Frenchmen are gazing in bewilderment at several pitchers, washbasins, and bars of soap sitting on a table outside the Crystal Palace. One says to the other, 'My goodness, Alphonse! Look. What is that machine over there called?' The other answers: 'Say, that's funny – but I don't know.' *Punch*'s respectable readership, with its famed compulsion for order and cleanliness, would certainly have recoiled in horror at the Frenchmen's unfamiliarity with such rudimentary methods of sanitation. The Frenchmen are depicted as buffoons, with baggy trousers and long capes. One man wears an eye-patch reminiscent of the ubiquitous pirate; the other puffs on a cigar. Unlike the trim top-hat of the Englishman behind the table, the French hats are rumpled and roguish. Juxtaposed against the neatly clad, clean-shaven Englishman, the Frenchmen, all of whom sport mustaches or beards, present an unkempt and suspicious threesome. For all the fine brocade, china, and other luxuries that the French exhibited at the Great Exhibition, water – to be poured from the pitchers and

A HINT TO THE COMMISSIONERS.

" MON DIEU, ALPHONSE ! REGARDEZ-DONC. COMMENT APPELE-T-ON CETTE MACHINE-LÀ ! "
" TIENS, C'EST DRÔLE—MAIS JE NE SAIS PAS."

60. Francophobia: John Leech, 'A Hint to the Commissioners'. *Punch* (26 April 1851).

washbasins and in the English Channel itself – separated Britain from all other peoples, culturally and geographically.

British writers worried that foreigners would cross all sorts of boundaries. The following by B. Clayton, who caricatured foreigners in his *Frolick & Fun or What was Seen and Done in London in 1851*, is revealing: 'We should say that few persons suffered more perplexity from the influx of strangers, than the door-keepers of Her Majesty's Theatre; for the rules prohibitory of coloured neck cloths and plaid trousers were found quite insufficient to meet the wants of the past season; they were, in fact, totally at a loss to define the boundary between full dress and *dishabille*.'[106] Accompanying these words was a drawing of an African king or prince covered only by a loincloth and fur cape draped across his shoulders (fig. 61). Her Majesty's Theatre, like the Crystal Palace itself, with its scale of admission prices, reflected, reinforced, created, and at times undermined the social hierarchies of Victorian society. Audiences were ordered by the amount they could pay, by where they sat, and by the clothes they wore. There were minimum standards of what was acceptable within Victorian society. Flaunting cultural norms of standards of dress, to quote from one historian, creates 'cultural anxiety.'[107] The fear captured in Clayton's *Frolick & Fun* was that the mythical African visitor to the theater, by appearing undressed, was crossing the boundaries that ordered Victorian society, and hence threatened the very order of that society. Submission to rules signifies acceptance of one's place in a hierarchy; by violating the dress codes of Her Majesty's Theatre, the African was revealing himself to be, literally and metaphorically, outside the boundaries of Victorian society, a true foreigner.

THE OPERA.

61. Crossing boundaries: dressing and undressing.

For all the worry that there would be a repeat of 1848, there was not a single episode of trouble. The only hint of an incident occurred in mid-May, when George Grey wrote to Albert's secretary Phipps, from the Home Office, that he had heard of an alleged distribution of placards in German near Leicester Square. He immediately sent the police to investigate, but they found no one, and Grey said there was reason to doubt whether any placards had been distributed at all.[108]

In fact, the number of foreigners in London during the exhibition was quite small. 'Where are the Foreigners?' asked *Punch* in mid-May, and *The Times* found 'no perceptible increase' in passengers on steamers from abroad.[109] *The Times* was wrong, however, because the census published a year later documented that the number of arriving 'foreigners and aliens' reported by ship captains in 1851 was three times that of the previous year, having increased from 22,301 in 1850 to 65,233 in 1851.[110] In their *First Report*, the Royal Commissioners estimated the number of foreign visitors at just under 60,000 (which, as the census revealed, was a remarkably accurate count), but dismissed this nonetheless as 'much below expectation.' About half of these came from France.[111] The Home Office kept track of the number of foreigners who visited the Royal Arsenal at Woolwich during the exhibition, and the numbers are small indeed.[112] Obviously not all foreigners who were in London toured the Royal Arsenal, but, since it was one of the premier attractions, the fact that so few went is further indication of how few foreigners there were in London during the exhibition. Not that the historian should be surprised by this. Although it is difficult in general to discern the number of foreigners in Britain from the 1851 census because they were classified according to place of birth or nationality, not race, foreigners as a whole constituted a minuscule portion of the populace in 1851. The census reported slightly more than 50,000 in England and Wales, or 0.28 percent of the population of eighteen million, and in London the percentage of foreigners was only slightly higher at 1.08 percent (25,500 out of a population of 2,362,000).[113]

Returning to Edwards' story and the notoriety of He-Sing, according to the census 110 London residents were born in China. Of these, seventy-eight were classified as 'foreigners' and thirty-two as 'British subjects.' There is no mention of Chinese in other parts of Britain. There were official references to Chinese seamen in Britain as early as 1814, though there were only a handful of them, employed by the East India Company. Chinese began to appear more frequently after the treaties of Nanking (1842) and Peking (1860), which opened up China to British trade, but throughout the nineteenth century the size of the Chinese population in Britain remained, in the words of one historian, 'negligible.'[114] The appearance of He-Sing, then, was a truly exceptional event; seeing him might well have been for many a once-in-a-lifetime experience, and it may be for this reason as well that he was accorded such respect at the opening of the Great Exhibition, even though contemporary depictions of Chinese people were generally quite demeaning.

How, then, to resolve the very contradictory evidence regarding the number and appearance of foreigners in London during the summer of 1851? Several considerations help explain why so many depictions of the Great Exhibition include foreigners, despite the fact that in all likelihood there were relatively few of them. First, many of them were drawn before the exhibition opened, at a time when people expected foreigners to attend in droves. Second, the ideology behind the exhibition was that it was a celebration of humanity as one large happy family, which included members of all nations. Thus many of these engravings reflect the ideological purpose of the exhibition in a way that no photograph could or would have. Third, while we now know that the number of foreigners in London was minimal, any sighting of a foreigner – particularly from the more exotic areas such as China, India, and Africa – was a rare and notable event given the even smaller number that Britons were accustomed to seeing. In fact, the commission's estimate of 60,000 extra foreigners in London during the exhibition would have more than doubled the number of foreigners in the city. Foreigners, then, were disproportionately prominent considering their small numbers.[115] Finally, the many visual representations of foreigners may be seen as expressions of deep anxieties about British national identity and status.

As for the rather ambivalent attitudes toward foreigners, they were a mixture of fear and fascination. Many of the fears can be attributed to memories of the revolutions of 1848, revived at the time of the exhibition by a particularly xenophobic sector of British society. They can also be explained by what the Duke of Argyll, George Douglas Campbell, described as 'The insular dislike of all foreigners, which is almost a feature in the English character.'[116] But, most of all, foreigners were different. George Augustus Sala, author of the humorous *Great Exhibition: 'Wot is to Be', or, Probable Results of the Industry of All Nations in the Year '51'*, which parodied foreigners at the exhibition, poked fun at Britain having become a haven for refugees by describing the nightly gatherings of foreigners in cafés for *Household Words*: 'hooded, tasselled and braided garments of unheard of fashion; hats of shapes to make you wonder to what a state the art of squeezability had arrived; trousers with unnumbered pleats; boots made as boots were never made before; finger and thumb-rings of fantastic fashion; marvellous gestures, Babel-like tongues; voices anything but (Englishly) human.'[117] The attitudes of an indigenous population toward an immigrant group frequently have little to do with the reality of the relationship between them, but rather with the perception of differences or otherness. Sala's writing, like the drawings of Africans or residents of the 'Cannibal Islands' as only a small step removed from monkeys (and this almost a decade before publication of Darwin's *Origin of Species*), suggests that many British writers characterized foreigners as barely human, and certainly not British.

Foreigners were not only different; they were curiosities, and as such they inspired in Britons both interest and revulsion. Charles Dickens' novel *The Old Curiosity Shop* reminds us that during the Victorian era interest in freaks was at its high point; P. T. Barnum's traveling show, which arrived in London in 1844 with Tom Thumb and the Fat Lady, makes the point further.[118] Freaks challenge conventional boundaries: between male and female, human and animal, large and small, self and other. They are one of us, but different.[119] The same is true of Britons' encounters with foreigners. The exhibition brought to Britain foreigners who were clearly different and alike at the same time, thus arousing both fear and fascination.

A number of issues and events combined to create the nationalist fervor that surrounded the exhibition. The Don Pacifico affair, the outcry over 'Papal Aggression', and the large increase in Irish immigration after 1845 made British men and women more anxious: protective of their nation and expressive of their collective identity. To affirm one's singularity is, by definition, to cultivate one's differences. The Great Exhibition was a convenient opportunity to celebrate the values and beliefs that, in the minds of British men and women, separated them from their neighbors. It is important to note, however, that these cultural boundaries were by no means fixed. Relationships were in constant motion; frontiers shifted.[120] Even as Britons liked to portray Americans as their 'brothers,' for example, slavery constituted an almost irreconcilable difference. France, an enemy in 1848, had returned to being Britain's closest neighbor by 1851, only to become a feared other again by 1852. Nevertheless, despite the shifting frontiers of international cultural relations, and the many possible ways of characterizing a given nation, or affirming British identity, on the occasion of the Great Exhibition, freedom, industry, progress, and Protestantism constituted normative reference points for British society.

RESULTS: INTERNATIONALISM REVISITED

In 1851, the Great Exhibition seemed to be more than just a museum of art and industry or another place 'to see and be seen.' It stood as a symbol of international brotherhood and mutual dependence that in the hopes of many would usher in an era of peace between nations. In organizing the exhibition, Prince Albert and the Royal Commission had routed the protectionist objections, putting free trade and international commerce and communication on a pedestal for everyone to see. And, as we have seen, to a large degree the organizers were successful in promulgating their vision of the exhibition as a festival of peace. Numerous writers followed the organizers' lead and asserted that international peace and understanding were at hand.

Not surprisingly, even after the exhibition closed the organizers persevered in their insistence that the exhibition had contributed to international peace and would continue to do so. Richard Cobden wrote to his friend Joseph Sturge at the conclusion of the exhibition: 'It is a glorious work, successful even to the end, and will bear fruit in spite of the Horse Guards, Admiralty and the Foreign Office.'[121] And Henry Cole, indefatigable as always, gave a lecture at the Royal Society of Arts 'On the International Results of the Exhibition of 1851'. He claimed that the Great Exhibition was likely to lead directly to a uniform international postage tariff; an international sanitary congress to discuss quarantine; increased visits from foreigners; open as opposed to secret diplomacy; an international and uniform system of weights, measures, and coinage; an international system of scientific classification; the abolition of passports; and international copyright. He spoke of international interactions being 'more reasonable, more civilized, less costly and more consistent with religious convictions, than the most scientific arguments of parks of artillery and squares of infantry, which in the long run do not settle any questions. . . . The old-fashioned, narrow suspicions and secrecy of diplomacy will be exchanged for public confidence and public discussion.'[122] Nor did Cole give up his dream. In early 1852 he wrote to Granville, who had just become Foreign Secretary, asking him to consider 'commencing those friendly international relations which are a natural result from the late exhibition.'[123]

Over the next fifty years writers continued to hold the organizers' view. James Hole wrote in 1853 of 'different nations, no longer rivalling each other in military contests or diplomatic chicane.'[124] Archibald Alison, the historian who wrote for *Blackwood's* on numerous issues including the census and free trade, remembered in the early 1880s: 'All the nations of the earth were to be there represented; but it was not in military array, but in civil garb: there were to be no more envyings, or jealousies, or strife, but only the generous and unselfish emulation of freemen.'[125] And just before the turn of the century, Charles Love, in his account of the four international exhibitions held in London up to that point, would boldly declare that the Great Exhibition had helped to 'inaugurate a new era of international *rapprochement* and world shrinkage.'[126]

Yet Britain was in a state of continuing belligerence. Only three years before the exhibition the country had been in the midst of an invasion scare; only three months before the exhibition Britons were in a frenzy about 'Papal Aggression'; and only a few months after the exhibition, Kossuth's arrival in Britain, coupled with the Russian repression of Hungary, produced a surge of popular Russophobia that quickly extinguished whatever momentum toward internationalism the exhibition might have generated. When the Duke of Wellington died and Louis Napoleon declared himself emperor almost simultaneously in early 1852, all the 'latent fears of Bonapartism' in England were awakened, and the paeans to peace that had dominated the political debate during the summer were drowned out by support for Russell's scheme for an expanded militia.[127] The mid-century years may have been years of peace (meaning the absence of international wars, although the revolutions of 1848 and the Crimean War, only six years apart, should perhaps make historians rethink that characterization), but they were certainly not years of international harmony, particularly from the British point of view. Indeed some, such as the conservative *Blackwood's*, the bane of Prince Albert's liberal, internationalist ideas, saw through all the pacifist cant about beating swords into plowshares: 'In short, war surrounds us on all sides,' wrote Archibald Alison in 1851, who thirty years later would nostalgically remember the exhibition as a festival of peace and civility. 'Its passions are raging throughout the world; an era of such hostile prognostications is scarcely to be found in the annals of mankind.'[128] For all the talk of peace, there was an awareness of the near inevitability of human conflict.

Historians have held two contradictory view about the exhibition. On the one hand, they have generally characterized it as a festival of peace, accepting at face value the language used by Albert, Cole, and numerous writers at the time in promoting the exhibition. On the other hand they have belittled the exhibition as a sham, highlighting its failure to bring about universal peace.[129] War played a vital part in the invention of the British nation after 1707,[130] and the Great Exhibition was no exception. Though much of the rhetoric surrounding the exhibition was of peace, the event itself was emphatically a war – of products and values – although this is not to say the conflict was such that British men and women did not learn enormously from it. But it was more than a peaceful competition; it was about consumers, and markets, and status, and ideology. The stakes were the British system of government and economy, which were compared, usually but not always favorably, with the governmental and economic institutions of other nations. At issue was Britain's future: whether it would decline like Greece, Italy, and Spain; whether it was superior in matters of democracy and production to France; and whether it would be overtaken economically by Germany and America. It is only by seeing the exhibition as a continuation of war between nations – by other means, to paraphrase Clausewitz – that the mid-century years, years of conflict not peace, make sense.

There is, then, another way to view the exhibition, and that is as a supremely nationalistic, even warlike event. The organizers may have hoped to foster peace and international harmony, and certainly promoted it on those grounds, but one of the most effective means of selling the idea to the British people was as a giant nationalistic competition that required the participation of all Britons. Moreover, there was a way in which the exhibition sold itself and took on new meanings in the hands of popular writers. Writers took the themes offered by the organizers, modified them, and diffused them. Whereas for Albert the exhibition might have been about reducing the cultural differences between nations, for popular writers it was a chance to expose those differences, mocking the foreign 'other' as a means of asserting British superiority and national identity.

PART III   MEMORY

CHAPTER 7

Palace of the People

O<small>N</small> 11 O<small>CTOBER</small> 1851, the last day of the Great Exhibition, some 53,000 people visited the Crystal Palace. Although there was 'a slight sprinkling of the humbler orders,' according to *The Times*, most 'belonged to the middle and wealthier classes, and consisted of *habitués* of the exhibition.' By the end of the day the transept, where people had gathered even more than usual, was 'packed with a dense mass of black hats' through which an occasional bonnet could be spotted. Just before five o'clock Osler's crystal fountain stopped and the crowd grew silent. The organs began to play the national anthem, and those in attendance turned their faces upward and sang along. Because of the size of the building and the distance between them, however, the organs were unable to stay together and so the singing of 'God Save the Queen' was, in the words of *The Times*, 'a very discordant demonstration of loyalty.' Then everyone cheered and slowly made their way to the exits to the pealing of bells.[1]

The history of the Great Exhibition splits into two strands after 1851: the story of the £186,000 surplus which went, after much debate, to buy land in South Kensington that was ultimately used for the Victoria and Albert and Natural History Museums, the Science Museum, the Imperial College of Science and Technology, and the Royal Albert Hall; and the story of the building, which was relocated to Sydenham, a London suburb, where it remained standing (and for a while quite popular) until it burned down in 1936. Intertwined with these two narratives are changing perceptions of British national identity as the Crystal Palace was transformed from a symbol of Britain's greatest successes to the most visible symbol of its failures.

WHAT IS TO BE DONE WITH THE CRYSTAL PALACE?

Two questions gripped London society during the summer of 1851: what was to be done with the Crystal Palace, and what was to be done with the surplus.[2] Joseph Paxton fired the first salvo in a short pamphlet, *What Is to Become of the Crystal Palace?* He advocated keeping it as a 'winter park and garden under glass,' a place of recreation and instruction, a 'public resort.' He wrote that the garden would provide an alternative to the 'murky' winter air by supplying the 'climate of southern Italy, where multitudes might ride, walk, or recline amidst groves of fragrant trees, and where they might leisurely examine the works of nature and art, regardless of the biting east winds or the drifting snow.' And, he claimed, it would give 'vigour to man's body and cheerfulness to his spirits.'[3] The popularity of Paxton's proposal may be gleaned from *Punch*'s cartoon, 'Mr John Bull in his Winter Garden' (fig. 62).

MR. JOHN BULL IN HIS WINTER GARDEN.

62. Support for Paxton's proposal to turn the Crystal Palace into a winter garden in Hyde Park. *Punch* (16 August 1851).

Henry Cole then added a volley of his own under the pseudonym 'Denarius' ('coal' in Latin), with a pamphlet titled *Shall We Keep the Crystal Palace, and Have Riding and Walking in all Weathers among Flowers, Fountains and Sculptures?* He too suggested a self-supporting winter garden for pedestrians and equestrians, along with a sculpture gallery, and urged people to write to the commissioners to let them know that there were many who wished to preserve the building. Cole emphasized that the popularity of the exhibition was 'mainly due' to 'the self-supporting and self-managing principle,' that it would have been far less popular and far less successful had it been carried out by the government instead of 'the public,' and that the winter garden should be funded in a similar fashion.[4] Here is another of those instances when people saw in the exhibition what they wanted, and used it to promote a broad social, political, or economic goal. Soon thereafter appeared *A Medical Man's Plea for a Winter Garden in the Crystal Palace*, which focused on the unhealthy air and living conditions in London. The author claimed that an enclosed winter garden would enable London residents to leave their dark, crowded houses in good and bad weather.[5]

Joining those in favor of keeping the building were *Punch* and the *Westminster Review*, along with the *Economist*, which asserted that while there were no reasons for its removal, there were thousands why it should be kept. The *Economist* likened the Crystal Palace in importance to St Paul's Cathedral and Westminster Abbey, calling it a monument and 'the crowning act of consolidation of a peace of thirty-five years' duration.'[6] Only a few months after it had opened, the Crystal Palace had already become an icon.

On the other side there were two camps, at least according to Francis Fuller: 'the legal and the local' and 'the engineering and the architectural.' The former, London residents who lived near the park, did not want to see their preserve 'spoiled,' that is, populated. The latter claimed that the building was not structurally sound, an unfounded fear that dated back to the construction of the building a year earlier.[7] Both views reached the public in *An Answer to 'What is to Become of the Crystal Palace'*, by 'Greville,' and in the anonymous *Reasons Why the Crystal Palace Should Not Be a Permanent Building*, both probably written in July 1851. The latter objected to the appropriation of the land in Hyde Park, and argued additionally that there would need to be extensive improvements made to the building, all at great expense to the taxpayer. When Lord Campbell attacked the advocates of retention in the House of Lords, asserting that the building would rapidly deteriorate, he drew an immediate rebuttal from Paxton in *The Times* (15 July 1851) and, ten days later, in his *Shall the Crystal Palace Stand or Not?*

Letters poured into the offices of the Royal Commission, and appeared in the London newspapers almost on a daily basis. The Metropolitan Sanitary Association recommended keeping the building for reasons of public health. Charles Hamilton of the British Museum proposed turning the Crystal Palace into a museum. One of the more fanciful proposals came from an architect, to convert the Crystal Palace into a 1,000-foot-high tower with elevators (fig. 63).[8] Leading the charge for those advocating removal was John Kelk, a real-estate developer who had invested £70,000 in a row of houses opposite the Crystal Palace and was having difficulty selling or renting them. In general, the strongest opposition came from South Kensington homeowners.[9] Even Charles Dickens was invited to join the fray, by his friend Eliot Warburton, an Irish writer and traveler, but Dickens declined, writing that the whole subject had become 'a horrible nuisance.' He admitted that he had been 'furtively lingering on the sea-shore for six months,' 'sequestering' himself from the crowds and commotion surrounding the exhibition.[10]

According to the terms of its appointment, the Royal Commission was required to return the Hyde Park site to the Commissioner of Woods and Forests at the conclusion of the exhibition. This position, quietly supported by Albert, prevailed, and, as required under the terms of the building contract, the commission served notice to the contractors in September that they would have to remove the building, coincidentally on the anniversary of the installation of the first column.[11] Nevertheless, as a result of the flurry of letters and pamphlets in favor of keeping the building the government appointed a commission to review the matter and to appease the proponents of retention. In February 1852, however, the commission bowed to the wishes of Albert and the Kensington homeowners, to the original promise made by the Royal Commission to return the park, and to financial realities, and recommended removing the Crystal Palace. On 29 April 1852 the House of Commons voted to affirm that decision.[12]

Paxton, astute as ever, had already made provisions for just such an event. Within weeks he had formed a corporation and secured £500,000 in capital, raised by selling £5 shares. Soon thereafter his company purchased the building from Fox & Henderson for £70,000, and a piece of land at the crest of one of the taller hills south of London, near the small country villages of Sydenham, Penge, and Norwood. The company dismantled the building and removed the materials to Sydenham, where it was soon rebuilt.

DESIGN FOR THE CONVERSION OF THE EXHIBITION-BUILDING INTO A TOWER 1000 FEET HIGH.
By Mr. C. Burton, Architect.

63. Design for conversion of the exhibition building into a tower.

The debate over whether to keep the Crystal Palace was, as far as the public was concerned, a debate about the meaning and importance of the exhibition. The *Economist* wrote that, when the exhibition was planned, the Hyde Park site granted, and the contract for the building signed, the public had no idea how grand the exhibition would be. It doubted whether even Paxton could have conceived of how popular the building and the exhibition would become. Given that public opinion had changed, the *Economist* recommended keeping the building which had in effect become too much of a national symbol to destroy.[13] On the other side was 'Greville,' who wrote unsentimentally that the building had served its purpose. He added, 'The building engages not our feelings.' *Fraser*'s concurred, reporting that the building was taken down 'without any evident signs . . . of national emotion.'[14] *Punch*, as always, captured both sides of the debate. While unequivocally in favor of preservation, it poked fun at those lamenting its destruction, suggesting that with this would come the destruction of 'learning, arts and commerce.' How sad it was, joked *Punch*, that the Crystal Palace, which had so bravely withstood Sibthorp's attacks, should be 'ignominiously "knocked down" by a common appraiser's hammer.'[15] Few knew that Albert had already decided that the building should be torn down.

WHAT SHALL WE DO WITH THE SURPLUS?

Much more important to Albert than the question of the building was the question of the surplus. His proposal, which he set out in a memorandum dated 10 August 1851, began with the presumption that the commission had to adhere to its objectives, and hence that the proposals to turn the Crystal Palace into a winter garden, museum, or promenade had 'no connection whatever with the objects of the exhibition.' Moreover, he stated that the relationship of the commission to the building was 'incidental,' that the commission was bound by its creation to remove the building. He was clearly not at all sentimental about the building, probably under great pressure from the residents of Belgravia to remove it (and the accompanying crowds), and much more interested in something that would benefit Britain's economic future.

In his memorandum he proposed purchasing an estate in Kensington for £50,000, and placing on it four institutions corresponding with the four sections of the exhibition. These institutions would be devoted 'to the furtherance of the industrial pursuits of all nations,' and toward that end would include a library, lecture and meeting rooms, and an exhibition space. Motivating his plan was his opinion that there were currently for each of these pursuits separate public societies that were unconnected and struggling for existence: the Geological Society, the Botanical Society, the Linnean Society, the Zoological Society, and the Agricultural Society. Albert wanted each of these organizations to sell their buildings and relocate to South Kensington.[16]

Albert's trial balloon did not get far. Three days after suggesting the idea he met with Cole, Reid, and Playfair at Osborne, all of whom, according to Cole, 'concurred strongly against the Prince's plan.'[17] In its place Playfair suggested that the money should be devoted to a single college of arts and manufactures, which would foster 'improvement and progress.' His plan, too, was designed to 'contribute to the furtherance of the industrial pursuit of all nations.' The college was to be modeled on the schools of design and the Ecole Centrale des Arts et Métiers in Paris, which annually sent 300 educated men to impart their knowledge of science to French manufacturers.[18] Both Cole and Reid – and, shortly thereafter, Albert – thought this a more practical approach.[19] Later that month Playfair drew up this proposal to circulate under Albert's name.

While the commission was preparing its report to the Queen on the surplus, it received numerous letters offering suggestions. The local committees in Newcastle and Gateshead petitioned the commission to use the surplus to cultivate the arts in large provincial towns; in short, to give something back to the provinces which had so strongly supported the exhibition. The Bolton local committee recommended using the surplus to purchase the building so that it could be rebuilt and opened to the public with free admission. The secretaries of the schools of design in

Manchester, Sheffield, and Newcastle-upon-Tyne all asked that the funds be used to endow the schools of design. One correspondent suggested that the commission fund 'studentships,' or fellowships, for skilled artisans and workers. Another suggested free hospitals for the poor of all nations.[20]

Francis Fuller offered one of the more carefully articulated suggestions for the surplus in his sixpenny pamphlet, *Shall We Spend £100,000 on a Winter Garden for London, or in Endowing Schools of Design... ?* He strongly supported using the money for the schools of design. He wrote that the surplus was the product of hard work; that it was the manufacturers and artisans who had made the exhibition; and that it was the middle and working classes who had supported the idea at a time when 'dandies sneered from Rotton Row.' Given that during his publicity trips to the provinces before the exhibition the appeal that had been most successful was the promise of improving British trade and manufacturing, it was only right to support the schools of design.[21]

The commissioners' report to the Queen, which they submitted on 6 November 1851, expressed their conviction that the Great Exhibition had indeed fulfilled its objectives, namely to promote industry and international understanding. They recommended improving industrial education and extending 'the influence of science and art upon productive industry.' They argued that the subscriptions were given 'absolute and definite,' but with the understanding that in the event of a surplus it should be used in accordance with the ends of the exhibition, or for the establishment of similar exhibitions for the future. With this in mind, they proposed that the surplus not be applied to future exhibitions because the Great Exhibition had proved that they could be self-supporting. Instead, the commission suggested that the surplus be used for 'the furtherance of every branch of human industry' and to promote 'kindly international feelings,' and that these benefits not be limited to Britain alone, but made available to all nations.[22]

The commission claimed in its report to have no 'comprehensive plan,' but this could not have been further from the truth. Even as this report was being prepared and submitted, the surplus committee was making plans to implement Playfair's suggestion for a central college of arts and manufactures – a plan which was consistent with the report to the Queen, but was not yet public. Although there was a delay in the granting of a supplementary commission to dispose of the surplus, time was of the essence regarding the Kensington Gore estate which Albert wanted to purchase for the new educational institution. Granville wrote to Cobden, appraising him of the situation: 'It is believed to be for sale. Circumstances at present unknown to the public, but which at any moment may well be published, make it probable that this land will very soon rise considerably in value.' Albert wanted to invest two-thirds of the surplus in the Kensington Gore estate, which, it seemed, would be profitable with a minimum of risk. Granville reassured Cobden that the purchase would not commit the commission to any particular course of action for the future.[23]

The reason that the commissioners did not publicize their plan for a central educational complex was fear of provincial opposition. As noted above, prominent and powerful men in the manufacturing towns wanted the surplus devoted to their own schools of design, and would have bristled at, if not opposed outright, the construction of a new school in London. Thomas Field Gibson, the Spitalfields silk merchant on the commission, wrote that it was 'scarcely possible to overestimate the importance of securing the active and healthy co-operation of the great manufacturing towns as a main element in the successful prosecution of the plan. We all know,' he continued, 'how great an amount of jealousy exists in these places (well or ill founded) of what is called centralization.' He referred back to the creation of the Government School of Design at Somerset House, an institution he said that had been 'all but abortive.' In contrast, the provincial schools, which were created a few years later, had 'found the co-operation of very influential and intelligent men in manufacturing areas.'[24] Once again, the tension between metropolis and provinces was a ruling consideration.

Cobden had even more substantive criticisms of the plan, which he seems to have revealed only privately, in a letter to Granville. His view is especially important because of its analysis of British industry:

> I have not been able to see the practical advantages likely to arise from the industrial establishment advocated by Dr L. Playfair, or Colonel Lloyd. Have they not lost sight of the fact that the minute and constantly extending subdivision of labour renders a *general mechanical knowledge* less necessary than when our artisans had a more varied field of employment? It is a better education, and better training, *for their children*, which are imperatively called for. . . .[25]

Cobden accurately perceived that the troublesome issue Britain had to face was not the quality of its designs, as so many art critics claimed, but the very structure of its production process. He knew that yet another school of design would do nothing, certainly not in the long term. What was needed was an entirely different approach, which he, unfortunately, could not provide.

Throughout 1852, General Charles Grey, Albert's new secretary, continued to express concerns about how Albert's plan would be revealed, what the public response would be, and what the commission could do about a negative reaction.[26] In many ways the search for support for Albert's plan resembled the search for support for the exhibition two years earlier. Cole made a tour of some of the major manufacturing towns, where he found mild support for the plan but stressed that the Royal Commission had to make clearer what the '*direct* interest' of the provinces would be.[27] Grey asked Playfair to present a more positive view of the commission's plan when unfavourable articles appeared in the press.[28] By late 1852 the commissioners had achieved success. An approving article appeared in the *Birmingham Journal* which praised the plan as being of the 'highest possible value to Birmingham . . . [from] a business point of view.'[29]

Not long after the commission filed its report, Queen Victoria granted the necessary supplemental charter according the Royal Commission the status of a permanent body, and giving it broad powers and the authority to prepare a plan to dispose of the surplus 'in accordance with the expectations which were held out to the subscribers at the time their aid was solicited.'[30] Eventually, with the surplus of £186,000 and another £150,000 granted by the government, the commission was able to purchase two estates in South Kensington. In 1856, Parliament appropriated £15,000 to construct a building on the south-east corner of the estate to house the exhibits given to the Royal Commission by exhibitors following the exhibition, and another £10,000 to move the Department of Science and Art to that same location.[31] In 1857 the South Kensington Museum opened with Henry Cole as its first director. Since then, Albert's dream of an educational complex has grown to include the Victoria and Albert Museum (the successor to the South Kensington Museum, which opened in 1909), the Science Museum, the Natural History Museum, the Imperial College of Science and Technology, and the Royal Albert Hall.

Beginning in 1891, the Royal Commission also began to finance scholarships for the promotion of science and art, a project which gradually supplanted its focus on capital expenditures. Its Science Research Scholarships were the first of their kind, and grew to include not just the United Kingdom, but Canada, New Zealand, Australia, South Africa, India, and Pakistan as well. Each year scholars from these countries continue their scientific training in London, and the former scholars include seven Nobel Laureates among their number. In 1911 the commission began providing stipends for scholars interested in careers in industry (a program that was discontinued in 1939), and they also inaugurated the Rome Scholarships in the Fine Arts, modeled on the French Prix de Rome. In short, the commission has strived to adhere to Prince Albert's interest in promoting both science and art.

SYDENHAM

While the South Kensington museum and educational complex became, over time, the most important outgrowth of the Great Exhibition, for years it was the rebuilt Crystal Palace in Sydenham that continued to capture the nation's imagination.[32] Its significance and appeal, however, were different from those of its Hyde Park predecessor. Whereas the Hyde Park exhibition had symbolized the mixing of the classes and the masses, the Sydenham site was clearly for the masses; whereas the former, at least on the surface, promised peace and international understanding, that latter instead carried forward the Great Exhibition's nationalistic undercurrent; and whereas the Great Exhibition was designed to educate British men and women about industrialization and tasteful consumption, the Sydenham Crystal Palace was, quite frankly, designed to amuse. In the final analysis, the arts manufactures that were so prominently on display in 1851 were the concern of the few, not the many, and so the Crystal Palace was transformed from a school to a playground.

The Sydenham Crystal Palace was built on an even larger scale than the original one, covering almost one hundred more acres and with an additional three stories (fig. 64). It opened in June 1854 (a year late, following a construction accident which killed fifteen men), to strains of the national anthem and Handel's 'Hallelujah Chorus'. The Queen and 40,000 others were present. Although the building was similar, the Sydenham Crystal Palace, a resort and theme park more than anything else, had a very different focus to that of the Great Exhibition. Samuel Laing MP, director of the Brighton Railway and chairman of the Crystal Palace Company, elucidated three objectives at its opening: amusement and recreation, instruction, and commercial utility. Note that only the second of these overlapped with the imperatives behind the Great Exhibition, although in the end the exhibition had indeed become a site of amusement, recreation, and commerce as well. The first of these goals was to be achieved by the enlargement of the building, and the inclusion of fountains and a terraced garden. The second was to be met by means of a complete historical illustration of sculpture and architecture from the earliest works of Egypt and Assyria to modern times. The directors looked forward to the Crystal Palace 'becoming an

64. The Crystal Palace, Sydenham.

illustrated encyclopaedia of this great and varied universe.'[33] Once again, as at the Great Exhibition, the Crystal Palace become a site for the systemization of knowledge. As for the third objective – commercial utility – there was little discussion of how this would come about.

If the Crystal Palace in Hyde Park was a microcosm of British industry, then the new Sydenham version was a tribute to Victorian leisure. It was vastly greater in both size and popularity than the Vauxhall Gardens, and, lacking the pressures of competitive exhibiting, there was a much more relaxed atmosphere which mixed together its educational and recreational purposes.[34] Its goals were to amuse and to educate, but not so much about industry as about the Beautiful. Towards this end the promoters assembled originals and copies of great works of art, especially statues. There were 'courts,' each illustrating the art and architecture of a great period in history, the most spectacular of which was the Egyptian court with high pillars, sphinxes, mummies, and enormous statues (fig. 65). There were also industrial pavilions representing several of the larger British manufacturing towns; carriages and machinery were in the basement. Science was important too, the idea being to 'combine scientific accuracy with popular effect': there was a natural history department with pictures illustrating the development of the human race; in the nave Paxton arranged a display of vegetation ordered from the tropical to the temperate; and in the gardens Waterhouse Hopkins and Richard Owen built models of dinosaurs (the first skeletal remains of which had been discovered in Sussex in 1822).[35]

There were high hopes when the new Crystal Palace opened. John Tallis wrote that the original Crystal Palace was 'the astonishment and delight of the millions who visited it,' and would remain a glorious memory for years to come, but that 'the new Palace of Glass – the Palace of the People – has, to an immeasurable extent, increased the attractions and advantages that belonged to its predecessor.'[36] The *Economist*

65. The north transept, Sydenham.

noted the placing of the first column in August 1852, and took the opportunity to assert its understanding of the meaning of the exhibition and its successor, namely, that private enterprise succeeds not only without government help, but in spite of government hindrances.[37] Harriet Martineau got even further carried away in the *Westminster Review*. She rhapsodized about 'a magic spectacle,' 'a palace evolved from nothingness by the spirit of the time.' She described children standing in the natural history department, 'with their thumbs in their mouths, staring at the polar bear and the reindeer, or peeping into the Greenland hut,' and of the working man 'looking up vacantly at the "images", in which he sees, as yet, no beauty.' She raved that the band was 'an inestimable agency' capable at the same time of gratifying the trained musical ear and bewitching 'the dullest listener.' And she praised the new Crystal Palace for putting all these things 'within the reach of the poorest.' Her only criticism, but this was a serious one, was that it was too 'heterogeneous,' that 'the most prominent impression of ordinary visitors' was 'of eating and drinking.' The Crystal Palace had lost its focus.[38]

During its first thirty years the new Crystal Palace was visited by an average of two million people each year. There was a variety of activities and forms of entertainment, including musical festivals, firework displays, balloon flights (in 1898 Stanley Spencer attained the then record height of 27,000 feet in a hydrogen balloon launched from the Crystal Palace), and shows of all sorts. In 1868 the Crystal Palace presented the first demonstration of moving pictures to a large audience. As late as the winter of 1870–1 the Crystal Palace was still enough of a spectacle for Camille Pissarro, who had fled Paris during the Franco-Prussian War, to paint several oil paintings of it and the surrounding area (fig. 66).[39]

Although it had not been designed expressly for musical performances, the Crystal Palace in Sydenham was throughout the second half of the nineteenth century the most important venue for public music-making in the United Kingdom. Arthur Manns' weekly performances introduced thousands of British men and women to classical music and to new repertoire, and the large-scale performances of Handel's oratorios, especially the *Messiah*, transformed musical life in Britain. One of the most spectacular of the Handel festivals occurred in 1857, when, over the course of three days, some 81,319 people heard the *Messiah* and *Israel in Egypt* performed by 2,765 singers in the choir and 457 instrumentalists in the orchestra (fig. 67). Manns' Saturday concerts stimulated the growth of English music in the period that would later come to be known as the English Musical Renaissance.[40]

Throughout this period the Crystal Palace retained its symbolic importance as a locus of nationhood and nationalism. In 1872, Disraeli chose the Crystal Palace as the location for a landmark speech in which he promoted the empire as central to the Conservative party as well as to the British nation. It is of no small significance that he used 'the palace of the people' as the site to claim that 'the Tory party, unless it is a national party, is nothing.' He asserted that the Conservative party was the party of social reform, the monarchy, and the empire. It was not 'a confederacy of nobles'

66. Camille Pissarro, *The Crystal Palace* (1871). The Art Institute of Chicago.

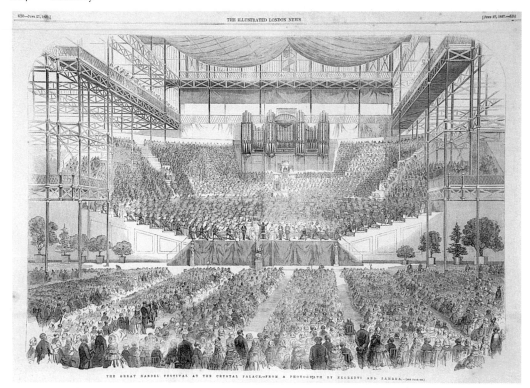

67. The Handel Festival of 1857, Sydenham Crystal Palace. *Illustrated London News* (27 June 1857).

or 'a democratic multitude,' he said, but rather 'a party formed from all the numerous classes in the realm – classes alike and equal before the law, but whose different conditions and different aims give vigour and variety to our national life.'[41] The Crystal Palace in Sydenham, like its predecessor, was still held up as a place for the orderly reconciliation of the different classes. But what had, in 1851, been essentially a liberal shibboleth, had become, by the time of Disraeli's speech, a point of national consensus like the issue of franchise reform itself. The new conservatism which he outlined paved the way for the electoral victory of the Tories two years later.

Disraeli's speech marked a radical realignment in British politics, not just of Disraeli, but of the working classes. As Chancellor of the Exchequer, Disraeli had derided the colonies as a 'millstone 'round our necks' and as 'deadweights.' Now he attacked a succession of Liberal governments for attempting to dismember the empire by the progressive granting of colonial self-rule. His subject was especially topical, coinciding as it did with H. M. Stanley's search for Livingston. It also came not long after the *Bee-Hive*, a working-class paper, advocated state-assisted emigration. Disraeli, then, captured what must have appeared to be a public mood in favor of imperial consolidation and development.[42] In so doing, he cemented the link between workers and the Conservative party that he had forged with his Reform Act of 1867.[43] For a decade Palmerston had stood as the symbol of populism and nationalism; following his death, the mantle passed to Disraeli and the Conservatives.[44]

One can see this continuing linkage between the Crystal Palace and British national identity in John Colcott Horsley's *Portrait Group of Queen Victoria and her Children* (fig. 68). In this painting, the future King Edward VII holds the architectural

68. John Colcott Horsley, *A Portrait Group of Queen Victoria and Her Children* (c. 1865). Forbes Magazine Collection, New York.

drawings of his father's *magnum opus*, the Crystal Palace, which appears in the background amid the trees. It remains a visible symbol of Britain's national successes. The empty chair at Queen Victoria's right, however, is a pointed reminder of Albert's death just a few years earlier. Here, as in the Winterhalter portrait of the royal family discussed earlier, Albert's personal and professional achievements are balanced against each other. Just as in marriage Victoria and Albert symbolized middle-class domesticity, even without her Prince, Victoria still reigns over both family and nation. She is now the grieving widow, responsible for a large brood of children, a plight with which the lower and middle classes would have identified.[45] It is hard to imagine a more potent symbol of British national identity in the mid-nineteenth century than this juxtaposition of the Crystal Palace, the royal family, and basic middle-class values.

In a related sense, one of the areas in which the Sydenham Crystal Palace differed most from the Great Exhibition was that it never had universalist, pacifist connotations. In this respect, it was the Great Exhibition that symbolized peace, not the Crystal Palace. This was especially evident in 1870 when *The Times* wrote of 'war fever . . . raging at Sydenham.' Apparently the most popular exhibits were those that were in some way or another connected with the Franco-Prussian War, which included a giant map of the war theater with forces marked with red and blue blocks of wood, and a newly designed court filled with rifles, sections of armor-plated warships and other war materials.[46] Whereas the Great Exhibition had presented at least the rhetoric of pacifist internationalism and commercial integration, the Sydenham reincarnation offered no such associations. Although the message had changed, the Crystal Palace nonetheless remained quite popular through the 1870s, as a place of leisure and as a symbol of British populism and nationhood.

DISENCHANTMENT AND DECLINE

As early as the 1860s, however, the Crystal Palace had, for many writers, come to symbolize not the triumph of progress but its failures. In Fyodor Dostoyevsky's *Notes from Underground* (1864), the Crystal Palace represents everything that is wrong with modernity. It is mechanical and rational, 'all ready-made and worked out with mathematical exactitude;' it is total, the last word, the ultimate truth; it has left nothing to doubt, meaning 'that every possible question will vanish in the twinkling of an eye, simply because every possible answer to it will be provided;' it is indestructible; and it is intended to intimidate, to force the spectator to 'become silent forever,' so that visitors can do nothing but say yes and shut up. As the Underground Man derisively tells his audience: 'You believe in a palace of crystal that can never be destroyed – a palace at which one will not be able to put out one's tongue or make a long nose on the sly. And perhaps that is just why I am afraid of this edifice, that it is of crystal and can never be destroyed and that one cannot put one's tongue out at it even on the sly.' It was, quite simply, 'inconsistent with the laws of nature.'[47]

Dostoyevsky's characterization of the Crystal Palace is so anomalous that one wonders if he ever even saw it.[48] First of all, as we have seen, the builders of the Crystal

Palace, far from presenting the building as permanent and indestructible, prided themselves on its transience. It was built in four months, and taken down in only three. Second, although it was worked out mathematically, it was one of the most visionary and adventurous buildings of the nineteenth century, rivaled only by the Eiffel Tower and the Brooklyn Bridge. Paxton's blotting-paper sketch, in fact, testifies to the inspiration, rather than calculation, that produced the Palace of Glass. Third, it was not destructive of nature, but harmonious with it. Thanks to Sibthorp's diatribes in the House of Commons, the transept was built over the trees, preserving them, even allowing them to flourish as in a greenhouse (which of course had been the model for the Crystal Palace). Fourth, as the analysis offered here has demonstrated, the Crystal Palace, far from offering the final silencing word, released a storm of dissent and opposition. Dickens, Ruskin, and Morris hated it, and their views were shared by a substantial portion of the press. Even the 'bourgeoisie,' the putative defenders of the liberal and progressive ethic proffered by the Crystal Palace, rejected its architectural innovations, preferring neo-Gothic buildings such as the Midland Hotel at St Pancras.

The 1860s, when Dostoyevsky wrote *Notes from Underground*, were a watershed in Russian history, the decade during which Russia began to modernize. Russia had lost the Crimean War in 1857, which led to a number of reforms, not the least of which was the decision by the Tsar to free the serfs in 1861. But modernization took longer than anyone expected. Dostoyevsky was both angry and defensive about the achievements of the West; he felt shame at his country's backwardness; the more impressive the achievement, the less Dostoyevsky was able to acknowledge it. What he was really reacting to, in *Notes from Underground*, was not the Western reality of modernization, which was full of conflict and debate, but the Russian *fantasy* of modernization as a means of silencing that very debate. Nor did all Russians view the Crystal Palace the way Dostoyevsky did. In 1859 the Russian critic Nikolai Chernyshevsky made a brief visit to London, and wrote about the Crystal Palace in his prison work *What Is to Be Done?* For the novel's heroine the Crystal Palace appears as a magical vision in a dream, 'a symbol of the new modes of freedom and happiness that Russians can enjoy if they make the great historical leap into modernity.'[49]

Dostoyevsky's general sentiments, however, were shared by other visitors from abroad, including Hippolyte Taine. Although he was overwhelmed by the size of the Crystal Palace, he suggested that 'this agglomeration of incongruous curiosities' was reminiscent of ancient Rome, where there were also 'pleasure palaces,' 'pantheons of riches and curios, bazaars in which the taste for novelty, variety and monstrosity replaced any feeling for simple beauty.' It made little difference for him that 'Rome supplied these collections by conquest, [whereas] England does so by industry.' He said that a Greek 'would have judged it good enough for a race of powerful barbarians trying to refine their taste and not having much success at it.' It should be clear that for Taine, as in 1851 for Wornum, Pugin, and Ruskin, the issue was the degradation of taste and, more broadly, antipathy to industrialization. As he put it, in world's fairs 'all the faults of the industrial system . . . are revealed.'[50]

As the nineteenth century progressed, British writers also grew increasingly disenchanted with the Crystal Palace. This was especially true of the novelist George Gissing, who featured the Sydenham site in his novel *The Nether World* (1888), a bleak, angry portrayal of artisans, factory girls, and slum dwellers in Clerkenwell.[51] The twelfth chapter is about Pennyloaf's and Bob's wedding, which takes place on the August Bank Holiday, when 'the slaves of industrialism' have the day off. They spend much of their day at the Crystal Palace, where early on they enjoy the gardens, boats, and merry-go-rounds, which Gissing mocked as circus-like games that appealed to the patriotism of the masses:

> Did you choose to 'shy' sticks in the contest for cocoa-nuts, behold your object was a wooden model of the treacherous Afghan or the base African. If you took up the mallet to smite upon a spring and make proof of how far you could send a ball flying upwards, your blow descended upon the head of some other recent foeman. Try your fist at the indicator of masculinity, and with zeal you smote full in the stomach of a guy made to represent a Russian.

Eventually the newlyweds tire of the grounds, only to find that inside the Palace was 'sweltering,' with dust rising from the floorboards. They pay a shilling for refreshments in the tea room, where 'there reigned a spirit of imbecile joviality.' It was in this context, after Bob gets into a fight and is quieted only by the military brass band, that Gissing offered his remedy for the ills of society: 'an entire change of economic conditions.' He wrote that there was 'no chance of a better world until the old be utterly destroyed.' At the Crystal Palace, 'the People' were 'respectable,' 'sober,' and 'dull.' Girls were 'worn out,' their shoulders stooped from too much work. None showed any taste in dress. As for middle-aged women, they were 'animal, repulsive, absolutely vicious in ugliness.' Men's faces were deformed by ill-health, their legs twisted out of shape. 'Since man came into being,' Gissing cried out, 'did the world ever exhibit a sadder spectacle?'

Evening brings fireworks, dancing, and pickpockets. Back home, Bob's and Pennyloaf's wedding chamber is a 'black hole.' The day ends with Bob, stupefied by drink and exhausted from a street fight, 'breathing stertorously.' His wife, also bloody, lies awake. Down below she can hear her father punching her mother, who has once again celebrated a bank holiday by breaking her vow of total abstinence. As Pennyloaf stares into the darkness, she is already thinking about pawning her wedding ring. She is seventeen; he is nineteen. Their marriage is ill conceived and off to a bad start. Although she had won Bob away from a much more sexually alluring woman, he had run into the woman again at the Crystal Palace and, drunk, had begun to flirt with her. Is it merely coincidence or symbolic that this descent into 'the nether world' is precipitated by a visit to the Crystal Palace? Whereas in 1851 there had been songs about love in the Crystal Palace, by the 1880s, at least for one author, it marked the breakdown in working-class family life. For Gissing, the promise of 1851 was unfulfilled.

The glamour of the Crystal Palace had clearly begun to wane in the later nineteenth century. Henry Cole wrote in 1884 that it had attracted 'millions of gratified visitors and greatly influenced the growth of public taste,' but there may be more than a touch of bravado here.[52] Although he was surely correct in his assessment of the number of visitors who had enjoyed a visit, by most accounts the Crystal Palace in Sydenham exercised little if any effect on taste and design, and as an educational center there is little doubt that it was superseded by other organizations and institutions. Attendance dropped considerably after the Lord's Day Observance Society won an injunction to have the palace and grounds closed on Sundays. And, with the continued growth of the railways and a general increase in wages, seaside resorts became more attractive, especially for the masses.[53] Visits fell off precipitously in the

1870s.[54] By the end of the century the building had become quite dilapidated. As one observer wrote in 1908, the 'education value of the art and architecture collections' had been 'overshadowed by the reputation of the palace as a resort for fireworks, football, and other attractions.'[55] Amusement had supplanted instruction. The Crystal Palace had been transformed from a museum into a pleasure park.

One of the underlying causes of its decline was its increasing loss of focus. The Sydenham grounds became a forum for the expression of all sorts of political views, and, as is so often the case with sites that mean everything, eventually it came to mean very little. In 1868 there was a demonstration 'in defence of the Throne, Church and Constitution,' and 'in support of the Established Church in Ireland and . . . other National Protestant Institutions,' and *The Times* noted a general feeling of 'regret' at the growing practice of holding political and party demonstrations at the Crystal Palace.[56] In 1903 the Cooperative Festival was held there, to exhibit goods produced in cooperative workshops, and 'to show what an addition could be made to working-class happiness if the principle of co-operation were extended more largely to the social and recreative side of a workman's life.'[57]

The first attempt to revive the declining fortunes and popularity of the Crystal Palace came in 1877, when the Lord Mayor of London convened a meeting at the Mansion House to consider the best means of maintaining and preserving the Crystal Palace 'for the use of the people, in fulfillment of the objects for which it was originally formed.' Although he did not specify what these were, Francis Fuller spoke about 'the necessity for places of popular recreation for the great masses of people.' Fuller claimed that during the past twenty-three years more than thirty-eight million people had visited the Crystal Palace, 'and not one person in a million' had been reprimanded by the police for drunkenness or disorderly behavior, even though such behavior was on the increase in London. He said that a public effort was needed to put the Crystal Palace on a solid foundation 'as an institution permanently devoted to the promotion and cultivation of art and science,' rather than leaving it subject to the 'vicissitudes' of 'an ordinary trading company.' Toward this end a joint-stock company had been formed, the Crystal Palace of Arts of All Nations Ltd, with almost £2 million in capital, in order to purchase the site, renovate it, construct new buildings and technological schools, fund scholarships, and provide 'pure and wholesome recreation for the people, with a view of establishing in connection therewith a series of art unions, tending to the development of arts, sciences and manufactures.'[58] Twenty-five years after the Great Exhibition, the production of tasteful arts manufactures remained an intractable problem. As *The Nether World* taught, so too did 'rational recreation.'

Fuller's high hopes for the Crystal Palace grounds were left unrealized. In 1879 a committee of inquiry elected by the Crystal Palace company reported that, with the exception of the portions frequented by the public, 'neglect and decay' were prominent throughout the building. There was a general lack of supervision, and the 'recreations and amusements' had become 'vulgarized,' as well as prohibitively expensive. Stockholders were not being paid, and Fuller's proposal that annual international art exhibitions would bring in new works, and hence more people, appeared not to be succeeding.[59] There was another attempt to refurbish the building in 1908 – the Lord Mayor visited the Crystal Palace and said it would be a 'national disaster' if it fell 'into the hands of a speculative builder,' and urged the government to preserve the site for the public as a 'national possession' – but it took another five years, until just before the First World War, for anything to come of this.[60] When the fiftieth anniversary of the Great Exhibition came along in 1901, there was barely mention of it in *The Times*.[61]

Nevertheless, by the early twentieth century, the Crystal Palace had become integrally linked with what might be called the propaganda of empire.[62] In 1851 only about 500 out of nearly 14,000 exhibitors were colonial. As the nineteenth century progressed, however, the presence of the empire at the Crystal Palace became more and more pronounced. This process had begun, of course, with the very construction and layout of the building, which, by including displays from the Egyptian, Assyrian, Greek, and Roman empires, implicitly attributed coherence to the British empire and put it on a level with the great ancient empires. There were also the annual brass-band festivals, which featured large numbers of military bands playing patriotic songs and marches.[63]

But the Crystal Palace did not reach its apogee as an imperial site until the Colonial and Indian Exhibition was held there in 1905. The goal of this exhibition was, to quote from the official announcement, 'to offer to the people of the United Kingdom an object lesson which would demonstrate that the British Empire produces all the necessaries and luxuries of life in quantities large enough to supply the wants of all its inhabitants. . . .' It was designed 'to promote inter-Imperial trading,' a point which the organizers emphasized in order to differentiate it from the many international exhibitions that had been held during the previous three decades. The implication here is that interest in world's fairs may have been waning at this point, but that an appeal to empire might prove more fruitful. Whereas the Great Exhibition had been promoted on the ground that it would benefit world trade (and not necessarily imperial trade), the focus has now shifted to commerce based on the empire. The organizers' decision that there was 'no better site . . . for this Imperial undertaking than the vast house of glass constructed for the epoch-making exhibition of 1851' reinforced the ever-tightening links between the Crystal Palace and the empire.[64]

These imperial associations were cemented by the Crystal Palace Exhibition of 1911, known variously as the Festival of Empire and the Coronation Exhibition. There was certainly no mistaking its propagandistic qualities. As one official publication put it, it was intended 'to demonstrate to the somewhat casual, oftentimes unobservant British public the real significance of our great self-governing Dominions, to make us familiar with their products, their ever-increasing resources, their illimitable possibilities.' The exhibits were housed in scale models of the Dominions' parliament buildings, connected by 'The All-Red Tour,' a train journey through the empire. There was a Jamaican sugar plantation, a Malay village, and, representing India, a jungle (with a variety of animals running wild), a palace (inlaid with gold and jewels), and a bazaar.[65] Although even this display paled in comparison with the Wembley Empire Exhibition of 1924–5, the 100,000 schoolchildren who attended the coronation party of King George V at the Crystal Palace could hardly have failed to make the linkage between the Crystal Palace and the imperial ideal.

What is especially interesting, if not surprising, about the 1911 Festival of Empire is that observers regarded it as the successor to the Great Exhibition, even though the 1851 event had not at the time been generally regarded as a testament to the empire. *The Times* described the Great Exhibition as the 'counterpart' to the Festival of Empire, noting that Queen Victoria had been 'attended by all that is most representative of the dignity and authority of the Empire.' Without a trace of irony, the paper characterized the Crystal Palace as 'the visible witness of the faith in a universal peace,' ignoring the Indian Mutiny, the Boer War, and the many other instances of violence that were by-products of Britain's imperial ambitions.[66] Once again, there was dissonance between the underlying principles and the associations of the Crystal Palace, in this case between its connotations of peace and those of empire.

Despite the popular empire exhibitions held there in 1905 and 1911, the Crystal Palace had, in the words of *The Times*, become a 'white elephant,' and suffered from a 'chequered career.'[67] A public appeal in 1913 to raise funds to purchase the building, however, revealed deep nostalgic feelings. Although there could not have been many who remembered the 1851 exhibition, *The Times* nonetheless received letters from, among others, an eighty-nine-year-old pensioner who had helped build the Crystal Palace, and an elderly woman who had been at the opening as a young girl, though she remembered that day as 'a long, fatiguing one.'[68] Lord Plymouth put up £230,000 in order to preserve the site, and, after a lengthy public appeal, the building was finally purchased by the government, which used it as a naval supply depot during the First World War.[69] This only led to its further deterioration.

One last attempt was made to refurbish the building after the war, but money was too scarce to do the job well. King George V and Queen Mary opened the Imperial War Museum there in 1920, rather ironically marking 'the return of the Crystal Palace to the uses of peace.' The king declared that it would have been an irreparable loss to the capital of the empire if the Crystal Palace had ceased to be available for public use and enjoyment.[70] Despite some optimism, however, the Crystal Palace had become a mockery of its former grand self. Instead of great music festivals performing Handel and Mendelssohn, there were brass-band competitions and jazz-age beauty pageants, and a sizeable chunk of the once elegant gardens had been used to make a cinder race track.[71] C. A. Bell-Knight, an amateur historian, remembered a visit to the Crystal Palace in the mid-1930s: 'It presented a most woe-begone picture, peeling and sunblistered paintwork, the glass grimy, ironwork encrusted with rust and stonework suffering from erosion. Over all was a film of black dust. . . . The fountains had ceased to function, possibly an economy drive, newspaper and wrappings floated disconsolately upon the oily waters of the lakes and pools.'[72] The Crystal Palace had become a relic of a bygone age.

Late in the evening of 30 November 1936 a fire broke out in one of the offices of the Crystal Palace. Within an hour the building was an inferno as the exhibits caught fire, first shattering and then melting the glass (fig. 69). The fire was visible as far away as Brighton, more than forty miles to the south, as well as to airplanes flying over Britain at the time. By morning there was nothing left but molten glass, twisted iron, and a pile of ash and rubble (fig. 70). As with so many other aspects of the Great Exhibition story, what is significant about this event is less what happened than how people interpreted it. The morning after the fire, the London *News Chronicle* contained a small box on its front page with the headline, 'Is it a Portent?'

The Crystal Palace was built in 1851 'for the promotion of universal happiness and brotherhood', to summon all nations 'to the peaceful field of a noble competition where all might strive who could do most to embellish, improve and elevate their common humanity.

Last night the Palace was in ruins.

69. The fire, 20 November 1936.

70. After the fire: the remains.

That same day the paper reported that German troops had landed in Spain.[73] Winston Churchill, never one to miss the momentousness of an event, commented, upon surveying the ruins, 'This is the end of an age.'[74] Bell-Knight wrote that 1936 was a tragic year, as fascism in Germany, Italy, and Spain threatened world peace, unemployment was rife, and hunger all too present. Edward VIII was to abdicate just nine days after the fire. As Bell-Knight wrote, 'The demise of the Crystal Palace . . . heralded the end of an era – it was to be the final break in the last lingering link with the age of Victoria.'[75]

As always, however, there were a number of possible meanings buried in the ashes of the Crystal Palace. Robert Cockayne wrote in the *Star* about what the Crystal Palace meant to Londoners, reporting that he was saddened not because, as a friend of his suggested, it was 'the burning of the Victorian Valhalla,' but because it had been a part of his childhood, 'Happy days that won't come any more. . . .'[76]

From its construction in 1854 until its destruction in 1936, the Crystal Palace in Sydenham, far more than the memory of the Great Exhibition in Hyde Park, remained an enduring symbol of the nation. It was the icon that foreigners such as Dostoyevsky and Taine and nationals such as Disraeli and Gissing pointed to as the barometer of Britain's successes and failures, its character and orientation. Certainly up until the First World War the Great Exhibition itself was a relatively unimportant symbol, having been supplanted in the imagination of writers and politicians by its Sydenham successor. But the total destruction of the Crystal Palace in 1936, combined with a massive re-evaluation of the Victorian era after the First World War, let loose a flood of reminiscences about 1851, and it is now the Great Exhibition of 1851 and the original Crystal Palace that have come to symbolize not only the Victorian era, but modernity itself.

CHAPTER 8

Legacy and Nostalgia

Even though the Great Exhibition concluded its short life in 1851, its legacy has carried on to the present day, and not only in the form of Crystal Palace memorabilia – commemorative coins, sewing kits, stationery – that were widely available during the summer of 1851 (fig. 71). In 1992 the *Independent* reported on yet another set of plans to renovate the Sydenham site, which would turn overgrown and abandoned stone terraces into a Kuwaiti-owned hotel, complete with bowling alley, multi-screen cinema, night club, and restaurants. What had once been a symbol of 'Victorian confidence, creativity and industrial might' had become 'relics of a lost theme park,' fist-sized chunks of molten glass to be auctioned at Christie's at £40–£50 apiece, perhaps the quintessential symbol of British decline.[1]

Memories of the exhibition have always been mixed, as contemporaries and historians alike have seen in it what they have wanted. Already by the time of the 1862 South Kensington exhibition, the legacy of 1851 was being contested, although for the most part memories of the exhibition were positive and nostalgic until the First World War. During this time, the Crystal Palace in Sydenham had the effect of deflecting attention away from the Great Exhibition. While the buildings were similar, the significance ascribed to the Crystal Palace in Sydenham was different to that attributed to the Great Exhibition, and for the most part the two were not conflated. The Sydenham Crystal Palace left memories of the Great Exhibition nearly pristine, as it absorbed much of the criticism by writers such as Dostoyevsky and Gissing. Sentiments toward the Great Exhibition began to shift after Queen Victoria's death, when Bloomsbury writers started to debunk their Victorian parents, and by the mid-1930s writers had become dismissive of the significance and lasting impact of the first world's fair. By the time of the Festival of Britain in 1951, conceived as a means of commemorating the centennial of the Great Exhibition and occurring just fifteen years after the Crystal Palace had burned down, the Great Exhibition had been virtually forgotten.

Analysis of writings on the Great Exhibition reveals three phases of remembering, each of which evaluates not only the Great Exhibition itself but also its liberal underpinnings. During the first nostalgic phase, which lasted from the end of the exhibition until the First World War, reminiscences of the exhibition reveal a vague wistful longing for what were perceived to be its certainties. During the second and much briefer phase, writers dismissed the significance of the exhibition, in effect marking the failure of its liberal ethos. Finally, at the time of the Festival of Britain, the Great Exhibition was virtually ignored altogether, as nineteenth-century liberalism no longer seemed relevant in the post-war, democratic-socialist society. In memory, as at the time, the exhibition has served as a projection screen for assertions of British national identity.

* * *

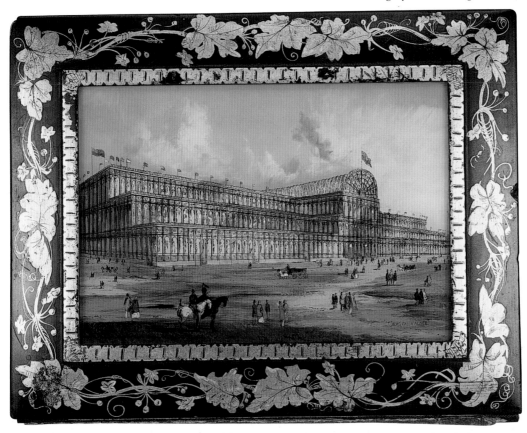

71. Crystal Palace memorabilia: blotting-book cover inset with painted glass over silver foil. Museum of London.

REMEMBERING: FROM SOUTH KENSINGTON TO WEMBLEY

The first substantial reconsideration of 1851 came during the preparations for the International Exhibition of 1862, held in South Kensington. Once again the exhibition took place in a building constructed especially for the occasion, only this time it was not a 'Crystal Palace' but the 'Brompton Boilers' (fig. 72). It was built out of brick, had two large iron domes courtesy of Brunel, and bore a striking resemblance to the building committee's unpopular and aborted plan for 1851. There was nothing visionary – or aesthetically appealing – about it. For Edmund Yates, art critic for *Temple Bar*, it merely demonstrated how special 1851 was. '[I]ts place in the memory is like a fairy vision,' he wrote of the Hyde Park Crystal Palace, and, for him, it was the reconstructed Crystal Palace in Sydenham, not the 1862 exhibition, that was the true successor to 1851.[2] It was the building itself, unique, a pleasure palace for the people, that was an essential element of the legacy of 1851.

The idea of a successor international exhibition was first discussed by the Royal Society of Arts in 1858, looking toward 1861 and every ten years thereafter. The plan was to show the progress made in industry and art during each decade, which 'would tend greatly to the encouragement of arts, manufactures and commerce.' Toward this end the exhibits would be arranged not according to country, as they had been in 1851, but according to classes (in 1851 only the British exhibits were organized by class, and only in the *Official Catalogue*, not at the exhibition itself). The council of the RSA produced a report with statistics showing the extent to which commerce had grown during the previous decade, and there was certainly a sense that the Great Exhibition had been a significant contributor to this economic expansion. Garibaldi's campaign for a unified Italy, however, caused the planners to delay the exhibition to 1862, though they were still optimistic that it would go a long way toward 'extending the blessings of peace and promoting the progress of civilization,' and that this would be especially welcome during 'a season of strife and warfare.'[3]

At the time of the 1862 South Kensington exhibition, assessments of progress since 1851 were largely positive, as were re-evaluations of the Great Exhibition itself. Not that this should be surprising, given that many of those doing the assessing had themselves been involved in the 1851 exhibition and had a personal interest in its legacy. According to Richard Cobden, French visitors and jurors with whom he had spoken were unanimous in their opinion that British manufacturers had made enormous advances since 1851, and the French Minister of Commerce was so concerned about the improvements in British design and production that he was forced to 'reorganize and awaken up the energies of the French schools of design . . . [which] could not afford to sleep in the face of such a competition.'[4] Edmund Yates also believed that British taste had made 'great progress' since 1851, though he wrote that British taste in arts manufactures still lagged behind that of other exhibiting countries.[5]

For both Disraeli and Granville, as for Cobden, the exhibition had stimulated invention and refined taste and produced positive results. Granville, for example, pointed out that even though the new building was 33 percent larger than the Hyde Park Crystal Palace, the organizers still had to turn away six out of every seven possible British exhibits, which suggested to him that the exhibition of 1851 had demonstrated to manufacturers the worth of such endeavors. Where the two men differed was in their assessment of how well Britain had competed in 1851. Disraeli characterized the Great Exhibition as a 'great lesson,' in which 'England learned many things of which before she was ignorant, and unlearned some things which perhaps she had practised too long.'[6] Granville, however, implied that Britain had held the leading position in 1851, although he worried that there was 'some danger' that this supremacy might be lost if British manufacturers did not get organized and apply themselves to the forthcoming exhibition. It is not clear whether he was truly concerned about Britain's industrial supremacy, or whether he was just rousing support for the exhibition. Both men, however, shared the view that the exhibition of 1851 had been at least in some measure a success for Britain.[7]

The Times, on the other hand, discerned little improvement in the quality of British arts manufactures, although it too was nostalgic about 1851.[8] The diplomat Viscount Canning provided a similarly mixed assessment of the Great Exhibition in a letter to Granville regarding the forthcoming 1862 exhibition:

> I think your exhibition for 1862 is a mistake. I do not believe that advances in arts and manufactures have been sufficiently marked to be appreciated by the common herd, and to be successful you must make impression upon them. Nor has there been time for them to forget 1851, and they will judge you relatively. . . . As to India, we shall make a bad show. . . . In upper India they say that they received no benefit from the exhibition of 1851.[9]

72. The 'Brompton Boilers'. South Kensington Exhibition, 1862. *Illustrated London News* (24 May 1862).

On the one hand, manufactures had not changed enough to guarantee support from Britons or to make another exhibition worth having, nor had the exhibition had enough of an impact on international trade to garner support from parts of India. On the other hand, there were still such positive feelings about the exhibition of 1851 that a successor would pale by comparison.

Outside the realm of arts manufactures, there was an even wider sense at the time of the South Kensington exhibition that the Great Exhibition had had a positive impact. The *Globe* cited the underwater telegraph, the screw-propeller on steamships, the removal of various duties, and the perfection of photography as proof of progress. Moreover, the declared value of exported manufactures had risen from £65,756,000 in 1851 to £122,155,000 in 1857, to a great extent due to the opening of trade with China and Japan and the development of colonial resources. At the 1862 exhibition, in fact, the British colonies produced three times as many exhibitors as they had in 1851.[10] There were now some 7,000 Indian exhibits which alone occupied 277 pages of the catalogue. So, although arts manufactures remained a continuing concern, in other areas the Victorian belief in progress and the expansion of empire held firm.

Only in one area – assessing the link between exhibitions and peace – was there a substantial re-evaluation. Yates acknowledged that in 1851 he had believed that 'in commerce was at last found the true link to bind together all the races of man in common brotherhood.' Now, following the Crimean War, the Indian Mutiny, the American Civil War, and the Wars of Italian Unification, that seemed to be 'a former age.'[11] And the anonymous reviewer of the 1862 exhibition for *Bentley's Miscellany* wrote rather sarcastically that the array of armaments on display in South Kensington was much more likely to guarantee peace – through deterrence, as it were – than was 'the affectation of good will and charity which we displayed rather too ostentatiously in 1851.'[12] The pacifist internationalism of the Great Exhibition, therefore, was the first casualty, though in fact there had been just as many examples of weaponry in 1851 as there were in 1862.

Following the 1862 exhibition, references to the Great Exhibition were generally nostalgic until the early twentieth century. Charles Knight, in the mid-1860s, looked back on it 'with pleasurable feelings that never before or since have been called up, in an equal degree, by any public display of national power and wealth.' The Crystal Palace especially had a profound effect on him. He described it as a tribute to free trade and fiscal reform, 'a palace of untaxed glass.' The exhibition as a whole was 'a true symbol of what *had been accomplished* and what *was to be accomplished* by wise legislation.'[13] In 1872 Jane Budge wrote that 1851 had been 'the brightest year of all Victoria's reign, when . . . [t]he world was at peace; and England, prosperous at home and honoured abroad, saw men of almost every nation gather in friendly rivalry to her shores.'[14] And in 1913, when *The Times* provided a brief history of the Crystal Palace as part of a fund-raising appeal for its preservation, the paper suggested that 'an almost Elizabethan halo' surrounded the Great Exhibition and the mid-Victorian years. There was, in *The Times*' words, 'a spirit of passionate devotion to the young Queen and her Prince Consort, which touched the whole enterprise of the Fair of the Nations with a colour of romance.' The exhibition was an 'enormous success . . . the earliest and one of the greatest of the peaceful triumphs of the reign of Queen Victoria.'[15]

Soon after Victoria's death, however, as the values that were associated with her name began to recede further into the past, attitudes toward the exhibition began to shift. Although there had always been those who had refused to glorify the exhibition, their presence became much more pronounced during the years immediately preceding, and in the decades following, the First World War. Robert Edward Francillon, for example, visited the exhibition when he was ten, and wrote about the experience on the eve of the First World War:

> About that time occurred an experience that ought to be, but is not, among the principal of my memories – a visit to the Great Exhibition of 1851. I was by no means too young or too ignorant, certainly anything but too apathetic, to take an intelligent and enduring interest in what I saw, and [it] was the talk and wonder of the world in a way with which not even the most ambitious of its subsequent imitations can remotely compare. But it remains in my mind a mere formless blur of colour, heat and crowd, with a delightful iced drink for its solitary detail. We took it on our way to Littlehampton for the summer holidays; and far more distinct than all the fondly supposed triumph of peace and industry (though in fact the harbinger of over sixty years of almost incessant war) remains the feudal keep of Arundel, with its guardian owls.[16]

What is so interesting about Francillon's recollection is his sense that he 'ought' to have remembered the exhibition more clearly and fondly than he did, which suggests how pervasive nostalgia toward the exhibition was as late as the First World War. Like many before him, he was skeptical of the internationalist rhetoric that had surrounded it, and in his memory, at least, his experience was nothing but a jumble.

Even as late as the Wembley British Empire Exhibition of 1924, *The Times* gave 'a fond backward glance at 1851,' although no one was more nostalgic than King George V, who opened the Wembley exhibition. 'Our thoughts go back to the Great Exhibition of 1851,' he said, 'and to the brilliant hopes of international peace and friendship with which it was inaugurated.' His language testifies to the enduring legacy of 1851: He spoke of the Wembley Exhibition as a 'picture,' a means by which 'to take stock of the resources, actual and potential, of the Empire,' just as Albert had spoken of the Great Exhibition as 'a true test and a living picture.' The King also asserted that the Wembley Exhibition represented to the world 'a graphic illustration of that spirit of free and tolerant co-operation which has inspired peoples of different races, creeds, institutions, and ways of thought, to unite in a single commonwealth and to contribute their varying national gifts to one great end.' Here too there are obvious references to 1851. But 1924 was not 1851, and the King knew this. Britain, he said, was no longer 'quite so ambitious' as it had been.[17] Insofar as the King was in any way representative of his subjects, the exhibition of 1851 was still looked upon fondly, even though there was a profound awareness that many of its promises had remained unfulfilled.

Within a decade, however, these nostalgic attitudes had been replaced by disillusionment, not just with 1851, but with the entire Victorian age. Violet R. Markham, in a book about Paxton and the Duke of Devonshire, wrote in 1935, 'The Great Exhibition of 1851: I am very conscious that to write its name is to invite a yawn.' According to Markham, the exhibition conjured up in people's minds 'a confused impression of Albert the Good, a giant glass house, some antiquated machinery and a litter of Victorian furniture and works of art.'[18] The culmination of reappraisals of the significance and majesty of the Great Exhibition came with Christopher Hobhouse's *1851 and the Crystal Palace*, published in 1937, in which he wrote:

> As for the importance of the Great Exhibition, it had none. It did not bring international peace; it did not improve taste. Imperceptibly it may have promoted free trade: a few manufacturers may have learned a few lessons from their foreign rivals. The Russell Government and the Prince both gleaned a little popularity from it. But first and foremost it was just a glorious show. . . .[19]

The date of Hobhouse's book is important, immediately following the destruction of the Crystal Palace, and barely a generation after the appearance of Lytton Strachey's witty and debunking *Eminent Victorians* (1918). The Victorians were no longer in vogue, and the Great Exhibition, from beginning to end the epitome of the Victorian age, suffered along with its creators. Not only had it failed to foster peace; it had also done nothing to improve taste.

Thus the Great Exhibition functioned as a litmus test for attitudes toward the Victorians. During the second half of the nineteenth century, memories were nostalgic, as those who mentioned the exhibition in their memoirs did so with fondness, seeing 1851 as a time when the possibilities for Britain, both at home and abroad, seemed limitless. By the First World War the glow of the Great Exhibition had begun to fade. It was still regarded as an important event, but there was an increasing sense that it was not as significant as its organizers, or those who attended, had claimed it was. In 1924, it continued to be a reference point for the King, who, while acknowledging that times had changed, nevertheless invoked the exhibition as a means of representing the ideals toward which Britain should continue to strive, especially the ideal of cooperation. Even as late as 1936, the Great Exhibition was still a significant marker, important enough for Christopher Hobhouse to proclaim its irrelevance. But once the Crystal Palace had burned down, and with the massive assault on the Victorian belief in liberalism wrought by communism and fascism, the Great Exhibition lost its relevance.

* * *

FORGETTING: THE FESTIVAL OF BRITAIN

At no point was the legacy of the Great Exhibition more ambiguous than at the Festival of Britain in 1951. Ostensibly created to mark the centennial of the first world's fair, the festival ended up more as a celebration of the achievements of the Labour government and a demonstration of Britain's recovery from the Second World War than as a commemoration of the Great Exhibition. It was only at the last moment that the organizers remembered to include a tangible reminder of 1851, so far from memory had the exhibition receded.[20] The Great Exhibition was irrelevant to the Labour party because the values it had come to represent, especially free trade, a minimalist government, and an expanding empire, were anathema to Labour policies. The Labour organizers cannot have ignored the exhibition by accident; they ignored it because it did not serve their purposes. Just as the organizers of 1851 had used the Great Exhibition to promote liberal values, so did the organizers of 1951 use the Festival of Britain to foster Labour values. Ironically, the principles that the Labour government was trying to promote – a public–private partnership between government and labor, and a commitment to reducing class tensions – were, as we have seen, very much a part of the Great Exhibition. The Festival of Britain, it turns out, was a missed opportunity to highlight certain legacies of the Great Exhibition. Each of the two events, in a sense, marks a paradigm shift, or branch, in modern British history: one, in 1851, toward liberalism; the other, in 1951, away from it.

In 1943, the Royal Society of Arts, ever mindful of its role in having brought to fruition the Great Exhibition, urged the government to begin to plan an exhibition along similar lines, to commemorate its centennial in 1951.[21] Such a proposal, of course, required a considerable amount of faith, for it presumed not only that Britain and its allies would win the war, but that Britain would be sufficiently recovered by 1951 to stage such a spectacle. Two years later, in September 1945, with the war over and Labour in power, Gerald Barry, editor of the *News Chronicle*, wrote an open letter to Stafford Cripps, President of the Board of Trade, advocating a trade and cultural exhibition to commemorate the centennial of the Great Exhibition and promote British products. Although the centennial may have served as the impetus and was a convenient reference point, it was clear that the underlying reasons for holding such an exhibition were to promote British-made goods and to raise people's spirits, to be 'a tonic to the nation.'

The government responded to Barry's letter by appointing the Ramsden Committee to consider the feasibility of organizing such an exhibition. Its report, published in 1946, recommended a 'universal international exhibition' to demonstrate to the rest of the world that Britain had fully recovered from the effects of the war. As a reminder that the event was to commemorate the centennial of the Great Exhibition, the committee proposed holding the event in Hyde Park, a suggestion which the government immediately rejected as unfeasible. *The Times* was relieved that the government abandoned its 'monstrous threat to build over some acres of Hyde Park,' not realizing the irony of its opposition: one hundred years before, of course, the paper had just as fervently opposed the construction of the original Crystal Palace in Hyde Park, the very location that contributed so greatly to the success of the Great Exhibition.[22] The following year, in 1947, with Britain's economy ravaged by widespread shortages and the rising cost of nationalization and social services, Cripps was forced to abandon as well the idea of an international exhibition as too expensive. In the end, the Festival of Britain would be little more than a national trade fair and arts festival. So, whereas the Great Exhibition of 1851 had begun with a proposal for a national exhibition and developed into an international exhibition, a century later the process was reversed, as what began as a proposal of international scope became an event that was entirely national.

Once it was clear that the focus of the Festival would be national rather than international, responsibility for planning it shifted from Stafford Cripps at the Board of Trade to Herbert Morrison, Lord President of the Council, who had served as Home Secretary during the war. Under Morrison's guidance, the Festival became not just a national show but a nationalistic one, designed to illustrate the British contributions to 'civilization,' past, present, and future, in the arts, science, technology, and industrial design. It seems clear that making the Festival popular was high on Morrison's list of priorities given the bleak austerity of the immediate post-war years, though as an astute politician he cannot have failed to expect that the Labour party itself stood to gain politically from its popularity (although in this he was proved wrong, with the Conservatives returning to power in September 1951).

Morrison formally announced the proposal to the House of Commons in 1947, but it was Charles Barry who was appointed Director-General and who, in concert with an executive committee and the Festival Council – the equivalent of the Royal Commission for 1851 – planned the festival. The Festival Council consisted of eminent artistic and political figures, and was chaired by Lord Ismay, who had served as Chief of Staff to the Minister of Defence and Deputy Secretary to the War Cabinet in 1940–5. Other notables on the council included Kenneth Clark, T. S. Eliot, and Malcolm Sargent. But whereas in 1851 the commission was widely praised for representing all classes and all interests – even if it in fact did not – in 1951 the festival was derided as 'a paternalistic enterprise' organized by 'a cultural elite.' Certainly, as one historian has pointed out, the members of the council 'spoke the same language' and had similar concerns and 'progressive sympathies.'[23]

When the government announced its plans for a Festival of Britain, its stated intention was 'to mark the centenary of the Great Exhibition of 1851 by a national display illustrating the British contribution to civilization in the arts, science and technology, and industrial design.'[24] The links between the Festival of Britain and the Great Exhibition, however, were tenuous from the outset, and receded even further as the festival plans progressed. It has even been suggested that for the organizers of the 1951 exhibition the Great Exhibition was a 'red herring' and little more than a 'pretext.' The plans for the South Bank site were well advanced before anyone noticed that there were no references to 1851 or the Crystal Palace. So, at the last minute, the organizers commissioned a scale model of the Crystal Palace, the only indication that the Festival of Britain actually marked the centennial of the Great Exhibition (fig. 73).[25] *The Times'* article announcing the proposed international exhibition for 1951 did not even mention its Hyde Park antecedent, even though the stated purposes of the two events were so similar, especially the 'promotion of Britain's export trade.'[26]

The contrast between the two events is striking. Whereas the Great Exhibition had been emphatically centered in London, and as such caused a great deal of provincial jealousy despite the proliferation of local committees, the Festival of Britain just as explicitly reached out to the towns outside of London: to Glasgow, where there was an exhibition of industrial power; to Belfast, where there was a display on Farm and Factory; to Worcester, where the popular 'three choirs' festival was incorporated into

73. Scale model of the Crystal Palace, centenary pavilion, Festival of Britain 1951. Public Record Office.

the scheme; and to many other towns, which witnessed the traveling exhibition of items relating to industry. The incorporation of Ulster into the imagined nation is particularly noteworthy: Whereas a century earlier the organizers had, after an initial attempt, virtually written off Ireland's participation in the Great Exhibition, now, in 1951, Northern Ireland's participation was required, for political if not economic reasons.

More profoundly, whereas the Great Exhibition ostensibly focused primarily on economic prowess and only secondarily on culture and ideas, in 1951 the order was reversed. As in the mid-nineteenth century when the organizers of the Great Exhibition had used economic success to demonstrate the worth of what they perceived to be British values, a century later the organizers of the Festival of Britain used so-called British values to promise economic recovery and success. It is worth recalling the extent to which 'traditional' British culture and ideas had come under assault in the 1930s and 1940s by the fascists and communists. The festival, even more than the Great Exhibition, overtly projected such values as freedom, democracy, and tolerance, and these must be seen in the context of the aftermath of the Second World War and the onset of the Cold War.

Inasmuch as the various British exhibitions after 1851 had charted the increasing prominence of the British empire, the apex of which occurred at the Wembley Empire Exhibition of 1924, the Festival of Britain both reflected and heralded the decline of the empire and Britain's retreat from world power. The exhibition itself was inward-looking, national, not international, and there was little direct imperial content. Britain had recently withdrawn from Palestine and the Indian sub-continent, and the imperial and Commonwealth exhibits were excluded from the South Bank site, located instead at the Imperial Institute. If the Great Exhibition of 1851 had marked the burgeoning of Britain's massive and formal overseas empire, then the Festival of Britain more or less symbolized its end.[27] Nothing symbolized this better than the Festival's official poster where Abram Games' design of Britannia surmounting the Festival Star shows her surveying not the globe, as she did in 1851, but the British Isles (fig. 74).

Given that the empire was no longer a central feature of British national identity, the organizers had to find other bases on which to promote a national image. According to Basil Taylor, who wrote the 1951 exhibition guide, the Festival of Britain was to provide 'the autobiography of a nation,' a 'record' of what the British thought of themselves in 1951, the work not of any individual or of any one city, but of the entire nation. There were three sections of the exhibition: 'The Land of Britain,' which described how the British Isles were formed and cultivated both agriculturally and industrially; 'The People of Britain,' which discussed their origins, character, and traditions; and 'British Achievements in Science, Technology and Industrial Design.' In addition to the South Bank site the London portion of the show included the Festival Gardens in Battersea, with a formal garden, amphitheater, acrobats, a dance pavilion, amusement park, zoo, Punch and Judy theater, beer garden, tea garden, and nightly displays of fireworks.

The Festival of Britain painted a very different picture of the composition of the British nation from that offered by the Great Exhibition. As Robert Henriques wrote in *Field*, 'Here we are presented as a mixed race compounded of invaders, each of whom in turn was assimilated by the invaded' – a 'synthesis.'[28] The idea, at least as conceptualized by Gerald Barry, was to 'provide a picture not only of the essential unity of our democracy, but also of the rich diversity within that unity which is an essential ingredient of it, and which, if allowed to wither, would deprive our national life of much of its vitality and colour.'[29] In 1948, in response to assertions by former colonies of their right to regulate immigration, Britain proclaimed its continuing commitment to free entry in the British Nationality Act. All citizens of the colonial empire or Commonwealth were recognized as also having British citizenship, giving them the right to move to Britain. Already by the time of the festival this movement of people was beginning to have an effect on British society, and the organizers clearly perceived a need to shore up so-called traditional British values in the face of the new, increasingly multi-ethnic society.

In this context it is fair to say that the Great Exhibition was more effective at creating a sense of national identity, and one that was longer lasting, than the Festival of Britain, in part because of the imperialist character of the event and the 'othering' that went along with it. Despite, or even because of, its internationalism, the Great Exhibition made it all too clear to British men and women how they differed from 'foreigners.' The Festival of Britain, on the other, made clear that 'foreigners' were a part of Britain. Moreover, in contrast to the great efforts of the organizers of 1851 to build bridges to various sub-sections within Victorian society in order to forge a liberal consensus, the Labour government in the late 1940s had recently won a landslide election victory, and thus did not need to engage in the sort of coalition-building of the sort undertaken by the Royal Commission for 1851.

74. The official Festival poster. Museum of London.

75. Remembering the Great Exhibition: advertisement for Huntley & Palmer Biscuits. *Illustrated London News* (12 May 1951).

Everywhere there were signs of progress, signs that Britain was recovering from the war. The leading example was the exhibition of architecture at Lamsbury, a former slum, which was rebuilt after the Blitz. Now it was 'a new urban landscape in which the buildings are growing together as a community.' Though no one seems to have made the connection at the time, this was clearly the modern equivalent of Albert's working-class housing. There was also the Dome of Discovery, the Power and Production Pavilion, which included everything from raw materials to finished products (just as in the Great Exhibition), and the Lion and Unicorn Pavilion, which featured 'some of the leading ideas, beliefs, traditions and eccentricities' which had shaped British social history. Featured among them were freedom (religious and civil), justice, democracy, pride in independence and craftsmanship, and love of sport, home, nature, and travel.[30] At least on the surface the festival was celebratory of progress and forward looking in orientation.

Underneath all the pomp, however, it was quite clear that Britain was suffering a severe national identity crisis. The mood in 1951 was dramatically more somber than it had been a century earlier. As the Archbishop of Canterbury summed up in one of his speeches:

> The chief governing purpose of the Festival is to declare our belief and trust in the British way of life, not with any boastful self-confidence nor with any aggressive self-advertisement, but with sober and humble trust that by holding fast to that which is good and rejecting from our midst that which is evil we may continue to be a nation at unity in itself and of service to the world.[31]

And the *Economist* wrote rather grimly that 'Whatever the pleasures of the Festival of Britain we shall not experience the awe, the wonder and the faith which caused our forefathers to break into torrents of emotional praise.' Gone were the hopes for international peace, the faith in the beneficence of scientific and industrial progress, the certainty of national superiority, and the delight in cheapness and plenty.[32] Gone, quite clearly, was the heady optimism of the Victorian age.

Observers also discerned differences in the way the two exhibitions promoted aesthetics and the arts. W. Y. Carman, for example, a working man and ex-soldier, was disappointed not to find at the festival the kind of stylistic lead that the exhibition of 1851 had offered, although given the polyglot assortment of styles diffused through the Crystal Palace one has to wonder what he had in mind. And Hugh Casson, the Director of Architecture for the Festival, observed that whereas in 1851 so much had seemed novel – though with the exception of the Crystal Palace itself almost all art critics, including Wornum, Ruskin, and Morris, would have disagreed with him – this was certainly not the case in 1951. Indeed, art historians have detected in the 1951 displays a pervasive anti-Victorianism, and 'a classless style for the masses' consisting of the council flat and the semi-detached house.[33] So, although in its origins it harkened back to 1851, in many ways the Festival of Britain could not have been more different than its predecessor.

Charles Plouviez, who worked in the Foreign Office, deplored the chauvinism of the Festival compared to the internationalism of the 1851 exhibition: 'It might almost be said to mark the beginning of our "English disease" – the moment at which we stopped trying to lead the world as an industrial power, and started being the world's entertainers, coaxing tourists to laugh at our eccentricities, marvel at our traditions and wallow in our nostalgia.'[34] Aside from the gloom and pervasive sense of imminent decline, what is interesting about Plouviez' comments is the way he character-ized the Great Exhibition, for as we have seen, while it was certainly dominated by internationalist and pacifist rhetoric, it was at heart a profoundly nationalistic and chauvinistic event. This was not the way it was remembered, however, and the inter-nationalist gloss is one of the most enduring interpretations.

Nevertheless, despite the differences – or perhaps because of them – King George VI repeatedly invoked the Great Exhibition in his opening address. He called its creators 'far-sighted men who looked forward to a world in which the advances of art and science would uplift civilization in enduring peace and prosperity,' and asserted that the Festival of Britain, as with its predecessor, had been planned 'as a visible sign of national achievement and confidence.' He did, however, note 'the con-trast between the calm security of the Victorian age and the hard experience' of his own. The peace that the Great Exhibition had promised had not endured, and much of the wealth that was associated with it had 'dissipated in fire and slaughter,' but the King nevertheless remained optimistic that the festival would be 'a symbol of Britain's abiding courage and vitality.' *The Times* added in its leader that there was nothing wrong with the Victorian ideal, and that at least in one sense the prophets of 1851 had been vindicated: 'Man's power over his material surroundings has increased to even greater proportions than they foresaw.'[35] Although the Labour government forgot the 1851 exhibition, the King and *The Times*, as well as a number of compa-nies, ever attived to potential marketing opportunities, chose to remember it, such as Huntley & Palmer which explicitly invoked the exhibition in its advertisement for biscuits (fig. 75).

There are several possible explanations for the failure, or refusal, of the organizers of the Festival of Britain to remember the Great Exhibition, but foremost among them is that the Great Exhibition, associated as it so often was with liberalism, free trade, and British power, did not accord with their vision of Britain. The publisher and author Ernest Benn, who had expressed his strong individualist views in *The Confessions of a Capitalist* (1925), derided the Festival of Britain as 'a perfect piece of Socialism.' In contrast to the Great Exhibition, the Festival of Britain was state funded and centrally planned; there was no competition to select either a builder of the exhibition site or the exhibits. Whereas the Great Exhibition was portrayed by most contemporaries as a testament to volu...

(although protectionists and Chartists surely resisted this assessment), the Festival of Britain, at least according to Benn, was designed to disguise. Its overarching premise, he claimed, was not to put side by side the produce of the world so that they might be compared, but rather for the various ... ground to ... select the items for display, in effect telling the viewing public what was good for them.' Most impor-tantly, Britain's economy and its place in the world ... had changed so dramatically between 1851 and 1951 that in any comparison with ... Festival of Britain could only come up short, revealing not its ... triumphs ... but its failures and defeats. Hoping to demonstrate Britain's recovery from the war and the efficacy of its own policies, the Labour gov... had distanced itself from the Great Exhibition.

* * *

CONCLUSION

The Festival of Britain in 1951 marked both the nadir of attitudes toward the Great Exhibition and the beginning of their revival. That same year Yvonne Ffrench published the first full-length narrative study of the exhibition, whiggish and celebratory except regarding design issues, about which she was in accord with Nikolaus Pevsner, whose *High Victorian Design*, also published in 1951, represented the last of the anti-Victorian accounts. In 1959 Asa Briggs wrote that the Great Exhibition had 'proclaimed . . . the triumphant facts of industrial progress,' and represented confidence based on economic strength and social balance.[37] Anthony Wood, a year later, held up the exhibition as a symbol of free trade, constitutional reform, international peace, a growing empire, thrift, hard work, and 'high moral endeavour.'[38] The Great Exhibition had become the leading icon of the Victorian age. In Walter Arnstein's *Britain Yesterday and Today* (1988) it served as the symbol of mid-Victorian material progress, self-satisfaction, economic efficiency, the gospel of free trade, universal peace 'and the glories of the British constitution.'[39] In popular imagination as well the exhibition has by and large remained a positive, celebratory, whiggish event. In 1991 Rupert Steiner wrote in *The Times* that the Crystal Palace was 'a showcase of all that was great about Britain at the height of the Industrial Revolution.'[40]

By the late 1980s, however, historians who took for granted its importance finally began to question the exhibition's meaning. Paul Greenhalgh's *Ephemeral Vistas* (1988) argued that the exhibition was not simply a cultural event aimed at educating and enlightening, but a purveyor of coded messages about the alleged racial superiority of European civilization. It was a display that not only glorified but domesticated and rationalized the empire. For Greenhalgh, the exhibition was a legitimizing structure that served the interests of the ascendant middle class. It was 'saturated with Liberal ideology,' 'a giant counter-revolutionary measure,' 'an immense show of strength designed to intimidate potential insurrectionists.' He concluded: 'The negative ideology the exhibitions espoused is still with us; sadly, the beauty of the façades has gone forever.'[41] Two years later, in *The Commodity Culture of Victorian England*, Thomas Richards claimed that the exhibition was a commodity spectacle which 'advanced a peculiarly middle-class vision.' It was 'an extraordinary collective bluff,' the genesis of advertising and a 'commodity culture.'[42] The Great Exhibition was still a landmark, but of what?

Historians have interpreted the Great Exhibition in many different ways because, even at the time, it contained so many different meanings. What is important about the exhibition is what people have seen in it, what they have projected on to it, how they have interpreted it. This process of imparting meaning to the exhibition began at the very first organizational meeting in 1849, if not before, and continued not only throughout its duration, but even after it closed. From beginning to end, Britons projected on to the Great Exhibition their hopes and fears, values and beliefs.

At its core, the Great Exhibition was a political event, the product of a manifestly political process. The organizers as a group stood for something that can best be described as liberalism. They held an expansive and inclusive view of the nation; they spanned traditional distinctions between the middle and upper classes. Holding what was back in the late 1840s a minority view, they attempted to use the Great Exhibition to promulgate their vision of Britain society and economy. They carefully gauged the likely appeal of their plan; they attempted to build a consensus around their vision, reaching out to a diversity of regions and interests, smoothing over differences; they incorporated the views of some of their constituents and excluded the views of others as they forged a groundswell of public opinion in their favor; they co-opted some of their political opponents; they changed their appeal to fit their audience; and they ultimately ignored those they could or would not incorporate. They attempted to make the exhibition as broadly appealing as possible, but always within certain limits.

The organizers were astute politicians, and, if their actions are indicative, they knew that the key to the exhibition's success was that it should be inclusive enough to claim representativeness, but not so inclusive that it risked alienating certain critical constituencies. At least at a glance, the organizers reached out to all geographical regions, social classes, political parties, and economic concerns. This reflected their patently liberal orientation, but it was also smart politics. There was very little that the exhibition obviously excluded. But it needs to be underscored that the exhibition did, in fact, exclude certain geographical regions, or, at least, that it privileged some at the expense of others. Scotland, for example, was deemed more fertile recruiting ground than Ireland or Wales. The organizers did not ignore Ireland and Wales, they just did not devote as much attention to those areas. In contrast, there were English and Scottish commercial industrial towns to which the organizers traveled over and over again.

The organizers also excluded certain social groups and political views, despite their paeans to inclusivity. Although what astounded observers at the time was the amount of integration that took place inside the Crystal Palace, no one had any difficulty differentiating one class from another. The rhetoric was of all classes peaceably congregating inside the exhibition building, but the reality was one of segregation and exclusion. Heading the list of those left out were the radical working classes, the Chartists, the 'ragged classes,' although the organizers never defined precisely who these people were. They were, if nothing else, those who could not afford the shilling price of admission. But the organizers also left out people when they decided not to hold evening meetings in Tower Hamlets, fearing that too many Radicals would attend. Throughout the planning and duration of the exhibition, in fact, the organizers had an uneasy relationship with the working classes, and the Great Exhibition indicates a considerable degree of underlying class tensions and wariness, if not outright antagonism.

On the surface, the Great Exhibition was about consensus. It was designed to be a national common denominator, abstract enough to collapse differences into similarities. It allowed different social and political groups to appropriate it and claim to be its only authoritative interpreters and to connect it with a specific, localized worldview.[43] This is apparent in the organizers' portrayal of the event as a tribute to international peace, rather than free trade. This allowed free-traders to celebrate the event one way and protectionists another. Similarly, in promoting the exhibition as a celebration of 'the dignity of labor,' the organizers enabled middle-class liberals to support the event as an occasion that would demonstrate to workers the benefits of hard work, while Chartists such as Henry Vincent could appropriate the language offered by the organizers as a means of fostering a sense of working-class solidarity. The organizers' greatest achievement was to construct the exhibition in such a way as to maximize support and minimize opposition, thus insuring not only its popularity, but its claim to represent British national identity.

The organizers promoted the exhibition as a tribute to peace, progress, and prosperity; to social integration, to internationalism, to voluntarism, and to laissez-faire economics. But their construction of the exhibition cannot be taken entirely at face value; there are, in essence, several stories to tell about the Great Exhibition. Despite all their efforts, it is still possible to discern in the exhibition a high level of social segregation, strident nationalism, and state involvement in economic affairs. While they emphasized that the exhibition would celebrate Britain's commercial successes, in point of fact they organized it to rectify Britain's economic deficiencies. There was, then, a disjuncture between what the organizers intended the exhibition to be, how they promoted and publicized it, and how it was interpreted.

The exhibition reflected all sorts of agendas: centralized and localized, individual and corporate, public and private, industrial and agricultural, religious and secular. The process of putting together the exhibition worked in two different directions: from the top down, that is from the organizers to the British populace; and from the bottom up, that is from the grassroots level to the organizers. In many areas, the exhibition took on meanings different from what its organizers intended. It did embody a set of shared values, and even sought to inculcate those values, but it also allowed for the expression of values that were not shared.[44] Albert and Cole, for example, intended the exhibition to be about arts manufactures, or tasteful consumerism. Instead, for many exhibitors and visitors, it became a trade fair, a shopping mall, a profoundly commercial event. In fact, although the improvement of taste was clearly one of the organizers' goals for the exhibition, they rarely used it as a means of promoting it. The lure of sales was much more effective, but in the end it proved costly, as many regarded the exhibition as a testament to commerce and as an opportunity to profit, rather than as a means of improving taste. Although the organizers intended the event to make long-term improvements in the British economy, many manufacturers and retailers instead used it as an opportunity to bolster short-term profits. And whereas Albert, Cole, Cobden, and several others on the commission hoped the exhibition would usher in an era of international peace and economic free trade, in the writings of many popular writers it became a supremely nationalistic event, a competition not only of products but of values, pitting the British against the foreign and exotic 'other.'

The exhibition was both a planned and a spontaneous event, and it is this totality, the interaction of the planned and the unplanned, that should be analyzed as a symbolic whole. There is, perhaps, no better example of this than the centerpiece of the exhibition, the collection of exhibits. Collections are often viewed simply as assemblages of objects in space, arranged according to some rationale. But a collection is also an event, a history of thousands of minute decisions and links of which the objects are simply the remainder. The organizers of the exhibition clearly had in mind a general sense of what they wanted the exhibition to look like, but they consistently refused to dictate. Instead, in patently liberal ways, they established general guidelines – an overarching system of classification – and then delegated most of the responsibility for generating the thousands of exhibits to local committees and individual exhibitors.

Ultimately, what is so fascinating about the Great Exhibition is that it sheds light on many different controversies within mid-Victorian Britain. There were rancorous debates about the proper relationship between metropolis and province, commerce and culture, social integration and segregation, nationalism and internationalism, as well as the process of industrialization and the role of the state. British society was complex, and thus it should come as no surprise that the Great Exhibition cannot be reduced to a single, unequivocal truth. Embedded within the exhibition were a multiplicity of meanings and identities that can be disclosed only by reinserting it into the historical context from which it emerged, by refusing to regard its creation in a teleological manner, and by giving credence not only to those who supported and promoted the event, but also to those who opposed it. If the Great Exhibition reveals anything about mid-Victorian Britain, it was that a number of astute observers were worried about their country's economic performance vis-à-vis other countries and the direction Britain's economy was headed; that British society could not be easily or clearly divided into social classes; that liberalism did not yet reign supreme; and that British national identity was a hotly contested issue.

It is a misnomer, then, to speak of the 'meaning' of the exhibition, for it has had many meanings, and its meanings have changed over time. For some observers in 1851 it was a symbol of progress; for others it embodied everything that was wrong with Victorian society. For some it was the eighth wonder of the world, an Arabian nights' palace; for others it was 'ugly,' full of 'old things.' All of these debates, both at the time of the exhibition and since, have really been about the nature, or identity, of Britain. That the exhibition put Britain on display there is little doubt. What is, and always will be, open to question is just which visions and versions of Britain it exhibited.

ABBREVIATIONS

BL Add. MSS	British Library, Additional Manuscripts
DNB	Leslie Stephen and Sidney Lee, eds, *The Dictionary of National Biography*, 22 vols (London: Oxford University Press, 1917)
Collection of Printed Documents	*Collection of Printed Documents and Forms used in carrying on the business of the Exhibition of 1851 . . .* , 8 vols, Victoria and Albert Museum
Hansard	*Hansard's Parliamentary Debates*
Manchester Committee	Records of the Royal Manchester Institution, Great Exhibition of 1851, Archives Section, Local Studies Unit, Manchester Central Library, M6/3/1–24
Official Catalogue	*Official Descriptive and Illustrated Catalogue*, 3 vols (London: Spicer Brothers, 1851)
PRO	Public Record Office, Kew
RCE/EC	Archives of the Royal Commission for the Exhibition of 1851, Imperial College of Science, Technology and Medicine; Exhibition Correspondence
RCE/WA	Archives of the Royal Commission for the Exhibition of 1851, Material on loan from Windsor Archives
RSA	Royal Society of Arts
Russell Collection	John Scott Russell's Collection of Papers Relating to the Great Exhibition of 1851, 5 vols, RSA
Tallis	John Tallis, *Tallis' History and Description of the Crystal Palace, and the Exhibition of the World's Industry in 1851*, 3 vols (London: John Tallis & Co., [1852])

NOTES

INTRODUCTION

1. *The Times*, 2 May 1851.
2. Christopher Hobhouse, *1851 and the Crystal Palace* (London: John Murray, 1937); Yvonne Ffrench, *The Great Exhibition, 1851* (London: Harvill Press, 1951); Patrick Howarth, *The Year Is 1851* (London: Collins, 1951); Kenneth Luckhurst, *The Great Exhibition of 1851* (London: Royal Society of Arts, 1951); John W. Dodds, *The Age of Paradox* (London: Victor Gollancz, 1953); Tom Corfe, *The Great Exhibition* (Cambridge: Cambridge University Press, 1979); Anthony Wood, *Nineteenth Century Britain* (London: Longman, 1960), pp. 174-7.
3. J. E. Preston Murdock, *The Romance and History of the Crystal Palace* (London: L. Upcott Gill, 1911), pp. 1-12.
4. John McKean, *Crystal Palace: Joseph Paxton and Charles Fox* (London: Phaidon, 1994), p. 20; Bradley James Macdonald, 'William Morris and the Aesthetic Foundations of Political Theory' (PhD thesis, University of California at Los Angeles, 1991), esp. pp. 65-6, 73, 76-7.
5. The phrase is from G. M. Trevelyan, *British History in the Nineteenth Century and After (1782-1919)*, 2nd edn (London: Longman, 1937), p. 295.
6. Asa Briggs, *The Making of Modern England, 1783-1867: The Age of Improvement* (New York: Harper & Row, 1959), pp. 398, 402; Wood, *Nineteenth Century Britain*, p. 176; Walter L. Arnstein, *Britain Yesterday and Today*, 5th edn (Lexington, MA: D. C. Heath, 1988), pp. 71-3.
7. W. L. Burn, *The Age of Equipoise* (New York: W. W. Norton, 1965).
8. G. M. Young, *Victorian England: Portrait of an Age*, 2nd edn (Oxford: Oxford University Press, 1977), p. 69.
9. Gertrude Himmelfarb, *The Idea of Poverty: England in the Early Industrial Age* (New York: Random House, 1983), p. 364; Paul Greenhalgh, *Ephemeral Vistas: The Expositions Universelles, Great Exhibitions, and World's Fairs, 1851-1939* (Manchester: Manchester University Press, 1988); Thomas Richards, *The Commodity Culture of Victorian England* (Stanford: Stanford University Press, 1990); Adrian Forty, *Objects of Desire: Design and Society since 1750* (London: Thames & Hudson, 1986); George F. Chadwick, *The Works of Sir Joseph Paxton* (London: The Architectural Press, 1961), p. 122.
10. Richards, *Commodity Culture*, pp. 4-5; Asa Briggs, *Victorian People*, rev. edn (Chicago: University of Chicago Press, 1972), p. 20. See also Eric Hobsbawm, *Industry and Empire* (Harmondsworth: Penguin, 1969), p. 92; Martin J. Wiener, *English Culture and the Decline of the Industrial Spirit, 1850-1980* (Cam-

bridge: Cambridge University Press, 1981), p. 28; Utz Haltern, *Die Londoner Weltaustellung von 1851* (Münster: Verlag Aschendorff, 1971).
11. Himmelfarb, *Idea of Poverty*, pp. 364-5; the motto is from Briggs, *Victorian People*, p. 41.
12. See, among many, William Weber, 'The Muddle of the Middle Classes,' *Nineteenth-Century Music* 3 (1979): 175-85; Raymond Williams, *Keywords: A Vocabulary of Culture and Society*, rev. edn (New York: Oxford University Press, 1983), pp. 65-6; Peter Gay, *The Bourgeois Experience: Victoria to Freud*, vol. I: *Education of the Senses* (New York: Oxford University Press, 1984), pp. 18-22, 31; Walter L. Arnstein, 'The Myth of the Triumphant Middle Class,' *Historian* 37 (1975): 205-21; R. S. Neale, ed., *History and Class* (Oxford: Basil Blackwell, 1983); Harold Perkin, *Origins of Modern English Society* (London: Routledge & Kegan Paul, 1969); W. D. Rubinstein, 'The Victorian Middle Classes: Wealth, Occupation, and Geography,' *Economic History Review*, 2nd ser., 30 (1977): 602-23; G. D. H. Cole, 'The Conception of the Middle Classes,' *British Journal of Sociology* 1 (1950): 275-90; Peter Bailey, '"A Mingled Mass of Perfectly Legitimate Pleasures:" The Victorian Middle Class and the Problem of Leisure,' *Victorian Studies* 21 (1977): 7-28.
13. Benedict Anderson, *Imagined Communities: Reflections on the Origin and Spread of Nationalism*, rev. edn (London: Verso, 1991). The best book on the formation of British national identity is Linda Colley, *Britons: Forging the Nation, 1707-1837* (New Haven: Yale University Press, 1992). More broadly, see Liah Greenfeld, *Nationalism: Five Roads to Modernity* (Cambridge, MA: Harvard University Press, 1992). On the construction of national identity at world's fairs, see Robert W. Rydell, *All the World's a Fair: Visions of Empire at American International Expositions, 1876-1916* (Chicago: University of Chicago Press, 1984), and Mauricio Tenorio-Trillo, *Mexico at the World's Fairs: Crafting a Modern Nation* (Berkeley: University of California Press, 1996).
14. Alon Confino, 'The Nation as a Local Metaphor: National Memory and the German Empire, 1871-1918,' *History and Memory* 5 (1993): 44.
15. *Ibid.*

CHAPTER 1: ORIGINS: CONCEIVING THE EXHIBITION

1. Luckhurst, *Great Exhibition*, p. 1; Tallis, I:5-6; Greenhalgh, *Ephemeral Vistas*, pp. 3-5, 9-10; Lever, *Suggestions*, pp. 17-18.
2. Luckhurst, *Great Exhibition*, p. 2. On local

exhibitions at mechanics' institutes, see Toshio Kusamitsu, 'Great Exhibitions before 1851', *History Workshop* 9 (1980): 70–89.

3. Peter Mathias, *The First Industrial Nation: An Economic History of Britain, 1700–1914* (New York: Charles Scribner's Sons, 1969).

4. A. C. Howe, *Free Trade and Liberal England, 1846–1946* (Oxford: Clarendon Press, 1997), pp. 54–5; Paul Kennedy, *The Rise and Fall of the Great Powers* (New York: Random House, 1987), pp. 151–8.

5. See, among many, Michael Argles, *South Kensington to Robbins: An Account of English Technical and Scientific Education since 1851* (London: Longman, Green & Company, 1964); R. J. Montgomery, *Examinations* (London: Longman, Green & Company, 1965), esp. p. 76; Quentin Bell, *The Schools of Design* (London: Routledge & Kegan Paul, 1963); Mabel Tylecote, *The Mechanics' Institutes of Lancashire and Yorkshire before 1851* (Manchester: Manchester University Press, 1957). It is interesting to note that all of the above were published within a decade of each other, at a time when the British were clearly struggling with the erosion of their manufacturing base in the aftermath of the Second World War (see Kennedy, *Rise and Fall*, pp. 424–5, 480–1).

6. Henry Brougham [William Davis, pseud.], 'Hints to Philanthropists; or a Collective View of Practical Means of Improving the Condition of the Poor and Labouring Classes of Society,' *Edinburgh Review* 41 (October 1824): 96–122; Argles, *South Kensington*, pp. 1–2.

7. James Hole, *An Essay on the History and Management of Literary, Scientific, and Mechanics' Institutions* (London: Longman, Brown, Green & Longmans, 1853), pp. 14–16.

8. Tylecote, *Mechanics' Institutes*, p. 27.

9. *Ibid.*, pp. 1–47 *passim*; Argles, *South Kensington*, p. 7; Montgomery, *Examinations*, p. 74.

10. Argles, *South Kensington*, p. 5.

11. Thomas Baines, *History of the Commerce and Town of Liverpool* (London: Longman, Brown, Green & Longmans, 1852), p. 649; Hole, *Essay*, p. 17; Tylecote, *Mechanics' Institutes*, pp. 258–86.

12. Kusamitsu, 'Great Exhibitions,' pp. 70–89; Altick, *Shows of London*, p. 435.

13. Maxine Berg, *The Age of Manufactures, 1700–1820*, 2nd edn (London: Routledge, 1994), p. 39; William Page, ed., *Commerce and Industry* (London: Constable, 1919), II: 132–3, 136–7. Tables of imports and exports of wholly or mainly manufactured articles indicate many 5–10-year periods during which growth was flat, at a time when imports were increasing.

14. Bell, *Schools of Design*, pp. 46–8, 60; Argles, *South Kensington*, pp. 8–9; Montgomery, *Examinations*, pp. 80–1; J. A. Lloyd, *Proposals for Establishing Colleges of Arts and Manufactures for the Better Instruction of the Industrial Classes* (London: Clowes & Sons, 1851), p. 5.

15. Richard Redgrave, *A Memoir*, ed. F. M. Redgrave (London: Cassell & Company, 1891), p. 62.

16. Quoted in Luckhurst, *Great Exhibition*, pp. 6–7.

17. On the ancient origins of fairs, see Burton Benedict, ed. *The Anthropology of World's Fairs* (Berkeley: Scholar Press, 1983), p. 3; Charles Lowe, *Four National Exhibitions in London and their Organizer* (London: T. Fisher Unwin, 1892), p. 25. For the medieval and early modern periods, see Ellen Wedermeyer Moore, *The Fairs of Medieval England* (Toronto: Pontifical Institute of Medieval Studies, 1985); Fernand Braudel, *The Wheels of Commerce* (New York: Harper & Row, 1982), pp. 81–94; O. Verlinden, 'Markets and Fairs,' *The Cambridge Economic History of Europe*, vol. III (Cambridge: Cambridge University Press, 1963), pp. 119–53; Robert W. Malcolmson, *Popular Recreations in English Society, 1700–1850* (Cambridge: Cambridge University Press, 1973), pp. 21–5; J. A. Sharpe, *Early Modern England: A Social History, 1550–1760* (London: Edward Arnold, 1997), p. 146.

18. Derek Hudson and Kenneth Luckhurst, *The Royal Society of Arts, 1754–1954* (London: John Murray, 1954), pp. 11, 15–16, 34, 125, 176–7; Henry Trueman Wood, *A History of the Royal Society of Arts* (London: John Murray, 1913).

19. Kusamitsu, 'Great Exhibitions;' Peter Berlyn, *A Popular Narrative of the Origin, History, Progress and Prospects of the Great Industrial Exhibition, 1851* (London: n.p., 1851).

20. Luckhurst, *Great Exhibition*, pp. 1–2. A few 'progressively minded educationalists' managed to convince King George IV to provide some modest backing for an annual industrial exhibition along the lines of the French model, but what began in 1828 in the Royal Mews in Trafalgar Square lasted only until 1833. In Ireland, the Royal Dublin Society, which 'did much in the way of promoting and encouraging the arts and manufactures of that country prior to the date of the Union [1801],' began a series of triennial exhibitions commencing in 1829, organized by its committee of manufacturers. See Ellis Lever, *Suggestions for a Grand International Exhibition of the Industrial Arts, Manufactures, Fine Arts, Scientific Inventions, Discoveries, and Natural Products of all Countries to be held in Manchester in the Year 1882* (Manchester: Guardian Letterpress and Lithographic Works, 1881), p. 20.

21. Richard D. Altick, *The Shows of London* (Cambridge, MA: Harvard University Press, 1978), pp. 2–3, 421–3, 443.

22. Royal Charter of Incorporation of the Society for the Encouragement of Arts, Manufactures and Commerce, 1847, *Collection of Printed Documents*, I:1.

23. Hudson and Luckhurst, *Royal Society of Arts*, pp. 6, 27–8.

24. *Ibid.*, pp. 11–16, 176–7; Francis Fuller, *Memoranda Relative to the International Exhibition of 1851* (n.p., n.d.), pp. 5–6.

25. Henry Cole, *Fifty Years of Public Work* (London: George Bell & Sons, 1884), I:119; Hudson and Luckhurst, *Royal Society of Arts*, pp. 188–9.

26. RSA, Minutes of Council, 21 and 28 May 1846.

27. Theodore Martin, *The Life of His Royal Highness the*

Prince Consort, 5th edn (London: Smith, Elder & Co. 1880), I:119–24, IV:13–15.

28. Russell Collection, I:46/2/4.

29. John Scott Russell, 'Statement of Proceedings Preliminary to the Exhibition of Industry of All Nations, 1851,' 8 February 1850, *Collection of Printed Documents*, I:5.

30. R. J. Morris, 'Leeds and the Crystal Palace,' *Victorian Studies* 13 (1970): 285.

31. B. R. Mitchell, *British Historical Statistics* (Cambridge: Cambridge University Press, 1988), p. 541. There were 6,266 miles of track in 1851, up from 3,036 five years earlier.

32. There was considerable controversy about Whishaw's contribution to the Great Exhibition, with Scott Russell appropriating for Albert credit for the idea of the exhibition. This is somewhat ironic because in the late 1840s it was Albert who, although always supportive of the idea, strongly urged caution in the planning of a large (at that time national) exhibition. See Scott Russell, 'Statement of Proceedings . . .;' Russell Collection, II:636ff; 'Origin of the Great Exhibition,' *Mining Journal*, 1 November 1851. The issue of Whishaw's contribution continued into 1852, and his case was discussed many times by Grey, Cole, and Phipps, who implied that Whishaw was raising the issue in the hope of garnering some sort of financial compensation or renumeration, having fallen on hard times. Whishaw to Bowring, 5 November 1851, RCE/EC; Grey to Cole, 10 January 1852; Cole to Phipps, 14 January 1852, Cole Papers. Charles Babbage, *The Exposition of 1851; or, Views of the Industry, the Science and the Government of England* (London: John Murray, 1851), p. 25; [Richard Burnet], *To Her Majesty's Commissioners for the Exhibition, 1851* (London, n.p., [1850]).

33. Scott Russell, 'Statement of Proceedings. . . .'

34. Luckhurst, *Great Exhibition*, pp. 4–6; Ffrench, *Great Exhibition*, pp. 15–16.

35. Cole, *Fifty Years*, pp. 1–97 *passim*; Bell, *Schools of Design*, pp. 212–15, 256; John Martin Robinson, *The Wyatts: An Architectural Dynasty* (Oxford: Oxford University Press, 1979), p. 207.

36. Cole, *Fifty Years*, pp. 24, 34.

37. Cobden to John Cassell, 25 September 1850, Cobden Papers, BL Add. MSS 43668 f. 106.

38. Scott Russell, 'Statement of Proceedings. . . .'

39. Luckhurst, *Great Exhibition*, p. 7. While this might be attributable to cultural insecurity of the sort described by Gerald Newman in *The Rise of English Nationalism: A Cultural History, 1740–1830* (London: Weidenfeld & Nicolson, 1987), as noted earlier (n. 13) there was economic evidence supporting manufacturers' sense that business was not as good as it had been, even if they did not fully understand the reasons for this.

40. Russell, 'Statement of Proceedings. . . .'

41. See, among many, Neil McKendrick, John Brewer, and J. H. Plumb, *The Birth of a Consumer Society* (Bloomington: Indiana University Press, 1985); Lorna Weatherill, *Consumer Behaviour and Material Culture in Britain, 1660–1760* (London: Rout-ledge, 1988), p. 193; Carole Shammas, 'Changes in English and Anglo-American Consumption from 1550 to 1800,' in John Brewer and Roy Porter, eds, *Consumption and the World of Goods*, (London: Routledge, 1993), pp. 177–205.

42. According to Richards, *Commodity Culture*, advertising did not even begin on a widespread, national, consumer-society level until the 1850s.

43. Neil McKendrick, 'Josiah Wedgwood and the Commercialization of the Potteries', in McKendrick, Brewer, and Plumb, eds, *Birth of a Consumer Society*, p. 100; Leonore Davidoff and Catherine Hall, *Family Fortunes* (Chicago: University of Chicago Press, 1987), pp. 375–6; Asa Briggs, *Victorian Things* (Chicago: University of Chicago Press, 1988), esp. pp. 213–59.

44. Page, *Commerce and Industry*, I:155; N. F. R. Crafts, *British Economic Growth during the Industrial Revolution* (Oxford: Clarendon Press, 1985), pp. 89–114; Mathias, *First Industrial Nation*, pp. 213–23, 375–81; Howe, *Free Trade*, pp. 38–49.

45. Cole to Phipps, 3 January 1848, Cole Papers; Cole, *Fifty Years*, p. 120.

46. Phipps to Cole, 6 February 1848, Cole Papers.

47. Cole, *Fifty Years*, p. 122; Scott Russell, 'Statement of Proceedings . . .;' RSA, Minutes of Council, 24 February 1848.

48. Bell, *Schools of Design*, p. 181.

49. *Ibid.*, pp. 219–21.

50. *Ibid.*, pp. 109–38, quote on p. 224. See also Stafford Northcote's review of the Select Committee's report, 'Schools of Design,' *Edinburgh Review* 90 (October 1849): 473–96.

51. Cole to Granville, 15 February 1849, Granville Papers, PRO 30/29/23/1.

52. Hudson and Luckhurst, *Royal Society of Arts*, p. 195.

53. RSA, Minutes of Council, 29 May 1849.

54. Wood, *History of the RSA*, pp. 408–9.

55. Matthew Digby Wyatt, 'A Report on the Eleventh French Exposition of the Products of Industry Submitted to the President and Council of the Society of Arts,' RCE/WA I:40.

56. The narrative for this section is from Cole, *Fifty Years*, pp. 123–5; Scott Russell, 'Statement of Proceedings . . .;' Ffrench, *Great Exhibition*, pp. 19–21.

57. George S. Emerson, *John Scott Russell* (London: John Murray, 1977), p. 76.

58. Cole, *Fifty Years*, pp. 123–5.

59. RCE/WA I:7.

60. Ffrench, *Great Exhibition*, p. 24.

61. 15 July 1849, in *The Prince Consort and his Brother: Two Hundred New Letters*, ed. Hector Bolitho (London: Cobden-Sanderson, 1933), p. 110.

62. Cole to Phipps, 16 July 1849, RCE/WA I:3.

63. Phipps to Cole, 17 July 1849, RCE/WA I:4.

64. Albert to Grey, 31 July 1849, PRO HO45/2888; minutes of meeting at Balmoral, 3 September 1849, RCE/WA I:26. Grey replied affirmatively on 1 August 1849. See Cole, *Fifty Years*, I:128.

65. Scott Russell, 'Statement of Proceedings. . . .'

66. Fuller, *Memoranda*, pp. 16–17.

67. RSA, Minutes of Council, 6 November 1849; Cole, *Fifty Years*, II:345.

68. Fuller, *Memoranda*; Ffrench, *Great Exhibition*, pp. 27–30.

69. Cole, *Fifty Years*, II:126–7.

70. Scott Russell, 'Statement of Proceedings . . .;' Cole, *Fifty Years*, II:127.

71. *The Times*, 6 September 1849.

72. Normanby to Phipps, 20 September 1849, RCE/WA II:38; George Bacon to John Scott Russell, 3 November 1849, RSA; Russell Collection, II: 34, 47–51.

73. *The Times*, 18 October 1849.

74. RCE/WA I:33.

75. *The Times*, 18 October 1849; RCE/WA I:33; Cole, *Fifty Years*, pp. 134–44.

76. Cole, *Fifty Years*, I:149; Phipps to Cole, 4 July 1849, Cole Papers; RCE/WA I:2, 8–10, 64; Labouchere to Phipps, 11, 14, 15, 18, 23 December 1849, RCE/WA II: 74–5, 89–91; Cole to Phipps, RCE/WA II: 56, 67–9; Cole, Diary, 11 December 1849.

77. Grey to Cole, 29 November 1849, Cole Papers.

78. This is one of many important issues that historians of the Great Exhibition have ignored. See, for example, Ffrench, *Great Exhibition*, pp. 35–6; Hobhouse, *1851*, p. 11.

79. Cole to Grey, 27 November 1849, RCE/WA I:62.

80. Albert to Labouchere, 30 November 1849, RCE/WA I:65.

81. Cole to Grey, 27 November 1849, RCE/WA I:62.

82. Cole to Phipps, 14 December 1849, Cole Papers.

83. Royal Commission, *First Report* (London: William Clowes & Sons for HMSO, 1852), pp. viii–ix.

84. *The Times*, 4 January 1850. Cole repeated this view in *Fifty Years*, I:149.

85. DNB. Jonathan Smith ' "The Abyss of the Heavenly Wilderness:" Thomas De Quincey, J. P. Nichol, and the Earl of Rosse Confront the Great Nebula in Orion' (paper presented at the annual meeting of the Northeast Victorian Studies Association, Rutgers University, New Brunswick, NJ, 24–26 April 1992); Rosse to Lord John Russell, 22 December 1849, RCE/WA I:102.

86. Pusey's younger brother was Edward Pusey, a prominent participant in the Oxford Movement. See Paul Sieveking, ed., *British Bibliographical Archive* (London: K. G. Saur, 1984), microfiche. Others on the commission with an interest in science and technological innovation included Albert, Lyell, Cubitt, and Peel, whose interest in science had been piqued by Playfair's decision to study in Germany. See Lyon Playfair, *Memoirs and Correspondence of Lyon Playfair*, ed. Thomas Wemyss Reid, (Jemimaville, Scotland: P. M. Pollack, 1976), pp. 77–87.

87. Gladstone's role on the commission has also been greatly underestimated by historians. He is not even mentioned in Asa Briggs' chapter on the Great Exhibition, 'The Crystal Palace and the Men of 1851,' in *Victorian People*, pp. 15–51, and received only a mention in Ffrench, *Great Exhibition*, and Hobhouse, *1851*. Although he was 'distracted' from public affairs during the first half of 1850, in part as a consequence of the death of his daughter in April, he still dutifully attended the Mansion House dinner, admiring and praising Albert's speech as a '5th Gospel, a New Evangel.' And although he was in Italy from November 1850 until the opening, his diary that summer reads like a list of meetings on his work for the exhibition: he attended almost half of the meetings of the Royal Commission; he served on several key sub-committees; he attended a meeting of St Martin's Parish on model dwellings for the working classes in connection with the exhibition; he met with Cole and Northcote a number of times; he visited the building site at least twice; and he continued to visit the exhibition and participate in meetings throughout the summer and autumn of 1851. Gladstone also kept abreast of the many pamphlets circulating about the exhibition. See William Gladstone, *The Gladstone Diaries*, vol. IV (1848–1854), ed. M. R. D. Foot and H. C. G. Matthew (Oxford: Clarendon Press, 1974); Richard Shannon, *Gladstone*, vol. I (1809–1865) (London: Hamish Hamilton, 1982), pp. 220 *et seq*.

88. On the great divide between the worlds of commerce and finance on the one hand and industry on the other, see P. J. Cain and A. G. Hopkins, *British Imperialism: Innovation and Expansion, 1688–1914* (London: Longman, 1993); W. D. Rubinstein, *Men of Property: The Very Wealthy in Britain since the Industrial Revolution* (New Brunswick: Rutgers University Press, 1981) and *Elites and the Wealthy in Modern British History* (New York: St Martins Press, 1987). On the tight-knit world of the aristocracy, see J. V. Beckett, *The Aristocracy in England, 1660–1914* (Oxford: Basil Blackwell, 1986).

89. Peter Mandler, *Aristocratic Government in the Age of Reform: Whigs and Liberals, 1830–1852* (Oxford: Clarendon Press, 1990), pp. 161–3.

90. There is considerable debate over the origins of the Liberal party in Victorian Britain. See T. A. Jenkins, *The Liberal Ascendancy, 1830–1886* (London: Macmillan, 1994), and Michael Bentley, *The Climax of Liberal Politics: British Liberalism in Theory and Practice, 1868–1918* (London: Edward Arnold, 1987). Norman Gash, *Aristocracy and People* (Cambridge, MA: Harvard University Press, 1979), claims that a recognizable Liberal party was actually in being by 1841; Jonathan Parry, *The Rise and Fall of Liberal Government in Victorian Britain* (New Haven: Yale University Press, 1993) suggests that there was one in existence even earlier than that. Peter Mandler, on the other hand, pushes the date into the 1850s as the earliest in *Aristocratic Government*, and Jonathan Vincent argues in *The Formation of the Liberal Party* (New York: Charles Scribner's Sons, 1966) that a Liberal party did not come into existence until the 1860s. See also J. B. Conacher, *The Peelites and the Party System, 1846–1852* (Hamden: Archon Books, 1972); William Devereux Jones and Arvel B. Erickson, *The Peelites, 1846–1857* (Columbus: Ohio State University Press, 1972); Eugenio F. Biagini, *Liberty, Retrenchment and Reform: Popular Liberalism in the Age of Gladstone, 1860–1880* (Cambridge: Cambridge University Press, 1992);

T. W. Heyck, *The Peoples of the British Isles*, vol. II (Belmont, CA: Wadsworth, 1992), pp. 290, 310–12; Donald Southgate, *The Passing of the Whigs, 1832–1866* (London: Macmillan, 1965).

91. Jenkins, *Liberal Ascendancy*, p. 45.
92. *Ibid.*, p. ix; Michael J. Winstanley, *Gladstone and the Liberal Party* (London: Routledge, 1990), p. 28.
93. Parry, *Rise and Fall*, esp. pp. 1–7.
94. C. A. Bell-Knight, *The Crystal Palace: Its Rise – Its Decline – Its Fall* (Bath: n.p., 1977), pp. 6–7; McKean, *Crystal Palace*, p. 48.

CHAPTER 2: OBSTACLES: PLANNING THE EXHIBITION

1. *The Times*, 15 April 1851.
2. Royal Commission, *First Report*, p. xix.
3. [E. A. Moriarty], 'Official Catalogue of the Great Exhibition,' *Edinburgh Review* 94 (October 1851): 569.
4. Matthew Digby Wyatt, for example, came from a family of prominent architects that had received a considerable amount of royal patronage. See Robinson, *Wyatts*.
5. Royal Commission, Minutes, 11 January 1850.
6. Cole to Phipps, 19–20 December 1849, RCE/WA I:86–8.
7. Mayor of Manchester to Labouchere, 2 and 10 January 1850, RCE/WA III:8, 16.
8. *Literary Gazette*, 5 January 1851.
9. Fuller, *Memoranda*, pp. 86–8.
10. Cole, Diary, 21 November 1849.
11. RCE/WA I:91.
12. *Ibid.*
13. *Patent Journal*, 29 December 1849.
14. [W. B. Adams], 'Industrial Exhibition,' *Westminster Review* 55 (July 1851): 351.
15. Tallis, I:7. See also the *First Report* of the Royal Commission, p. xvi.
16. On 22 November 1850 the Mundays were repaid the £22,500 they had advanced for the prize fund and for general expenses. The issue of compensation for loss of time and risk was referred by mutual consent to Robert Stephenson who, on 21 July 1851, decided that the Royal Commissioners should pay £5,120 plus costs, or a total of £6,435, to the Mundays. George Drew to Prince Albert, 7 December 1849, RCE/WA I:70; Bowring to Grey, 22 July 1851, RCE/WA VII:130; Royal Commission, *First Report*, p. xvii; Peel Papers, BL Add. MSS 40603 ff. 205–6, 209, 239, 243.
17. Luckhurst, *Great Exhibition*, p. 15.
18. Royal Commission, *First Report*, pp. xvii, xx.
19. G. P. Mabon, 'John Scott Russell and Henry Cole: Aspects of a Personal Rivalry at the Society of Arts,' *Journal of the Royal Society of Arts* 115 (February–March 1967): 204–8, 299–302.
20. Cole, Diary, 4 November, 12 December 1849.
21. Cole wrote on 9 March 1850 (*ibid.*): 'Colonel Reid complained of Russell . . . [that] Russell was the wrong point of the needle.' On 26 April he wrote that 'Northcote said some of the commissioners had found out that Russell did not speak the truth.'
22. *Ibid.*, 1 January 1850; Russell Collection, II:584.
23. Emerson, *John Scott Russell*, pp. 2–13.
24. *Ibid.*, pp. 2–13, 27–9, 33.
25. L. T. C. Rolt, *Isambard Kingdom Brunel* (New York: St Martin's Press, 1957), described him as a 'strange character,' a 'megalomaniac,' and an 'evil genius' (pp. 233–312 *passim*).
26. *Life, Letters, and Diaries of Sir Stafford Northcote*, ed. Andrew Lang (Edinburgh: William Blackwood & Sons, 1890), I:60.
27. *Ibid.*, I:81–2, 92.
28. *Ibid.*, I:66–78. Following the exhibition Northcote co-authored the Northcote–Trevelyan Report (1854), which began the process of civil service reform. He eventually became one of the leaders of the Conservative party. Despite these contributions, historians have been quite critical of his activities. See Lang, Northcote, pp. xi–xv; Emerson, *John Scott Russell*, p. 39; Bell, *Schools of Design*, pp. 211–12.
29. Northcote to Cole, 3 January 1850, Cole Papers.
30. Northcote to Cole, 27 February 1852, 8 February 1850, Cole Papers.
31. Peel to Playfair, 15 February [1850], Playfair Papers; Northcote to Peel, 15 January 1850, Peel Papers, BL Add. MSS 40603.
32. Cole to Grey, 25 January 1850, Cole Papers; Cole, Diary, 23–25 January 1850.
33. Cole, Diary, 26 January 1850; Grey to Cole, 29 January 1850, Cole Papers.
34. Cole, *Fifty Years*, I:161.
35. Cole, Diary, 24–26 January, 5–8 February, 24 December 1850; Emerson, *John Scott Russell*, pp. 40–1.
36. RCE/WA II:56.
37. Emerson, *John Scott Russell*, p. 41.
38. Cole, *Fifty Years*, I:155–61.
39. Reid to Phipps, 8 September 1850, RCE/WA IV:21.
40. Granville to Grey, 8 March 1850, RCE/WA II:96.
41. Cole, Diary, 19–20 February, 11 June 1850.
42. Playfair, *Memoirs*, p. 114.
43. Russell Collection, II:240; Emerson, *John Scott Russell*, pp. 41–2.
44. Emerson, *John Scott Russell*, p. 44.
45. Wood, *History of the RSA*, p. 359.
46. Royal Commission, *First Report*, p. xx.
47. Cole, *Fifty Years*, I:163.
48. McKean, *Crystal Palace*, pp. 8–9.
49. Cole, *Fifty Years*, I:163.
50. Phipps to Cole, 8 July 1849, Cole Papers.
51. Tallis, I:6–7.
52. Royal Commission, *First Report*, p. xxiv; Ffrench, *Great Exhibition*, pp. 72–3.
53. *The Times*, 2 March 1850; Royal Commission, *First Report*, p. xxiv.
54. Peter Berlyn and Charles Fowler, *The Crystal Palace: Its Architectural History and Constructive Marvels* (London: James Gilbert, 1851), pp. 6–8; *Collection of Printed Documents*, II:354; Tallis, I:8–9; *The Times*, 3 June 1850.

55. Tallis, I:8–9.
56. McKean, *Crystal Palace*, p. 9.
57. 'Greville,' *An Answer to 'What is to Become of the Crystal Palace?'* (London: John Ollivier, 1851), p. 5.
58. *John Bull*, 6 July 1850; *The Times*, 10 July 1850; George Douglas Campbell, *Autobiography and Memoirs*, ed. Dowager Duchess of Argyll (London: John Murray, 1906), I:340; Ffrench, *Great Exhibition*, pp. 77–9.
59. *Hansard*, 3rd ser., 109:1085; 112:744, 867–9.
60. Ffrench, *Great Exhibition*, p. 76.
61. Sydney D. Bailey, 'Parliament and the 1851 Exhibition,' *Parliamentary Affairs* 4 (1951): 312.
62. J. N. P. Watson, *Horse and Carriage: The Pageant of Hyde Park* (London: The Sportsman's Press, 1990), pp. 13, 58; John Ashton, *Hyde Park* (London: Downey & Co., 1896), p. 28; Ethel Brilliana Tweedie, *Hyde Park: Its History and Romance*, rev. edn (London: Besant & Co., 1930), p. 63; Harold P. Clunn, *The Face of London: The Record of a Century's Changes and Developments* (London: Simpkin, Marshall & Co., 1932), p. 315.
63. Leslie Jones, *Hyde Park and Free Speech* (London: Museum of Labour History, [1981]); Eric Dancy, *Hyde Park* (London: Methuen, 1937), pp. 99, 106, 110–11, 114.
64. Fuller, *Memoranda*, pp. 160–1.
65. Cole, Diary, 4 July 1850.
66. [W. B. Adams], 'The Industrial Exhibition of 1851', *Westminster Review* 53 (April 1850): 95; Dancy, *Hyde Park*, p. 120.
67. Wood to Grey, 4 July 1850, RCE/WA IV:43.
68. *Economist* 8 (6 July 1850): 733; RCE/WA IV:20; Sarah Foote to the Royal Commission, June 1850, RCE/EC.
69. 18 and 28 June; 1, 4, 12, 25, 26 and 29 July; 1, 6, 19 and 12 August. See *Hansard*, 3rd ser., 112:699–786, 870, 874, 903, 1300; 114:106.
70. PRO WORK 6/126/1/4–6, 8.
71. *Hansard*, 3rd ser., 112:72–3.
72. *Ibid.*, 112:604–9.
73. Cole, Diary, 21 July 1850.
74. *Ibid.*, 4 July 1850.
75. Albert to Ernst, 4 July 1850, in *Prince Consort and his Brother*, p. 117.
76. Northcote to Grey, 4 July 1850, RCE/WA IV:40.
77. Lord John Russell to Albert, 4 July 1850, RCE/WA IV:44.
78. Francis Sheppard, *London, 1808–1870: The Infernal Wen* (London: Secker & Warburg, 1971), pp. 10, 89, 112, 382; Gareth Stedman Jones, *Outcast London* (New York: Pantheon, 1984); Judith R. Walkowitz, *City of Dreadful Delight: Narratives of Sexual Danger in Victorian London* (Chicago: University of Chicago Press, 1992), pp. 27–34, 50–1.
79. Cole, Diary, 29 June–2 July 1850; *Fifty Years*, I:165–6.
80. Royal Commission, Minutes, 11 July 1850.
81. Cole, *Fifty Years*, I:163–4.
82. Paxton to Sarah Paxton, 22 June 1850, Paxton Papers, 576.1, 576.2; Granville to Paxton, undated, Paxton Papers, 575.
83. Paxton to Sarah Paxton, 24 June 1850, Paxton Papers, 576.3.
84. John Crace to Granville, 29 June 1850, Paxton Papers, 578.
85. George F. Chadwick, *The Works of Sir Joseph Paxton* (London: The Architectural Press, 1961), pp. 106–7.
86. *Ibid.*; Graham Reeves, *Palace of the People* (London: Bromley Library Service, 1986), p. 5; Tallis, I:10–11; 'The Private History of the Palace of Glass,' *Household Words* 43 (18 January 1851): 388.
87. Paxton Papers, 578.1.
88. Luckhurst, *Great Exhibition*, pp. 24–25.
89. *Illustrated London News*, 6 July 1850.
90. Paxton to Sarah Paxton, 24–5 June 1850, Paxton Papers, 576.3–4.
91. Chadwick, *Works of Paxton*, pp. 106–7.
92. *The Times*, 15 July 1850.
93. Granville to Albert, 12 July 1850, RCE/WA IV:62.
94. Peto made this offer formally in a 12 July 1850 letter to Grey, RCE/WA IV:61.
95. Cole, *Fifty Years*, I:168–9; Luckhurst, *Great Exhibition*, pp. 18–21.
96. Peto to Grey, 12 July 1850, RCE/WA IV:61.
97. Paxton to Sarah Paxton, 12 July 1850, Paxton Papers, 583.1.
98. Cole, Diary, 6–16 July 1850; Paxton Papers, 584.
99. Blanche Paxton to Joseph Paxton, undated, Paxton Papers, 585.
100. G. N. Browne to Paxton, 17 July 1850, Paxton Papers, 588.1.
101. Duke of Devonshire, Diary, 25 July 1850, Devonshire Collection.
102. 'Greville,' *Answer*, pp. 7–8.
103. Paxton to Devonshire, 15 October 1850, Paxton Papers, 632.
104. Albert to Prince William of Prussia, 29 December 1850, in *Letters of the Prince Consort, 1831–1861*, ed. Kurt Jagow, trans. E. T. S. Dugdale (London: John Murray, 1938), p. 175.

CHAPTER 3: ORGANIZATION: SELLING THE EXHIBITION

1. [W. E. Aytoun], 'The Proposed Exhibition of 1851', *Blackwood's* 68 (September 1850): 279.
2. [Moriarty], 'Official Catalogue,' pp. 565–6. See also *The World's Metropolis, or Mighty London* (London: [Read & Co., 1855]), p. 10.
3. 'A Report to the Society of Arts', Russell Collection, II:218.
4. Donald Read, *The English Provinces c. 1760–1960: A Study in Influence* (New York: St Martin's Press, 1964), p. 1; Asa Briggs, *Victorian Cities* (Berkeley: University of California Press, 1993), p. 363.
5. Phipps to Scott Russell, 18 December 1849, Letters from Prince Albert and the Emperor Ferdinand to John Scott Russell Regarding the 1851 Exhibition, RSA.

6. Bramley Moore to George Grey, 5 and 13 November 1849, RCE/WA I:52.

7. Gibson to Granville, 20 November 1851, RCE/EC.

8. The arguments of some historians notwithstanding, for example Read, *English Provinces*, it is hard to overestimate London's importance, if not predominance, in almost every respect throughout the nineteenth century. See H. J. Dyos, 'Greater and Greater London: Metropolis and Provinces in the Nineteenth and Twentieth Centuries', in David Cannadine and David Reeder, eds, *Exploring the Urban Past* (Cambridge: Cambridge University Press, 1982), pp. 39, 47; Cain and Hopkins, *British Imperialism,* esp. pp. 125–34, 141–60. John Fisher Murray provided an astute characterization of London in *The World of London* (Edinburgh: William Blackwood & Sons, 1843), when he described it as 'the head, the brain, the heart, the noble viscus of our body politic', adding that 'we in the provinces are but outlying extremities, subsidiary, secondary; we are hardly allowed to know whether our toes are cold until we are so instructed by leading articles from London' (I:7).

9. RCE/WA I:33.

10. Royal Commission, Minutes, 9 May 1850.

11. Cain and Hopkins, *British Imperialism*, pp. 22, 25, 41.

12. Richard Price, 'Does the Notion of Victorian England Make Sense?', in Derek Fraser, ed., *Cities, Class and Communication* (New York: Harvester Wheatsheaf, 1990), pp. 164–5; Briggs, *Victorian Cities*, p. 43.

13. Howe, *Free Trade*, pp. 1–69; Robert Stewart, *The Politics of Protection: Lord Derby and the Protectionist Party, 1841–1852* (Cambridge: Cambridge University Press, 1971), esp. pp. 45, 77, 143.

14. A. C. Howe, 'Free Trade and the City of London, c. 1820–1870', *History* 77 (1992): 391–410.

15. *The Times*, 18 October 1849; *The Art Journal Illustrated Catalogue* (London: Virtue & Co., 1851), p. xv.

16. All references to the 17 October 1849 meeting at the Mansion House, unless noted otherwise, are from *The Times*, 18 October 1849.

17. Ronald K. Huch and Paul R. Ziegler, *Joseph Hume: The People's MP* (Philadelphia: American Philosophical Society, 1985).

18. RCE/WA I:33.

19. *The Times*, 18 October 1849.

20. All references to the 25 January 1850 meeting at the Mansion House, unless noted otherwise, are from *The Times*, 26 January 1850.

21. *Ibid.*

22. *Sun*, 26 January 1850.

23. All references to the 21 March 1850 Mansion House meeting, unless noted otherwise, are from *The Times*, 22 March 1850.

24. RCE:WA III:9–10.

25. Cole to Grey, 25 January 1850, Cole Papers.

26. *Scotsman*, RCE:WA VII:102.

27. 'The Proposed New National Galleries and Museums,' *Fraser's Magazine* 47 (March 1853): 341–2.

28. Horace Greeley, *Glances at Europe* (New York: Dewitt & Davenport, 1851), pp. 20–1, 71.

29. Robert Rhodes James, *Albert, Prince Consort* (London: Hamish Hamilton, 1983), pp. xi–xii, 62–76, 87–9, 102–8; Dorothy Thompson, *Queen Victoria: Gender and Power* (London: Virago Press, 1990), pp. 24–5, 33–41.

30. James, *Albert*, pp. 151–3, 199.

31. Campbell, *Autobiography and Memoirs*, I:320. See also David W. Bartlett, *What I Saw in London; or, Men and Things in the Great Metropolis* (Auburn: Derby & Miller, 1852), pp. 214–15.

32. Malcolm Warner, *The Victorians: British Painting, 1837–1901* (Washington, DC: National Gallery of Art, 1996), pp. 17–18, 76–7.

33. *Collection of Printed Documents*, II:275.

34. *Ibid.*, II:277; *Derby Reporter*, 31 May 1850, in *Collection of Printed Documents*, II:281. See also John Tod, 'Visit to London and "The Exhibition," June 21st 1851,' National Library of Scotland, Acc. 9211. Tod, an otherwise anonymous engineer from Lasswade, Scotland, wrote in his diary that 'party feeling and selfishness' were forgotten and overcome.

35. [Aytoun], 'Proposed Exhibition.' See also *idem.*, 'The Congress and the Agapedome,' *Blackwood's* 70 (September 1851): 359–78 and 'Autumn Politics,' *Blackwood's* 70 (November 1851): 607–28, and [J. S. Barty], 'The Experiment,' *Blackwood's* 70 (October 1851): 488–504. There is no question that these articles reached their intended audience as well. Herbert Spencer (*An Autobiography* [London: Williams & Norgate, 1904], I:373) wrote of 'the divergent opinions which were entertained concerning this industrial show and its consequences.' He remembered in particular an article by [William Henry Smith], 'Voltaire and the Crystal Palace,' *Blackwood's* 70 (August 1851): 142–53.

36. [Aytoun], 'Proposed Exhibition.'

37. *Blackburn Standard*, 11 September 1850, in *Collection of Printed Documents*, VIII:1129.

38. *John Bull*, undated, in RCE/WA III:15.

39. *Ibid.*, 8 June and 7 December 1850.

40. *Collection of Printed Documents*, II:277.

41. *Britannia*, 21 December 1850.

42. *Economist* 8 (13 April 1850): 395.

43. *Collection of Printed Documents*, II:275; PRO HO 45/3623.

44. *Morning Herald*, 22 March 1850. So palatable was this core definition of the exhibition that the commissioners received a ringing endorsement from the otherwise radical and skeptical paper, *John Bull* (23 March 1850), which refused, for once, to find fault with the details of the project so enamored was it – and the public – with the core ideology underlying the plan.

45. *Collection of Printed Documents*, II:268.

46. All references to this meeting, as well as one in Marylebone with a similar orientation, are from *ibid.*, II:170, 277, unless otherwise noted.

47. *Ibid.*, II:283.

48. The Duchess of Sutherland to Queen Victoria, undated, RCE/WA II:78.

49. RCE/WA II:88; *The Times*, 12 April 1850. There was also a ladies' committee in Bristol, but it raised only £6.

50. On mechanics' institutes, see R. J. Morris, *Class, Sect and Party: The Making of the British Middle Class, Leeds, 1820–50* (Manchester: Manchester University Press, 1990), pp. 241–2, 249–61; Edward Royle, 'Mechanics Institutes and the Working Classes, 1840–1860', *Historical Journal* 14 (1971): 305–21; Tylecote, *Mechanics' Institutes;* Hole, *Essay.* Similar sentiments were expressed by the Basingstoke Mechanics' Institute; see *Collection of Printed Documents,* I:70b, II:184.

51. Sally Mitchell, 'Sentiment and Suffering: Women's Recreational Reading in the 1860s', *Victorian Studies* 21 (1977): 31; Richard Altick, *The English Common Reader* (Chicago: University of Chicago Press, 1957), pp. 82–3, 318, 332–3.

52. Granville to Phipps, 16 February 1850, RCE/WA II:74; G. A. Cranfield, *The Press and Society* (London: Longman, 1978), p. 155.

53. Grey to Cole, 12 January 1850, Cole Papers.

54. Cole, Diary, 14 August 1849. Cole also courted the *Art Journal.* See Cole to Scott Russell, 23 September 1849, Russell Collection, II:67.

55. *Stone the First at the Great Glass House* (London: William Edward Painter, n.d.), p. 25.

56. *Collection of Printed Documents,* V:554–5.

57. Granville to Grey, 15 June 1850, RCE/WA III:132.

58. [Adams], 'Industrial Exhibition of 1851,' p. 10.

59. See also the *Weekly Dispatch,* 24 March 1850; *The British Advertiser. An Illustrated Hand-Book of the Great Exhibition* (London: Jackson & Cooper, 1851).

60. Henry Mayhew and George Cruikshank, *1851; or, the Adventures of Mr. and Mrs. Sandboys and Family who came to London to 'Enjoy Themselves' and to see the Great Exhibition* (London: David Bogue, [1851]), p. 131.

61. S. P. Newcombe, *Little Henry's Holiday at the Great Exhibition* (London: Houlston & Stoneman, [1851]), p. 33. See also *The House that Albert Built* (n.p., n.d.): *The English and Continental Guide to London, in English and French* (London: W. and T. Piper, 1851), p. 42.

62. Hugh McCorquodale to Wellington, 5 April 1851, Wellington Papers, University of Southampton Library, 2/168/169. Compare his statement with the following, from *The Royal Exchange and the Palace of Industry* (London: William Jones, 1851), p. 163: 'The Palace of Industry was the Temple of Peace.'

63. Tod, 'Visit to London.'

64. *Britannia,* 21 December 1850; 25 January, 26 April 1851.

65. *Mechanics' Magazine,* 12 January and 2 March 1850.

66. *Reynold's Newspaper,* 8 June, 11 August, 12 October 1851. See also the *Operative,* 1 February, 5 July 1851.

67. McKean, p. 20; *Crystal Palace,* Macdonald, 'William Morris,' p. 76.

68. Royal Commission, *First Report,* pp. xxi–xxii.

69. Grey to Cole, 5 June 1850, Cole Papers.

70. Cole, Diary, 24 May 1850.

71. *Collection of Printed Documents,* I:58, 73; II:61, 68. Wyatt was in fact something of an ombudsman in the preparations for the exhibition. It was Wyatt who wrote the report on the 1849 Paris Exposition that had been well received by, among others, Robert Peel, which got him appointed secretary to the executive committee. He was also the 'superintendent architect' for the Crystal Palace, responsible for drawing up the contracts with Fox and Henderson, regulating the accounts, directing some of the work on the building and arranging the exhibits inside the building, although he received considerable assistance. See Robinson, *Wyatts,* pp. vi, 204–8.

72. Playfair, *Memoirs,* pp. 112–14.

73. *Ibid.,* pp. 63–6, 109–14; Playfair to Peel, 18 February 1850, Peel Papers, BL Add. MSS 40603 f. 86; Peel to Albert, 19 April 1850, RCE:WA III:52; DNB.

74. Henry Cole and Francis Fuller, 'Report made to H.R.H. Prince Albert . . . into the Willingness of Manufacturers and Others to Support Periodical Exhibitions of the Works of Industry of All Nations, 5 October 1849', pp. 11–14, RCE/WA I:37.

75. RCE/WA II:22, 32.

76. *Journal of the Exhibition of 1851,* 7 December 1850, p. 52.

77. RCE/WA IV:89.

78. These problems beset the organizational efforts in Maidstone, Rochester and Chatham, among others. See RCE/WA IV:53.

79. *Ibid.*

80. RCE/WA II:24.

81. Playfair to Granville, 1 November 1850, RCE/WA V:25.

82. Playfair to Granville, 4 August 1850, RCE/WA IV:106; Playfair to Reid, 1 and 27 September, 5 October 1850, RCE/WA IV:136–7, 141.

83. John Johnson Collection.

84. Playfair to Granville, 15 June 1850, RCE/WA IV:4.

85. RCE/WA IV:107.

86. Royal Commission, Minutes, 14 March 1850.

87. RCE/WA IV:89.

88. [Aytoun], 'Proposed Exhibition,' pp. 278–9.

89. Cole to Grey, 26 January 1850, Cole Papers.

90. W. W. Rundell to Northcote, Alexander Lowe to Playfair, 4 November 1851, RCE/EC; Lloyd to Granville, 31 May 1850, RCE/WA III:301.

91. Fuller, *Memoranda,* p. 28.

92. Herbert Byng Hall, *The West of England and the Exhibition, 1851* (London: Longman & Company, 1851), pp. 330–1. For a brief discussion of the varied responses found by the executive committee in the provinces, see [Moriarty], 'Official Catalogue,' p. 566.

93. Briggs, *Victorian Cities,* p. 89.

94. *Ibid.,* pp. 105–26; V. A. C. Gatrell, 'The Commercial Middle Class in Manchester, c. 1820–1857' (PhD thesis, University of Cambridge, 1971), esp. pp. 78, 105–6.

95. John Seed, ' "Commerce and the Liberal Arts:" The Political Economy of Art in Manchester, 1775–1860,' in Janet Wolff and John Seed, eds, *The Culture of*

Capital: Art, Power, and the Nineteenth-Century Middle Class (Manchester: Manchester University Press, 1988), pp. 45–81.

96. Royal Commission, *First Report*, Appendix XL.

97. *Manchester Guardian*, 7 November 1849; Fuller, *Memoranda*, p. 86.

98. Morris, 'Leeds and the Crystal Palace,' p. 288. Morris argued that this was actually a drawback.

99. *Manchester Guardian*, 7 November 1849.

100. *Ibid.*

101. William Entwisle's bank donated £200; Alexander Henry's firm gave £105, as did Thomas Bazley and John Potter; J. A. Turner's company gave £50; Joseph Brotherton gave £10 10s; and the Lord Bishop gave £30.

102. *Manchester Committee*, M6/3/4/7.

103. Gatrell, 'Commercial Middle Class,' pp. 154–210, 273; Thomas Heywood, *A Memoir of Sir Benjamin Heywood* (Manchester: Thomas Fargie, n.d.), pp. 57, 68, 73, 162–3, 176–7; Alan J. Kidd, 'Introduction: The Middle Class in Nineteenth-Century Manchester,' in Kidd and K. W. Roberts, eds, *City, Class and Culture: Studies of Social Policy and Cultural Production in Victorian Manchester* (Manchester: Manchester University Press, 1985), pp. 10–11.

104. Heywood, *Heywood*, pp. 40–1; Gatrell, 'Commercial Middle Class,' pp. 375–9.

105. Gatrell, 'Commercial Middle Class,' pp. 174–186.

106. Royal Commission, *First Report*, pp. 53–4.

107. Newall to Fuller, 4 April 1850, RCE/WA III:34; *Manchester Guardian*, 23 January 1850.

108. Two examples are the speeches by Milner Gibson at a meeting in Kensington on 20 March 1850 and John Smith at a meeting in Westminster on 19 February 1850. *Collection of Printed Documents*, II:170.

109. E. M. Sigsworth, 'The West Riding Wool Textile Industry and the Great Exhibition,' *Yorkshire Bulletin of Economic and Social Research* 4 (1952): 21–2; Briggs, *Victorian Cities*, pp. 139–57.

110. Briggs, *Victorian Cities*, p. 151; Morris, 'Leeds and the Crystal Palace,' p. 284; Derek Fraser, ed., *A History of Modern Leeds* (Manchester: Manchester University Press, 1980).

111. Sigsworth, 'West Riding Wool', p. 23.

112. Morris, 'Leeds and the Crystal Palace,' pp. 299–300.

113. Theodore Koditschek, *Class Formation and Urban-Industrial Society: Bradford, 1750–1850* (Cambridge: Cambridge University Press, 1990).

114. Morris, *Class, Sect and Party*.

115. Sigsworth, 'West Riding Wool,' p. 29; Royal Commission, *First Report*, Appendix XL.

116. Sigsworth, 'West Riding Wool,' p. 24.

117. *Leeds Mercury*, 15 April, 3 May 1851, quoted in Sigsworth, 'West Riding Wool,' p. 29.

118. E. J. Connell and M. Ward, 'Industrial Development, 1780–1914', in Fraser, ed., *History of Modern Leeds*, pp. 156–7.

119. Fuller, *Memoranda*, p. 86; Playfair to Granville, 29 May 1850, RCE/WA III:98.

120. Playfair to Gray, 31 May 1850; Playfair to Granville, 2 June 1850, RCE/WA III:104, 106.

121. Thomas Ellison, *Gleanings and Reminiscences* (Liverpool: Henry Young & Sons, 1905), pp. 309–11.

122. *Liverpool Mercury*, 31 May 1850.

123. *Journal of the Exhibition of 1851*, 18 January 1851, p. 109; *The Times*, 3 April 1851.

124. Playfair to Granville, 2 June 1850, RCE/WA III:106.

125. Mary Ede, 'Bath and the Great Exhibition of 1851,' *Bath History* 3 (1990): 139, 156–7.

126. *Ibid.*, p. 156.

127. *Collection of Printed Documents*, I:70a.

128. Ede, 'Bath,' pp. 141–2.

129. Charles Booth, *Condition and Occupations of the People of the Tower Hamlets, 1886–1887* (London: Edward Stanford, 1887), p. 4.

130. *Ibid.*, pp. 8–27.

131. Sir W. Clay to Granville, 9 March 1850, RCE/WA II:99.

132. Royal Commission, *First Report*, Appendix XL.

133. Manchester Committee, M6/3/10/4; Cole to Grey, December 1849, Cole Papers.

134. Lord Londonderry to Grey, 26 February 1850, RCE/WA II:90.

135. *Ibid.* Despite this gloomy outlook, Playfair was nevertheless able to report to Granville on 7 July 1850, RCE/WA IV:52, that in Durham the local committee had raised £140, including £70 from small donations (indicating breadth of support), £50 from the dean of the cathedral, and £20 from the carpet manufacturers, who represented Durham's one substantial industry.

136. Lloyd to Granville, 31 May 1850, RCE/WA III:101.

137. *Punch* 20 (24 May 1851): 212.

138. *Collection of Printed Documents*, II:281; *The Times*, 29 May 1851.

139. Lloyd to Granville, 22 June 1850, RCE/WA IV:12.

140. *Ibid.*

141. RCE/EC IV:53.

142. RCE/WA IV:89; Royal Commission, *First Report*, Appendix XL.

143. Cole, *Fifty Years*, I:128–9; Matthew Digby Wyatt, 'Further Report made this 14th day of November, 1849, to His Royal Highness the Prince Albert . . . of preliminary inquiries into the willingness of manufacturers and others to support periodical exhibitions of the works of industry of all nations' (n.p., n.d.). On the significance, definition, and historians' neglect of the Celtic fringe, see J. C. D. Clark, 'English History's Forgotten Context: Scotland, Ireland, Wales,' *Historical Journal* 32 (1989): 211–28; J. G. A. Pocock, 'British History: A Plea for a New Subject,' *Journal of Modern History* 47 (1975): 601–21, and 'The Limits and Divisions of British History,' *American Historical Review* 87 (1982): 311–36; Linda Colley, 'Britishness and Otherness: An Argument,' *Journal of British Studies* 31 (1992): 309–29.

144. Playfair to Grey, 2 May 1850, RCE/WA III:64; Playfair to Granville, 8 July 1850, RCE/WA IV:110; Playfair to Granville, 4 August 1850, RCE/WA IV:106. On the pervasiveness of class consciousness and

conflict in Scotland during the nineteenth century, see, among many, T. C. Smout, *A Century of the Scottish People, 1830–1950* (London: Collins, 1986), esp. p. 5.

145. Playfair to Granville, 8 July 1850, RCE/WA IV:110; Royal Commission, *First Report*, Appendix XL. For material on Dundee, which presents a similar story, see Playfair to Granville, 4 August 1850, RCE/WA IV:106.

146. Smout, *Century of Scottish People*, pp. 85–95, 109–113.

147. *Collection of Printed Documents*, II:306.

148. David Williams, *A History of Modern Wales* (London: John Murray, 1950), pp. 213–28; Gareth Elwyn Jones, *Modern Wales: A Concise History, c. 1485–1979* (Cambridge: Cambridge University Press, 1984), pp. 151–82.

149. *Cardiff and Merthyr Guardian*, 19 January 1850.

150. *Cambrian*, 11 January 1850.

151. *Reports by the Juries on the Subjects in the Thirty Classes into which the Exhibition was Divided* (London: William Clowes & Sons, 1852), I:67, 231; II:766, 809, 1241; Royal Commission, *First Report*, Appendix XL, pp. 180–95.

152. *Nation*, 24 May, 4 October, 25 October 1851. The *Evening Mail*, conservative and supportive of the Church of England, did provide more coverage, especially of the opening, but for this paper too the exhibition lacked immediacy.

153. W. E. Vaughan, ed., *A New History of Ireland*, vol. V: *Ireland under the Union, I: 1801–70* (Oxford: Clarendon Press, 1989), pp. 137–57; Michael Hechter, *Internal Colonialism: The Celtic Fringe in British National Development, 1536–1966* (Berkeley: University of California Press, 1975), pp. 92–3.

154. Hechter, *Internal Colonialism*, p. 141.

155. Although R. J. Morris has argued that 'the main work of rousing the provinces was done by approaching each town as a community rather than approaching individuals, and working through the community network of formal organizations' ('Leeds and the Crystal Palace,' p. 284), there is much evidence to suggest otherwise. For example, the circular Wyatt sent out to the Mayor of Manchester asked him to schedule a meeting with 'the chief members of any chambers of commerce, agricultural associations, literary or scientific bodies, and generally such individuals as should seem, from their position, most likely to become interested in this matter.' In Leeds, Dilke was distraught that none of the Marshall family attended the first organizational meeting, and in Durham County the organizational effort was handled by Lord Londonderry, who in turn contacted not formal organizations, but two individuals, the Duke of Cleveland and Mr Burdon, the Chairman of the Quarter Sessions.

156. Morris, 'Leeds and the Crystal Palace,' p. 286.

157. Elizabeth Hammerton and David Cannadine, 'Conflict and Consensus on a Ceremonial Occasion: The Diamond Jubilee in Cambridge in 1897,' *Historical Journal* 24 (1981): 112–13.

CHAPTER 4: COMMERCE AND CULTURE

1. Tallis, I:207.

2. Benjamin Silliman, *A Visit to Europe in 1851* (New York: G. P. Putnam & Co., 1854), II:426.

3. Few historians have successfully analyzed this conglomeration of objects. See Briggs, *Victorian Things*, ch. 1; Richards, *Commodity Culture*, ch. 1; Nikolaus Pevsner, *High Victorian Design: A Study of the Exhibits of 1851* (London: The Architectural Press, 1951). Only Thomas Parke Hughes ('Industry through the Crystal Palace' [PhD thesis, University of Virginia, 1953]) has explored the machinery in any depth.

4. Manchester Committee, M6/3/8/47–8.

5. Royal Commission, *First Report*, pp. 51–3; *Collection of Printed Documents*, I:119, II:328–38, 416–19, 422–3, 427, 431, 436–7; Royal Commission, *Minutes*, 16 May 1850; Cole, *Diary*, 26–27 August 1850; Reid to Grey, 29 May 1850, RCE/WA III:97; Granville to Phipps, 20 July 1850, RCE/WA IV:93; *The Times*, 23 November 1850.

6. Briggs, *Victorian Things*, p. 54. For a discussion of earlier classification systems, see Richard Yeo, 'Reading Encyclopedias: Science and the Organization of Knowledge in British Dictionaries of Arts and Sciences, 1730–1850', *Isis* 82 (1991): 24–49.

7. Playfair, *Memoirs*, p. 115; Russell Collection, III:68–96, 107 *passim*; RCE/WA I:40; Playfair to Peel, 5 February 1850, RCE/WA II:76.

8. Playfair, *Memoirs*, p. 116.

9. For a complete accounting of the various editions of the *Catalogue*, see Elizabeth M. Mitchell, 'The Great Exhibition of 1851: A Select Bibliography' (MA thesis University of London, School of Librarianship, 1950). The more portable one-volume shilling edition of the catalogue sold well, reaching approximately one out of every twenty visitors to the exhibition. At the time of the publication of the Royal Commission's *First Report* in early 1852, a total of 286,000 copies of the one-volume shilling edition had been sold, plus another 13,000 copies in French and German at 2s 6d. There was also a synopsis available for sixpence, which sold 84,000 copies, and a twopenny popular guide which sold best on the shilling days, reaching a total sales of 26,000. The *Official Descriptive and Illustrated Catalogue*, however, for all its symbolism and significance for historians, was a sales disaster, with the publishers claiming losses of almost £8,000. Each of the five parts cost ten shillings; the three volumes together cost £3 3s. Although more than 400 copies were sold on the first day of the exhibition, after the first three days only once did sales reach twenty copies. See the Royal Commission, *First Report*, pp. 132–8; Spicer Brothers and Clowes & Sons to the Royal Commission, 30 December 1851; Harrison and Rurington [comptrollers at Her Majesty's Stationery Office] to J. R. McCulloch, 15 June 1852; McCulloch to Bowring, 22 June 1852; Clowes & Sons to Bowring, 28 October 1852, RCE/EC.

10. These included Robert Owen, Philip Pusey, J. Forbes

Royle, Justus Liebig, and I. K. Brunel. The editors could add scientific annotations, but could not offer criticism.

11. *Official Catalogue*, pp. vi, viii.

12. Quoted in Bruce Mazlish, *The Fourth Discontinuity: The Co-Evolution of Humans and Machines* (New Haven: Yale University Press, 1993), p. 8.

13. On this point more broadly, see Tony Bennett, 'The Exhibitionary Complex,' *New Formations* 4 (1988): 73–102.

14. On this latter point about the numerous 'paths' to industrialization, see, among many, Patrick K. O'Brien and Caglar Keyder, *Economic Growth in Britain and France, 1780–1914* (London: George Allen & Unwin, 1978); N. F. R. Crafts, 'British Industrialization in an International Context,' *Journal of Interdisciplinary History* 19 (1989): 415–28; Alexander Gerschenkron, *Economic Backwardness in Historical Perspective* (New York: Frederick A. Praeger, 1962); Whitney Walton, *France at the Crystal Palace: Bourgeois Taste and Artisan Manufacture in the Nineteenth Century* (Berkeley: University of California Press, 1992); David S. Landes, *The Unbound Prometheus* (Cambridge: Cambridge University Press, 1969), esp. pp. 124–92.

15. Many contemporaries used the word 'spectacle' in their accounts of the Crystal Palace, but on the broader meanings of the term, see Richards, *Commodity Culture*, ch. 1; Guy Debord, *Society of the Spectacle* (Detroit: Black and Red, 1983).

16. Lewis Carroll to Elizabeth Carroll, 5 July 1851, in Lewis Carroll, *The Letters of Lewis Carroll*, ed. Morton N. Cohen (New York: Oxford University Press, 1979), I:17–18; [Newcombe], *Little Henry's Holiday at the Great Exhibition*, pp. 43–4, 47, 80–1; Zadok Thompson, *Journal of a Trip to London, Paris, and the Great Exhibition of 1851* (Burlington: Nichols & Warren, 1852), p. 99; *The Times*, 4 June 1851. This contemporary evidence overwhelmingly suggests, contrary to what Philip Langdon has argued in 'Great Exhibitions: Representations of the Crystal Palace in Mayhew, Dickens, and Dostoyevsky,' *Nineteenth-Century Contexts* 20 (1997), that working men and women were not participants 'in an experience of regulated spectatorship' (p. 28). At a minimum, they were free to move about the Crystal Palace however they chose.

17. James Ward, *The World in its Workshops*, 2nd edn (London: William S. Orr & Co., 1851), p. 3. Modern critics such as Benjamin and Adorno have termed this state of 'vertigo induced by the teeming and random miscellany of commodities in an uncircumscribed and otherwise seemingly featureless space' 'phantasmagoria.' See Larry D. Lutchmansingh, 'Commodity Exhibitionism at the London Great Exhibition of 1851,' *Annals of Scholarship* 7 (1990): 204.

18. Williams, *Keywords*, pp. 165–8. Carlyle wrote of 'leaders of industry' in 1843; Disraeli of 'our national industries' in 1844.

19. *The Times*, 2 May 1851. Historians have almost uniformly failed to recognize the purpose and focus of the exhibition because they have largely used 'industry' in its twentieth- rather than its mid-nineteenth-century meaning. See Arnstein, *Britain Yesterday and Today*, p. 72; Landes, *Unbound Prometheus*. For a useful corrective, see Raphael Samuel, 'Workshop of the World: Steam Power and Hand Technology in Mid-Victorian Britain,' *History Workshop* 3 (1977): 6–72. See also Adrian Forty, *Objects of Desire: Design and Society since 1750* (London: Thames & Hudson, 1986), p. 43, and Berg, *Age of Manufactures*.

20. McLean to Wyatt, 29 January 1851, RCE/EC. The table appeared in Class XXVI, no. 386.

21. S. P. Newcombe, *Fireside Facts from the Great Exhibition: Object Lessons in the Food and Clothing of All Nations in 1851* (London: Peter, Duff & Co., [1851]), p. 245. It is important to note that in 1851 'working men' did not only mean the working classes. John Tallis, in his guide to the exhibition, provided brief biographies of famous 'working men,' among whom he included James Watt and Josiah Wedgwood (II:80ff).

22. Tallis, I:57–8.

23. 'The Great Exhibition,' *Eclectic Review* 1 (June 1851): 742. In the anonymous satiric fable *The Enchanted Hive, or, The Island of the Bees*, an obvious reference to Mandeville's *Fable of the Bees*, the father tries to teach his son the importance of hard work, and cautioned against the 'dreadful effects of idleness.'

24. Thomas Carlyle, *Past and Present*, ed. Richard D. Altick (New York: New York University Press, 1965), p. 196; Houghton, *Victorian Frame of Mind*, pp. 242–62.

25. Carlyle, *Past and Present*, p. 180; Macdonald, 'William Morris', pp. 71–2.

26. *Official Catalogue*, p. 1.

27. Siegfried Giedion, *Mechanization Takes Command* (New York: Oxford University Press, 1948).

28. *Official Catalogue*, p. 119.

29. *Ibid*.

30. E. A. Wrigley, *Continuity, Chance and Change: The Character of the Industrial Revolution in England* (Cambridge: Cambridge University Press, 1988), pp. 5, 37, 95.

31. *Official Catalogue*, p. 87.

32. Thomas Richards, *The Imperial Archive* (London: Verso, 1993); Bernard S. Cohn, *Colonialism and its Forms of Knowledge* (Princeton: Princeton University Press, 1996).

33. *Collection of Printed Documents*, II:326–7; Playfair to Grey, 13 June 1850, RCE/WA III:128.

34. *Official Catalogue*, IV:9. Roman numerals indicate the class, arabic numerals the item number within each class.

35. *Ibid*., I:427.

36. *Ibid*., I:509.

37. The Duke's exhibits were handled by Henry Cadell, his mining engineer in the years 1849–55, through the Edinburgh committee. See the Cadell of Grange Papers, Box 35.

38. Partha Mitter, *Much Maligned Monsters: A History*

of European Reactions to Indian Art (Chicago: University of Chicago Press, 1992), p. 221.

39. *Official Catalogue*, p. 857; J. Forbes Royle, *On the Culture and Commerce of Cotton in India* (London: Smith, Elder & Co., 1851); India Office, India and Bengal Dispatches, 7 January 1850, IOR E/4/803; Ray Desmond, *The India Museum, 1801–1879* (London: HMSO, 1982).

40. Jonathan Sweet, 'The Face of Australia: Colonial Design and Representation at International Exhibitions, 1851–1888' (MA thesis, Royal College of Art, 1991).

41. *Official Catalogue*, III:988–9.

42. Greenhalgh, *Ephemeral Vistas*, pp. 52–5.

43. *Official Catalogue*, p. 949; Benedict, *et al.*, *Anthropology of World's Fairs*, p. 46.

44. *Illustrated London News*, 26 April 1851.

45. *Art Union* 29 (1851): 1845.

46. The difficulties the British had governing their empire are legendary. For a suggestive overview, see Ged Martin, 'Was There a British Empire?', *Historical Journal* 15 (1972): 562–9; Richards, *Imperial Archive*, pp. 1–9.

47. *Official Catalogue*, III:992.

48. Everett to Royal Commission, 4 April 1851, RCE/WA V:71.

49. Cain and Hopkins, *British Imperialism*, and also their earlier articles, 'The Political Economy of British Expansion Overseas, 1750–1914,' *Economic History Review*, 2nd ser., 33 (1980), 463–90; 'Gentlemanly Capitalism and British Expansion Overseas, 1688–1850: I, The Old Colonial System,', 463–90 *Economic History Review*, 2nd ser., 39 (1986), 501–25; 'Gentlemanly Capitalism and British Expansion Overseas, 1850–1945: II, The New Imperialism,' *Economic History Review*, 2nd ser., 40 (1987), 1–26; M. Daunton, ' "Gentlemanly Capitalism" and British Industry,' *Past & Present* 122 (1989): 119–58. For one recent critique, which also emphasizes the problems associated with dividing the financial and service sectors from the industrial sector, see David Cannadine, 'Review Article: The Empire Strikes Back,' *Past & Present* 147 (1994): 180–94. 'Gentlemanly Capitalists' also stood to benefit from free trade after 1846, and pushed hard for repeal of protectionist measures throughout the 1840s. See Howe, *Free Trade*, pp. 12–18.

50. India Office, IOR L/F/2/150.

51. Desmond, *India Museum*, pp. 36–41.

52. *Official Catalogue*, p. 209.

53. Surprisingly, this has been the section most ignored by historians. The exception is Hughes. This chapter argues in part that the reason for this neglect is that historians have focused on the manufactures either for design issues or, more recently, for their bearing on the formation of a consumer or commodity culture. Thomas Richards, for example, asserted incorrectly that 'no one could possibly mistake the Crystal Palace for a factory' because, 'aside from a few moving mechanical parts, the commodities in the Crystal Palace were at a standstill' (*Commodity Culture*, p. 30). Nothing could be further from the truth.

54. *The Times*, 9 June 1851.

55. *Official Catalogue*, p. 210.

56. Robert Askrill, *The Yorkshire Visitors' Guide to the Great Exhibition* (Leeds: Joseph Buckton, 1851), p. 38; Mayhew and Cruikshank, *1851*, pp. 160–1.

57. Tallis, I:234.

58. James David Forbes, for example, made two trips to the Great Exhibition to examine and purchase some of the machinery for the University of Edinburgh, which allotted him £100 for this purpose. Competition was fierce for some items: in one case Forbes lost out to the Museum of Practical Geology, but the Low Moor Iron Works which had manufactured the item in question offered to furnish him with a few samples. Forbes also managed to acquire a model of a bridge and a marine oscillating engine after deciding to forgo a set of propellers and some pumps in which he had also been interested. See James Whitelaw to Forbes, 18 September; Airy to Forbes, 24 September; Forbes to John Lee, 23 October; Forbes to Delewil, 4 October; Biddell to Forbes, 6 and 8 October, 4 and 14 November; William and John Freeman to Forbes, 13 and 22 October; Walter and John Cooke to Forbes, 13 January 1852; W. Wilson to Biddell, 31 October; Benjamin Webster to Forbes, 12 November; C. A. Deane to Biddell, 13 November; Low Moor Iron Works to Forbes, 7 October; James David Forbes Papers. See also John Campbell Shairp, Peter Guthrie Tait, and A. Adams-Reilly, eds, *Life and Letters of James David Forbes* (London: Macmillan, 1873), pp. 353–5.

59. Ward, *World in its Workshops*, p. 1.

60. *Official Catalogue*, VI:448.

61. Tallis, I:165, II:200–1.

62. *Official Catalogue*, V:434.

63. Askrill, *Yorkshire Visitors' Guide*, pp. 12–13.

64. *A Guide to the Great Exhibition; containing a description of every principal object of interest* (London: George Routledge & Co., 1851), pp. 38–9.

65. Quoted in C. R. Fay, *Palace of Industry, 1851* (Cambridge: Cambridge University Press, 1951), p. 57.

66. *Scientific American* 6 (31 May 1851): 290.

67. Mayhew and Cruikshank, *1851*, p. 161; Royal Commission, *First Report*, Appendix II, p. 8.

68. Royal Commission, *First Report*, Appendix XVIII, pp. 92–100; Susan H. Curtland to the Royal Commission, 11 May 1851, RCE/EC.

69. *The Times*, 20 May 1851.

70. Reid to Grey, 2 April 1850, RCE/WA III:29.

71. Ward, *World in its Workshops*, p. 12; Tallis, I:63.

72. Quoted in Tallis, II:198.

73. Wiener, *English Culture*, pp. 27–9; James Raven, 'Viewpoint: British History and the Enterprise Culture,' *Past & Present* 123 (1989): 185–6. This point is illustrated visually by a series of colored engravings published in 1851 under the title *Recollections of the Great Exhibition of 1851* (London: Lloyd Brothers & Co., Simkin, Marshall & Co., 1851), which emphasize the more exotic foreign courts – India, China, Persia, Turkey, Russia, even France and the United States – rather than the industrial sections. The fine arts alone were the central subject in six of the twenty-five engravings. Ironi-

cally, the engraving that dealt most closely with industry depicted the Agricultural Court. The only other appearance of machinery in these drawings was De La Rue's stationery stand and envelope machine.

74. Nasmyth to Colquhoun, 8 April 1851, RCE/EC.

75. *Official Catalogue*, p. 429.

76. J. C. Whish, *The Great Exhibition Prize Essay* (London: Longman, Brown, Green & Longmans, 1851), p. 8.

77. Tallis, I:115; [Moriarty], 'Official Catalogue', p. 559. For a parody of these absurdities, see the anonymous *Mr. Goggleye's Visit to the Exhibition of National Industry to be Held in London on the 1st of April 1851* (London: Timothy Takemin, n.d.).

78. *Official Catalogue*, XXVI:9.

79. *Ibid.*, XXVII:124; Memorandum from the Committee of the Society for Improving the Condition of the Labouring Classes, 20 December 1850, RCE/WA V:73. Prince Albert's was not the only model working-class house exhibited, only the most famous. C. Bruce Allen displayed a laborer's cottage 'with improvements in construction to lessen expense, adapted for agricultural districts' (*Official Catalogue*, XXVII:68).

80. *Plans and Suggestions for Dwellings Adapted to the Working Classes, including the model house for families built by command of His Royal Highness the Prince Albert, K.G., in connection with The Exposition of the Works of Industry of All Nations, 1851* (London: The Society for Improving the Condition of the Labouring Classes, 1851).

81. Martin, *His Royal Highness*, II:227–9; S. Martin Gaskell, *Model Housing: From the Great Exhibition to the Festival of Britain* (London: Mansell, 1986), p. 4; RCE/WA V:73.

82. *The Times*, 13 June 1851.

83. *Plans and Suggestions for Dwellings*. The brochure, obviously targeting prospective builders, cost sixpence. It estimated that the houses would cost £440–£480 to construct, and could be rented at 3s 6d to 4s per week for a 7 percent return after deducting taxes.

84. Henry Roberts to Grey, 23 October 1851, RCE/WA IX:1.

85. *Official Catalogue*, XXII:690; Dodds, *Age of Paradox*, p. 402.

86. *Ibid.*, XXIII:105.

87. Quoted in Briggs, *Victorian Things*, p. 53; William Morris, 'How I became a Socialist', *Justice*, 16 June 1894, p. 6.

88. Ralph Nicholson Wornum, 'The Exhibition as a Lesson in Taste', in *The Art Journal Illustrated Catalogue* (London: George Virtue, 1851), pp. V–VI***. For discussions of the decorative aspects of the arts manufactures, see, among many, Pevsner, *High Victorian Design*, and Ann Ferebee, *A History of Design from the Victorian Era to the Present* (New York: Van Nostrand Reinhold, 1970), esp. p. 25.

89. A. Welby Pugin, *The True Principles of Pointed or Christian Architecture* (London: John Weale, 1841), pp. 23–4. Pugin's work grew out of the Select Committee on Design (1836) and the creation of the first School of Design (1837).

90. Nasmyth to Lieutenant-Colonel Colquhoun, 8 April 1850, RCE/EC.

91. Landes, *Unbound Prometheus*, pp. 124–92. Wornum would have agreed with Nasmyth on this point.

92. *Official Catalogue*, p. 819.

93. Tallis, I:38–9, 202–3; *The Crystal Palace, and its Contents* ([London]: W. M. Clark, 1851), p. 36.

94. Among the many examples of a more modern critique along the same lines, see Nikolavs Pevsner, *Pioneers of Modern Design*, 2nd edn. (New York: Museum of Modern Art, 1949), pp. 8, 20–1, 24; Mazlish, *Fourth Discontinuity*.

95. Most modern critics have repeated these same views. See Pevsner, *Pioneers*, p. 20; Joan Gloag, *Victorian Taste: Some Social Aspects of Architecture and Industrial Design from 1820–1900* (New York: Macmillan, 1962), pp. 9, 136; E. H. Gombrich *The Sense of Order: A Study in the Psychology of Decorative Art* (Ithaca: Cornell University Press, 1979), p. 34.

96. Adam Smith, *Wealth of Nations* (London: Everyman's Library, 1954), II:263–4.

97. Granville to Grey, 20 March 1851; Granville to Ashley, 20 March 1851, RCE/WA VI:35–6.

98. The Medieval Court included exhibitors 529–36 in Class XXVI, 'furniture'. On the firm of Crace, Minton and Potter who joined with Pugin to produce the Medieval Court, see Megan Aldrich, ed., *The Craces: Royal Decorators, 1768–1899* (Brighton: The Royal Pavilion Art Gallery and Museums, 1990), pp. ix, 62–86.

99. *Express*, 29 March 1851.

100. Tallis, I:227. See also *The Crystal Palace, and its Contents*, p. 215.

101. 'The Great Exhibition', *Eclectic Review* 1 (June 1851): 748.

102. On the broader issues raised here, see Gombrich, who wrote of 'the menace of the machine' (*Sense of Order*, p. 33), and Walter Benjamin, 'The Work of Art in an Age of Mechanical Reproduction' (1936) in Hannah Arendt, ed., *Illuminations* (New York: Harcourt, Brace & World, 1968), pp. 223, 236.

103. See Select Committee on Arts and Manufactures, Minutes of Evidence, *Parliamentary Papers* IX (1836): 108, ¶1431; Charles Eastlake, *Hints on Household Taste*, 3rd edn (London: Longman, 1872), p. 106.

104. Samuel 'workshop;' Berg, *Age of Manufactures*; Forty, *Objects of Desire*, pp. 43–51; Lorna Weatherill, *The Pottery Trade and North Staffordshire, 1660–1760* (New York: Augustus M. Kelley, 1971), pp. 59–75.

105. See Bell, *Schools of Design*, and Kusamitsu, 'Great Exhibitions.'

106. Wornum, 'Exhibition as a Lesson in Taste'.

107. Pevsner, *High Victorian Design*, p. 73. The criticisms of Pugin, Ruskin, and Wornum, as well as more modern contempt, is also the product of a pronounced antipathy towards the middle class. Pevsner wrote that the exhibits appealed to a philistine, industrially based middle class that was uneducated and had no leisure time in which to learn to appreciate culture (*ibid.*, p. 116). Joan Gloag wrote that 'ornament appeased the anxious appetite of the new rich

and prosperous middle classes for visible evidence of their social status' (*Victorian Taste*, p. 136). See also Perry Anderson, 'Origins of the Present Crisis,' *New Left Review* 23 (1964): 26–54, and Wiener, *English Culture*, This view of the industrial manufacturer or capitalist as a puritanical, uncultured philistine interested in little other than profit is both outdated and inaccurate. Recently historians have detailed the extent to which industrialists and bankers patronized the arts and promoted various cultural institutions. See Wolff and Seed, eds, *Culture of Capital*.

108. Quoted in Pevsner, *High Victorian Design*, pp. 11–12.

109. Henrietta M. A. Ward, *Memories of Ninety Years*, ed. Isabel G. McAllister (London: Hutchinson & Co., [1924]), pp. 64–5, 67.

110. Quoted in C. H. Gibbs-Smith, *The Great Exhibition of 1851*, 2nd edn (London: HMSO, 1981), p. 20.

111. John Ruskin, *The Seven Lamps of Architecture* (London: Smith, Elder & Co., 1849), p. 56.

112. Pevsner, *High Victorian Design*, pp. 152–3; Charlotte Gere, *Nineteenth-Century Decoration: The Art of the Interior* (New York: Harry N. Abrams, 1989), p. 276.

113. Peter Stansky, *Redesigning the World: William Morris, the 1880s, and the Arts and Crafts* (Princeton: Princeton University Press, 1985), p. 5.

114. Tallis, I:5.

115. Phipps to Edwin Chadwick, 3 October 1850, Chadwick Papers, University College London Library, 1577; Playfair to Babbage, 2 June 1851, Babbage Papers, BL Add. MSS 37194 f. 539.

116. Smedley to Scott Russell and Northcote, 13 March 1850, RCE/EC.

117. *The Times*, 5 December 1850, 13 February 1851.

118. *Economist* 8 (13 April 1850): 396.

119. *Collection of Printed Documents*, I:70c.

120. *Economist* 9 (28 June 1851): 701.

121. Babbage, *Exposition of 1851*, pp. 70, 81.

122. *The Times*, 8 January 1851; *Collection of Printed Documents*, VI:891a.

123. Forty, *Objects of Desire*, pp. 29–30; Neil McKendrick, 'Josiah Wedgwood and the Commercialization of the Potteries,' in McKendrick, Brewer, and Plumb, eds, *Birth of a Consumer Society*, pp. 99–145.

124. 'Bills and Cards of Exhibitors', BL 1890.e.12.

125. One guidebook, published before the opening, promoted the exhibition on these very grounds, citing previous exhibitions at which manufacturers had secured large orders for goods. See the *Guide-Book to the Industrial Exhibition; with Facts, Figures and Observations on the Manufactures and Produce Exhibited* (London: Partridge & Oakey, 1851), p. 4. As for the Great Exhibition itself, at least one agricultural firm received £5,000 in orders for equipment (*The Crystal Palace, and its Contents*, p. 124). See also [George Troup], *Art and Faith, in Fragments from the Great Exhibition* (London: Partridge, 1852), pp. 3–4. There should also be no doubt that increased sales were clearly an objective of many exhibitors. At a meeting of 200 exhibitors in August, many emphasized that they wanted the reports of the juries made public, before the exhibition closed, in order that they might 'reap the benefit to which they were justly entitled.' See *The Times*, 30 August 1851.

126. *Express*, 15 October 1851; *The Times*, 5 June, 13 October 1851; *John Bull*, 7 June 1851; *Punch* 22 (10 April 1852): 146. Seymour to Commissioner of Treasury, 31 October 1851, PRO WORK 6 6/126/1/61–2; Paxton to Devonshire, 20 November 1851, Paxton Papers 698.

127. Several historians have characterized the Crystal Palace as the first department store. See Fay, *Palace of Industry*, p. 91; Richards, *Commodity Culture*, p. 17.

128. Richards, *Commodity Culture*, p. 40.

129. Advertisements at the back of the *Official Catalogue* clearly targeted a prosperous, educated, leisured class. Booksellers advertised recent releases such as G. R. Porter's *Progress of the Nation* and a *Family Arabian Nights*; resort hotels sought to capitalize on or perhaps promote the new tourism mania; and predominantly middle-class societies such as the Sacred Harmonic Society of Exeter Hall, the Religious Tract Society, and the Governesses' Benevolent Institution made their appeals for members and donations. Additionally, the prices of goods advertised were well out of the range of affordability for most people who would have been considered working class (that is, those earning about £50 per year).

130. William Felkin, *The Exhibition in 1851 of the Products and Industry of all Nations, its Probable Influence upon Labour and Commerce* (London: Arthur Hall, Virtue & Co., 1851; Benedict *et al.*, *Anthropology of World's Fairs*, p. 2.

131. Britain and France were highly competitive in the mid-nineteenth century, despite their different economic systems. Several economic historians have even suggested that French productivity levels were actually higher than those of Britain. See O'Brien and Keyder, *Economic Growth*, pp. 146, 171, 192–3. Rather than being 'a core of cultural opposition' and a cause of British decline, aesthetics may have been one of the keys to Britain's economic success at the time. Wiener has argued (*English Culture*, esp. pp. 28–9,) that commerce and culture were mutually exclusive, that the Great Exhibition was the highpoint of commerce and industry, but from that point on the British turned to 'culture.' He implicitly associates industry and commerce with modern values and culture with pre-modern values. But at the Great Exhibition commerce and culture were complementary, not contradictory, as the organizers viewed culture as a means of improving commerce.

132. See Chapter 3; Minutes of the Sub-Committee for Canvassing, Manchester Committee, M6/3/1, M6/3/4/7; *The Times*, 26 January 1850.

133. Cain and Hopkins, *British Imperialism*, p. 15.

134. Landes, *Unbound Prometheus*, p. 124; Kennedy, *Rise and Fall*, pp. 151–8.

135. Samuel, 'workshop;' Eric Richards, 'Margins of the Industrial Revolution,' in Patrick O'Brien and Roland Quinault, *The Industrial Revolution and British Society* (Cambridge: Cambridge University

Press, 1993), p. 204; Crafts, 'British Industrialization,' and *British Economic Growth*, esp. pp. 3–7; C. H. Lee, *The British Economy since 1700: A Macroeconomic Perspective* (Cambridge: Cambridge University Press, 1986), esp. pp. 125–41. Even Landes admits that the pace of change was slow (*Unbound Prometheus*, pp. 105, 118, 120–2). For a broad overview of interpretations of the Industrial Revolution, see David Cannadine, 'The Present and the Past in the English Industrial Revolution, 1880–1980,' *Past & Present* 103 (1984): 131–72.

136. *The Times*, 29 July 1851; Wornum, 'Exhibition as a Lesson in Taste,' pp. vii***–viii***; Tallis, II:259; 'Philoponus,' *The Great Exhibition of 1851; or, the Wealth of the World in its Workshops* (London: Edward Churton, 1850), pp. 35–42, 47–57, 89–91, 133; Ward, *World in its Workshops*, pp. 21, 28–9; Archibald Alison, *Some Account of my Life and Writings* (Edinburgh: William Blackwood & Sons, 1883), pp. 28–9. The notable exception to this assessment came from [Adams], 'Industrial Exhibition', p. 391.

137. Tallis, I:151–4; 'Philoponus', *Great Exhibition*, pp. 56–63. See also *Guide to the Exhibition*, pp. 41–2; *The Times*, 7 June 1851.

138. *The Crystal Palace, and its Contents*, pp. 12–14; *The Times*, 27 September 1851; Bartlett, *What I Saw in London*, pp. 322, 324. As Lee has pointed out, America had already overtaken Britain in gross domestic production per head by the mid-nineteenth century (*British Economy*, p. 6).

139. Hobsbawm, *Industry and Empire*; Roderick Floud and David McCloskey, eds., *The Economic History of Britain since 1700* (Cambridge: Cambridge University Press, 1981), II: 1–2; Michael Dintenfass, *The Decline of Industrial Britain, 1870–1980* (London: Routledge, 1992), esp. p. 4.

140. Hobsbawm, *Industry and Empire*, pp. 172–81; Landes, *Unbound Prometheus*, pp. 231–358.

141. Hobsbawm, *Industry and Empire*, pp. 172–5.

142. Robert Hunt, ed., *Hunt's Handbook to the Official Catalogues of the Great Exhibition* (London: Spicer Brothers and W. Clowes, [1851]), II:501; *Official Catalogue*, pp. 1184–6.

143. Dr Lardner, *The Great Exhibition, and London in 1851* (London: Longman, Brown, Green & Longmans, 1852), pp. 84, 107.

144. *Official Catalogue*, V:661; Hughes, 'Industry through the Crystal Palace,' pp. 65–7, 82.

145. Celia Brunel Noble, *The Brunels* (London: Cobden-Sanderson, 1938), p. 200.

146. Charles Babbage, *Reflections on the Decline of Science in England and on Some of its Causes* (London: B. Fellowes, 1830). See *idem., Exposition of 1851*, and *Passages from the Life of a Philosopher* (London: Longman, Green, Longman, Roberts & Green, 1864). The broader issue of British attitudes towards science, particularly in the modern period, has been covered in W. D. Rubinstein, *Capitalism, Culture and Decline in Britain, 1750–1990* (London: Routledge, 1993), pp. 94–7. But, as Rubinstein himself noted, even if there has been no *a priori*

antipathy to science in British culture, Britain's record of translating scientific inventions into commercial successes has been lacking. The issue is not the few top scientists who have won Nobel prizes, but the broader population who have been in a position to make practical use of various scientific inventions.

147. Quoted in Tallis, I:194–7.

148. J. A. Bennett, *Science at the Great Exhibition* (Cambridge: Whipple Museum of the History of Science, 1983); Sheppard, *London*, pp. 233–4.

149. Quoted in Tallis, II:195.

150. This discussion about the socio-economic transformations that societies need to undergo in order for industrialization to take place, and about an elite that spurs industrial transformation, is developed from W. W. Rostow, *The Process of Economic Growth*, 2nd edn (New York: W. W. Norton, 1962), pp. 275–8, and *The Stages of Economic Growth: A Non-Communist Manifesto* (Cambridge: Cambridge University Press, 1960), pp. 26–8. See also Alexander Gerschenkron, 'Social Attitudes, Entrepreneurship, and Economic Development,' in *Economic Backwardness in Historical Perspective*, pp. 52–71.

151. In France the economy was based to a much greater degree than in Britain on workshop production, it was marked by the survival of the village economy, and there were millions of self-employed artisans up to the late nineteenth century. Nor is it clear that the path followed by the French between 1780 and 1914 was inferior to that taken by the British; it was simply different. The French also took away from the exhibition very different lessons than the British, viewing it 'as a vindication of small-scale manufacturing.' See O'Brien and Keyder, *Economic Growth*, pp. 194–5; Walton, *France at the Crystal Palace*, p. 3.

152. Michael J. Fiore and Charles F. Sabel, *The Second Industrial Divide* (New York: Basic Books, 1984).

153. *The Times*, 13 October 1851. For an analysis of the French response, see Walton, *France at the Crystal Palace*.

154. Kennedy, *Rise and Fall*, pp. 148–58, 228.

155. See, among many, Cain and Hopkins, *British Imperialism*; Lee, *British Economy*; Rubinstein, *Capitalism, Culture and Decline*.

156. Lee, *British Economy*, p. 74.

157. Britain's failure to innovate is amply demonstrated by Dintenfass, *Decline of Industrial Britain*.

158. Cain and Hopkins, *British Imperialism*, pp. 113–14.

CHAPTER 5: INTEGRATION AND SEGREGATION

1. Tallis, I:102.

2. *Ibid.*, I:101; the now familiar phrase 'to see and be seen' is from *The Times*, 24 May 1851.

3. *The Times*, 5 May 1851.

4. *Ibid.*, 23 May 1851.

5. *Ibid.*, 28 May 1851.

6. Tallis, I:27.

7. 'The Dangers of the Exhibition,' *Economist* 8 (26 October 1850): 1180.

8. Houghton, *Victorian Frame of Mind*, p. 56; Young, *Victorian England*, pp. 30–7. See also Briggs, *Making of Modern England*, esp. p. 302; Gash, *Aristocracy and People*, pp. 214–18; Edmund Burke's *Reflections on the French Revolution* (1790), Robert Southey's *Sir Thomas More: or, Colloquies on the Progress and Prospects of Society* (1829) and Thomas Carlyle's *The French Revolution* (1837) both testify to the dread that an uprising of the masses would overthrow the established order and confiscate private property.

9. Thomas Babington Macaulay, 'The People's Charter,' in *The Works of Lord Macaulay Complete*, vol. VIII, ed. Lady Trevelyan (London: Longmans, Green & Co., 1866), p. 221.

10. Himmelfarb, *Idea of Poverty*, pp. 253–69; John Saville, *1848: The British State and the Chartist Movement* (Cambridge: Cambridge University Press, 1987), esp. pp. 207–8; Edward Royle, *Chartism* (London: Longman, 1980), p. 23; David Large, 'London in the Year of Revolutions, 1848,' in John Stevenson ed., *London in the Age of Reform* (Oxford: Basil Blackwell, 1977), pp. 177–211.

11. Saville, *1848*, pp. 24–6, 105; Large, 'London,' pp. 185–7, 192. The estimates of crowd size range from a low of about 10,000 to a high of 250,000. The latter figure is inconceivable, given that Kennington Common could hold no more than about 50,000.

12. John Stevenson, *Popular Disturbances in England, 1700–1870* (London: Longman, 1979), esp. pp. 245–74; Audrey Short, 'Workers under Glass in 1851,' *Victorian Studies* 20 (1966): 193–202.

13. Cole, Diary, 5 and 20 October 1850.

14. Charles Grey to Henry Cole, 7 June 1850, Cole Papers; Martin, *His Royal Highness*, II:46–8, 227–9. See also Robert Stephenson, *The Great Exhibition; its Palace, and its Principal Contents* (London: George Routledge & Co., 1851), pp. 49–50.

15. Samuel Wilberforce, *On the Dignity of Labour* (London: Bradbury & Evans, [1850]); *Daily News*, 23 February 1850.

16. Briggs, *Victorian People*, p. 41.

17. Reginald G. Wilberforce, ed., *Life of the Right Reverend Samuel Wilberforce*, vol. II (London: John Murray, 1881), pp. 30–1; Charles Knight, 'Three May-Days in London,' *Household Words* III (3 May 1851): 123; *The Times*, 22 March 1850; Bartlett, *What I Saw in London*, pp. 196–8.

18. Wilberforce, *Wilberforce*, II:30–1; Cole, *Fifty Years*, I:190. Wilberforce already knew many of those serving on the Royal Commission, including Charles Lyell, who in early February invited him to serve on the Council of the Geological Society for 1850. See Lyell to Wilberforce, 6 February 1850, Wilberforce MSS, c.10.39–40; Henry Vincent to Wilberforce, 18 March 1850, d.17/3/430. According to an undated letter from Granville to Cole, Cole Papers, Robert Peel approved of Wilberforce's appointment to the committee.

19. Royal Commission, Minutes, 9 May 1850; Cole, *Fifty Years*, I:188–93; Cole to Grey, 14 May 1850, Cole Papers.

20. Wilberforce, *Wilberforce*, II:31; Carlyle to Wilberforce, Wilberforce MSS, c.10.50–1.

21. Cole, *Fifty Years*, I:191–2; Cole to Grey, 7 June 1850, Cole Papers; Cole, Diary, 12, 15 June 1850.

22. Cole to Grey, 7 June 1850, RCE/WA III:118.

23. Cole, *Fifty Years*, I:190–3; William Lovett, *The Life and Struggles of William Lovett* (London: Trübner & Co., 1876), pp. 364–5; Graham Storey, Kathleen Tillotson, and Nina Burges, eds, *The Letters of Charles Dickens*, vol. VI (Oxford: Clarendon Press, 1988), p. 57; Grey to Cole, 5 June 1850, Cole Papers.

24. Cole to Grey, 6 June 1850, RCE/WA III:110.

25. *Illustrated London News*, 22 March 1851, p. 239; *A Short Statement of the Nature and Objects of the proposed Great Exhibition of the Works of Industry of All Nations* (London, 1850), p. 6.

26. See, among many, Williams, *Keywords*, pp. 176–9, 334–7; Harold Perkin, *Origins of Modern English Society* (London: Routledge & Kegan Paul, 1969), pp. 231–4; Himmelfarb, *Idea of Poverty*, pp. 288–304.

27. *Chambers'*, 1 March 1851, p. 129.

28. Martin F. Tupper, 'The Great Exhibition of 1851,' in Anon., *Guide to the Great Exhibition*, pp. 27–8.

29. [John Critchley Prince], 'A Voice from the Factory,' *Household Words* 3 (5 April 1851): 36.

30. See especially Gareth Stedman Jones, *Languages of Class* (Cambridge: Cambridge University Press, 1983); Geoffrey Crossick, 'From Gentlemen to the Residuum: Languages of Social Description in Victorian Britain', in Penelope J. Corfield, ed., *Language, History and Class* (Oxford: Basil Blackwell, 1991), pp. 150–78.

31. G. Julian Harney, *The Friend of the People*, no. 22, 10 May 1851, p. 152.

32. *Ibid.*, pp. 189–90.

33. Peter Bailey, ' "Will the Real Bill Banks Please Stand Up?" Towards a Role Analysis of Mid-Victorian Working-Class Respectability,' *Journal of Social History* 12 (1979): 336–53; *idem.*, *Leisure and Class in Victorian England* (London: Routledge & Kegan Paul, 1978), p. 177.

34. Geoffrey Crossick, 'The Labour Aristocracy and its Values: A Study of Mid-Victorian Kentish London,' *Victorian Studies* 19 (1976), 301–28; Simon Cordery, 'Friendly Societies and the Discourse of Respectability in Britain, 1825–1875,' *Journal of British Studies* 34 (1995): 35–58.

35. Cordery, 'Friendly Societies,' p. 41.

36. *Punch* 18 (13 April 1850): 145.

37. *Ibid.* 20 (1 Feb. 1851): 42.

38. Granville to Grey, 9 June 1850, RCE/WA III:117.

39. Cole, *Fifty Years*, I:193.

40. Grey to Cole, 7 June 1850, Cole Papers.

41. Granville to Grey, 9 June 1850, RCE/WA III:117.

42. Lloyd to Granville, 22 June 1850, RCE/WA IV:12.

43. RCE/WA IV:89.

44. Attempts to define the labor aristocracy and discussions of the usefulness of the term may be found in E. J. Hobsbawm, *Labouring Men* (New York: Basic Books, 1964); John Foster, *Class Struggle and the*

Industrial Revolution (New York: St Martin's Press, 1974); Robert Q. Gray, *The Labour Aristocracy in Victorian Edinburgh* (Oxford: Clarendon Press, 1976); Geoffrey Crossick, *The Lower Middle Class in Britain, 1870–1914* (London: Croom Helm, 1977), and *An Artisan Elite in Victorian Society: Kentish London, 1840–1880* (London: Croom Helm, 1978); H. F. Moorehouse, 'The Marxist Theory of the Labour Aristocracy,' *Social History* 3 (1978): 61–82; and J. Field, 'British Historians and the Concept of the Labour Aristocracy,' *Radical History Review* 19 (Winter 1978–9): 61–84. The term 'ragged classes' is from Himmelfarb, *Idea of Poverty*, pp. 371–400.

45. Morris, *Class, Sect and Party*, pp. 241–2, 249–61; Royle, 'Mechanics Institutes and the Working Classes;' *Collection of Printed Documents*, I:70b, II:184. See also Tylecote, *Mechanics' Institutes*, and Hole, *Essay*.

46. *Collection of Printed Documents*, VI:922.

47. Royal Commission, Minutes, 16 May 1850.

48. Babbage, *Exposition of 1851*, pp. 28–9.

49. *The Times*, 4 March, 5 April 1850. The workers at De La Rue's printing company forwarded £5 5s directly to the Royal Commission, and Thomas Cubitt's employees did likewise with the amount of £14 5s 6d.

50. See especially Samuel, 'Workshop;' Robert Gray, *Labour Aristocracy*; Patrick Joyce, *Work, Society, and Politics: The Culture of the Factory in Later Victorian England* (New Brunswick: Rutgers University Press, 1980); W. D. Rubinstein, *The Very Wealthy in Britain since the Industrial Revolution* (New Brunswick: Rutgers University Press, 1981); Morris, *Class, Sect and Party*; and, for an excellent overview, Alastair J. Reid, *Social Classes and Social Relations in Britain, 1850–1914* (Cambridge: Cambridge University Press, 1992).

51. Samuel, 'Workshop;' *Illustrated Exhibitor*, 23 August 1851; *Official Catalogue*, I:52.

52. Patrick Joyce, 'Work,' in *The Cambridge Social History of Britain, 1750–1950*, ed. F. M. L. Thompson (Cambridge: Cambridge University Press, 1990), esp. II:163–7.

53. RCE/WA IV:109.

54. [Askrill], *Yorkshire Visitors' Guide*, p. 25.

55. Altick, *Shows of London*, p. 442; [J. F. Murray], 'The World of London,' *Blackwood's* 51 (1842): 419; Hugh Cunningham, *Leisure in the Industrial Revolution* (London: Croom Helm, 1980), esp. pp. 104–5. Cunningham defines 'rational recreation' as 'ordered, disciplined, improving, educational leisure' that was generally motivated by guilt as well as fear (p. 91); the Great Exhibition certainly qualifies under this definition. More generally, see Bailey, *Leisure and Class*. Although F. M. L. Thompson, 'Social Control in Victorian Britain,' *Economic History Review*, 2nd ser., 34 (1981): 189–208, has largely laid to rest the issue of social control, meaning 'the imposition of opinions and habits by one class upon another,' he and other historians have acknowledged the usefulness and validity of the concept particularly for the decades preceding the Great Exhibition. See also Gareth Stedman Jones, 'Class Expression versus

Social Control? A Critique of Recent Trends in the Social History of "leisure,"' *History Workshop* 4 (1977): 162–70; Reid, *Social Classes*, p. 37.

56. RCE/WA V:82.

57. *The Times*, 20 August 1850; Royal Commission, *First Report*, p. xlv; *Journal of the Exhibition*, 18 January 1851.

58. Fay, *Palace of Industry*, pp. 73–4; A. B. Rae, 'Visitors by Railway to the Great Exhibition of 1851' (MPhil thesis, Open University, 1987), pp. 93, 229–30. Rae has calculated that some four million people over and above the average annual increase in railway traffic during the late 1840s used the railways in 1851, the majority to visit the Great Exhibition. That would comprise 19 per cent of the population of Great Britain in 1851. The 6,039,195 entrances include 773,766 visits by the 25,605 season ticket holders, and there is ample evidence from diaries and biographies that many middle- and working-class visitors who did not have season tickets entered more than once.

59. John R. Isaac Collection of material relating to three inventions by John R. Isaac to be exhibited at the Great Exhibition of 1851; Collection of Material relating to the Liverpool Excursion Club for Enabling the Working Classes to Visit London in 1851, Yale Center for British Art, Folio A/T/8, B/T/7; *Collection of Printed Documents*, VI:934; Morris, 'Leeds and the Crystal Palace,' pp. 290–1; *Leeds Times*, 4 January 1851; *Collection of Printed Documents*, VI:939; *Illustrated London News*, 6 September 1851, p. 275.

60. P. H. J. H. Gosden, *Self-Help: Voluntary Associations in the 19th Century* (London: B. T. Batsford, 1973); Morris, *Class, Sect and Party*, pp. 280–317.

61. In addition to those works cited above, n. 44, see G. Kitson Clark, *The Making of Victorian England* (Cambridge, MA: Harvard University Press, 1962), pp. 118–23.

62. Tod, 'Visit to London.' More generally, see Wolfgang Schivelbusch, *The Railway Journey: The Industrialization of Time and Space in the 19th Century* (Berkeley: University of California Press, 1986).

63. Piers Brendon, *Thomas Cook* (London: Secker & Warburg, 1991), pp. 57–8; E. G. Barnes, *The Rise of the Midland Railway, 1844–1874* (London: George Allen & Unwin, 1966), p. 137; John Pudney, *The Thomas Cook Story* (London: Michael Joseph, 1953), p. 105; *Express*, 22 March 1851.

64. *Cook's Excursionist*, 3 May 1851.

65. Brendon, *Thomas Cook*, pp. 5, 58.

66. Pudney, *Thomas Cook Story*, pp. 105–6; Jack Simmons, *The Victorian Railway* (London: Thames & Hudson, 1991), p. 276; Rae, 'Visitors by Railway,' pp. 47–9. The London & North Western Railway (L&NWR) appointed an agent of its own, Henry Marcus of Liverpool, to oversee and encourage exhibition traffic on its behalf. Although Marcus has largely disappeared from history, and obviously had nowhere near the impact that Cook did, he nonetheless reported to the directors of the L&NWR that he had arranged for 90,000 people to attend the exhibition on 145 trains, which brought in £61,805 in

receipts for the company. See London & Northwest Railway, General Road and Traffic Committee, 11 March 1851, 6 February 1852 in PRO RAIL 410/140. For his efforts Marcus received £300.

67. Reid to Phipps, 17 September 1850, RCE/WA IV:127–8.

68. 'Memorandum on Railway Accommodation,' 17 December 1850, *Collection of Printed Documents*, VI:935–6; *The Times*, 21 November 1850; *Leader*, 16 November 1850. The executive committee also tried to work with the railway directors through the Railway Clearing House. See Joint Committee of the London and Northwest Railway and the Midland Railway, 14 March, 30 April, 8 May 1851, PRO RAIL 406/7; Rae, 'Visitors by Railway,' pp. 78–9; Philip S. Bagwell, *The Railway Clearing House in the British Economy, 1842–1922* (London: George Allen & Unwin, 1968), pp. 44–5, 56–7; Simmons, *Victorian Railway*, p. 275.

69. Joint Committee of the London & Northwest Railway and the Midland Railway, 12 February 1851, PRO RAIL 406/7.

70. See Rae, 'Visitors by Railway,' pp. 32–45.

71. *Herepath's*, 25 January 1851, p. 87; 8 February 1851, pp. 141–2.

72. It was not until 21 June 1851 that *Herepath's* reported that 'The Exhibition appears now to be producing some of its long expected fruits on railways,' though two weeks earlier the *Railway Times*, 7 June 1851, stated that the entire country 'was alive with excursion trains.' For the period from 1–26 May, see the *Railway Times*, 18 October 1851; *The Times*, 9 May 1851; Board Minutes of the Great Western Railway, 15 May 1851, PRO RAIL 250/5.

73. *The Times*, 13 August 1851; Charles H. Grinling, *The History of the Great Northern Railway, 1845–1895* (London: Methuen & Co., 1898), pp. 99–103; T. R. Gourish, *Mark Huish and the London & North Western Railway* (Leicester: Leicester University Press, 1972), pp. 164, 202; Henry Grote Lewin, *The Railway Mania and its Aftermath, 1845–1852* (London: The Railway Gazette, 1936), pp. 428–38. The one exception seems to have been the York, Newcastle, and Berwick Railway Company, which had a monopoly in that part of the country.

74. Rae, 'Visitors by Railway,' pp. 107, 109, 229–30. For the figures, see Royal Commission, *First Report*, pp. 111–12; Mark Huish, 'Railway Accidents,' *Minutes of Proceedings of the Institution of Civil Engineers; with Abstracts of the Discussions*, vol. XI (20 April 1852): 447; *Address of Robert Stephenson, Esq., M.P., on his election as President of the Institution of Civil Engineers, Session 1855–1856* (London: Clowes & Sons, 1856), pp. 24–5.

75. Most of the major London-based railway companies, such as the L&NWR and Great Western, profited from the exhibition, as the enormous number of people who took the railways to the Great Exhibition made up for the very low fares they paid. Several of the smaller provincial railways, however, such as the South Devon, the Eastern Union, and the North Staffordshire, reported a much less rosy picture, and in some cases an actual loss. Overall, *Herepath's* calculated a net gain of £355,512 for the railway companies as a whole from the exhibition. See *Herepath's*, 25 October 1851, pp. 1120–41; *Railway Times*, 18 October 1851, p. 1057; 15 (1852): 70, 73, 210–11, 243, 247.

76. Brendon, *Thomas Cook*, p. 57. See also Simmons, *Victorian Railway*, p. 273; Geoffrey Best, *Mid-Victorian Britain, 1851–75* (London: Fontana, 1971), p. 294.

77. Cunningham, *Leisure*, p. 157; Bailey, *Leisure and Class*, p. 56.

78. Simmons, *Victorian Railway*, p. 277.

79. Sheppard, *London*, p. 135.

80. Royal Commission, Minutes, 12 May 1851.

81. *Ibid.*; Francis D. Lewis to Granville, 4 June 1851, RCE/EC.

82. 'Accommodations for Artisans,' undated, RCE/WA IV:120.

83. Simon Nowell-Smith, *The House of Cassell, 1848–1958* (London: Cassell & Company, 1958), pp. 29–30.

84. 'Great Exhibition … To members of Christian congregations …' (London: [John Cassell, 1851]). According to the *Express*, 12 April 1851, Cassell's listing service also included more lavish lodgings in Russell Square and St Pancras, some with drawing-room and piano privileges, that cost several guineas per week. There were in fact a number of private listing services, a testament to the spirit of voluntarism that surrounded the exhibition. Henry Burnett opened one aimed at foreign visitors, and already by March 1851 claimed to be taking in about 3,000 tourists a week from the continent, a figure which is highly suspect. And Horace Greeley recommended to his readers the name of John Chapman, an American bookseller in the Strand, who kept lists of rooms to let at reasonable prices. *Journal of the Exhibition*, 8 March 1851; Horace Greeley, *Glances at Europe* (New York: Dewitt & Davenport, 1851), p. 46.

85. Nowell-Smith, *Cassell*, pp. 31–2.

86. Cobden to Cassell, 21 October 1850, Cobden Papers, BL Add. MSS 43668 f. 118.

87. *Guide to the Great Exhibition*, p. 63.

88. Tallis, I:27–8.

89. *The Times*, 8 July 1851, issued a reminder 'for the industrial classes' still pouring into London about the Renalgh Club, which the paper said had been formed under the auspices of the Royal Commission, that could accommodate 1,000 people per night, and was conveniently located on the north side of the Thames only one mile from the exhibition.

90. Harrison to Albert, 10 October 1851, RCE/EC; Royal Commission, *First Report*, Appendix XXIV, p. 116. On his behalf, Harrison said that he had provided good accommodation for 13,000 people without 'drunkenness, riot, or even the loss of sixpence by theft.'

91. Harrison to Albert, 10 October 1851; Harrison to Granville, 11 October 1851; Reid to Grey, 16 October 1851, RCE/EC.

92. Enid Porter, ed., *Victorian Cambridge: Josiah*

Chater's Diaries, 1844–1884 (London: Phillimore & Co., 1975), p. 77.

93. *Journal of the Exhibition*, 1 February 1851.

94. *Illustrated London News*, 25 October 1851, p. 534.

95. Mayhew and Cruikshank, *1851*.

96. Royal Commission, *First Report*, Appendix XXIV, p. 116.

97. *Journal of the Exhibition*, 23 November 1850.

98. Tallis, I:28.

99. Fuller to Granville, 22 January 1851, RCE/EC; Granville to Grey, 17 January 1851, RCE/WA V:102; Bazley to Granville, 22 January 1851, RCE/EC.

100. *The Times*, 23 January 1851; Paxton to Sarah Paxton, 21 January 1851, Paxton Correspondence 655.

101. Granville to Grey, 24 January 1851, RCE/WA V:110; Paxton to Grey, 25 January 1851, RCE/WA V:111; *The Times*, 23 January 1851.

102. *Guide to the Great Exhibition*, p. 43.

103. *The Times*, 25 January 1851.

104. Cole, Diary, 8 May 1851; Royal Commission, Minutes, 10 May 1851.

105. *The Times*, 28 July 1851.

106. *Ibid.*, 31 July 1851.

107. T. Bauhart to Royal Commission, 25 February 1851, RCE/EC. See also John Brookes to the Royal Commission, undated (late February 1851), and J. H. Mauro to Granville, 28 January 1851, RCE/EC.

108. Thomas to Albert, 28 January 1851, RCE/EC. For a discussion of anti-Popery and the agitation over Catholicism in Britain at the time of the Great Exhibition, see Chapter 6.

109. RCE/EC; Royal Commission, Minutes, 5 March 1851.

110. *The Times*, 13 February 1851.

111. *Daily News*, 29 August 1850.

112. In light of this, assertions by historians such as Hugh Cunningham that 'Class and not the divisions within classes continued to be of prime importance for an understanding of leisure' (*Leisure*, p. 100) need to be re-evaluated. See also Best, *Mid-Victorian Britain*, pp. 220–1.

113. Norman McCord, 'Some Difficulties of Parliamentary Reform,' *Historical Journal* 10 (1967): 376–90.

114. William A. Drew, *Glimpses and Gatherings* (Augusta, ME: Homan & Manley, 1852), p. 195.

115. PRO HO 45/4299; Granville to Grey, 19 November 1850, RCE/WA V:54.

116. Reid to Grey, 20 December 1850, RCE/WA V:79.

117. Metropolitan Police Office to executive committee, 19 May 1851, RCE/EC.

118. PRO HO 45/4299; Royal Commission, *First Report*, p. xlv; Bowring to Grey, 27 May 1851, RCE/WA VII:77.

119. 'Eighteen Hundred and Fifty-One,' *Fraser's Magazine* 45 (January 1852): 22–3.

120. *The Times*, 27 May 1851.

121. *The Life and Letters of Lord Macaulay*, ed. George Otto Trevelyan, vol. II (New York: Harper & Brothers, 1876), p. 249.

122. 'The Multitude at the Exhibition,' *Economist* 9 (31 May 1851): 586.

123. *Ibid.*

124. Royal Commission, *First Report*, p. iii.

125. Playfair estimated that there would be some two million paid entrances in a letter to Granville, 11 July 1850, RCE/WA IV:60. *The Times*, 20 October 1851, suggested rather vaguely that there might have been 'more than three million visitors;' Fay, *Palace of Industry*, p. 73, estimated four million. See above, n. 58.

126. *Census of Great Britain, 1851*, Population Tables, vol. I: 'Numbers of the Inhabitants,' p. xxiv.

127. Royal Commission, *First Report*, pp. 88–9; Tallis, I:254–5.

128. *The Times*, 13 October 1851.

129. *Daily News*, 24 June 1865, in R. H. Love, 'A Memorial of the Great Exhibition,' BL Add. MSS 35255 f. 34–9.

130. *The Times*, 7 October 1851; Cole, *Fifty Years*, I:198–9.

131. Tallis, II:95; *Economist* 9 (27 September 1851): 1070; *The Times*, 23 September 1851; *Illustrated London News*, 25 October 1851, p. 522. See also [Caroline Gascoyne], *Recollections and Tales of the Crystal Palace* (London: W. Shoberl, 1852), p. 36, for a description of the many different kinds of people who could be found in the Crystal Palace.

132. *Journal of the Exhibition*, 10 May 1851; *The Times*, 8 October 1851.

133. *Leeds Times*, 12 July 1851.

134. *Jimmy Trebilcock; or, the Humorous Adventures of a Cornish Miner at the Great Exhibition, what he saw and what he didn't see* (Cambridge, n.p., 1862); Tod, 'Visit to London;' Porter, ed., *Victorian Cambridge*; Valerie Chancellor, ed., *Master and Artisan in Victorian England: The Diary of William Andrews and the Autobiography of Joseph Gutteridge* (London: Evelyn, Adams & Mackay, 1969), p. 142; Henry Watson, 'Journal of a Journey to London,' Strathclyde Regional Archives, Mitchell Library, Glasgow, TD120/1; Rae, 'Visitors by Railway,' p. 178.

135. *Illustrated London News*, 19 July 1851, p. 101.

136. *The Times*, 9 September 1851; *Herepath's*, 13 September 1851, p. 987.

137. *Punch* 21 (1 November 1851): 176.

138. *The Times*, 26 August 1851.

139. Julie Salis-Schwabe, *Reminiscences of Richard Cobden* (London: T. Fisher Unwin, 1895), p. 160.

140. *The Times*, 20 September 1851.

141. Most historians have overlooked or simply not discussed the possibility that the workers attending the exhibition were of a very respectable sort. See, for example, Best, *Mid-Victorian Britain*, pp. 252–3. One historian who has noted the respectable nature of the working classes is F. M. L. Thompson, *The Rise of Respectable Society* (Cambridge, MA: Harvard University Press, 1988), p. 261.

142. For example, the directors of the Imperial Insurance Company gave each clerk a two-day holiday to visit the exhibition, plus two shillings for the admission; likewise at the Church of England Life and Fire Assurance Trust and Annuity Institution, where clerks received a four-day leave of absence and nine guineas. See the Minute Book, vol. 16 (14 May 1851),

Court of Directors, Imperial Insurance Co., and Minute Book, vol. 2 (9 May 1851), Board of Directors, Church of England Life and Fire Assurance Trust and Annuity Institution, Guildhall Library 12,160A and 12,160D. According to the *Leader*, 12 July 1851, the directors of the Great Northern gave all their staff a five-day leave to visit the exhibition, each with a free pass to travel on the company's railway lines, and with permission for married men to take their wives and for unmarried men to take a friend.

143. *Illustrated London News*, 7 June 1851, p. 513.

144. *Journal of the Exhibition*, 24 May 1851.

145. *The Times*, 4 June 1851.

146. *Journal of the Exhibition*, 10 May 1851.

147. *The Times* and *Morning Chronicle*, 11 September 1851.

148. *Journal of the Exhibition*, 17 and 31 May 1851.

149. *The Times*, 7 December 1850; *Illustrated London News*, 11 January 1851.

150. Tallis, II:95.

151. *The Times*, 26–29 May 1851.

152. Society for Promoting Christian Knowledge, *The Industry of Nations, as exemplified in the Great Exhibition of 1851* (London: n.p., 1852), p. 241. The Society reported that on 26 May, 'The visitors appeared chiefly to belong to the middle class of society, and few fustian jackets were observed among them.' *The Times*, 27 May 1851, reported as well that 'the visitors appeared chiefly to belong to the middle class of society.'

153. Edward Frederick Leveson Gower, *Bygone Years* (London: John Murray, 1905), pp. 42–3.

154. Drew, *Glimpses and Gatherings*, pp. 336–8, 373.

155. *Economist* 9 (17 May and 31 May 1851): 531, 587.

156. See Joyce, 'Work,' pp. 163–7; *Illustrated London News*, 28 June 1851, p. 608; 19 July 1851, pp. 100–2; 17 May 1851, p. 438.

157. Society for Promoting Christian Knowledge, *Industry of Nations*, pp. 245–6.

158. *The Times*, 12 June 1851.

159. Silliman, *Visit to Europe*, II:422.

160. Royal Commission, *First Report*, pp. 122–5, suggested that crime statistics were lower in 1851 than in previous years, taking into account the average yearly increase; *The Times*, 29 May 1851.

161. Gideon Mantell, *The Journal of Gideon Mantell*, ed. E. Cecil Curwen (London: Oxford University Press, 1940), p. 273.

162. *Ibid.*

163. *Punch* 21 (5 July 1851): 16.

164. Tallis, III:51–5.

165. *Ibid.*, I:101.

166. *The Times*, 29 May 1851.

167. *Punch* 20 (7 June 1851): 240.

168. Tallis, I:56, 101.

169. *Remembrances of The Great Exhibition* (London: Ackerman & Co., [1852]); *Recollections of the Great Exhibition of 1851* (London: Lloyd Brothers & Co.; Simkin, Marshall & Co., 1851). There was even a 'Ladies' Department', which consisted of lace, needlepoint and knitting. This was virtually the only department or class with any number of women exhibitors. See Tallis, III:39–44.

170. Palmerston (Broadland) Papers, Southampton University Library, D/12.

171. Lyn H. Lofland, *The World of Strangers* (New York: Basic Books, 1973), pp. ix–x, 2–55, 66–82.

172. *The Times*, 8 October 1851.

173. See Ross McKibbin, *The Ideologies of Class: Social Relations in Britain, 1880–1950* (Oxford: Oxford University Press, 1990).

174. Margot C. Finn, *After Chartism: Class and Nation in English Radical Politics, 1848–1874* (Cambridge: Cambridge University Press, 1993), p. 1.

175. *Life and Letters of Lord Macaulay*, II:248.

CHAPTER 6: NATIONALISM AND INTERNATIONALISM

1. RCE/WA I:7.

2. Charles Babbage characterized the exhibition in almost identical terms in his *Exposition of 1851*, pp. 41–3.

3. Henry Sutherland Edwards, *An Authentic Account of the Chinese Commission, which was sent to report on the Great Exhibition; wherein the opinion of China is shown as not corresponding at all with our own* (London: H. Vizitelly, n.d.), p. 29.

4. [Moriarty], 'Official Catalogue,' p. 593. See also [Adams], 'Industrial Exhibition,' pp. 386–7.

5. The *Illustrated London News* (29 March 1851, pp. 251–2) provided sketches of the American warship *St Lawrence* unloading its goods and the British steamer *Singapore* taking on troops, both at the Southampton Docks, which were 'striking pictures of the missions of peace and war: one charged with contributions of the competitive industry of the whole world; the other bearing armed authority to repress political rebellion. The contrast is not without its moral.'

6. *The Royal Exchange and the Palace of Industry* (London: William Jones, 1851), pp. 162–3.

7. *The Times*, 22 March 1850.

8. *Short Statement*, p. 7.

9. Tallis, I:103; *The Royal Exchange and the Palace of Industry*, pp. 162–3.

10. *The World's Fair; or, Children's Prize Gift Book* (London: Thomas Dean & Son, [1851]), p. 3.

11. *Guide to the Great Exhibition*, p. 13.

12. *Ibid.*, p. 1.

13. *Ibid.*, pp. 11–12. His sentiments were echoed by John Tallis, who wrote that the Exhibition 'was the blessed offspring of forty years' peace' between Britain and the other European nations (III:110).

14. Ward, *World in its Workshops*, pp. 5–7.

15. *Economist* 9 (26 July 1851): 813.

16. Sidney Pollard, *The Integration of the European Economy since 1815* (London: George Allen & Unwin, 1981), pp. 25–9; *Official Catalogue*, III: 1046.

17. William D. Grampp, *The Manchester School of Economics* (Stanford: Stanford University Press, 1960), pp. 5–15.

18. Jeremy Bentham, 'A Plan for an Universal and Perpetual Peace,' from *Principles of International Law*, in *The Works of Jeremy Bentham*, vol. II, ed. John Bowring (Edinburgh: William Tait, 1843), p. 559.

19. The other 'apostle of peace' at the time of the exhibition was John Bright (1811–89). A Lancashire cotton-mill owner and Liberal MP from 1843 who pushed hard for franchise reform, Bright was also Cobden's lieutenant in the Anti-Corn Law League. Although he shared many of the same views as Cobden, because of his fervent support of the working class and franchise reform he was largely marginalized from the exhibition. See Peter Brock, *Pacifism in Europe to 1914* (Princeton: Princeton University Press, 1972), pp. 350–2; Keith Robbins, *John Bright* (London: Routledge & Kegan Paul, 1979), esp. pp. 70–1; Grampp, *Manchester School of Economics*, pp. 2–3, 62–4.

20. *Guide to the Great Exhibition*, pp. 12–13.

21. The many expressions of international peace at the time of the exhibition, and especially those voiced by Richard Cobden, need to be regarded in the context of the series of peace conferences held in Europe between 1848 and 1853, and, more broadly, in the context of the nineteenth-century peace movement as a whole. See David Nicholls, 'Richard Cobden and the International Peace Congress Movement, 1848–1853,' *Journal of British Studies* 30 (1991): 351–76; Alexander Tyrell, 'Making the Millennium: The Mid-Nineteenth Century Peace Movement,' *Historical Journal* 20 (1978): 75–95; Brock, *Pacifism in Europe to 1914*; W. H. van der Linden, *The International Peace Movement, 1815–1874* (Amsterdam: Tilleul Publications, 1987); A. C. F. Beales, *The History of Peace* (New York: The Dial Press, 1931); F. S. L. Lyons, *Internationalism in Europe, 1815–1914* (Leyden: A. W. Sythoff, 1963); Gavin B. Henderson, 'The Pacifists of the Fifties,' *Journal of Modern History* 9 (1937): 314–41.

22. On the bipolar nature of the conflict between Cobden and Palmerston, see Kenneth Bourne, *The Foreign Policy of Victorian England, 1830–1902* (Oxford: Clarendon Press, 1970), p. 83.

23. Briggs, *Making of Modern England*, p. 350.

24. *Hansard*, 3rd ser., XCVII:122.

25. See Dolphus Whitten, 'The Don Pacifico Affair,' *Historian* 48 (1986): 255–67. Pacifico was eventually compensated by the Greek government to the amount of £5,000.

26. *Hansard*, 3rd ser., CXII:444.

27. Martin, *His Royal Highness*, II:285.

28. Cobden's reply to Palmerston was a vintage plea for non-interventionist foreign policy: 'I believe the progress of freedom depends more upon the maintenance of peace, the spread of commerce, and the diffusion of education, than upon the labours of Cabinets and Foreign Offices. . . . If I have one conviction stronger than another, it is in favour of the

principle of non-intervention in the domestic concerns of other nations.' MPs on both sides of the House jeered him nonetheless. See *Hansard*, 3rd ser., CXII:673–4.

29. Grampp, *Manchester School of Economics*, p. 24; Wendy Hinde, *Richard Cobden: A Victorian Outsider* (New Haven: Yale University Press, 1987), p. 213; B. Kingsley Martin, *The Triumph of Lord Palmerston: A Study of Public Opinion in England before the Crimean War* (London: George Allen & Unwin, 1924), p. 64; Bourne, *Foreign Policy*, p. 83.

30. Bourne, *Foreign Policy*, pp. 45, 82; Parry, *Rise and Fall*, esp. pp. 167–94; Nicholas Edsall, *Richard Cobden: Independent Radical* (Cambridge, MA: Harvard University Press, 1986), p. 244.

31. It is useful to view the debate between Cobdenite internationalism and Palmerstonian interventionism as one of the early skirmishes of a war between two groups within Britain that fought with each other throughout the second half of the nineteenth century and well into the twentieth. Paul Kennedy, 'Idealists and Realists: British Views of Germany, 1864–1939,' *Transactions of the Royal Historical Society* 25 (1975): 137–56, has labeled these two camps the Idealists and the Realists. The former, ethical, preached a gospel of international morality and goodwill. The latter, practical, argued for the morality of the state and the need to defend national interests. The former disliked war; the latter defended and even glorified it. The former urged arbitration and conciliation; the latter scorned this approach as an affront to national honor. The former emphasized freedom of the individual; the latter stressed a sense a duty to the state. In nineteenth-century terms, this was the debate between free trade and protectionism, between anti-imperialism and imperialism. This battle, as the Great Exhibition illustrates, also cut across traditional Liberal/Conservative party lines.

32. *Hansard*, 3rd ser., LX:619.

33. Bourne, *Foreign Policy*, pp. 84–6.

34. Quoted in Martin, *Triumph of Lord Palmerston*, p. 48.

35. The literature in the area is expanding rapidly, but see especially Ernest Gellner, *Nations and Nationalism* (Ithaca: Cornell University Press, 1983), pp. 1–7; Anderson, *Imagined Communities*, pp. 6, 15; Greenfeld, *Nationalism*; Peter Alter, *Nationalism*, 2nd edn (London: Edward Arnold, 1994); Anthony D. Smith, *National Identity* (Reno: University of Nevada Press, 1991); E. J. Hobsbawm, *Nations and Nationalism since 1780*, 2nd edn (Cambridge: Cambridge University Press, 1992); Eric Hobsbawm and Terence Ranger, eds, *The Invention of Tradition* (Cambridge: Cambridge University Press, 1983), esp. pp. 1–14, 101–64.

36. See Greenhalgh, *Ephemeral Vistas*; Robert W. Rydell, *All the World's a Fair: Visions of Empire at American International Expositions, 1876–1916* (Chicago: University of Chicago Press, 1984); John M. MacKenzie, *Propaganda and Empire* (Manchester: Manchester University Press, 1984); Ozouf, *Festivals and the French Revolution*; Walton, *France at the*

Crystal Palace; Benedict *et al.*, *Anthropology of World's Fairs.*

37. *The Exhibition Lay* (London: Groombridge & Sons, 1852), p. 30.

38. This vitally important and fascinating issue will have to remain unexplored here, but see Hechter, *Internal Colonialism*; Clark, 'English History's Forgotten Context;' Pocock, 'British History: A Plea for a New Subject,' and 'The Limits and Divisions of British History;' Colley, 'Britishness and Otherness.'

39. Ward, *World in its Workshops*, p. 12; 'Philoponos,' *Great Exhibition*, pp. 13–14.

40. F. W. N. Bayley, *The Little Folks' Laughing Library. The Exhibition* (London: Darton & Co., 1851), pp. 13–14.

41. William Johnston, *England as It Is, Political, Social and Industrial, in the Middle of the Nineteenth Century* (London: John Murray, 1851), p. 213.

42. Joseph Turner, *Echoes of the Great Exhibition* (London: William Pickering, 1851), p. 2. Freedom was, according to E. P. Thompson, the leading ingredient in 'the common Englishman's "birthright".... Freedom from absolutism (the constitutional monarchy, freedom from arbitrary arrest, trial by jury, equality before the law, the freedom of the home from arbitrary entrance and search, some limited liberty of thought, of speech, and of conscience, the vicarious participation in liberty (or in its semblance) afforded by the right of parliamentary opposition and by elections and election tumults ... as well as freedom to travel, trade, and sell one's own labor.' See *The Making of the English Working Class* (New York: Random House, 1963), p. 79.

43. [Gascoyne], *Recollections and Tales*, pp. 7–8.

44. Peter Sahlins, *Boundaries: The Making of Spain and France in the Pyrenees* (Berkeley: University of California Press, 1989), p. 271.

45. *World's Fair*, pp. 71, 76. See also B. B. Baker, a nautical assessor at the Board of Trade, who wrote of 'autocratic Russia,' and 'France the land of elegance and witty elocution, whose skilful hands make all things well, except a constitution,' in *Verses on the Exhibition of 1851* (Ventnor: James Briddon, [1871]), pp. 4–5.

46. *Britannia*, 2 November 1850.

47. Drew, *Glimpses and Gatherings*, pp. 357–8; *Harthill's Guide through London and to the Industrial Exhibition* (London: Effingham Wilson, [1851]), p. 9.

48. John Johnson Collection.

49. Sigmund Freud, *Civilization and its Discontents*, trans. and ed. James Strachey (New York: W. W. Norton and Co., 1961), p. 61.

50. *Punch* 20 (24 May 1851): 209.

51. *Punch* 20 (7 June 1851): 236.

52. *Chaff; or, The Yankee and Nigger at the Exhibition* (London: Edward Stanford, 1853), p. 16.

53. Drew, *Glimpses and Gatherings*, p. 358. He noted, however, that among the British exhibits there were many that were 'useless and costly, adapted only to the means of the aristocratic few.'

54. *Collection of Printed Documents*, II:283.

55. *The Times*, 1 May 1851; Tallis, I:67ff.

56. Stephenson, *Great Exhibition*, pp. 9–10.

57. Mayhew and Cruikshank, *1851*, p. 137.

58. *The Times*, 2 October 1851.

59. Gilbert A. Cahill, 'British Nationalism and Nativism, 1829–1848: "No Popery" and British Popular Culture,' *Journal of Popular Culture* 3 (1969) 480–91; Frank H. Wallis, *Popular Anti-Catholicism in Mid-Victorian Britain* (Lewiston, NY: Edwin Mellen Press, 1993); G. F. A. Best, 'Popular Protestantism in Victorian Britain', in Robert Robson, ed., *Ideas and Institutions of Victorian Britain* (London: G. Bell & Sons, 1967), pp. 115–42; D. G. Paz, 'Popular Anti-Catholicism in England, 1850–1851,' *Albion* 11 (1979): 331–59; Walter L. Arnstein, *Protestant versus Catholic in Mid-Victorian England: Mr Newdegate and the Nuns* (Columbia, MO: University of Missouri Press, 1982); Robert J. Klaus, *The Pope, the Protestants, and the Irish: Papal Aggression and Anti-Catholicism in Mid-Nineteenth Century England* (New York: Garland Publishing, 1987); John Wolffe, *The Protestant Crusade in Great Britain, 1829–1860* (Oxford: Clarendon Press, 1991). On the eighteenth century, see Colley, *Britons*. This entire section questions J. C. D. Clark's view that Catholic emancipation in 1829 destroyed the Protestant character of Britain. Although 1829 may represent a turning point, even the death-knell for the 'theoretic hegemony of the ancien regime' (*English Society, 1688–1832* [Cambridge: Cambridge University Press, 1985], p. 429) the war was by no means over, and the battles over Britain's religious identity raged on throughout the early Victorian years.

60. Religions Tract Society, *The Palace of Glass and the Gathering of the People* (London: W. Jones, 1851), pp. 53, 55–60. See also J. A. Emerton, *A Moral and Religious Guide to the Great Exhibition* (London: Longman, Brown, Green and Longmans, 1851), p. 27.

61. Thomas Aveling, *Great Sights; A Discourse delivered in Kingsland Chapel on the Sabbath Evening Preceding the Opening of the Great Exhibition* (London: Snow, [1851]), pp. 13–15.

62. *Protestant Magazine*, March 1851, quoted in Klaus, *Pope, Protestants, and Irish*, p. 283.

63. Granville to Ashley, RCE/WA VI:36.

64. Granville to Grey, 20 and 28 March 1851, RCE/WA VI:35, 43; Alexander Wedgwood, 'The Medieval Court,' in Paul Atterbury and Clive Wainwright, eds, *Pugin: A Gothic Passion* (New Haven: Yale University Press, 1994), p. 239. See also the letter to *The Times* by 'A Protestant Clergyman,' 15 May 1851. As Cole put it in a letter to Pugin, displaying the cross in such a prominent location went 'beyond the scope of the exhibition.' Cole to Pugin, 18 March 1851, Cole Papers.

65. Pevsner, *High Victorian Design*, p. 50; John Summerson, 'Architecture,' in *The Cambridge Cultural History of Britain*, vol. vii, ed. Boris Ford (Cambridge: Cambridge University Press, 1992), p. 45.

66. Wallis, *Popular Anti-Catholicism*, pp. 54–6, 68–9;

Paz, 'Popular Anti-Catholicism,' p. 332; Klaus, *Pope, Protestants, and Irish*, pp. 10, 173.

67. Wallis, *Popular Anti-Catholicism*, pp. 53–4; Best, 'Popular Protestantism,' pp. 197–9.

68. Klaus, *Pope, Protestants, and Irish*, pp. 8–9; Arnstein, *Protestant versus Catholic*, pp. 40–2.

69. Robert Blake, *Disraeli* (New York: St Martin's Press, 1966), pp. 171–2; Peter Fuller, 'Fine Art,' in Ford, ed., *Cambridge Cultural History*, pp. 182–4; Leslie Parris, ed., *The Pre-Raphaelites* (London: Tate Gallery, 1984). Rossetti exhibited *Ecce Ancilla Domini*, which showed a terrified Virgin Mary cowering in bed, and Millais sent *Christ in the Carpenter Shop*, a painting which may in fact have been inspired by a Tractarian sermon.

70. See Mark Girouard, *The Return to Camelot: Chivalry and the English Gentleman* (New Haven: Yale University Press, 1981).

71. Timothy Hilton, *The Pre-Raphaelites* (New York: Harry N. Abrams, 1970), pp. 66–7.

72. Girouard, *Return to Camelot*, pp. 115–16.

73. Klaus, *Pope, Protestants, and Irish*, p. 173; Arnstein wrote that 'Rome seemed to lie immediately across the Irish sea' (*Protestant versus Catholic*, p. 6).

74. Wallis, *Popular Anti-Catholicism*, pp. 211–13; Klaus, *Pope, Protestants, and Irish*, p. 10. More broadly, see Gordon Allport, *The Nature of Prejudice* (Cambridge, MA: Addison-Wesley, 1954).

75. On the links between liberalism and anti-Catholicism, see Eugenio F. Biagini, *Liberty, Retrenchment and Reform: Popular Liberalism in the Age of Gladstone, 1860–1880* (Cambridge: Cambridge University Press, 1992), pp. 14, 16.

76. Wallis, *Popular Anti-Catholicism*, pp. 21–2; Arnstein, *Protestant versus Catholic*, p. 212; Best, 'Popular Protestantism,' pp. 118–22; Wolffe, *Protestant Crusade*, p. 121; Tallis, I:131. See also John Pemble, *The Mediterranean Passion: Victorians and Edwardians in the South* (Oxford: Oxford University Press, 1988), pp. 228–40.

77. Klaus, *Pope, Protestants, and Irish*, p. 171; Arnstein, *Protestant versus Catholic*, p. 214; Colley, *Britons*, pp. 11–54.

78. Tod, 'Visit to London,' pp. 41–2, 86–7. Henry Mayhew, always sensitive to the pulse of John Bull, wrote in *1851* of 'Chinamen, with their peculiar slanting eyes, and old-woman-look and dress' (p. 132).

79. Tzvetan Todorov, *The Conquest of America: The Question of the Other*, trans. Richard Howard (New York: Harper & Row, 1984), pp. 42, 185.

80. Terry Castle, *Masquerade and Civilization: The Carnivalesque in Eighteenth-Century English Culture and Fiction* (London: Methuen, 1986), pp. 4–5, 116.

81. *Ibid.*, p. 86. See also Sigmund Freud, 'Negation' (1925), in *General Psychological Theory: Papers on Metapsychology*, ed. Philip Rieff (New York: Collier Books, 1963), pp. 213–17.

82. Queen Victoria's *Journal*, 1 May 1851, quoted in Gibbs-Smith, *Great Exhibition*; *The Times*, 2 May 1851; Ffrench, *Great Exhibition*, pp. 191, 196–7; John

W. Dodds, *The Age of Paradox* (London: Victor Gollancz, 1953), pp. 461–2; *The Letters and Private Papers of William Makepeace Thackeray*, ed. Gordon N. Ray (Cambridge, MA: Harvard University Press, 1945–6), II:767–9.

83. Edward Said, *Orientalism* (New York: Random House, 1978), pp. 1–3.

84. Hobsbawm, *Nations and Nationalism*, p. 91.

85. There is now a significant body of historiography acknowledging, and even arguing, that national identities obscured and at times even replaced class allegiances during the mid-Victorian period. See Foster, *Class Struggle*, pp. 239–43; Gareth Stedman Jones, 'Class Struggle and the Industrial Revolution,' in *Languages of Class*, pp. 72–4; Patrick Joyce, *Visions of the People* (Cambridge: Cambridge University Press, 1991), p. 11.

86. 'I was struck by the number of foreigners in the streets,' Macaulay wrote in his diary on opening day. See *Life and Letters of Lord Macaulay*, p. 550.

87. Ward, *Memories of Ninety Years*, pp. 63–4.

88. Silliman, *Visit to Europe*, II:421–2.

89. Society for the Promotion of Christian Knowledge, *Industry of Nations*, pp. 245–6.

90. See Colin Holmes, *John Bull's Island: Immigration and British Society, 1871–1971* (London: Macmillan, 1988); Bernard Porter, *The Refugee Question in Mid-Victorian Politics* (Cambridge: Cambridge University Press, 1979); James Walvin, *Passage to Britain: Immigration in British History and Politics* (Harmondsworth: Penguin, 1984).

91. PRO HO 45/3623/5.

92. *John Bull*, 7 December 1850.

93. *Express*, 12 April 1851.

94. John Patterson to Wellington, 8 February 1851, Wellington Papers 2/168/37–8.

95. Hugh McCorquodale to Wellington, 5 April 1851, Wellington Papers 2/168/89. But if McCorquodale saw the exhibition as a potential tower of Babel, the Rev. J. C. Whish saw it as just the opposite, as 'compensation for the Tower of Babel . . . the means of promoting the brotherly union, the peace and the prosperity of mankind' (*Great Exhibition Prize Essay*, p. 8).

96. Russell to Wellington and Wellington to Russell, 2 April 1851; Wellington to Russell, 9 April 1851, Wellington Papers 2/168/82–4, 100.

97. Francis W. H. Cavendish, *Society, Politics and Diplomacy, 1820–1864* (London: T. Fisher Unwin, 1913), p. 199.

98. *John Bull* and *Morning Post*, 29 March 1851.

99. *The Times*, 10 April 1851.

100. *Household Words* 3 (26 April 1851): 99ff. See also George Augustus Sala, 'The Foreign Invasion,' *Household Words* 4 (11 October 1851): 60.

101. *Punch* 20 (1851): 104.

102. Temple to Palmerston, 3 April 1851, RCE/WA VI:50. See also Lord Bloomfield to Palmerston, 2 April 1851; Arthur Magenis to Palmerston, 5 April 1851; Lord Normanby to Palmerston, 10 and 14 April 1851, RCE/WA VI:49 51, 59, 62.

103. Frederick William of Prussia to Albert, 8 April 1851,

RCE/WA VI:56; Albert to Frederick William, 14 April 1851, in *Letters of the Prince Consort: 1831–1861*, ed., Kurt Jagow, trans E. T. S. Dugdale (London: John Murray, 1938) pp. 175–6. Many of the other princes and statesmen of Europe were cautious about the exhibition and the disasters that might accompany it. King Leopold of Belgium, another of Victoria's uncles, declined to attend the opening because of the risk involved. In fact, only Frederick Wilhelm and his family took the risk, and even then only after having received Albert's personal guarantee that they would be protected. Leopold eventually traveled to London later in the summer, after the exhibition had proved safe, but he was the only other head of state to do so. See also Anthony Bird, *Paxton's Palace* (London: Cassell, 1976), pp. 27, 102. Napoleon Bonaparte, Napoleon's nephew, visited the exhibition just before it closed, but his cousin, Louis Napoleon, already President of France and soon to be Emperor, did not (*Morning Chronicle*, 10 October 1851).

104. Dr [George Frederick] Collier, *The Philosopher's Mite to the Great Exhibition of 1851* (London: Houlston & Stoneman, n.d.); J. C. H. Freund, *A Small Contribution to the Great Exhibition of 1851* (London: Groombridge & Sons, 1851). *Punch* 19 (21 December 1850): 239 prescribed that every Frenchman 'be washed from head to foot before entering London.'

105. Mary Douglas, *Purity and Danger: An Analysis of Concepts of Purity and Taboo* (New York: Praeger, 1966); Elaine Showalter, *Sexual Anarchy: Gender and Culture at the Fin de Siècle* (New York: Viking Penguin, 1990), esp. pp. 188–208.

106. [B. Clayton], *Frolick & Fun or What was Seen and Done in London in 1851* (London: Dean & Son, [1852]).

107. Marjorie Garber, *Vested Interests: Cross-Dressing & Cultural Anxiety* (New York: Routledge, Chapman & Hall, 1992).

108. George Grey to Phipps, 12 May 1851, RCE/WA VII:52.

109. *Punch* 20 (17 May 1851): 207; *The Times*, 21 May 1851.

110. *Census of Great Britain*, 1851, Population Tables, vol. I: 'Numbers of the Inhabitants,' p. xxv.

111. Royal Commission, *First Report*, pp. 112–14. *Herepath's*, 12 July 1851, also reported that the number of foreigners in London was much lower than had been expected.

112. PRO HO 45/4299. Included were 2,009 Prussians, 1,163 French, 720 Belgians, 596 Austrians, 593 Italians, 267 Swiss, 211 Germans, 161 Americans, and 821 others, for a total of 6,541.

113. *Census of Great Britain*, 1851, vol. II, pp. ciii, cclxxxviii.

114. Kwee Choo Ng, *The Chinese in London* (Oxford: Oxford University Press, 1968), p. 5.

115. The popularity of black-face minstrels also suggests how rare and exotic dark-skinned foreigners were. See George F. Rehin, 'Blackface Street Minstrels in Victorian London and its Resorts: Popular Culture and its Racial Connotations as Revealed in Polite Opinion,' *Journal of Popular Culture* 15 (1981): 19–38; Henry Mayhew, *London Labour and the London Poor* (New York: Dover, 1968), III:191; James Walvin, *Black and White: The Negro and English Society 1555–1945* (London, 1973), pp. 197–203.

116. Campbell, *Autobiography and Memoirs*, I:320.

117. 'Perfidious Patmos,' *Household Words* 7 (12 March 1853): 27.

118. Neil Harris, *Humbug: The Art of P. T. Barnum* (Chicago: University of Chicago Press, 1973), esp. pp. 43, 49–50, 93–8.

119. Leslie Fiedler, *Freaks: Myths and Images of the Secret Self* (New York: Simon & Schuster, 1978), p. 24.

120. See, for an earlier period, but for an excellent discussion of the notion of 'shifting frontiers' (p. 22), Bernard Bailyn and Philip D. Morgan, *Strangers within the Realm: Cultural Margins of the First British Empire* (Chapel Hill: University of North Carolina Press, 1991).

121. Cobden to Sturge, 9 October 1851, quoted in Hinde, *Richard Cobden*, p. 220.

122. *Lectures on the Results of the Great Exhibition of 1851, Delivered before the Society of Arts, Manufactures, and Commerce* (London: David Bogue, 1852–3), II:428–45; Cole, *Fifty Years*, I:242–55; Cole to Granville, 12 January 1852, Granville Papers.

123. Cole to Granville, 12 January 1852, Granville Papers, PRO 30/29/23/2/5–12. Later in the century, Gladstone, who had also been on the Royal Commission, wrote that 'It was a great work of peace on earth: not of that merely diplomatic peace which is honey-combed with suspicion, which bristles with the apparatus and establishments of war on a scale far beyond what was formerly required for actual belligerence, and which is potentially war, though still only on the tiptoe of expectation for an actual outbreak. It was a more stable peace, founded on social and mental unison, which the Exhibition of 1851 truly, if circuitously, tended to consolidate.' William E. Gladstone, 'Life of the Prince Consort', in *Gleanings of Past Years, 1843–1878* (London: John Murray, 1879), I:67–8.

124. Hole, *Essay*, p. 1. See also Tallis, II:94.

125. Archibald Alison, *Some Account of my Life and Writings* (Edinburgh: William Blackwood & Sons, 1883), p. 28.

126. Love, 'Memorial,' p. 25.

127. Edsall, *Richard Cobden*, pp. 252–8.

128. 'The Dangers of the Country,' *Blackwood's* 69 (February 1851): 204.

129. See, for example, Arnstein, *Britain Yesterday and Today*, p. 73; Briggs, *Making of Modern England*, pp. 376–7, and *Victorian People*, pp. 41–2; A. J. P. Taylor, *The Struggle for Mastery in Europe, 1848–1918* (Oxford: Clarendon Press, 1954), p. 46, and *The Trouble Makers: Dissent over Foreign Policy, 1792–1939* (London: Hamish Hamilton, 1957), pp. 57–8; Violet R. Markham, *Paxton and the Bachelor Duke* (London: Hodder & Stoughton, 1935), pp. 230–1.

130. Colley, *Britons*, pp. 367–8.

CHAPTER 7: PALACE OF THE PEOPLE

1. *The Times*, 13 October 1851.
2. *Ibid.*, 26 August 1851; Charles Greville, *The Greville Memoirs, 1814–1860*, ed. Lytton Strachey and Roger Fulford (London: Macmillan, 1938), VI:296.
3. Joseph Paxton, *What Is to Become of the Crystal Palace?* (London: Bradbury & Evans, 1851).
4. Henry Cole [Denarius, pseud.], *Shall We Keep the Crystal Palace, and Have Riding and Walking in all Weathers among Flowers, Fountains and Sculptures?* (London: John Murray, 1851). Lyon Playfair confirmed that 'Denarius' was Cole, it being the Latin word for coal (*Playfair*, pp. 124–5).
5. [F. Seymour Haden], *A Medical Man's Plea for a Winter Garden in the Crystal Palace* (London: John Van Voorst, 1851).
6. [Adams], 'Industrial Exhibition of 1851;' *Punch* 21 (5 July 1851): 13; *Economist* 9 (12 July 1851): 754.
7. Francis Fuller, *Shall We Spend £100,000 on a Winter Garden for London, or in Endowing Schools of Design . . . ?* (London: John Ollivier, 1851).
8. Metropolitan Sanitary Association to the Royal Commission, 15 July 1851; Charles Newton to the Royal Commission, 1 August 1851, RCE/EC; *A Collection of One Hundred and Six Engravings* (London: n.p., n.d.), Victoria and Albert Museum, no. 53; *The Builder* (10 May 1852), pp. 280–1. See also Tallis, III:98–9.
9. John Kelk to the Royal Commission, 4 July 1851, RCE/EC; Commission Appointed to Inquire into the Cost and Applicability of the Exhibition in Hyde Park, *Report* (London: George Edward Eyre & William Spottiswoode, 1852), pp. 31–2; *The Times*, 18 July 1851; George F. Chadwick, *The Works of Sir Joseph Paxton* (London: Architectural Press, 1961), pp. 140–1.
10. Dickens to Warburton, 23 October 1851, *Letters of Charles Dickens*, VI:525–6.
11. *The Times*, 29–30 September 1851.
12. Cole to Phipps, 17 September 1851, Cole Papers; Chadwick, *Works of Paxton*, pp. 141–4.
13. *Economist* 9 (2 August 1851): 840–1.
14. 'The Proposed New National Galleries and Museums,' p. 342.
15. *Punch* 21 (25 October 1851): 178–9; 22 (3 April 1852): 136; 22 (1 May 1852): 181–2.
16. RCE/EC.
17. Cole, Diary, 14 August 1851.
18. 'Draft of H.R.H.'s Scheme for Surplus,' Playfair Papers, 706:1–3; Playfair to De la Beche, 20 August 1851, Playfair Papers 219.
19. Cole, Diary, 13, 19 August 1851.
20. *The Times*, 20 September 1851; Thomas Agnew to RC, 27 October 1851; Edward Bramley to RC, 13 October 1851; Benjamin Wightman to Northcote, 9 December 1851; Henry W. Phillips to Scott Russell, 8 October 1851; Thomas Burnet to RC, 8 October 1851; Thomas Buckland to RC, 31 May 1851, RCE/EC.
21. Fuller, *Shall We Spend £100,000 . . . ?*
22. Report of the Royal Commission to the Queen, 6 November 1851, PRO HO 45/3623; *The Times*, 7 November 1851. The report was written by Playfair, and represented a combination of his and Albert's ideas. See Phipps to Playfair, 27 September 1851, RCE/WA VIII:60.
23. Granville to Cobden, 17 November 1851, Cobden Papers, BL Add. MSS 53688 f. 144.
24. Thomas Field Gibson to Granville, 19 November 1851, RCE/EC.
25. Cobden to Granville, 19 November 1851, RCE/EC.
26. Grey to Playfair, 19 June, 29 July, 5 and 7 December 1852, Playfair Papers, 779–82, 788–90.
27. Cole to Grey, 13 December 1852, RCE/WA XI:1; draft copy, Cole to Grey, 13 December 1852, Cole Papers. See also the Royal Commission, *Second Report* (London: William Clowes & Sons for HMSO, 1852), pp. 45–55.
28. Grey to Playfair, 5 September 1852, Playfair Papers, 788–9.
29. *Birmingham Journal*, 8 January 1853; *Economist* 10 (25 December 1852): 1427–9.
30. Royal Commission, *First Report*, p. xviii; *Second Report*.
31. Proof of letter by Henry Cole, November 1874, Cole Papers.
32. The history of the Sydenham Crystal Palace, as with the South Kensington educational and museum complex, remains to be told.
33. *The Times*, 10 June 1904.
34. Michael Musgrave, *The Musical Life of the Crystal Palace* (Cambridge: Cambridge University Press, 1995).
35. Markham, *Paxton and the Bachelor Duke*, pp. 239–46; Bell-Knight, *Crystal Palace*, pp. 39–44; Reeves, *Palace of the People*, pp. 22–3, 31–3; *World's Metropolis*, p. 233.
36. Tallis, III:103–4.
37. *Economist* 10 (7 August 1852): 869; 12 (17 June 1854): 643–4.
38. [Harriet Martineau], 'The Crystal Palace,' *Westminster Review* 62 (October 1854): 534–50.
39. Reeves, *Palace of the People*, pp. 31–3; Bell-Knight, *Crystal Palace*, p. 49; Maurice Bristow, *The Postal History of the Crystal Palace* (London: Postal History Group, 1983), pp. 32–3; Nicholas Reed, *Camille Pissarro at the Crystal Palace* (London: London Reference Books, 1987).
40. Musgrave, *Musical Life*.
41. Benjamin Disraeli, *Speech of the Right Hon. B. Disraeli, M.P., at the Banquet of the National Union of Conservative and Constitutional Associations at the Crystal Palace, on Monday, June 24, 1872* (London: R. J. Mitchell & Sons, 1872).
42. Paul Smith, *Disraeli: A Brief Life* (Cambridge: Cambridge University Press, 1996), pp. 163–4.
43. W. F. Monypenny and George Earle Buckle, *The Life of Benjamin Disraeli*, vol. V (London: John Murray, 1920), p. 194.
44. Bernard Porter, *Britannia's Burden* (London: Edward Arnold, 1994), pp. 52–7.
45. Susan P. Casteras, *Victorian Childhood* (New York: Henry M. Abrams, 1986), pp. 8–9.
46. *The Times*, 24 August 1870.

47. Fyodor Dostoyevsky, *Notes from the Underground* (New York: Dover, 1992), pp. 17, 23–5.

48. Marshall Berman, *All That is Solid Melts into Air* (New York: Penguin, 1988), pp. 236–41.

49. *Ibid.*, p. 220.

50. Hippolyte Taine, *Taine's Notes on England*, trans. Edward Hyams (London: Thames & Hudson, 1957), pp. 188–90.

51. George Gissing, *The Nether World*, ed. Stephen Gill (Oxford: Oxford University Press, 1992); *The Collected Letters of George Gissing*, ed. Paul F. Mattheisen, Arthur C. Young, and Pierre Coustillas (Athens, OH: Ohio University Press, 1991), II:87–8, III:198.

52. Cole, *Fifty Years*, I: 171.

53. Bell-Knight, *Crystal Palace*, p. 44; *Punch* 23 (3 July 1852): 11; (30 October 1852): 195.

54. *The Times*, 21 July 1871.

55. *Ibid.*, 25 July 1908.

56. *Ibid.*, 7 and 18 August 1868.

57. *Ibid.*, 11 July 1903.

58. *Ibid.*, 8 February 1877.

59. *Ibid.*, 3 November 1879.

60. *Ibid.*, 10 July 1908.

61. *Ibid.*, 1 May 1901.

62. MacKenzie, *Propaganda and Empire*.

63. *Ibid.*, pp. 31–2.

64. *The Times*, 12 October 1904.

65. MacKenzie, *Propaganda and Empire*, pp. 106–7.

66. *The Times*, 13 May 1911.

67. *Ibid.*, 2 June 1911.

68. *Ibid.*, 4 July 1913.

69. *Ibid.*, 30 June 1913.

70. *Ibid.*, 10 June 1920.

71. Bell-Knight, *Crystal Palace*, pp. 44–8; Bristow, *Postal History*, pp. 37–41; Murdock, *Romance and History of the Crystal Palace*, pp. v–vii; Gibbs-Smith, *Great Exhibition*, p. 28.

72. Bell-Knight, *Crystal Palace*, p. 48.

73. *London News Chronicle*, 1 December 1936.

74. Quoted in Musgrave, *Musical Life*, p. 3.

75. Bell-Knight, *Crystal Palace*, pp. 54–5.

76. *London Star*, 1 December 1936.

CHAPTER 8: LEGACY AND NOSTALGIA

1. *Independent*, 8 April 1992, 16 October 1993.

2. Edmund Yates, 'The International Exhibition,' *Temple Bar* 5 (May 1862): 205.

3. *The Times*, 17 November 1859.

4. Cobden to Cole, 30 July 1862, Cole Papers.

5. Edmund Yates, 'Taste at South Kensington,' *Temple Bar* 5 (1862): 471, 479–80.

6. *The Times*, 29 April 1862.

7. *Ibid.*, 29 April, 6 June 1861.

8. *The Times*, 25 April 1862.

9. Canning to Granville, 3 March 1861, *The Life of Granville George Leveson Gower*, ed. Edmund Fitz-Maurice (London: Longman, Green & Co., 1905), pp. 389–93.

10. *The Exhibition of 1861. Why it Should Be. What it Should Be. Where it Should Be* (London: Bradbury & Evans, 1859), John Johnson Collection, Exhibitions Box 3; Yates, 'International Exhibition,' pp. 209–10.

11. Yates, 'International Exhibition,' pp. 121–31.

12. 'The World's May Meeting,' *Bentley's Miscellany* 51 (1862): 609.

13. Charles Knight, *Passages of a Working Life during Half a Century* (London: Bradbury & Evans, 1864–5), III:122.

14. [Jane Budge], *Great Events in England's History* (London: John Marshall, 1872), p. 222.

15. *The Times*, 30 June 1913.

16. R. E. Francillon, *Mid-Victorian Memories* (London: Hodder & Stoughton, 1914), pp. 49–50.

17. *The Times*, 23–24 April 1924.

18. Markham, *Paxton and the Bachelor Duke*, p. 183. Her account, written contemporaneously with Strachey and Hobhouse, though just before the Crystal Palace burned down, was by and large a positive one. She was also Paxton's granddaughter, and so presumably had a lot invested in saving, or boosting, his reputation.

19. Hobhouse, *1851*, pp. 149–50.

20. Mary Banham and Bevis Hillier, eds, *A Tonic to the Nation: The Festival of Britain, 1951* (London: Thames & Hudson, 1976) p. 8.

21. The details and chronology for the section are from the following sources: [Basil Taylor], *The Festival of Britain, 1951* (London: HMSO, [1951]); F. M. Leventhal, '"A Tonic to the Nation:" The Festival of Britain, 1951,' *Albion* 27 (1995): 445–53; Gerald Barry, 'The Festival of Britain, 1951,' *Journal of the Royal Society of Arts* 100 (1952): 667–704.

22. *The Times*, 6 December 1947.

23. Leventhal, 'Tonic to the Nation,' pp. 447–8.

24. *The Times*, 6 December 1947.

25. Banham and Hillier, eds, *Tonic to the Nation*, pp. 7, 12.

26. *The Times*, 4 April 1946.

27. MacKenzie, *Propaganda and Empire*, p. 98.

28. Robert Henriques, 'A Portrait of Britain,' *Field* (5 May 1951): 671.

29. Barry, 'Festival of Britain,' p. 677.

30. [Taylor], *Festival of Britain*.

31. *Ibid.*

32. *Economist* 158, (2 May 1951): 1019–20. See also [Taylor], *Festival of Britain*, p. 3; *The Times*, 6 December 1947.

33. Banham and Hillier, eds, *Tonic to the Nation*, pp. 9, 183.

34. *Ibid.*, pp. 10–11.

35. *The Times*, 4 May 1951.

36. Ernest Benn, 'The Festival of Britain and the "Mess of Centuries,"' *Quarterly Review* 290 (1952): 315–28.

37. Briggs, *Making of Modern England*, pp. 398, 402.

38. Wood, *Nineteenth Century Britain*, p. 176.

39. Arnstein, *Britain Yesterday and Today*, pp. 71–3.

40. Rupert Steiner, 'Leisure-Age Crystal Palace Gets a Tudor Pub and Bowling alley,' *The Times*, 7 August 1991.

41. Greenhalgh, *Ephemeral Vistas*, esp. pp. 27–9, 52–4, 226. Surprisingly given his overall argument, Greenhalgh wrote that there was 'little real evidence of concern with national profile in 1851 when industry and empire guaranteed Britain's position as most powerful country' (p. 120). The present work has argued just the opposite.

42. Richards, *Commodity Culture*, pp. 1–72.

43. Confino, 'Nation as a Local Metaphor,' pp. 50, 74–5.

44. On this point see Hammerton and Cannadine, 'Conflict and Consensus;' Michael Robertson, 'Cultural Hegemony Goes to the Fair: The Case of E. L. Doctorow's *World Fair*,' *American Studies* 33 (1992): 31–44.

SELECT BIBLIOGRAPHY

I. Manuscript Collections

Bodleian Library, Oxford University
  John Johnson Collection of Printed Ephemera
  Samuel Wilberforce MSS

British Library
  Charles Babbage Papers
  Richard Cobden Papers
  Robert Peel Papers
  Joseph Sturge Papers
  R. H. Love, 'A Memorial of the Great Exhibition,' 1851,
    BL Add. MSS 35255.

Chatsworth
  Devonshire Collection
  Joseph Paxton Papers

Churchill College Archives, Cambridge
  Dilke Family Papers

Guildhall Library
  Imperial Insurance Company
  Church of England Life and Fire Assurance Trust and
    Annuity Institution
  Union Assurance Company
  London and County Banking Company
  London and Westminster Bank
  National Provincial Bank of England

Imperial College of Science, Technology, and Medicine
  Archives of the Royal Commission for the Exhibition
    of 1851
  Lyon Playfair Papers

India Office Library
  India & Bengal Dispatches E/4/803, 813
  Finance and Home Committee Correspondence
    L/F/2/130–51

Manchester Central Library
  Records of the Royal Manchester Institution, Great
    Exhibition of 1851

National Art Library, Victoria and Albert Museum
  Henry Cole Papers and Diary

National Library of Scotland
  Cadell of Grange Papers
  Traill Papers
  John Tod, 'Visit to London and "The Exhibition"', 21
    June 1851

Public Record Office
  British Transportation Archive, RAIL 250, 406, 410,
    491, 635
  Home Office, HO 45/3623, 4299
  Granville Papers, PRO 30/29
  Russell Papers, PRO 30/22
  Woods and Forest, WORK 6

Royal Society of Arts
  John Scott Russell's Collection of Papers Relating to the
    Great Exhibition . . . , 5 vols
  Letters from Prince Albert and the Emperor Ferdinand
    to John Scott Russell
  Minutes of Council

St Andrews University Library
  James David Forbes Papers

Strathclyde Regional Archives, Mitchell Library, Glasgow
  Henry Watson, 'Journal of a Journey to London'

University College, London
  Brougham Collection
  Edwin Chadwick Collection
  Francis Galton Papers

University of Southampton, Hartley Library
  Palmerston (Broadland) Papers
  Wellington Papers

Yale Center for British Art
  John R. Isaac Collection of Material Relating to the
    Great Exhibition of 1851
  Collection of Material Relating to the Liverpool
    Excursion Club for Enabling the Working Classes to
    Visit London in 1851

II. Newspapers and Periodicals

Athenaeum	*Journal of the Exhibition of*
Bentley's Miscellany	*1851*
Blackwood's	*Leader*
Britannia	*Leeds Mercury*
Cambrian	*Leeds Times*
Cardiff and Merthyr	*Liverpool Mercury*
Guardian	*Manchester Guardian*
Catholic Standard	*Mechanics Magazine*
Chambers'	*Mining Journal*
Christian Times	*Morning Chronicle*
Cook's Excursionist	*Morning Herald*
Daily News	*Nation (Dublin)*
Eclectic Review	*Northern Star*
Economist	*Post*
Edinburgh Review	*Punch*
Express	*Railway Times*
Fraser's Magazine	*Reynold's Weekly Newspaper*
Herepath's Railway and	*Scotsman*
Commercial Journal	*Sun*
Household Words	*Temple Bar*
Hull Advertiser	*The Times*
Illustrated London News	*Weekly Dispatch*
John Bull	*Westminster Review*

III. Published Autobiographies, Diaries, Letters, and Reminiscences

Albert. *Letters of the Prince Consort, 1831–1861*. Ed. Kurt Jagow. Trans. E. T. S. Dugdale. London: John Murray, 1938.

——. *The Prince Consort and his Brother: Two Hundred New Letters*. Ed. Hector Bolitho. London: Cobden-Sanderson, 1933.

Alison, Archibald. *Some Account of my Life and Writings*. 2 vols. Edinburgh: William Blackwood & Sons, 1883.

Astley, John Dugdale. *Fifty Years of my Life*. 2 vols. London: Hurst & Blackett, 1894.

Babbage, Charles. *Passages from the Life of a Philosopher*. London: Longman, Green, Longman, Roberts & Green, 1864.

Berlioz, Hector. *Life and Letters of Berlioz*. Ed. H. Mainwaring Dunstan. 2 vols. London: Remington, 1882.

Bright, John. *The Diaries of John Bright*. Ed. R. A. J. Walling. London: Cassell, 1930.

Campbell, George Douglas [8th Duke of Argyll]. *Autobiography and Memoirs*. Ed. Dowager Duchess of Argyll. Vol. I. London: John Murray, 1906.

Carroll, Lewis. *The Letters of Lewis Carroll*. Vol. I (1837–1885). Ed. Morton N. Cohen. New York: Oxford University Press, 1979.

Cavendish, Francis W. H. *Society, Politics and Diplomacy, 1820–1864: Passages from the Journal of Francis W. H. Cavendish*. London: T. Fisher Unwin, 1913.

Chancellor, Valerie E., ed. *Master and Artisan in Victorian England: The Diary of William Andrews and the Autobiography of Joseph Gutteridge*. London: Evelyn, Adams & Mackay, 1969.

Cole, Henry. *Fifty Years of Public Work*. 2 vols. London: George Bell & Sons, 1884.

Cooper, Thomas. *The Life of Thomas Cooper*. London: Hodder & Stoughton, 1872.

Crompton, R. E. *Reminiscences*. London: Constable, 1928.

Dickens, Charles. *The Letters of Charles Dickens*. Ed. Graham Storey, Kathleen Tillotson and Nina Burges. Vol. VI (1850–1852). Oxford: Clarendon Press, 1988.

Ellison, Thomas. *Gleanings and Reminiscences*. Liverpool: Henry Young & Sons, 1905.

Francillon, Robert Edward. *Mid-Victorian Memories*. London: Hodder & Stoughton, 1914.

Fullerton, Georgiana. *Life of Lady Georgiana Fullerton*. Ed. Pauline Marie Craven. Trans. Henry James Coleridge. London: Richard Bentley, 1888.

Gissing, George. *The Collected Letters of George Gissing*. 6 vols. Ed. Paul F. Mattheisen, Arthur C. Young, and Pierre Coustillas. Athens, OH: Ohio State University Press, 1991.

Gladstone, William. *The Gladstone Diaries*. Vol. IV (1848–1854). Ed. M. R. D. Foot and H. C. G. Matthew. Oxford: Clarendon Press, 1974.

Gower, Edward Frederick Leveson. *Bygone Years*. London: John Murray, 1905.

Greville, Charles. *The Greville Memoirs, 1814–1860*. 8 vols. Ed. Lytton Strachey and Roger Fulford. London: Macmillan, 1938.

Guest, Charlotte. *Lady Charlotte Guest: Extracts from her Journal, 1833–1852*. Ed. Earl of Bessborough. London: John Murray, 1950.

Humphrey, A. W., ed. *Robert Applegarth: Trade Unionist, Educationalist, Reformer*. New York: Garland Press, 1984.

Kingsley, Charles. *His Letters and Memories of his Life*. 2 vols. Ed. Frances E. Kingsley. London: Henry S. King & Co., 1877.

Knight, Charles. *Passages of a Working Life during Half a Century*. 3 vols. London: Bradbury & Evans, 1864–5.

Lovett, William. *The Life and Struggles of William Lovett*. London: Trübner & Co., 1876.

Loyd, Samuel Jones [Baron Overstone]. *The Correspondence of Lord Overstone*. 3 vols. Ed. D. P. O'Brien. Cambridge: Cambridge University Press, 1971.

Lyell, Charles. *Life, Letters and Journals of Sir Charles Lyell*. 2 vols. London: John Murray, 1881.

Macaulay, Thomas Babington. *The Life and Letters of Lord Macaulay*. Ed. George Otto Trevelyan. New York: Harper & Bros., 1876.

Mantell, Gideon. *The Journal of Gideon Mantell*. Ed. E. Cecil Curwen. London: Oxford University Press, 1940.

Morris, William, 'How I Became a Socialist', *Justice* (16 June 1894).

Northcote, Stafford. *Life, Letters and Diaries of Sir Stafford Northcote*. 2 vols. Ed. Andrew Lang. Edinburgh: William Blackwood, 1890.

Norton, Charles Eliot, ed. *The Correspondence of Thomas Carlyle and Ralph Waldo Emerson, 1834–1872*. 2 vols. London: Chatto & Windus, 1883.

Palmerston, Henry John Temple. *Opinions and Policy of Viscount Palmerston*. Ed. George Henry Francis. London: Colburn, 1852.

Pease, Edward. *The Diaries of Edward Pease*. Ed. Alfred E. Pease. London: Headley Brothers, 1907.

Playfair, Lyon. *Memoirs and Correspondence of Lyon Playfair*. Ed. Thomas Wemyss Reid. Intro. Colin Armstrong. Jemimaville, Scotland: P. M. Pollack, 1976.

Porter, Enid, ed. *Victorian Cambridge: Josiah Chater's Diaries, 1844–1884*. London: Phillimore & Co., 1975.

Redgrave, Richard. *A Memoir*. Ed. F. M. Redgrave. London: Cassell & Company, 1891.

Salis-Schwabe, Julie. *Reminiscences of Richard Cobden*. London: T. Fisher Unwin, 1895.

Spencer, Herbert. *An Autobiography*. 2 vols. London: Williams & Norgate, 1904.

Taine, Hippolyte. *Taine's Notes on England*. Trans. Edward Hyams. London: Thames & Hudson, 1957.

Thackeray, William Makepeace. *The Letters and Private Papers of William Makepeace Thackeray*. 4 vols. Ed. Gordon N. Ray. Cambridge, MA: Harvard University Press, 1945–6.

Thompson, Zadock. *Journal of a Trip to London, Paris, and the Great Exhibition of 1851*. Burlington: Nichols & Warren, 1852.

Victoria. *The Letters of Queen Victoria*. Vol. II. Ed. Arthur Christopher Benson and Viscount Esher. London: John Murray, 1907.

Vignoles, Charles Blacker. *Life of Charles Blacker Vignoles*. Ed. Olinthus J. Vignoles. London: Longman, 1889.

Walmsley, Joshua. *The Life of Sir Joshua Walmsley*. Ed.

Hugh Mulleneux Walmsley. London: Chapman & Hall, 1879.

Ward, Henrietta M. A. *Memories of Ninety Years.* Ed. Isabel G. McAllister. London: Hutchinson & Co., 1924.

Wilberforce, Reginald G., ed. *Life of the Right Reverend Samuel Wilberforce.* Vol. II. London: John Murray, 1881.

IV. Official Reports and Publications

Commission Appointed to Inquire into the Cost and Applicability of the Exhibition in Hyde Park. *Report.* London: George Edward Eyre & William Spottiswoode, 1852.

Commission for the Promotion of the Exhibition of the Works of Industry of All Nations. *Prospectus: 21 February 1850.* London: Vacher & Sons, 1850.

Institution of Civil Engineers. *Minutes of Proceedings.* London: The Institution. Vols IX–XI, 1849–52.

Royal Commission for the Exhibition of the Works of Industry of All Nations. *Catalogue of a Collection of Samples of Raw and Partly-Manufactured Produce Shown in the Exhibition of 1851 . . . for Transmission to Foreign Countries.* London: William Clowes & Sons, 1853.

——. *Collection of Printed Documents and Forms Used in Carrying on the Business of the Exhibition of 1851.* 8 vols. London: n.p., 1847–53.

——. *First Report.* London: William Clowes & Sons for HMSO, 1852.

——. *Second Report.* London: William Clowes & Sons for HMSO, 1852.

——. *Reports by the Juries on the Subjects in the Thirty Classes into which the Exhibition was Divided.* London: William Clowes & Sons, 1852.

V. Printed Primary Sources

The Art Journal Illustrated Catalogue. 16 vols. London: George Virtue, 1851.

Askrill, Robert. *The Yorkshire Visitors' Guide to the Great Exhibition.* Leeds: Joseph Buckton, 1851.

Aveling, Thomas. *Great Sights; A Discourse delivered in Kingsland Chapel on the Sabbath Evening Preceding the Opening of the Great Exhibition.* London: Snow, 1851.

Babbage, Charles. *The Exposition of 1851; or, Views of the Industry, the Science and the Government of England.* London: John Murray, 1851.

——. *Reflections on the Decline of Science in England, and on Some of its Causes.* London: B. Fellowes, 1830.

Baker, B. B. *Verses of the Exhibition of 1851.* Ventnor: James Briddon, 1871.

Bartlett, David W. *What I Saw in London; or, Men and Things in the Great Metropolis.* Auburn: Derby & Miller, 1852.

Baxter, George. *Baxter's Gems of the Great Exhibition.* London: n.p., 1854.

Bayley, F. W. N. *The Little Folks' Laughing Library, The Exhibition.* London: Darton & Co., 1851.

Beasland's London Companion during the Great Exhibition; 1851. London: Ro. Donaldson, 1851.

Berlyn, Peter. *A Popular Narrative of the Origin, History, Progress and Prospects of the Great Industrial Exhibition, 1851.* London: n.p., 1851.

Berlyn, Peter and Charles Fowler. *The Crystal Palace: Its Architectural History and Constructive Marvels.* London: James Gilbert, 1851.

Bills and Cards of Exhibitors. N.p., n.d.

The Book of Wonders. London: John Griffin, 1851.

Booth, Charles. *Condition and Occupations of the People of the Tower Hamlets, 1886–1887.* London: Edward Stanford, 1887.

'The Bramah Lock Controversy: Extracts from the Press'. London: n.p., 1851.

The British Advertiser. An Illustrated Hand-Book of the Great Exhibition. London: Jackson & Cooper, 1851.

Brougham, Henry [William Davis, pseud.]. 'Hints to Philanthropists; or a Collective View of Practical Means of Improving the Condition of the Poor and Labouring Classes of Society.' *Edinburgh Review* 41 (1824): 96–122.

Burnet, Richard. *To Her Majesty's Commissioners for the Exhibition, 1851.* London: n.p., 1850.

Carlyle, Thomas. *Past and Present.* Ed. Richard D. Altick. New York: New York University Press, 1965.

Cassell, John. *Great Exhibition . . . to Members of Christian Congregations . . .* London: John Cassell, 1851.

——. *Great Industrial Exhibition. Accommodations for Visitors . . .* London: John Cassell, 1851.

A Catalogue of the Highly Important and by far the greater portion of the valuable and interesting collection as exhibited by the honourable East India Company at the Great Exhibition of 1851 . . . London: Cox Brothers & Wyman, 1852.

Chaff; or, The Yankee and Nigger at the Exhibition. London: Edward Stanford, 1853.

Chamerovzow, Louis Alexis. *The Industrial Exhibition of 1851. Being a Few Observations upon the General Advantages which may be Expected to Arise from it.* London: T. C. Neuby, n.d.

Clayton, B. *Frolick & Fun or What Was Seen and Done in London in 1851.* London: Dean & Son, 1852.

Coalbrookdale Company Specimen Catalogue. Northampton: W. W. Lae, 1851.

Cole, Henry. *Observations on the Expediency of carrying out the Proposals of the Commissioners for the Exhibition of 1851, for the promotion of institutions of science and art at Kensington, rather by the public themselves than by the Government.* London: Chapman & Hall, 1853.

—— [Denarius, pseud]. *Shall We Keep the Crystal Palace, and Have Riding and Walking in All Weathers among Flowers, Fountains, and Sculptures?* London: John Murray, 1851.

Collier, George Frederick. *The Philosopher's Mite to the Great Exhibition of 1851.* London: Houlston & Stoneman, n.d.

Collier, William. *Sights of London, and How to See Them.* London: Vickers, n.d.

The Crystal Palace and its Contents. [London]: W. M. Clark, 1851.

The Crystal Palace: A Little Book for Little Boys. London: James Nisbett & Co., 1851.

Cummings, John. *The Great Exhibition, Suggestive and Anticipative.* London: John Farquhar Shaw, 1851.

Dickinsons' Comprehensive Pictures of the Great Exhibition of 1851. London: Dickinson, Brothers, 1854.

Disraeli, Benjamin. *Speech of the Right Hon. B. Disraeli, M. P., at the Banquet of the National Union of Conservative and Constitutional Associations at the Crystal Palace, on Monday June 24, 1872.* London: R. J. Mitchell & Sons, 1872.

Dostoyevsky, Fyodor. *Notes from The Underground.* Trans. Richard Pevear and Larissa Volokhonsky. New York: Dover, 1992.

Downes, Charles and Charles Couper. *The Building Erected in Hyde Park for the Great Exhibition of the Works of Industry of All Nations, 1851 . . . from the working drawings of the contractors, Messrs. Fox, Henderson and Co.* London: John Weale, 1851.

Doyle, Richard. *An Overland Journey to the Great Exhibition Showing a few extra articles and visitors.* London: Chapman & Hall, n.d.

Drew, William A. *Glimpses and Gatherings.* Augusta, ME: Homan & Manley, 1852.

Edwards, Henry Sutherland. *An Authentic Account of the Chinese Commission, which was sent to report on the Great Exhibition; wherein the opinion of China is shown as not corresponding with our own.* London: H. Vizitelly, n.d.

Emerton, J. A. *A Moral and Religious Guide to the Great Exhibition.* London: Longman, Brown, Green & Longmans, 1851.

E.M.G. *The Crystal Palace, The London Season. Two Satires for 1851.* London: John Ollivier, 1851.

The English and Continental Guide to London, in English and French. London: W. and T. Piper, 1851.

Excelsior. *The Dial of the World.* London: Ward & Co., 1851.

The Exhibition Lay. London: Groombridge & Sons, 1852.

The Exhibition of 1851. Why it Should Be. What it Should Be. Where it Should Be. London: Bradbury & Evans. 1859.

'Exhibition on a Sunday Night'. London: H. Disley, 1851?.

Felkin, William. *The Exhibition of 1851 of the Products and Industry of All Nations, its Probable Influence upon Labour and Commerce.* London: Arthur Hall, Virtue & Co., 1851.

A Frenchman's Visit to England, and the Crystal Palace. All he saw there, with his remarks upon England and the English people in general, and London in particular, translated into English by a Belgian, revised and corrected by an American, printed by a Prussian, published everywhere, and dedicated to everybody. London: W. N. Wright, 1851.

Freund, J. C. H. *A Small Contribution to the Great Exhibition of 1851.* London: Groombridge & Sons, 1851.

Friendly Observations . . . to the Sculptors and Artists of Great Britain. London: John Farquhar Shaw, 1851.

Fuller, Francis. *Memoranda Relative to the International Exhibition of 1851.* N.p., n.d.

——. *Shall We Spend £100,000 on a Winter Garden for London, or in Endowing Schools of Design . . . ?* London: John Ollivier, 1851.

Gascoyne, Caroline. *Recollections and Tales of the Crystal Palace.* London: W. Shoberl, 1852.

Gibbs, W. *The Handbook of Architectural Ornament Illustrating and Explaining the Various Styles of Decoration Employed in the Great Exhibition of 1851.* London: Ackermann, 1851.

Gissing, George. *The Nether World.* Ed. Stephen Gill. Oxford: Oxford University Press, 1992 [1888].

The Great National Exhibition of 1851: A Description of the Building Now Erecting in Hyde Park by messrs. Fox and Henderson, from Designs by Mr. Paxton. London: H. G. Clarke & Co., 1850.

Greeley, Horace. *Glances at Europe.* New York: Dewitt & Davenport, 1851.

'Greville'. *An Answer to 'What is to Become of the Crystal Palace'.* London: John Ollivier, 1851.

Guide-book to the Industrial Exhibition; with Facts, Figures and Observations on the Manufactures and Produce Exhibited. London: Partridge & Oakey, 1851.

A Guide to the Great Exhibition; containing a description of every principal object of interest. London: George Routledge & Co., 1851.

Haden, F. Seymour. *A Medical Man's Plea for a Winter Garden in the Crystal Palace.* London: John Van Voorst, 1851.

Hall, Herbert Byng. *The West of England and the Exhibition, 1851.* London: Longman & Company, 1851.

Hall, Rev. John. *The Sons of Toil and the Crystal Palace: in reply to Mr. Mayhew.* London: John Snow, 1853.

Hammersby, J. A. *An Address on the Preparations on the Continent for the Great Exhibition of 1851 and the Condition of Continental Schools of Art.* Nottingham: n.p., 1850.

Harthill's Guide through London and to the Industrial Exhibition. London: Effingham Wilson, 1851.

Hole, James. *An Essay on the History and Management of Literary, Scientific, and Mechanics' Institutions.* London: Longman, Brown, Green & Longmans, 1853.

The House that Albert Built. Illus. Henning. N.p., n.d.

Hunt, Robert. *Hunt's Hand-Book to the Official Catalogues of the Great Exhibition.* 2 vols. London: Spicer Brothers and W. Clowes, 1851.

Jerrold, William Blanchard. *How to See the Exhibition. In Four Visits.* London: Bradbury & Evans, 1851.

Jimmy Trebilcock; or, the Humorous Adventures of a Cornish Miner at the Great Exhibition, What he saw and What he didn't see. Cambridge: n.p., 1862.

Johnston, William. *England as It Is, Political, Social, and Industrial, in the Middle of the Nineteenth Century.* 2 vols. London: John Murray, 1851.

Lardner, Dr. *The Great Exhibition, and London in 1851.* London: Longman, Brown, Green & Longmans, 1852.

Lectures on the Results of the Great Exhibition of 1851, Delivered before the Society of Arts, Manufactures, and Commerce. 2 vols. London: David Bogue, 1852–3.

Limner, Luke. *The Rejected Contributions to the Great Exhibition of All Nations.* London: David Bogue, 1851.

Lloyd, J. A. *Proposals for Establishing Colleges of Art and Manufactures for the Better Instruction of the Industrial Classes.* London: Clowes & Sons, 1851.

Mama's Visit with her Little Ones, to the Great Exhibition. London: Darton, 1852.

Mayhew, Henry and George Cruikshank. *1851; or, the Adventures of Mr. and Mrs. Sandboys and Family who came to London to 'Enjoy Themselves' and to see the Great Exhibition.* London: David Bogue, 1851.

Mr. Goggleye's Visit to the Exhibition of National Industry to be Held in London on the 1st of April 1851. London: Timothy Takemin, n.d.

Murray, John Fisher. *The World of London.* 2 vols. Edinburgh: William Blackwood & Sons, 1843.

Napier, Mrs. *The Lay of the Palace.* London: John Ollivier, 1852.

Newcombe, S. P. *Fireside Facts from the Great Exhibition: Object Lessons in the Food and Clothing of All Nations in 1851.* London: Peter, Duff & Co., 1851.

——. *Little Henry's Holiday at the Great Exhibition.* London: Houlston & Stoneman, 1851.

——. *The Royal Road to Reading through the Great Exhibition; in which those who were too young to visit the Exhibition may learn to read about it.* London: Houlston & Stoneman, n.d.

Official Descriptive and Illustrated Catalogue. 3 vols. London: Spicer Brothers, 1851.

Onwhyn, Thomas. *Mr. and Mrs. John Brown's Visit to London to see the Great Exposition of all Nations.* London: Ackerman, n.d.

Paxton, Joseph. *What Is to Become of the Crystal Palace?* London: Bradbury & Evans, 1851.

'Philoponos'. *The Great Exhibition of 1851; or, the Wealth of the World in its Workshops.* London: Edward Churton, 1850.

Plans and Suggestions for Dwellings Adapted to the Working Classes, including the model house for families built by command of His Royal Highness the Prince Albert, K. G., in connection with The Exposition of the Works of Industry of All Nations, 1851. London: The Society for Improving the Condition of the Labouring Classes, 1851.

Pugin, A. Welby. *The True Principles of Christian or Pointed Architecture.* London: John Weale, 1841.

Recollections of the Great Exhibition of 1851. London: Lloyd Brothers & Co., Simpkin; Marshall & Co., 1851.

Religious Tract Society. *The Palace of Glass and the Gathering of the People.* London: W. Jones, 1851.

——. *A Walk through the Crystal Palace.* London: The Religious Tract Society, n.d.

Remembrances of the Great Exhibition. London: Ackerman & Co., 1852.

The Removal of the Crystal Palace. London: Houlston & Stoneman, 1852.

Richardson, John. *The Exhibition London Guide.* London: Simpkin, Marshall & Co., 1851.

——. *The Real Exhibitors Exhibited; or, An Inquiry into the Condition of those Industrial Classes who have Really Represented England at the Great Exhibition.* London: Wertheim & Macintosh, 1851.

The Royal Exchange and the Palace of Industry. London: William Jones, 1851.

Royal Exhibition Song Book. Vols I–XIII. London: T. Woode, 1851.

Royle, J. Forbes. *On the Culture and Commerce of Cotton in India.* London: Smith, Elder & Co., 1851.

Ruskin, John. *The Opening of the Crystal Palace considered in some of its relations to the prospects of Art.* London: Smith, Elder & Co., 1854.

——. *The Seven Lamps of Architecture.* London: Smith, Elder & Co., 1849.

St Clair, William. *The Great Exhibition of 1851: A Poem.* London: Partridge & Oakley, 1850.

Sala, George A. [Vates Secundus, pseud]. *Great Exhibition: 'Wot is to Be,' or, Probable Results of the Industry of All Nations in the Year '51. Showing What is to be Exhibited, Who is to Exhibit, in short, How it's all Going to be Done.* London: The Committee for Keeping Things in Their Places, 1850.

Sharp, Granville. *Prize Essay on the Adoption of Recent Inventions Collected at the Great Exhibition of 1851 to the Purposes of Practical Banking.* N.p., n.d.

Silliman, Benjamin. *A Visit to Europe in 1851.* 2 vols. New York: G. P. Putnam & Co., 1854.

Smith, William. *Advertise. How? When? Where?* London: Routledge, Warne & Routledge, 1863.

Society for Promoting Christian Knowledge. *An Address to Foreigners Visiting the Great Exhibition of Arts in London, 1851.* London: Gilbert & Rivington, 1851.

——. *The Industry of Nations, as exemplified in the Great Exhibition of 1851.* London: n.p., 1852.

Stephenson, Robert. *The Great Exhibition; its Palace, and its Principal Contents.* London: George Routledge & Co., 1851.

Stone the First at the Great Glass House. London: William Edward Painter, n.d.

Tallis, John. *Tallis's History and Description of the Crystal Palace, and the Exhibition of the World's Industry in 1851.* 3 vols. London: John Tallis & Co., 1852.

Taylor, Basil. *The Festival of Britain, 1951.* London: HMSO, 1951.

The Theology and Morality of the Great Exhibition. London: Edward Painter, 1851.

Thomas, W. Cave. *Suggestions for a Crystal College or New Palace of Glass, for combining the intellectual talent of all nations; or, a sketch of a practical philosophy of education.* London: Dickinson, 1851.

Troup, George. *Art and Faith, in Fragments from the Great Exhibition.* London: Partridge, 1852.

Turner, Joseph. *Echoes of the Great Exhibition.* London: William Pickering, 1851.

Voices from the Workshop on the Exhibition of 1851. N.p., n.d.

Wallace, R. W. *The History of the Steam Engine, from the Second Century before the Christian Era to the Time of the Great Exhibition.* London: John Cassell, 1852.

Wallis, George. *The Future Uses of the Crystal Palace.* London: n.p., 1851.

Ward, James. *The World in its Workshops.* 2nd edn. London: William S. Orr & Co., 1851.

Weir, John. *The New Crystal Palace and the Christian Sabbath.* London: N. H. Cotes, 1852.

Whish, J. C. *The Great Exhibition Prize Essay.* London: Longman, Brown, Green & Longmans, 1851.

Wilberforce, Samuel. *On the Dignity of Labour.* London: Bradbury & Evans, 1850.

The World's Fair; or, Children's Prize Gift Book. London: Thomas Dean & Son, 1851.

The World's Metropolis, or Mighty London. London: Read & Co., 1855.

Wornum, Ralph Nicholson. 'The Exhibition as a Lesson in Taste.' In *The Art Journal Illustrated Catalogue.* London: George Virtue, 1851.

Wyatt, Matthew Digby. *Views of the Crystal Palace and Park, Sydenham.* London: Day and Son, 1854.

VI. PUBLISHED SECONDARY WORKS

Abbott, Albert. *Education for Industry and Commerce in England.* Intro. Eustace Perry. Oxford: Oxford University Press, 1933.

Aldrich, Megan, ed. *The Craces: Royal Decorators, 1768–1899.* Brighton: The Royal Pavilion Art Gallery and Museums, 1990.

Alexander, Edward P. *Museum Masters: Their Museums and their Influence.* Nashville: American Association for State and Local History, 1983.

——. *Museums in Motion: An Introduction to the History and Function of Museums.* Nashville: American Association for State and Local History, 1979.

Allport, Gordon. *The Nature of Prejudice.* Cambridge, MA: Addison-Wesley, 1954.

Alter, Peter. *Nationalism,* 2nd edn. London: Edward Arnold, 1994.

Altick, Richard. *The English Common Reader.* Chicago. University of Chicago Press, 1957.

——. *Punch: The Lively Youth of a British Institution, 1841–1851.* Columbus: Ohio State University Press, 1997.

——. *The Shows of London.* Cambridge, MA: Harvard University Press, 1978.

Ames, Winslow. *Prince Albert and Victorian Taste.* New York: Viking Press, 1968.

Anderson, Benedict. *Imagined Communities: Reflections on the Origin and Spread of Nationalism.* Rev. edn. London: Verso, 1991.

Argles, Michael. *South Kensington to Robbins: An Account of English Technical and Scientific Education since 1851.* London: Longmans Green & Company, 1964.

Arnstein, Walter L. *Britain Yesterday and Today,* 5th edn. Lexington, MA: D. C. Heath, 1988.

——. 'The Myth of the Triumphant Middle Class.' *Historian* 37 (1975): 205–21.

——. *Protestant versus Catholic in Mid-Victorian Britain: Mr. Newdegate and the Nuns.* Columbia, MO: University of Missouri Press, 1982.

Ashley, Evelyn. *The Life of Henry John Temple, Viscount Palmerston, 1846–65.* 2 vols. London: Richard Bentley, 1876.

Ashton, John. *Hyde Park.* London: Downey & Co., 1896.

Atterbury, Paul and Clive Wainwright, eds. *Pugin: A Gothic Passion.* New Haven: Yale University Press, 1994.

Bagwell, Philip S. *The Railway Clearing House in the British Economy, 1842–1922.* London: George Allen & Unwin, 1968.

Bailey, Edward. *Charles Lyell.* London: Thames Nelson, 1962.

Bailey, Peter. *Leisure and Class in Victorian England.* London: Routledge & Kegan Paul, 1978.

——. '"A Mingled Mass of Perfectly Legitimate Pleasures": The Victorian Middle Class and the Problem of Leisure.' *Victorian Studies* 21 (1997): 7–28.

——. '"Will the Real Bill Banks Please Stand Up?" Towards a Role Analysis of Mid-Victorian Working-Class Respectatility.' *Journal of Social History* 12 (1979): 336–53.

Bailey, Sidney D. 'Parliament and the 1851 Exhibition.' *Parliamentary Affairs* 4 (1951): 311–25.

Bailey, Victor. 'The Metropolitan Police, the Home Office, and the Threat of Outcast London.' In *Policing and Punishment in Nineteenth-Century Britain.* London: Croom Helm, 1981, pp. 94–125.

Bailyn, Bernard and Philip D. Morgan. *Strangers within the Realm: Cultural Margins of the First British Empire.* Chapel Hill: University of North Carolina Press, 1991.

Baines, Thomas. *History of the Commerce and Town of Liverpool.* London: Longman, Brown, Green & Longmans, 1852.

Banham, Joanna, Sally MacDonald, and Julia Porter. *Victorian Interior Design.* London: Cassell, 1991.

Banham, Mary and Bevis Hillier, eds. *A Tonic to the Nation: The Festival of Britain, 1951.* London: Thames & Hudson, 1976.

Barnes, E. G. *The Rise of the Midland Railway, 1844–1874.* London: George Allen & Unwin, 1966.

Barry, Alfred. *The Life and Works of Sir Charles Barry.* London: John Murray, 1867.

Barry, Gerald. 'The Festival of Britain, 1951.' *Journal of the Royal Society of Arts* 100 (1952): 667–704.

Beales, A. C. F. *The History of Peace.* New York: The Dial Press, 1931.

Beckett, J. V. *The Aristocracy in England, 1660–1914.* Oxford: Basil Blackwell, 1986.

Bell, Quentin. *The Schools of Design.* London: Routledge & Kegan Paul, 1963.

Bell-Knight, C. A. *The Crystal Palace: Its Rise – Its Decline – Its Fall.* Bath: n.p., 1977.

Benedict, Burton, ed. *The Anthropology of World's Fairs.* Berkeley: Scholar Press, 1983.

Benjamin, Walter. 'The Work of Art in an Age of Mechanical Reproduction.' In Hannah Arendt, ed., *Illuminations.* New York: Harcourt Brace & World, 1968, pp. 217–51.

Benn, Ernest. 'The Festival of Britain and the "Mess of Centuries".' *Quarterly Review* 290 (1952): 315–28.

Bennett, J. A. *Science at the Great Exhibition.* Cambridge: Whipple Museum of the History of Science, 1983.

Bennett, Tony. *The Birth of the Museum: History, Theory, Politics*. London: Routledge, 1995.

Bennett, Tony. 'The Exhibitionary Complex.' *New Formations* 4 (1988): 73–102.

Bentley, Michael. *The Climax of Liberal Politics: British Liberalism in Theory and Practice, 1868–1918*. London: Edward Arnold, 1987.

Berg, Maxine. *The Age of Manufactures, 1700–1820*. 2nd edn. London: Routledge, 1994.

Berman, Marshall. *All That Is Sold Melts into Air: The Experience of Modernity*. New York: Penguin, 1988.

Best, Geoffrey. *Mid-Victorian Britain, 1851–75*. London: Fontana, 1971.

——. 'Popular Protestantism in Victorian Britain'. In Robert Robson, ed., *Ideas and Institutions of Victorian Britain*. London: G. Bell & Sons, 1967, pp. 115–42.

Biagini, Eugenio F. *Liberty, Retrenchment and Reform: Popular Liberalism in the Age of Gladstone, 1860–1880*. Cambridge: Cambridge University Press, 1992.

Biagini, Eugenio F. and Alastair J. Reid, eds. *Currents of Radicalism: Popular Radicalism, Organized Labour and Party Politics in Britain, 1850–1914*. Cambridge: Cambridge University Press, 1991.

Bird, Anthony. *Paxton's Palace*. London: Cassell, 1976.

Blake, Robert. *Disraeli*. New York: St Martin's Press, 1966.

Bourne, Kenneth. *The Foreign Policy of Victorian England, 1830–1902*. Oxford: Clarendon Press, 1970.

Braudel, Fernand. *The Wheels of Commerce*. New York: Harper & Row, 1982.

Breckenridge, Carol A. 'The Aesthetics and Politics of Colonial Collecting: India at World's Fairs.' *Comparative Studies in Society and Theory* 31 (1989): 195–216.

Brendon, Piers. *Thomas Cook*. London: Secker & Warburg, 1991.

Brewer, John and Roy Porter, eds. *Consumption and the World of Goods*. London: Routledge, 1993.

Briggs, Asa. *From Iron Bridge to Crystal Palace*. London: Thames & Hudson, 1979.

——. *The Making of Modern England, 1783–1867: The Age of Improvement*. New York: Harper & Row, 1959.

——. *Victorian Cities*. Berkeley: University of California Press, 1993.

——. *Victorian People*. Rev. edn. Chicago: University of Chicago Press, 1972.

——. *Victorian Things*. Chicago: University of Chicago Press, 1988.

Bristow, Maurice. *The Postal History of the Crystal Palace*. London: Postal History Group, 1983.

Brock, Peter. *Pacifism in Europe to 1914*. Princeton: Princeton University Press, 1972.

Buchanan, R. A. 'Gentlemen Engineers: The Making of a Profession.' *Victorian Studies* 26 (1983): 407–29.

Bud, Robert and Gerrylynn K. Roberts. *Science versus Practice: Chemistry in Victorian Britain*. Manchester: Manchester University Press, 1984.

Budge, Jane. *Great Events in England's History*. London: John Marshall, 1872.

Burn, W. L. *The Age of Equipoise*. New York: W. W. Norton, 1965.

Burrow, J. W. *Whigs and Liberals: Continuity and Change in English Political Thought*. Oxford: Clarendon Press, 1988.

Bury, J. B. *The Idea of Progress*. New York: Macmillan, 1932.

Bylsma, John R. 'Party Structure in the 1852–1857 House of Commons: A Scalogram Analysis.' *Journal of Interdisciplinary History* 7 (1977): 617–35.

Cahill, Gilbert. 'British Nationalism and Nativism, 1829–1848: "No Popery" and British Popular Culture.' *Journal of Popular Culture* 3 (1969): 480–91.

Cain, P. J. and A. G. Hopkins. *British Imperialism: Innovation and Expansion, 1688–1914*. London: Longman, 1993.

——. 'Gentlemanly Capitalism and British Expansion Overseas, 1688–1850: I, The Old Colonial System.' *Economic History Review*, 2nd. ser. 39 (1986): 501–25.

——. 'Gentlemanly Capitalism and British Expansion Overseas, 1688–1850: II, The New Imperialism.' *Economic History Review*, 2nd. ser. 40 (1987): 1–26.

——. 'The Political Economy of British Expansion Overseas, 1750–1915.' *Economic History Review*, 2nd. ser. 33 (1980).

Cannadine, David. 'The Making of the British Upper Class.' *Aspects of Aristocracy: Grandeur and Decline in Modern Britain*. New Haven: Yale University Press, 1994, pp. 9–36.

——. 'The Present and the Past in the English Industrial Revolution, 1880–1980.' *Past & Present* 103 (1984): 131–72.

——. 'Review Article: The Empire Strikes Back'. *Past and Present* 147 (1995): 180–94.

Carlton, Grace. *Friedrich Engels: The Shadow Prophet*. London: Pall Mall Press, 1965.

Casteras, Susan P. *Victorian Childhood*. New Haven: Henry M. Abrams, 1986.

Castle, Terry. *Masquerade and Civilization: The Carnivalesque in Eighteenth-Century English Culture and Fiction*. London: Methuen, 1986.

Chadwick, George F. *The Works of Joseph Paxton*. London: The Architectural Press, 1961.

Church, Roy A. 'Problems and Perspectives.' In Roy A. Church, ed., *The Dynamics of Victorian Business*. London: George Allen & Unwin, 1980, pp. 1–45.

Clark, G. Kitson. *The Making of Victorian England*. Cambridge, MA: Harvard University Press, 1962.

Clark, J. C. D. 'English History's Forgotten Context: Scotland, Ireland, Wales'. *Historical Journal* 32 (1989): 211–28.

Clunn, Harold P. *The Face of London: The Record of a Century's Changes and Development*. London: Simpkin, Marshall & Co., 1932.

Cole, G. D. H. 'The Conception of the Middle Classes.' *British Journal of Sociology* 1 (1950): 275–90.

Colley, Linda. 'The Apotheosis of George III: Loyalty, Royalty and the British Nation, 1760–1820.' *Past & Present* 102 (1984): 94–129.

——. 'Britishness and Otherness: An Argument.' *Journal of British Studies* 31 (1992): 309–29.

——. *Britons: Forging the Nation, 1707–1837*. New Haven: Yale University Press, 1992.

——. 'Whose Nation? Class and National Consciousness in Britain, 1750–1830.' *Past & Present* 113 (1986): 97–117.

Collins, Bruce and Keith Robbins, eds. *British Culture and Economic Decline.* Vol. I. New York: St Martin's Press, 1990.

Collins, Michael. *Banks and Industrial Finance in Britain, 1800–1939.* London: Macmillan, 1991.

Conacher, J. B. *The Peelites and the Party System, 1846–1852.* Hamden: Archon Books, 1972.

Confino, Alon. 'The Nation as a Local Metaphor: National Memory and the German Empire, 1871–1918.' *History and Memory* 5 (1993): 42–86.

Conway, Hazel. *People's Parks: The Design and Development of Victorian Parks in Britain.* Cambridge: Cambridge University Press, 1991.

Cooper, Jeremy. *Victorian and Edwardian Decor.* New York: Abbeville Press, 1987.

Cooper, Nicholas. *The Opulent Eye: Late Victorian and Edwardian Taste in Interior Design.* London: The Architectural Press, 1976.

Cordery, Simon. 'Friendly Societies and the Discourse of Respectability in Britain, 1825–1875.' *Journal of British Studies* 34 (1995): 35–58.

Corfe, Tom. *The Great Exhibition.* Cambridge: Cambridge University Press, 1979.

Corfield, Penelope J., ed. *Language, History, and Class.* Oxford: Basil Blackwell, 1991.

Corley, T. A. B. *Quaker Enterprise in Biscuits: Huntley and Palmers of Reading, 1822–1972.* London: Hutchinson, 1972.

Cowling, Mary. *The Artist as Anthropologist: The Representation of Type and Character in Victorian Art.* Cambridge: Cambridge University Press, 1989.

Crafts, N. F. R. *British Economic Growth during the Industrial Revolution.* Oxford: Clarendon Press, 1985.

——. 'British Industrialization in an International Context.' Journal of Interdisciplinary History 19 (1989): 415–28.

Cranfield, G. A. *The Press and Society.* London: Longman, 1978.

Crossick, Geoffrey. *An Artisan Elite in Victorian Society: Kentish London, 1840–1880.* London: Croom Helm, 1978.

——. 'The Labour Aristocracy and its Values: A Study of Mid-Victorian Kentish London.' *Victorian Studies* 19 (1976): 301–28.

Crouzet, François. *The Victorian Economy.* New York: Columbia University Press, 1982.

Cuncliffe, Marcus. 'America at the Great Exhibition of 1851.' *American Quarterly* 3 (1951): 115–27.

Cunningham, Hugh. *Leisure in the Industrial Revolution.* London: Croom Helm, 1980.

Dancy, Eric. *Hyde Park.* London: Methuen, 1937.

Dasant, Arthur Irwin. *John Thadeus Delane.* 2 vols. London: John Murray, 1908.

Daunton, M. '"Gentlemanly Capitalism" and British Industry.' *Past and Present* 122 (1989): 119–58.

Davidoff, Leonore, and Catherine Hall. *Family Fortunes.* Chicago: University of Chicago Press, 1987.

Davies, Alun C. 'Ireland's Crystal Palace, 1853.' In J. M. Goldstrom and L. A. Clarkson, eds, *Irish Population, Economy, and Society.* Oxford: Clarendon Press, 1981, pp. 249–70.

Debord, Guy. *Society of the Spectacle.* Detroit: Black and Red, 1983.

Desmond, Ray. *The India Museum, 1801–1879.* London: HMSO, 1982.

Dintenfass, Michael. *The Decline of Industrial Britain, 1870–1980.* London: Routledge, 1992.

Dodds, John W. *The Age of Paradox.* London: Victor Gollancz, 1953.

Douglas, Mary. *Purity and Danger: An Analysis of Concepts of Pollution and Taboo.* New York: Praeger, 1966.

Dyos, H. J. 'Greater and Greater London: Metropolis and Provinces in the Nineteenth and Twentieth Centuries.' In David Cannadine and David Reeder, eds, *Exploring the Urban Past.* Cambridge: Cambridge University Press, 1982.

Dyos, H. J. and Michael Wolff, eds. *The Victorian City.* Vol. I. London: Routledge & Kegan Paul, 1977.

Eastlake, Charles L. *Hints on Household Taste.* 3rd edn. London: Longman, 1872.

Ede, Mary. 'Bath and the Great Exhibition of 1851.' *Bath History* 3 (1990): 138–58.

Edsall, Nicholas. *Richard Cobden: Independent Radical.* Cambridge, MA: Harvard University Press, 1986.

Emerson, George S. *John Scott Russell.* London: John Murray, 1977.

Fay, C. R. *Palace of Industry, 1851.* Cambridge: Cambridge University Press, 1951.

Ferebee, Ann. *A History of Design from the Victorian Era to the Present.* New York: Van Nostrand Reinhold, 1970.

Feuchtwanger, E. J. *Gladstone.* London: Allen Lane, 1975.

Ffrench, Yvonne. *The Great Exhibition, 1851.* London: Harvill Press, 1951.

Fiedler, Leslie. *Freaks: Myths and Images of the Secret Self.* New York: Simon & Schuster, 1978.

Fielding, K. J. 'Charles Dickens and the Department of Practical Art.' *Modern Language Review* 48 (1953): 270–7.

Finn, Margot C. *After Chartism: Class and Nation in English Radical Politics, 1848–1874.* Cambridge: Cambridge University Press, 1993.

FitzMaurice, Edmond, ed. *The Life of Granville George Leveson Gower.* 2 vols. London: Longman, Green & Co., 1905.

Floud, Roderick and David McCloskey, eds. *The Economic History of Britain Since 1700.* 2 vols. Cambridge: Cambridge University Press, 1981.

Ford, Boris, ed. *The Cambridge Cultural History of Britain.* Vol. VII. Cambridge: Cambridge University Press, 1992.

Forty, Adrian. *Objects of Desire: Design and Society since 1750.* London: Thames & Hudson, 1986.

Foster, John. *Class Struggle and the Industrial Revolution.* New York: St Martin's Press, 1974.

Fraser, Derek. *Urban Politics in Victorian England.* Leicester: Leicester University Press, 1976.

——, ed. *A History of Modern Leeds.* Manchester: Manchester University Press, 1980.

Friebe, Wolfgang. *Buildings of the World Exhibitions.* Trans. Jenny Vowles and Paul Roper. Leipzig: Edition Leipzig, 1985.

Gash, Norman. *Aristocracy and People*. Cambridge, MA: Harvard University Press, 1979.

Gaskell, S. Martin. *Model Housing: From the Great Exhibition to the Festival of Britain*. London: Mansell, 1986.

Gay, Peter. *The Bourgeois Experience: Victoria to Freud.* Vol. I: *Education of the Senses*. New York: Oxford University Press, 1984.

Gelernter, David. *1939: The Lost World of the Fair*. New York: The Free Press, 1995.

Gellner, Ernest. *Nations and Nationalism*. Ithaca: Cornell University Press, 1983.

Gere, Charlotte. *Nineteenth-Century Decoration: The Art of the Interior*. New York: Harry N. Abrams, 1989.

Gerschenkron, Alexander, *Economic Backwardness in Historical Perspective*. New York: Frederick A. Praeger, 1962.

Gibbs-Smith, C. H. *The Great Exhibition of 1851*. 2nd edn. London: HMSO, 1981.

Giedion, Siegfried. *Mechanization Takes Command*. New York: Oxford University Press, 1948.

Girouard, Mark. *The Return to Camelot: Chivalry and the English Gentleman*. New Haven: Yale University Press, 1981.

Gladstone, William E. *Gleanings of Past Years, 1843–78.* Vol. I: *The Throne, and the Prince Consort; the Cabinet, the Constitution*. London: John Murray, 1879.

Gleason, John Howes. *The Genesis of Russophobia in Great Britain*. Cambridge, MA: Harvard University Press, 1950.

Gloag, Joan. *Victorian Taste: Some Social Aspects of Architecture and Industrial Design from 1820–1900*. New York: Macmillan 1962.

Gombrich, E. H. *The Sense of Order: A Study in the Psychology of Decorative Art*. Ithaca: Cornell University Press, 1979.

Gosden, P. H. J. H. *Self-Help: Voluntary Associations in the 19th Century*. London: B. T. Batsford, 1973.

Gourish, T. R. *Mark Huish and the London & North Western Railway*. Leicester: Leicester University Press, 1972.

Grampp, William. 'How Britain Turned to Free Trade.' *Business History Review* 61 (1987): 86–112.

——. *The Manchester School of Economics*. Stanford: Stanford University Press, 1960.

Gray, Robert Q. *The Labour Aristocracy in Victorian Edinburgh*. Oxford: Clarendon Press, 1976.

Greenfeld, Liah, *Nationalism: Five Roads to Modernity*. Cambridge, MA: Harvard University Press, 1992.

Greenhalgh, Paul. *Ephemeral Vistas: The Expositions Universelles, Great Exhibitions, and World's Fairs, 1851–1939*. Manchester: Manchester University Press, 1988.

Grindon, Leo H. *Manchester Banks and Bankers*. 2nd edn. Manchester: Palmer & Howe, 1878.

Grinling, Charles H. *The History of the Great Northern Railway, 1845–1895*. London: Methuen & Co., 1898.

Gurowich, P. M. 'The Continuation of War by Other Means: Party and Politics, 1855–1865.' *Historical Journal* 27 (1984): 603–31.

Hafter, Daryl M. 'The Business of Invention in the Paris Industrial Exposition of 1806.' *Business History Review* 58 (1984): 317–35.

Haltern, Utz. *Die Londoner Weltaustellung von 1851*. Münster: Verlag Aschendorff, 1971.

Hammerton, Elizabeth and David Cannadine. 'Conflict and Consensus on a Ceremonial Occasion: The Diamond Jubilee in Cambridge in 1897.' *Historical Journal* 24 (1981): 111–46.

Hayward, R. A. *Sir William Fairbairn*. Manchester: North Western Museum of Science and Industry, 1977.

Hechter, Michael. *Internal Colonialism: The Celtic Fringe in British National Development, 1536–1966*. Berkeley: University of California Press, 1975.

Henderson, Gavin B. 'The Pacifists of the Fifties.' *Journal of Modern History* 9 (1937): 314–41.

Henriques, Robert. 'A Portrait of Britain.' *Field* (5 May 1951): 671.

Heyck, T. W. *The Peoples of the British Isles*, vol. II. Belmont, CA: Wadsworth, 1992.

Heywood, Thomas. *A Memoir of Sir Benjamin Heywood*. Manchester: Thomas Fargie, n.d.

Hilton, Timothy. *The Pre-Raphaelites*. New York: Harry N. Abrams, 1970.

Himmelfarb, Gertrude. *The Idea of Poverty: England in the Early Industrial Age*. New York: Random House, 1983.

Hinde, Wendy. *Richard Cobden: A Victorian Outsider*. New Haven: Yale University Press, 1987.

Hix, John. *The Glass House*. London: Phaidon, 1974.

Hobhouse, Christopher. *1851 and the Crystal Palace*. London: John Murray, 1937.

Hobhouse, Hermione. *Prince Albert: His Life and Work*. London: Hamish Hamilton, 1983.

Hobsbawm, Eric. *Industry and Empire*. Harmondsworth: Penguin, 1969.

——. *Nations and Nationalism since 1780*. 2nd edn. Cambridge: Cambridge University Press, 1990.

Hobsbawm, Eric and Terence Ranger, eds. *The Invention of Tradition*. Cambridge: Cambridge University Press, 1983.

Hobson, J. A. *Richard Cobden: The International Man*. London: T. Fisher Unwin, 1918.

Hodder, Edwin. *The Life and Work of the Seventh Earl of Shaftesbury*. London: Cassell, 1892.

——. *The Life of a Century, 1800–1900*. London: George Newnes, 1901.

Holmes, Colin. *John Bull's Island: Immigration and British Society, 1871–1971*. London: Macmillan, 1988.

Houghton, Walter E. *The Victorian Frame of Mind, 1830–1870*. New Haven: Yale University Press, 1957.

Howarth, Patrick. *The Year Is 1851*. London: Collins, 1951.

Howe, A. C. 'Free Trade and the City of London, c. 1820–1870.' *History* 77 (1992): 391–410.

——. *Free Trade and Liberal England, 1846–1946*. Oxford: Clarendon Press, 1997.

Huch, Robert and Paul R. Ziegler. *Joseph Hume: The People's MP*. Philadelphia: American Philosophical Society, 1985.

Hudson, Bill. *Through Limestone Hills: The Peak Line – Ambergate to Chinley*. Sparkford, Somerset: W. Hudson & Haynes, 1989.

Hudson, Derek and Kenneth Luckhurst. *The Royal Society of Arts, 1754–1954*. London: John Murray, 1954.

Ingham, Geoffrey. *Capitalism Divided? The City and Industry in British Social Development*. New York: Schocken Books, 1984.

James, Robert Rhodes. *Albert, Prince Consort*. London: Hamish Hamilton, 1983.

Jeaffreson, J. C. *The Life of Robert Stephenson*. 2 vols. London: Longman, 1864.

Jenkins, T. A. *The Liberal Ascendancy, 1830–1886*. London: Macmillan, 1994.

Jones, Gareth Elwyn. *Modern Wales: A Concise History, c.1485–1979*. Cambridge: Cambridge University Press, 1984.

Jones, Gareth Stedman. 'Class Expression versus Social Control? A critique of recent trends in the social history of "leisure".' *History Workshop* 4 (1977): 162–70.

——. *Languages of Class*. Cambridge: Cambridge University Press, 1983.

——. *Outcast London*. New York: Pantheon, 1984.

Jones, Leslie. *Hyde Park and Free Speech*. London: Museum of Labour History, 1981.

Jones, William Devereux and Arvel B. Erickson. *The Peelites, 1846–1857*. Columbus: Ohio State University Press, 1972.

Joyce, Patrick. *Visions of the People: Industrial England and the Question of Class, 1848–1914*. Cambridge: Cambridge University Press, 1991.

——. 'Work.' In *The Cambridge Social History of Britain, 1750–1950*. Vol. II. Ed. F. M. L. Thompson. Cambridge: Cambridge University Press, 1990.

——. *Work, Society, and Politics: The Culture of the Factory in Later Victorian England*. New Brunswick: Rutgers University Press, 1980.

Kamm, Josephine. *Joseph Paxton and the Crystal Palace*. London: Metheun, 1967.

Kaplan, Flora E. S., ed. *Museums and the Making of 'Ourselves:' The Role of Objects in National Identity*. London: Leicester University Press, 1994.

Kasson, John F. *Civilizing the Machine*. New York: Viking Press, 1976.

Kennedy, Paul. 'Idealists and Realists: British Views of Germany, 1864–1939.' *Transactions of the Royal Historical Society* 25 (1975): 137–56.

——. *The Rise and Fall of the Great Powers*. New York: Random House, 1987.

Kidd, Alan J. and K. W. Roberts, eds. *City, Class and Culture: Studies of Social Policy and Cultural Production in Victorian Manchester*. Manchester: Manchester University Press, 1985.

Kihlstedt, Folke T. 'The Crystal Palace.' *Scientific American* (October 1984): 124–39.

King, Richard. 'Joseph Paxton and the Crystal Palace.' *Industrial Archaeology* 6 (1969): 124–31.

Klaus, Robert J. *The Pope, the Protestants, and the Irish: Papal Aggression and Anti-Catholicism in Mid-Nineteenth Century England*. New York: Garland Publishing, 1987.

Koditschek, Theodore. *Class Formation and Urban-Industrial Society: Bradford, 1750–1850*. Cambridge: Cambridge University Press, 1990.

Kusamitsu, Toshio. 'Great Exhibitions before 1851.' *History Workshop* 9 (1980): 70–89.

Landes, David. *The Unbound Prometheus*. Cambridge: Cambridge University Press, 1969.

Langdon, Philip. 'Great Exhibitions: Representations of the Crystal Palace in Mayhew, Dickens, and Dostoyevsky.' *Nineteenth-Century Contexts* 20 (1997): 27–59.

Large, David. 'London in the Year of Revolutions, 1848.' In *London in the Age of Reform*. Ed. John Stevenson. Oxford: Basil Blackwell, 1977.

Lasdun, Susan. *Victorians at Home*. Intro. Mark Girouard. London: Weidenfeld & Nicolson, 1981.

Lee, C. H. *The British Economy since 1700: A Macroeconomic Perspective*. Cambridge: Cambridge University Press, 1986.

Leventhal, F. M. *Respectable Radical: George Howell and Victorian Working-Class Politics*. Cambridge: Harvard University Press, 1971.

——. '"A Tonic to the Nation:" The Festival of Britain, 1951.' *Albion* 27 (1995): 445–53.

Lever, Ellis. *Suggestions for a Grand International Exhibition of the Industrial Arts, Manufactures, Fine Arts, Scientific Inventions, Discoveries, and Natural Products of all Countries to be Held in Manchester in the Year 1882*. Manchester: Guardian Letterpress and Lithographic Works, 1881.

Lewin, Henry Grote. *The Railway Mania and its Aftermath, 1845–1852*. London: The Railway Gazette, 1936.

Linden, W. H. van der. *The International Peace Movement, 1815–1874*. Amsterdam: Tilleul Publications, 1987.

Lofland, Lyn H. *A World of Strangers*. New York: Basic Books, 1973.

Longford, Elizabeth. *Wellington: Pillar of State*. London: Weidenfeld & Nicolson, 1972.

Lowe, Charles. *Four Exhibitions in London and their Organizer*. London: T. Fisher Unwin, 1892.

Luckhurst, Kenneth W. *The Great Exhibition of 1851*. London: Royal Society of Arts, 1951.

Lutchmansingh, Larry D. 'Commodity Exhibitionism at the London Great Exhibition of 1851.' *Annals of Scholarship* 7 (1990): 203–16.

Lyons, F. S. L. *Internationalism in Europe, 1815–1914*. Leyden: A. W. Sythoff, 1963.

Mabon, G. P. 'John Scott Russell and Henry Cole: Aspects of a Personal Rivalry at the Society of Arts,' *Journal of the Royal Society of Arts* 115 (February–March 1967): 204–8, 299–302.

McCarthy, Fiona. *A History of British Design, 1830–1970*. London: George Allen & Unwin, 1979.

McCord, Norman. 'Some Difficulties of Parliamentary Reform.' *Historical Journal* 10 (1967): 376–90.

Machlup, Fritz. *A History of Thought on European Integration*. New York: Columbia University Press, 1977.

MacKenzie, John. *Propaganda and Empire*. Manchester: Manchester University Press, 1984.

McKean, John. *Crystal Palace: Joseph Paxton and Charles Fox*. London: Phaidon, 1994.

McKendrick, Neil, John Brewer, and J. H. Plumb. *The Birth of a Consumer Society*. Bloomington: Indiana University Press, 1985.

Malcolmson, Robert W. *Popular Recreations in English Society, 1700–1850*. Cambridge: Cambridge University Press, 1973.

Mandler, Peter. *Aristocratic Government in the Age of Reform: Whigs and Liberals, 1830–1852*. Oxford: Clarendon Press, 1990.

Markham, Violet R. *Paxton and the Bachelor Duke*. London: Hodder & Stoughton, 1935.

Markow, Joyce. *Mr. and Mrs. Gladstone: An Intimate Biography*. London: Weidenfeld & Nicholson, 1977.

Martin, B. Kingsley. *The Triumph of Lord Palmerston: A Study of Public Opinion in England before the Crimean War*. London: George Allen & Unwin, 1924.

Martin, Theodore. *The Life of His Royal Highness the Prince Consort*. 5th edn. London: Smith, Elder & Co., 1880.

Mathias, Peter. *The First Industrial Nation: An Economic History of Britain, 1700–1914*. New York: Charles Scribner's Sons, 1969.

Matthew, H. C. G. *Gladstone, 1809–1874*. Oxford: Clarendon Press, 1986.

Messinger, Gary S. *Manchester in the Victorian Age*. Manchester: Manchester University Press, 1985.

Michie, Ranald C. 'Income, Expenditure and Investment of a Victorian Millionaire: Lord Overstone, 1823–83.' *Bulletin of the Institute for Historical Research* 58 (1985): 59–77.

Miller, Edward. *That Noble Cabinet: A History of the British Museum*. London: André Deutsch, 1973.

Mitter, Partha. *Much Maligned Monsters: A History of European Reactions to Indian Art*. Chicago: University of Chicago Press, 1992.

Montgomery, R. J. *Examinations: An Account of their Evolution as Administrative Devices in England*. London: Longmans, Green & Company, 1965.

Monypenny, W. F. and George Earle Buckle. *The Life of Benjamin Disraeli*. Vol. V. London: John Murray, 1920.

Moore, Ellen Wedermeyer. *The Fairs of Medieval England*. Toronto: Pontifical Institute of Medieval Studies, 1985.

Morley, John. *The Life of Richard Cobden*. London: T. Fisher Unwin, 1906.

Morris, R. J. *Class, Sect and Party: The Making of the British Middle Class, Leeds, 1820–50*. Manchester: Manchester University Press, 1990.

——. 'Leeds and the Crystal Palace.' *Victorian Studies* 13 (1970): 283–300.

Murdock, J. E. Preston. *The Romance and History of the Crystal Palace*. London: L. Upcott Gill, 1911.

Musgrave, Michael. *The Musical Life of the Crystal Palace*. Cambridge: Cambridge University Press, 1995.

Musson, A. E. *The Growth of British Industry*. New York: Holmes & Meier, 1978.

Neale, R. S. ed. *History and Class*. Oxford: Basil Blackwell, 1983.

Newman, Gerald. *The Rise of English Nationalism: A Cultural History, 1740–1830*. London: Weidenfeld & Nicolson, 1987.

Ng, Kwee Choo. *The Chinese in London*. Oxford: Oxford University Press, 1968.

Nicholls, David. 'Richard Cobden and the International Peace Congress Movement, 1848–1853.' *Journal of British Studies* 30 (1991): 351–76.

Noble, Celia Brunel. *The Brunels*. London: Cobden-Sanderson, 1938.

Nowell-Smith, Simon. *The House of Cassell, 1848–1958*. London: Cassell & Co., 1958.

Nye, John Vincent. 'The Myth of Free-Trade Britain and Fortress France: Tariffs and Trade in the Nineteenth Century.' *Journal of Economic History* 51 (1991): 23–46.

O'Brien, Patrick and Caglar Keyder. *Economic Growth in Britain and France, 1780–1914*. London: George Allen & Unwin, 1978.

O'Brien, Patrick and Roland Quinault, eds. *The Industrial Revolution and British Society*. Cambridge: Cambridge University Press, 1993.

Orosz, Joel L. *Curators and Culture: The Museum Movement in America, 1740–1870*. Tuscaloosa: University of Alabama Press, 1990.

Ozouf, Mona. *Festivals and the French Revolution*. Trans. Alan Sheridan. Cambridge, MA: Harvard University Press, 1988.

Page, William, ed. *Commerce and Industry*. 2 vols. London: Constable, 1919.

Parris, Leslie, ed. *The Pre-Raphaelites*. London: Tate Gallery, 1984.

Parry, Jonathan. *Democracy and Religion: Gladstone and the Liberal Party, 1867–1875*. Cambridge: Cambridge University Press, 1986.

——. *The Rise and Fall of Liberal Government in Victorian Britain*. New Haven: Yale University Press, 1993.

Paz, D. G. 'Popular Anti-Catholicism in England, 1850–1851.' *Albion* 11 (1979): 331–59.

Pemble, John. *The Mediterranean Passion: Victorians and Edwardians in the South*. Oxford: Oxford University Press, 1988.

Perkin, Harold. *Origins of Modern English Society*. London: Routledge & Kegan Paul, 1969.

Pevsner, Nikolaus. *High Victorian Design: A Study of the Exhibits of 1851*. London: The Architectural Press, 1951.

——. *Pioneers of Modern Design*. 2nd edn. New York: Museum of Modern Art, 1949.

Piore, Michael J. and Charles F. Sabel. *The Second Industrial Divide: Possibilities for Prosperity*. New York: Basic Books, 1984.

Platt, D. C. M. *Finance, Trade and Politics in British Foreign Policy, 1815–1914*. Oxford: Clarendon Press, 1968.

Pollard, Sidney. *The Integration of the European Economy since 1815*. London: George Allen & Unwin, 1981.

Porter, Bernard. *Britannia's Burden*. London: Edward Arnold, 1994.

——. *The Refugee Question in Mid-Victorian Politics*. Cambridge: Cambridge University Press, 1979.

Price, Richard. 'Does the Notion of Victorian England Make Sense?' In *Cities, Class and Communication*, ed. Derek Fraser. New York: Harvester Wheatsheaf, 1990.

Pudney, John. *The Thomas Cook Story*. London: Michael Joseph, 1953.

Read, Donald. *The English Provinces c. 1760–1960: A Study in Influence*. New York: St Martin's Press, 1964.

Rearick, Charles. 'Festivals in Modern France: The Experience of the Third Republic.' *Journal of Contemporary History* 12 (1977): 435–60.

Reed, Nicholas. *Camille Pissarro at the Crystal Palace*. London: London Reference Books, 1987.

Reeves, Graham. *Palace of the People*. London: Bromley Library Service, 1986.

Reid, Alastair J. *Social Classes and Social Relations in Britain, 1850–1914*. Cambridge: Cambridge University Press, 1992.

Richards, Thomas. *The Commodity Culture of Victorian England*. Stanford: Stanford University Press, 1990.

——. *The Imperial Archive*. London: Verso, 1993.

Ridley, Jasper. *Lord Palmerston*. London: Constable, 1970.

Robbins, Keith. *John Bright*. London: Routledge & Kegan Paul, 1979.

Robertson, Michael. 'Cultural Hegemony Goes to the Fair: The Case of E. L. Doctorow's *World Fair*.' *American Studies* 33 (1992): 31–44.

Robinson, John Martin. *The Wyatts: An Architectural Dynasty*. Oxford: Oxford University Press, 1979.

Robson, Robert, ed. *Ideas and Institutions of Victorian Britain*. London: G. Bell, 1967.

Roderick, G. W. and M. D. Stephens. *Education and Industry in the Nineteenth Century: The English Disease?* London: Longman, 1878.

Rolt, L. T. C. *George and Robert Stephenson*. London: Longman, 1960.

——. *Isambard Kingdom Brunel*. New York: St Martin's Press, 1957.

Rostow, W. W. *The Process of Economic Growth*. 2nd edn. New York: W. W. Norton, 1962.

——. *The Stages of Economic Growth: A Non-Communist Manifesto*. Cambridge: Cambridge University Press, 1960.

Royle, Edward. *Chartism*. London: Longman, 1980.

——. 'Mechanics Institutes and the Working Classes, 1840–1860.' *Historical Journal* 14 (1971): 305–21.

Rubinstein, W. D. *Capitalism, Culture and Decline in Britain, 1750–1990*. London: Routledge, 1993.

——. *Elites and the Wealthy in Modern British History*. New York: St Martin's Press, 1987.

——. 'The Victorian Middle Classes: Wealth, Occupation, and Geography.' *Economic History Review*, 2nd ser., 30 (1997): 602–23.

Rydell, Robert W. *All the World's a Fair: Visions of Empire at American International Expositions, 1876–1916*. Chicago: University of Chicago Press, 1984.

Sahlins, Peter. *Boundaries: The Making of France and Spain in the Pyrenees*. Berkeley: University of California Press, 1989.

Said, Edward. *Orientalism*. New York: Random House, 1978.

Samuel, Raphael. *Patriotism: The Making and Unmaking of British National Identity*, 3 vols. London: Routledge, 1989.

——. 'Workshop of the World: Steam Power and Hand Technology in Mid-Victorian Britain.' *History Workshop* 3 (1977): 6–72.

Saville, John. *1848: The British State and the Chartist Movement*. Cambridge: Cambridge University Press, 1987.

Schivelbusch, Wolfgang. *The Railway Journey: The Industrialization of Time and Space in the 19th Century*. Berkeley: University of California Press, 1986.

Searle, G. R. *Entrepreneurial Politics in Mid-Victorian Britain*. Oxford: Oxford University Press, 1993.

——. *The Liberal Party: Triumph and Disintegration, 1886–1939*. New York: St Martin's Press, 1992.

Seed, John. 'Unitarianism, Political Economy and the Antinomies of Liberal Culture in Manchester, 1830–1850.' *Social History* 7 (1982): 1–25.

Shairp, John Campbell, Peter Guthrie Tait, and A. Adams-Reilly. *Life and Letters of James David Forbes*. London: Macmillan, 1873.

Shannon, Richard. *Gladstone*. Vol. I (1809–1865). London: Hamish Hamilton, 1982.

Sheppard, Francis. *London, 1808–1870: The Infernal Wen*. London: Secker & Warburg, 1971.

Sherman, Daniel and Irit Rogoff. *Museum Culture: Histories, Discourses, Speculations*. Minneapolis: University of Minnesota Press, 1994.

Short, Audrey. 'Workers under Glass in 1851.' *Victorian Studies* 20 (1966): 193–202.

Sigsworth, E. M. 'The West Riding Wool Textile Industry and the Great Exhibition.' *Yorkshire Bulletin of Economic and Social Research* 4 (1952): 21–31.

Sime, Jonathan D. 'Creating Places or Designing Spaces?' *Journal of Environmental Psychology* 6 (1986): 49–63.

Simmons, Douglas A. *Schweppes: The First 200 Years*. London: Springwood Books, 1983.

Simmons, Jack. *The Victorian Railway*. London: Thames & Hudson, 1991.

Smith, Anthony D. *National Identity*. Reno: University of Nevada Press, 1991.

Smith, Paul. *Disraeli: A Brief Life*. Cambridge: Cambridge University Press, 1996.

Smith, Simon Nowell. *The House of Cassell, 1848–1958*. London: Cassell, 1958.

Smout, T. C. *A Century of the Scottish People, 1830–1950*. London: Collins, 1986.

Southgate, Robert. *The Passing of the Whigs, 1832–1866*. London: Macmillan, 1965.

Spall, Richard Francis Jr. 'Free Trade, Foreign Relations, and the Anti-Corn Law League.' *International History Review* 10 (1988): 405–32.

Sperber, Jonathan. 'Festivals of National Unity in the German Revolution of 1848–1849.' *Past & Present* 136 (1992): 114–38.

Spielmann, M. H. *The History of Punch*. London: Cassell & Co., 1895.

Stansky, Peter. *Redesigning the World: William Morris, the 1880s, and the Arts and Crafts*. Princeton: Princeton University Press, 1985.

Steegman, John. *Victorian Taste: A Study of the Arts and Architecture from 1830–1870*. London: Thomas Nelson, 1970.

Steele, E. D. *Palmerston and Liberalism, 1855–1865*. Cambridge: Cambridge University Press, 1991.

Stevenson, John. *Popular Disturbances in England, 1700–1850*. London: Longman, 1979.

Stewart, Richard. *Design and British Industry*. London: John Murray, 1987.

Stewart, Robert. *The Foundations of the Conservative Party, 1830–1867*. London: Longman, 1978.

——. *The Politics of Protection: Lord Derby and the Protectionist Party, 1841–1852*. Cambridge: Cambridge University Press, 1971.

Stocking, George W., Jr. *Victorian Anthropology*. New York: The Free Press, 1987.

Swinglehurst, Edmund. *The Romantic Journey: The Story of Thomas Cook and Victorian Travel*. London: Pica, 1974.

Taylor, A. J. P. *The Struggle for Mastery in Europe, 1848–1918*. Oxford: Clarendon Press, 1954.

——. *The Trouble Makers: Dissent over Foreign Policy, 1792–1939*. London: Hamish Hamilton, 1957.

Taylor, Miles. *The Decline of British Radicalism, 1847–1860*. Oxford: Clarendon Press, 1995.

Tencotte, Paul A. 'Kaleidoscopes of the World: International Exhibitions and the Concept of Culture-Place, 1851–1915.' *American Studies* 29 (1987): 5–29.

Tenorio-Trillo, Mauricio. *Mexico at the World's Fairs: Crafting a Modern Nation*. Berkeley: University of California Press, 1996.

Thompson, Dorothy. *Queen Victoria: Gender and Power*. London: Virago Press, 1990.

Thompson, E. P. *The Making of the English Working Class*. New York: Random House, 1963.

Thompson, F. M. L. *The Rise of Respectable Society*. Cambridge, MA: Harvard University Press, 1988.

——. 'Social Control in Victorian Britain.' *The Economic History Review*, 2nd ser., 34 (1981): 189–208.

Thorne, Robert. 'Paxton and Prefabrication.' *Architectural Design* 57 (1987): 23–8.

Todorov, Tzvetan. *The Conquest of America: The Question of the Other*. Trans. Richard Howard. New York: Harper & Row, 1984.

Trevelyan, George Macaulay. *British History in the Nineteenth Century and After (1782–1919)*. 2nd edn. London: Longman, 1937.

Turner, Michael J. 'Before the Manchester School: Economic Thought in Early Nineteenth-Century Manchester.' *History* 79 (194): 216–41.

Tweedie, Ethel Brilliana. *Hyde Park: Its History and Romance*. Rev. edn. London: Besant & Co., 1930.

Tylecote, Mabel. *The Mechanics' Institutes of Lancashire and Yorkshire before 1851*. Manchester: Manchester University Press, 1957.

Tyrell, Alexander. 'Making the Millennium: The Mid-Nineteenth Century Peace Movement.' *Historical Journal* 20 (1978): 75–85.

Vaughan, W. E., ed. *A New History of Ireland*, vol. V: *Ireland under the Union, I: 1801–70*. Oxford: Clarendon Press, 1989.

Verlinden, O. 'Markets and Fairs.' *The Cambridge Economic History of Europe*, vol. III. Cambridge: Cambridge University Press, 1963.

Vincent, Jonathan. *The Formation of the Liberal Party*. New York: Charles Scribner's Sons, 1966.

Walkowitz, Judith R. *City of Dreadful Delight: Narratives of Sexual Danger in Victorian London*. Chicago: University of Chicago Press, 1992.

Wallis, Frank H. *Popular Anti-Catholicism in Mid-Victorian Britain*. Lewiston, NY: Edwin Mellen Press, 1993.

Walton, Whitney. *France at the Crystal Palace: Bourgeois Taste and Artisan Manufacture in the Nineteenth Century*. Berkeley: University of California Press, 1992.

Walvin, James. *Passage to Britain: Immigration in British History and Politics*. Harmondsworth: Penguin, 1984.

Warner, Malcolm. *British Painting, 1837–1901*. Washington, D.C.: National Gallery of Art, 1996.

Watson, J. N. P. *Horse and Carriage: The Pageant of Hyde Park*. London: The Sportsman's Press, 1990.

Weatherill, Lorna. *Consumer Behaviour and Material Culture in Britain, 1660–1760*. London: Routledge, 1988.

——. *The Pottery Trade and North Staffordshire, 1660–1760*. New York: Augustus Kelley, 1971.

Weber, William. 'The Muddle of the Middle Classes.' *Nineteenth-Century Music* 3 (1979): 175–85.

White, R. J. *From Peterloo to the Crystal Palace*. London: William Heinemann, 1972.

Whitten, Dolphus. 'The Don Pacifico Affair.' *Historian* 48 (1986): 255–67.

Wiener, Joel. *William Lovett*. Manchester: Manchester University Press, 1989.

Wiener, Martin J. *English Culture and the Decline of the Industrial Spirit, 1850–1980*. Cambridge: Cambridge University Press, 1981.

Williams, David. *A History of Modern Wales*. London: John Murray, 1950.

Williams, Raymond. *Keywords: A Vocabulary of Culture and Society*, rev. edn. New York: Oxford University Press, 1983.

Wilson, John F. *British Business History, 1720–1994*. Manchester: Manchester University Press, 1995.

Winstanley, Michael J. *Gladstone and the Liberal Party*. London: Routledge, 1990.

Wolff, Janet, and John Seed, eds. *The Culture of Capital: Art, Power and the Nineteenth-Century Middle Class*. Manchester: Manchester University Press, 1988.

Wolffe, John. *The Protestant Crusade in Great Britain, 1829–1860*. Oxford: Clarendon Press, 1991.

Wood, Anthony. *Nineteenth Century Britain*. London: Longman, 1960.

Wood, Henry Trueman. *A History of the Royal Society of Arts*. London: John Murray, 1913.

Woodring, Carl. *Nature into Art: Cultural Transformations in Nineteenth-Century Britain*. Cambridge, MA: Harvard University Press, 1989.

Wright, D. G. *Popular Radicalism: The Working-Class Experience, 1780–1880*. London: Longman, 1988.

Wrigley, E. A. *Continuity, Chance and Change: The Character of the Industrial Revolution in England*. Cambridge: Cambridge University Press, 1988.

Wyatt, Matthew Digby. 'On the Architectural Career of the Late Sir Charles Barry.' *Transactions of the Royal Institute of British Architects* (1859–60), pp. 1–20.

Yeo, Richard. 'Reading Encyclopedias: Science and the Organization of Knowledge in British Dictionaries of Arts and Sciences, 1730–1850.' *Isis* 82 (1991): 24–49.

Young, G. M. *Victorian England: Portrait of an Age*. 2nd edn. Oxford: Oxford University Press, 1977.

VII. Unpublished Theses

Cooper, Ann. 'For the Public Good: Henry Cole, his Circle, and the Development of the South Kensington Circle.' PhD thesis, Open University, 1992.

Gatrell, V. A. C. 'The Commercial Middle Class in Manchester, c. 1820–1857.' PhD thesis, University of Cambridge, 1971.

Green, Charlotte Crack. 'The Great Exhibition of 1851 and the Mid-Century Works of Dickens, Kingsley, and Carlisle.' PhD thesis, Ohio State University, 1978.

Hughes, Thomas Parke. 'Industry through the Crystal Palace.' PhD thesis, University of Virginia, 1953.

Macdonald, Bradley James. 'William Morris and the Aesthetic Foundations of Political Theory.' PhD thesis, University of California at Los Angeles, 1991.

Mitchell, Elizabeth M. 'The Great Exhibition of 1851: A Select Bibliography.' MA thesis, University of London, School of Librarianship, 1950.

Rae, A. B. 'Visitors by Railway to the Great Exhibition of 1851.' MPhil thesis, Open University, 1977.

Short, Audrey. 'The Great Exhibition of 1851.' MA thesis, University of Cincinatti, 1965.

Sweet, Jonathan. 'The Face of Australia: Colonial Design and Representation at International Exhibitions, 1851–1888.' MA thesis, Royal College of Art, 1991.

INDEX

References to illustrations are in *italics*

ILLUSTRATION CREDITS

1 from Edward Forbes Robinson, *The Early History of Coffee Houses in England* (London, 1893); 2 and 6, courtesy of the National Portrait Gallery, London; 3, 4 and 58, Victoria and Albert Museum, London; 5 and 59, John Johnson Collection, Bodleian Library, University of Oxford; 7 from Peter Berlyn and Charles Fowler, *The Crystal Palace: Its Architectural History and Constructive Marvels* (London, 1851); 8–10, 16, 39, 45–7, 50–1, 53, 60, 62 from *Punch*; 13, 17, 19–20, 25, 29, 33, 38, 43–4, 67, 72, 75 from the *Illustrated London News*; 11, Devonshire Collection, Chatsworth, reproduced by permission of the Duke of Devonshire and the Chatsworth Settlement Trustees and the Courtauld Institute of Art; 12 and 69–70, Bromley Central Library; 15, 21, 24, 27–8, 31 and 36 from *Dickinson's Comprehensive Pictures of the Great Exhibition of 1851* (London, 1854); 18 and 54 (photograph: A.C. Cooper Ltd), The Royal Collection © 1999 Her Majesty Queen Elizabeth II; 22 is reproduced in *Studying the Victorians at the Victoria and Albert Museum* (London, 1994); 23 and 35 from *Tallis's History and Description of the Crystal Palace, and the Exhibition of the World's Industry in 1851*, 3 vols (London [1852]); 30, 48–9 from *Recollections of the Great Exhibition of 1851* (London, 1851); 34 from the *Official Descriptive and Illustrated Catalogue* (London, 1851); 37 and 40–2 from Henry Mayhew and George Cruikshank, *1851; or The Adventures of Mr. and Mrs. Sandboys* (London, [1851]); 52 Corcoran Gallery of Art, Washington, gift of William Wilson Corcoran; 55–6 from Thomas Onwhyn, *Mr. and Mrs. John Brown's Visit to London to see the Great Exposition of all Nations* (London, n.d.); 57 from Henry Sutherland Edwards, *An Authentic Account of the Chinese Commission which was sent to report on the Great Exhibition* (London, n.d.); 61 from B. Clayton, *Frolick & Fun, or What Was Seen and Done in London in 1851* (London, [1852]) and 63 from the *Builder* vol. X (1852), no. 482, pp. 280–1, Yale Center for British Art, Paul Mellon Collection; 64 © Crown Copyright, Royal Commission on Historical Monuments in England; 65 from Matthew Digby Wyatt, *Views of the Crystal Palace and Park, Sydenham* (London, 1854); 66, photograph © 1999 The Art Institute of Chicago, all rights reserved; 68, The Forbes Magazine Collection, New York, © all rights reserved; 71 and 74, courtesy of the Museum of London; 73, Public Record Office; Maps 1 and 3 from Harold Pollins, *Britain's Railways: An Industrial History* (Totowa, NJ, 1971), Map 2 prepared by the author.